The Selected Letters of George Oppen

George Oppen circa 1981. Photographer unknown.

The Selected Letters of George Oppen

Edited by Rachel Blau DuPlessis

Duke University Press   Durham and London 1990

Letters by George Oppen © Linda Oppen Mourelatos, by permission
Introduction, Notes, and Index © 1990 Duke University Press
All rights reserved.
Printed in the United States of America
on acid-free paper ∞
Library of Congress Cataloging-in-Publication Data
appear on the last printed page of this book.

Contents

Introduction

In an unusual work at the end of his *Collected Poems* George Oppen speaks of a scene of writing, and the "power of the scene." "Something wrong with my desk," he begins. He goes on to point alternatively to the "venture adventure" which gets defined both as "the sense / of the thing" and as a poet's credo for its exploration:

> say as much as I dare, as much as I can
> sustain I don't know how to say it
>
> I say all that I can
> [CP 255]

The tone of that exposed burst of feeling recalls Oppen's letters—situational, meditative, vulnerable, determined, proud. And then the poem pivots from the isolations of desk (and, not incidentally, shipwreck) into an alternative scene of writing: "the people standing at a little distance / from each other, or in small groups // would be the poem. . . ." This is a curious rhetorical condensation suggesting the tripled vitality for Oppen of a network of witnesses—constituting the object which is the poem, forming the subject of the poem, being the context for the poem. Oppen's formation of a community of "people . . . at a little distance . . . or in small groups," through the medium of letters, helped him define and sustain his major career as a writer.

Because many of the issues, stances, locutions, feelings raised in Oppen's poetry occur in the interactive arena of letters, Oppen's correspondence is an important part of his oeuvre.[1] Letters are both intimate and declarative—a curious mixture of semiprivate and semipublic utterance; letters come from need, and there is an immediacy of provocation and response to them which helps dramatize ideas and personalize social and moral trends. The controlled dialogue which letters provide—a forum for hearing oneself, as well as for conversation with others—was crucial to the composition process of a number of Oppen's works. Letters offer both a mirror of what thought one did not see until it was written and an arena for self-explanation and gloss, important because Oppen's writing hinged on self-knowledge: "in my life to know // what I have said to myself" (CP 242). Letters also can provide a place for authority and judgment made less pontifical, more "essaying," by virtue of the possibilities of debate and response.[2] Oppen's delight at "the pleasure of being heard, / the pleasure / of companionship" (CP 142) was announced first in a letter; the recipient, Charles Tomlinson, set that statement as a poem, which Oppen then took back (UCSD 16, 11, 12). While not repeated in such a graphic form again, this collaborative interaction whose subject is precisely the ideal interaction of speaker and listener summarizes the dual functions for Oppen's correspondence: at once to create dialogue and audience.[3]

Oppen first emerged as a member of the original "Objectivist" group (1929–35), that set of poets which included Louis Zukofsky, Charles Reznikoff, and William Carlos Williams (with Ezra Pound as an outrider), whose affiliation expressed itself in two presses: To Publishers and The Objectivist Press.[4] Louis Zukofsky was the intellectual and the poetic center of both enterprises. The work Zukofsky did in 1930 for the "Objectivists" issue of Poetry (published in February 1931) framed and named this moment. The affiliation to a poetics was an intellectual and moral commitment of life-long seriousness for Zukofsky, Reznikoff, Oppen. As well, it involved primary loyalties; the poets were a cohort, even though members of the group were joined in an uneven fashion. Some of its members were affiliated in both helpful and abrasive ways; others met late in life; some met only by mail, some not at all. Some exerted primary and deep influence upon each other (Niedecker-Zukofsky, and vice versa; Reznikoff-Oppen; Zukofsky-Oppen). Some were wary of each other's work (Oppen-Niedecker; Oppen-Rakosi; and once again, Oppen-Zukofsky). All wrote a poetry that draws upon the vanguard modernist pioneers in American poetry (William Carlos Williams, Marianne Moore, and Ezra Pound), creating a subtle, humane, socially and linguistically nuanced poetry.[5] The "Objectivists" have more than a bridge function in literary history—as, say, "between" Williams and Creeley. They explore, within avant-garde practices, the social statements poetry could make in a poetry compounded of Jewishness, democratic socialism, and the populist urbanity of city lives.[6]

Several of the central "Objectivists"—Oppen, Zukofsky, Rakosi— also have in common decade-long gaps in their writing and publishing careers. The artesian reemergence of a number of "Objectivist" writers after these long hiatuses has been characterized as a "third phase Objectivism"; their presence has the capacity to drastically alter our picture of American poetry and poetics.[7] The mature works of the "Objectivist" writers, along with certain—but not all—positions in the poetics of the New American Poetry, urge us to see that the term *objectivist* usefully designates a general aesthetic position in modern and contemporary poetry encompassing work based, generally, on "the real," on history not myth, on empiricism not projection, on the discrete not the unified, on vernacular prosodies and not traditional poetic rhetoric, on "imagism," not "symbolism" or "surrealism," and on particulars with a dynamic relation to universals. Indeed, this argument for *objectivist* as the main alternative to *symbolist* poetics has been put forward with eloquence and verve by the poet David Antin and critics Charles Altieri and Marjorie Perloff.[8] At the same time, taking any literary position for purposes of generalization veils the nuances of the position of objectivism both as it is contextualized and enacted in (specifically) Oppen's poetic judgments and meditations in epistolary conversation with friends and literary colleagues, and as it emerged in the mature bonds among this cohort—the aggressive likes and dislikes, the principled and accidental disagreements and conjunctures. The meaning of this collection of *The Selected Letters of George Oppen* lies in the threefold evidence it offers: first, for a reconstructed literary history with the "Objectivists" included; second, for an enriched sense of the poetics of modernism based upon Oppen's objectivist meditations; and third, for a contextualization of a unique and influential poetic career.

For unlike their older modernist mentors Eliot, Pound, Williams, and Moore, and unlike their younger but contemporaneous colleagues Creeley, Olson, and Duncan, the "Objectivist" cohort wrote very little justificatory prose. Only Louis Zukofsky produced a coherent and extensive body of critical writing. Now the function of poets' critical prose—of essays, manifestos, reviews, studies that occur in a public forum—is not only to work through particular positions, but also to position themselves in relation to an audience. Critical prose is of course part of poetic production, but it is part of poetic dissemination as well. Critical prose readies individual listeners and prepares and educates an audience for the reception of any poet's work. Hence the chariness of most, though not all, of the "Objectivist" cohort in producing critical prose, as well as, or in addition to, the long gaps in the production/publication of writing that characterized the careers of most, have both been factors contributing to their uneven critical reception. As a group, and as individuals, they remain under-read and shockingly under-anthologized.[9] But given the aggressive studies of the politics and poetics of canon formation current in the academy, given the interest in describing a historical context for individual literary achievement, and given current debates about mainstream poetry, there is cause to rethink individual "Objectivists" and to assemble the documents contributing to the poetics as a whole.

Oppen, as a specific case of the general "Objectivist" chariness, wrote one essay ("The Mind's Own Place"), one review (of Ginsberg, Olson, and McClure), and made several oblique and aphoristic statements of position for certain little magazines (e.g., West End, Agenda, Montemora). He also, often along with Mary Oppen, gave a number of interesting and subtle interviews in which he discussed his poetics and the meaning of his work.[10] However, Oppen's critical thought, his "manifestos," his meditations on poetry, poetics, and the poet's career, his studies of other writers, are not, in fact, absent. Instead of being public, they occur in two private forms: in working papers (a record of his reading and thinking very often an intersection of meditative poetics and meditative autobiography), and in his correspondence.[11] His letters are both "conversation" (as he said) with others, and as clearly a set of provocative writings that are essays in the oldest sense—a testing out or essaying of his poetics— created and sustained in a private, but interactive, forum. Not only his poetics, but a number of Oppen's poems form within, in relation to, and sometimes even because of the arena of dialogue of his correspondence. Oppen said occasionally that he thought he had "answered" a certain letter, but had done so without writing it down; not just a possible memory slip, this statement suggests that letters to others helped focus and impel Oppen's interior voices.

A Selected Letters of George Oppen provides access to the sustained, elegant, perceptive body of critical and aesthetic thinking which was done by Oppen throughout his poetic career. The combination of letters and working papers will, in toto, constitute Oppen's "selected essays."[12] Oppen's complex, and constantly renegotiated rejection of public stances, his intricate and oblique dealings with fame, as well as his fascination with questioning and conversation, make consistent and characteristic his choice of these mediums for his essayistic writing.

George Oppen (April 24, 1908–July 7, 1984) was born in New Rochelle, New York, to George August Oppenheimer (1881–1954), son of a wholesale diamond merchant, and Elsie Rothfeld ([1884]–1912).[13] When Oppen was four and his older sister Elizabeth (Libby) seven, their mother had a nervous breakdown and shot herself, a wound which caused her death. She left a suicide note (not apparently extant) whose terms haunted Oppen; he cites it, or reconstructs it, from memory in a 1960 letter to June Oppen Degnan. " 'We've been happy - - I love you -- I worry about the children and school and their clothes -- it seems -- since I did this and don't know why -- that I am not fitted for the business of life.' "[14] In March 1917 Oppen's father married Seville Shainwald (January 1891–May 1956), a woman from a very wealthy family. Oppen's half sister, June Frances, was born June 7, 1918; she and Oppen maintained a deep, complex, and mutually illuminating relationship for the greater part of their lives, especially important in the years from Oppen's return to a poetic career in 1958 until his death.

The family moved to San Francisco in 1918. Oppen's high school years were particularly fraught with tension. He attended Warren Military Academy; his sister Libby attended a Dominican convent school. He had a difficult and apparently abusive relationship with his stepmother which, he wrote in a rare statement, gave him both symptoms of asthma and a propensity to violent acting-out of his feelings.[15] His father was an elegant and seductive man.[16] Six weeks before he was due to graduate from high school in 1925, Oppen was the driver in a serious car accident in which one youth was killed. The Academy expelled him for drinking; his expected upper-class college career was aborted. After traveling in Europe, especially in England and Scotland, he returned to the States, attended a small preparatory school, graduated, and, on a whim, to accompany a friend, went north to Oregon State University at Corvallis and matriculated.

Two events of crucial importance then occur. George Oppen simultaneously met Mary Colby and Conrad Aiken's anthology of modern poetry, both in a course soon after he entered college (1926).[17] Both were life-transforming events. They left college as a consequence of their (incidentally unequal) punishments when they violated curfew rules. From the moment they met at about age eighteen, the Oppens had a life-long compact about being together and being artists. This has been movingly traced in a number of poems and interviews, as well as in Mary Oppen's memoir, Meaning a Life. Mary had an independent adolescence—in work, sexual experience, intransigence, and distance from her mother; George claimed that he was "saved" and "freed"—saved from the wounds and limits of his social class among other things—by Mary.

From 1927 to 1929—that is, until Oppen turned twenty-one and received an inheritance from his mother's and maternal grandmother's estates—the young couple had a relationship resistant to and wary of the wealth and expectations of Oppen's family.[18] They moved away from, and back to, the family: hitchhiking across the West in 1927, returning to a seductive life of wealth in San Francisco; driving to Detroit in 1928, and thereupon sailing in a catboat through the Great Lakes, the Erie Canal, and the Hudson River to New York City—where George worked briefly as a switchboard operator in a brokerage house, a job gotten through his uncles, Robert and Tracy Rothfeld. In Dallas, Texas, during their first trip out, on October 7, 1927, the Oppens married, George using the alias "David Verdi."[19]

Oppen's literary life can be glimpsed a little in his youth; a family legend has him, circa eight years old, describing a woman whose "cheeks are as smooth as the sidewalks of Pelham," a trope evincing a preternatural turn to the sincerity of an urban (as well as urbane) realism.[20] He said in his adolescence that he wanted to be a writer; he sent fairy tales to his younger sister from abroad. He also seems to have been writing through his adolescence. But since one of the motifs of the Oppens' lives is a kind of existential decidedness in which insight is attained, and one immediately, even radically, readjusts and sets one's course by that piercing knowledge, it is not narratively inconsistent that the Aiken anthology and the experience of hearing Carl Sandburg in their brief college careers initiated Oppen's poetic ambitions, for both George and Mary were writing in San Francisco in 1928 and in Texas, where early poems (not yet rediscovered) were published.[21] Further, "hitchhiking," noted Mary Oppen, "became more than flight from a powerful family—our discoveries themselves became an esthetic and a disclosure" (MAL 68). Oppen's active literary career intensified in 1928, in New York City, when he and Mary first read, then met, Louis Zukofsky, and through him Charles Reznikoff; by both he was decisively affected, with both decisively affiliated.

In 1929, Oppen began to write *Discrete Series*, and about a year later he had a thirty-two page manuscript, which he circulated in a private edition to a few people—among them Reznikoff, whose copy is preserved.[22] Interestingly, during his "second career," Oppen often returned to ponder this work and its meanings as a gesture of incipience, and as a foreshadowing of certain motifs for his oeuvre as a whole. For example, he was to note the coincidence of his and Heidegger's use of the term boredom in the same year, 1929. He also suggested that "Party on Shipboard," the final poem of *Discrete Series* to be completed, offered oblique statements about the idea of humanity that would be taken up in "Of Being Numerous."[23]

Soon after he turned twenty-one (in 1929), George and Mary Oppen went to France and settled in Le Beausset, in the Var. In October 1931, they formed To Publishers, with Oppen as publisher and Zukofsky, who received a salary of $100 per month, as editor. By 1932 they had published three notable modernist texts: Williams's *A Novelette and Other Prose (1921–1931)*, Pound's *How to Read*, and Zukofsky's *An "Objectivists" Anthology*.[24] However, a combination of factors—Oppen's cut in income, his suspicion of Pound's politics, an inability to distribute the books, much less break even, and a changing political climate—made the enterprise go under before it had carried out one of its major missions: the publication of a complete prose of Ezra Pound.

The Oppens returned to the United States in 1933. But the desire to see certain new work in print had not ended. In October 1933, a group of writers around Zukofsky, instigated by Zukofsky with the active interest of Pound, set up a short-lived publication cooperative called The Objectivist Press. Each book was self-financed. Despite being at the center of the group, Zukofsky did not have enough money to publish his own work, but the press brought out in 1934 Williams's *Collected Poems 1921–31*, Oppen's *Discrete Series*, and three books by Reznikoff—*Jerusalem the Golden, Testimony,* and *In Memoriam: 1933*; a Reznikoff book called *Separate Ways* appeared in 1936. The "Preface" by Ezra Pound and the review in *Poetry* by William Carlos Williams of Oppen's *Discrete Series* became talismanic documents for Oppen's future literary career.

In a major decision undertaken in winter 1935, at the time of the Popular Front, the Oppens joined the Communist Party; the political crisis of unemployment and poverty galvanized them. They worked as organizers for a social change which was democratic socialist and populist in its ultimate contours, but also committed to the class analysis of Marxism.[25] Their political coming-of-age in the Party during the Popular Front era paralleled the experience of a whole generation of American radicals. Because of his resistance to the instrumental use of artists within the Party, Oppen concealed his vocation and soon stopped writing.[26]

Thereupon began an almost twenty-five-year period of poetic silence (1934–58). There were complex, overlapping reasons for initiating this silence in the thirties, and for maintaining it through the forties and fifties: a critique of modernism which ran counter to contemporary critical, poetic, and academic thinking, a choice of activism in a deeply felt polit-

ical crisis, a process of self-testing, a war injury, and recovery; later these
were joined by a set of taboos and inhibitions around parenthood, and a
fear of his own power.[27] The silence existed in a relationship to his career
as a poet; it did not simply negate the career. In a late 1972 letter to Harvey
Shapiro, Oppen said that he stopped in midpoem when he (in effect)
realized that he had no experience to write from, and so he sought a forum
for his instruction in affiliations and actions outside of literary tradition:
"When I quit writing I was attempting a poem that began : [']twenty-first
birthday / stitch taken without thread' ('twenty-first' because twenty third
or fourth, whichever it was didn't go as smoothly)." Oppen's silence had
a situational necessity: "25 years to write the next poem means. . . It
means we knew we didn't know enough from the poetry that was being
written; from the poetry we had written. And when the [political] crisis
occurred we knew we didn't know what the world was and we knew we
had to find out so it was a poetic exploration at the same time that it was
an act of conscience."[28] The period of political activism and political consequences offered Oppen cultural instruction.

Some of the biographical information (mainly exact dates) about
this period of silence comes from whatever was not blackened out or excised by bureaucratic censor-readers of Oppen's FBI file, which was obtained in 1988 for purposes of this edition under the Freedom of Information Act. The Oppens' main period of political activity and active
membership went from 1936 to 1941; after the war they were "a little bit
active" but "very uncomfortable" and "ready to leave."[29] They were organizers for the Workers' Alliance and Oppen was "Kings County election
campaign manager for Communist Party in 1936 elections."[30] The stories
of their helping the Farmers' Union organize a milk strike around Utica,
New York (after their training in a Party school), are told in Meaning a Life.

Oppen's political opinions were also explicitly antifascist. His sis-
ter, June, remembered his guilt about not going to fight in the Spanish Civil
War. He was old but not overage for military service, with a young child,
Linda Jean (born 1940), and had a work exemption as a pattern maker in
Grumman Aircraft, Hempstead, Long Island, when he abruptly moved to
Detroit to provoke his induction in the U.S. Army (November 27, 1942).
His daughter also suggested that Oppen's negative opinions about the Hit-
ler-Stalin Pact (1939) were such that he was almost expelled from the
Party.[31] Oppen was trained in an antitank company, and, serving with the
411th Infantry in the 103rd Division, he saw active duty in the European
theater for the year between October 1944 and 1945, landing in Marseilles,

and fighting in the Battle of the Bulge, part of the Rhineland campaign (September 15, 1944–March 21, 1945, to win territory through France to the Rhine). Oppen also served in the Central Europe campaign, beginning on March 22, 1945, crossing the Rhine River into Germany; Germany surrendered on May 9, 1945. Only several weeks before, on April 22, 1945, Oppen had been gravely wounded in a foxhole receiving direct shell fire; his companions were killed. This frightening and transformative moment is reflected in a number of poems late in his career: "Of Hours," the third of "Some San Francisco Poems," "The Myth of the Blaze," and "Semite." Other aspects of the war experience infuse "Of Being Numerous" and "Route." For his war service he received full disability benefits from the Veterans' Administration and a number of medals, including the Purple Heart.[32] Oppen was, at later junctures (cf. CP 189), to suspect some of his motives and to feel guilt at the level of personal risk he took in his army service.

During the postwar era, after a cross-country trip with a homemade trailer, the Oppens moved to Redondo Beach, California, where George became a contractor and then a custom carpenter. The Oppens supported the campaign of Henry Wallace for president on the Independent Progressive ticket, and other local left candidates.[33] After the war, in 1946, Mary Oppen has said "we had left the Party (in our heads)," and when they lived in Redondo Beach they did not transfer to a local party branch.[34] However, neither did they hand in their membership cards. The growing climate of repression both in California (the Tenney Committee, the jailing of the Hollywood Ten) and then in the country as a whole meant that even former membership left one open to official harassment. Hence, they technically remained members of the CPUSA (yet did not follow its policies) straight through the McCarthy era.[35] As Mary Oppen said of the process of leaving the Party: "It was not a clear decision and then no more contact. McCarthy interfered. To leave the Party after June 1950 meant indictment and imprisonment or naming names."[36]

The FBI's career of Oppen-watching extended from 1941 to 1966, also, ironically, a twenty-five-year period. The FBI began serious harassment of Oppen in 1949 with two visits to the Oppens themselves; during the first, on May 13, 1949, Oppen had "not been reported to be currently active in Communist party affairs"; during the second, on June 24, Oppen was eloquently antagonistic about their intrusion upon political and civil rights.[37] It is important to remember that by January 1949 the Smith Act had been invoked to indict the leadership of the American Communist

Party on the grounds of conspiracy to teach or advocate the overthrow of the government by force.[38] Justice Department officials in 1950 threatened the prosecution of between 12,000 and 20,000 people under the Smith Act—names of those on the so-called "Security Index."[39] It should also be noted that the Los Angeles region had been the site of a bitter labor struggle between rival unions organizing the Hollywood work force (1945–46). One of the earliest uses of national hearings by the House Committee on Un-American Activities (HUAC) about political affiliations occurred in October 1947 with the charge—in causal relation to the union struggle—that the motion picture industry was "infiltrated by Communists." This was the general context in which the Oppens viewed their harassment by the FBI and its attempt to sever them from their neighborhood and community in Redondo Beach. The threat of general and widespread Smith Act prosecutions seemed reasonable at that time. Oppen implied that there was some reason for them to fear HUAC, aside from the general assault on civil rights and the climate of fear.[40] This may have been the fact that the Oppens had begun an unaffiliated, short-lived protest and petition campaign against the Korean War in 1950.[41] In any event, they would not have "cooperated"—in the sly metaphor of the times—with HUAC had they been called to testify, but had they made an issue of noncooperation, among other effects, it would have meant the possible abandonment of their daughter, Linda, to go to jail.[42] In June 1950, fearing further and increased levels of harassment, the Oppens went into political exile in Mexico, joining some of their friends.

Political exile did not mean the end of "FBI-like" harassment, for the Office of the Director of the FBI actively and assiduously sought to extend and disseminate his files (e.g., sending these reports to U.S. Embassy Legal Attaché in Mexico and France, and Department of State, Office of Security).[43] Periodically, all American political exiles living in Mexico might see their names on a standard—and static—list published in the English-language daily whenever a political flurry necessitated some reminder of "known subversives." There were six-month residence checks whose information was, through whatever channels, passed into Oppen's FBI file. In 1956 the Los Angeles office of the SACB (Subversive Activities Control Board) called for removing Oppen from the Security Index, but for reasons blanked out in his files the director of the FBI intervened to prevent it; later, on November 11, 1957, Oppen's name was indeed removed from the Security Index.[44]

While in Mexico, Oppen supervised work as a manufacturer of furniture in a cabinetmaker shop in a partnership with Carlos Ayala (begun 1951); he was barred, by law, from direct manual labor.[45] Oppen worked briefly for General Electric in Mexico (1957). He also briefly formed a corporation for investment in Mexican real estate, and, for three months, served as its treasurer (November 1957–January 1958; UCSD 16, 1, 1). Early on, from 1951, perhaps to the end of his eligibility in June 1955, Oppen used the G.I. Bill to attend a distinguished art school—Escuela de Pintura y Escultura Esmeralda—and did wood carvings in bas-relief. A few are still extant. However, he apparently wrote virtually nothing—no poems, not even letters; Linda Oppen Mourelatos remembers only a comic driver's manual produced for Charles Humboldt.[46] Of course, the American exiles were in absolute political échec and did not engage in political activities. The Oppens had originally hoped wholeheartedly to enter Mexican life; for a variety of reasons, including, with bitter irony, the inevitability of maintaining high bourgeois social class, they found they could not.[47]

The year 1958 was a turning point. The Oppens had applied for a U.S. passport less than a year after arriving in Mexico (in March 1951); it was granted seven years (and many political changes and court cases) later, in August 1958. This passport symbolized the end of McCarthyite harassment of United States citizens and guaranteed their right to travel. In 1958, very depressed, Mary initiated her own visits to a therapist, and George—in a decisive moment—had analyzed his "rust in copper" dream quickly, with the same therapist.[48] This was a dream connected with his father's instructions for preventing rust in copper; the dream's punch line, delivered in therapy—"you were dreaming that you don't want to rust"—and Oppen's strained, even suicidal, hilarity that the rust was supposed, ridiculously, to be in copper—formed a complex depth charge that unblocked Oppen the poet.[49] The association of "copper" with "Oppen" (and perhaps even with communist Oppen and Poppa) is very suggestive; Oppen not only could not rust, definitionally (as copper), he also had a paternal and sororal mandate that such rust was going to be prevented.

Also, in early 1958, Linda was admitted to Sarah Lawrence College; she matriculated in the autumn, and her parents visited her over Thanksgiving of that year. Oppen had some complex protective sense about fatherhood, exacerbated by the family's life in exile, which made him mute and censor the possibility of writing to protect Linda from his skepticism and his apocalyptic fears of the atomic age when Linda was a "child." The extension of this protection until Linda departed for college is a curiosity; Linda served, not willingly, as the final complex justification for Oppen's not writing. Oppen seems, throughout the time in exile, to have felt both power and fear at once; the Mexican photographs often show a saturnine and brooding face.

In May 1958, Oppen began writing again; his first work was "Blood from the Stone" (then titled "To Date"). When he typed up this and a few other completed poems in January 1959, he poignantly dated that one, in a slip, January 1949 (UCSD 16, 1, 1).[50] He began to work extremely hard on poetry, and began his significant correspondence—through which he built a literary and moral context, demanded a response to his writing, and set forth its claims. In February, March, and August 1959, Oppen initiated contact with publishers—his sister, June Oppen Degnan, who was affiliated with *The San Francisco Review*, James Laughlin, and Henry Rago of *Poetry Magazine*, where a number of his new poems were published. After a visit to New York in 1959, and a return trip to Mexico with the Zukofskys, the Oppens came back permanently to the United States in January 1960. Just about the time they were returning to the United States, his sister Libby died; Oppen assumed she had committed suicide.[51] This event focused his long-standing sense of possessive concern, as sole male, for the women in his extended family.

Amid the constant, and assiduous writing—a whole oeuvre created in the twenty years between 1958 and 1978—the Oppens traveled a good deal in Europe and the Caribbean and summered on Penobscot Bay in Maine (Little Deer Island and Eagle Island) where they sailed a small boat.[52] In 1961 he worked closely with Charles Reznikoff in the preparation of selected poems called *By the Waters of Manhattan*; in 1963 he performed a similar function for William Bronk and *The World, the Worldless*. This editorial work framed the completion and publication of *The Materials* in 1962.[53] In October 1964 Oppen delivered the manuscript of *This in Which* to San Francisco Review–New Directions; it was published a year later.[54] During the summer of 1965 Oppen reopened the poem "A Language of New York" and circulated it, in changed form, among some correspondents. That poem modulated into "Of Being Numerous" by early 1966—this being one of Oppen's central works, and one saturated with his political meditations and commitments, including his response to the assassination of Kennedy and his early opposition to and local activism against the Vietnam War. During the New York years Oppen was involved in the Academy of American Poets reading series at the Guggenheim Museum; he both read and introduced poets a number of times, and maintained a correspondence with Betty Kray, suggesting and proposing poets. His first book, *Discrete Series,* was republished in a (prefaceless) facsimile in 1966.

In December 1966, the Oppens moved from their Henry Street apartment in Brooklyn Heights to San Francisco. They bought a house at 2811 Polk Street into which they were able to move by the end of 1967. A number of letters meditate on the meanings of the two cities in his life and the feeling of such a transition back to the place where his family had lived during his adolescence, and to a place experiencing the end of 1960s hippie activism. Oppen began to write "Some San Francisco Poems" during 1967, and in March to April 1969 poems from and versions of that sequence were circulated by Oppen among Harvey Shapiro, Michael Heller, Linda Oppen Mourelatos, and Diane [Andy] Meyer.

Of Being Numerous was published in March 1968; in April of that year Oppen went to the University of Wisconsin-Madison as one of the "Objectivists" interviewed by L. S. Dembo. This was an important moment in the recognition of the continuing significance of these poets, and a moment that Oppen appreciated as such.[55] During 1968–69 he gave several poetry readings, and in June 1969 he remet Ezra Pound. But also in 1969, after Oppen was awarded the Pulitzer Prize for poetry in May, a crisis about fame and self-presentation came to a head. In November 1969 Oppen sent a multiple carbon mailing—what he called, in a pun, a "bad-form letter"—and canceled outright a reading tour involving a number of cross-country appearances.

The early 1970s were marked by depression over the failure of The Fulcrum Press in England to publish his *Collected Poems* for which Oppen had signed a contract in March 1969. After much rankling delay, the book was published in December 1972. During the early 1970s as well, Oppen contracted for *Seascape: Needle's Eye* to be published by a small press; unsatisfied with them, he withdrew it, and it was, happily, then published by Sumac Press in November 1972. Oppen also experienced difficulties defining the nature of his poetry after the summary of much of his life represented by "Of Being Numerous."

In 1973, Oppen undertook a major set of public appearances, residencies, and readings. He read in San Diego and at the San Francisco Museum of Modern Art with Robert Duncan.[56] In May, Oppen did a number of readings in England: at Gonville and Caius College, Cambridge; at the University of East Anglia; and finally at a "Modern American Poetry Conference" at the Polytechnic of Central London, at which he was honored as one of four notable American poets with Duncan, Rothenberg, and Ted Berrigan.[57] On his return to the States, Oppen then attended the National Poetry Festival at Thomas Jefferson College, Allendale, Michigan, in June.[58] Oppen always struggled with feelings of neglect and sympathized with poets who shared these feelings; he had an astonished flirtation with the possibility of fame. At the same time he participated irregularly and with some suspicion (but no rancor) in the public (and sometimes self-publicizing) gestures of the "poetry scene."

In 1974, Oppen prepared his *Collected Poems* for New Directions. This work was published in October 1975 with a paperback edition a year later in October 1976. During 1975, Mary was writing her memoir *Meaning a Life*, and George saw his work featured in an issue of *Ironwood*. In September to mid-October they were in residence at Mishkenot Sha'ananim in Jerusalem. This invitation to visit Israel corresponded with some pensive meditations upon Jewishness in such poems as "Semite" and "Disasters," meditations reflected in a number of letters from the mid 1970s. The return from Israel (and Greece) was approximately the beginning of a slowly emerging but marked change in Oppen's health, which became more clearly apparent in 1977, the final summer they spent in Maine.

In the fall of 1977 Oppen completed his final book, *Primitive*, a title with implications like *basis, basic,* or *first things.* Mary Oppen assisted him with secreterial help. This was atypical of their practice, and was related to Oppen's decline.[59] After that time Oppen could complete no more poems, although he wrote a large number of aphorisms.[60] His letters also decrease noticeably. In 1978 *Primitive* was published by Black Sparrow Press; the author's copy was sent to George on April 24, his seventieth birthday. In June of that year Mary's *Meaning a Life* was also published by Black Sparrow. In the early 1980s Oppen was honored for his work by the American Academy and Institute of Arts and Letters and by the National Endowment for the Arts; in 1982 he received the PEN/West Rediscovery Award.[61] Two special collections of essays, studies, and tributes were published, and his seventy-fifth birthday was celebrated publicly in 1983. In 1982, after years of puzzling symptoms, and much pain and grief in relation to their physical and mental manifestations, Oppen was diagnosed as having Alzheimer's Disease. He entered a nursing home in January 1984 and died in July of that year at the Idlewood Convalescent Home in Sunnyvale, California.

Editorial Comments

Criteria for Selection

These letters document Oppen's career as a writer, a critic, an encouraging presence to other writers, and a contributor to an objectivist poetics. The greatest emphasis has been given to statements about his poems and his poetics, and then to essaying comments of general interest which fit the criterion of working papers. Among these are Oppen's political meditations, especially as these provide a context for his poems. The collection continually confronts the reader with the questions of the relationship of political commitment to poetic process, production, and to poetic meaning—questions to which Oppen's career gives several complex answers, and questions which he never ceased to examine.

Oppen is sometimes asked, and always fairly willing to offer his definition of his cohort—the "Objectivist" poets—and his letters necessarily contain reflections on them as individuals. It is Louis Zukofsky with whom Oppen maintained the relationship of greatest stress, and there are both letters to him, and commentary about him throughout. There are, as well, letters to Carl Rakosi and a commentary about *Amulet*, letters to and even more comments about Charles Reznikoff, and some notes on both Lorine Niedecker and Basil Bunting. He developed a deeply felt colleagueship with Robert Duncan after his move to San Francisco, and maintained a strong bond to Harvey Shapiro. Oppen's letters are also filled with "letters to young poets"—in fact, many more than could be accommodated here—and with some blunt advice to all poets; these become a vital source for his poetics.[1]

Oppen drafted—and saved drafts of—some of his letters. Sometimes he apparently drafted letters that were not sent. Because I am interested in considering the letters as a form of his prose writing (as "essays"), these letters, when of intrinsic interest, will be included whether or not they were sent. Further, there is clearly general relation between some of the working papers and some letters. Letters sometimes began as notes in the working paper mode or turned into them (and then may not have been sent). It was beyond the scope of this collection to trace the instances of this practice.

While both his letters and his working papers could be continuations of discussions held in person, it should also be remembered that these letters do not reflect the extent of Oppen's relations with others, nor signal, in any special or exclusive way, his friends. Letters are an accident of place; one may write only sporadically, or be less likely to write at all, if one lives in the same city and sees a friend on a regular basis. There are a number of people who had extremely close ties with Oppen and yet whose contact occurred mainly in conversation; they are unreflected here.

In an amusingly unpromising remark, Oppen noted to himself (UCSD 16, 16, 2): "I have an offensive epistolary style. The result partly of compression. Or of bad character." Oppen's style is both elliptical and, while interrogative, also quite definite. It is "full of tentatives and hesitations," as he remarked (to F. Will in 1967); the "bad character" is revealed by his tendency "to omit" not only connectives both syntactic and rhetorical, but also to omit "the phrase 'I think.' "[2] Narrative and exposition are not, indeed, characteristic of Oppen's poetry; his letters are similar, and, like his working papers, some might be usefully seen as a species of poetic text. This is, in fact, an exaggeration of the general tendency in the genre of letters, which, as Sharon Hileman shows, may be abrupt, associative, quite conscious of "spatial or temporal gaps," and ungoverned by either the causalities or the climaxes of "sequentially structured narratives."[3]

Design of the Presentation

Every letter is headed with a fourfold notation, comprising (1) the name of the recipient, (2) the date, (3) information about the text, whether typed or autograph, and (4) the provenance of the letter.[4] The letterhead with address is excluded, because Oppen sometimes used older or uncorrected letterhead that did not indicate where he actually was.[5] All recipients are identified by a brief bio-bibliographic paragraph; these are grouped at the end of the collection. The letters with autograph inserts (beyond the correction of typographical errors) and autograph postscripts are always noted as such, in part because of the intense difficulty of reading Oppen's writing.[6] Notes appear at the end of the book and are numbered consecutively throughout the letters for each year.

There are three main sources for the letters which I have collected here. About half of the letters have their provenance in The Archive for New Poetry, The Mandeville Department of Special Collections of the University of California at San Diego, La Jolla, California. The Oppen Archive there consists of three components: (1) The George Oppen Papers, 1958–84, including letters to him. These papers sometimes include carbon copies and drafts of outgoing letters (Mss. 16, 33 boxes). (2) The papers of Linda Oppen Mourelatos, in which are preserved much family correspondence, including her letters from her father (Mss. 33, 3 boxes). (3) The literary papers of June Oppen Degnan, who worked as an editor of *The San Francisco Review*, and who received many letters from her brother (Mss. 17, 8 boxes). Diane Meyer's papers have gone to the Archive as well; this set of Oppen's letters to his niece is important (in Mss. 16). I have made extensive use of these materials, and the Archive has been unfailingly generous in support of this project. The Archive is now also the source of some letters of Oppen to Steven Schneider and William Bronk, although both of these had helpfully given copies of their letters to me prior to their acquisition by the Archive. This essential collection, comprising working papers and drafts of poems as well, will be abbreviated UCSD in the heading to individual letters.

The second main source for Oppen letters, close to the other half of the material I have collected since 1980, comes from individual correspondents who entrusted to me copies of their letters from Oppen. Although I gave all correspondents the option of excising material from their letters prior to passing them to me, only two correspondents did so. It is also my strong impression that very few—a scant handful—of the letters of any general literary interest were held back for private reasons. Although my search was extensive and repeated, there may have been correspondents whom I missed. I regret any omissions very much.

The third source, comprising numerically fewer letters than the above, was a variety of Special Collections in many university and college libraries. The librarians of those collections and the libraries richly deserve the individual thanks which I tender in the acknowledgments.

Gradations of Datability

One of the peculiarities of all the Oppen letters I collected or received from libraries is that virtually all—I would estimate between 90–95 percent—are undated in the body of the letter. Creating viable and defensible dates for almost every letter was one of the major challenges of the edition.

My notation indicates gradations of datability. Letters fully dated by Oppen—by month, day, and year—will always bear the notation "(dated)" to signal this fact. Dates on the majority of the rest of the letters will be factually inferred, in various ways which I shall outline below. *All of these dates will be given in square brackets even if there is reasonable assurance of their accuracy.*[7] It should also be noted that the sequencing of letters, in the majority of this edition, is based on inferred dates. In many cases my task was aided by internal historical references, but anyone who wishes to base a critical argument on the exact sequence of Oppen's letters should be forewarned that most dates have been editorially inferred.

Given the difficulty of establishing dates, some discussion of how these "factually inferred" dates were created seems necessary. The reader should note that often a combination of the tactics listed below were brought into play for any individual letter whose postmark was not available.

(a) Use of postmark. In some cases, envelopes were made available to me; in some cases postmark dates were written on letters. While it appears that Oppen usually wrote and sent letters on the same day, nonetheless postmark dates are given in square brackets. June Oppen Degnan wrote postmark dates on her brother's letters.

(b) Date of receipt. A few correspondents (such as James Laughlin and Donald Davie) noted the date of receipt of a letter and even sometimes the date of response. I have used these dates to establish a "date" for the letter.

(c) The "Letters-In" file. The Oppen collection at The Archive for New Poetry has twelve boxes of letters to Oppen with between forty to sixty folders in each box. Some of these letters correspond to the answers Oppen sent, or respond to what Oppen said, and if those letters are dated, an approximate date (often month and year) can be established for an Oppen letter. Some of these dates will be given as, e.g. "[before February 7, 1974]" which may be translated: on February 7, the correspondent replied explicitly to issues Oppen raised; Oppen's letter preceded it by an undetermined amount of time.

(d) Some correspondents had kept dated carbon copies of their letters to Oppen which they kindly provided to me; this facilitated the dating of, inter alia, the letters of John Crawford, Michael Heller, and Hugh Seidman.

(e) Some letters will allude to verifiable events (i.e., the Pulitzer Prize award, a poetry reading, a political event), and a date can be assigned. Some letters allude to events in process—books to be published, items forthcoming. The correspondents themselves, and certain reference works such as almanacs and *Facts on File*, have been used to date (often by month and year) letters which allude to these events. For all information about Oppen's life I prepared a chronology with assistance from Mary Oppen, June Oppen Degnan, Linda Oppen Mourelatos, and others. This document, on which I drew for my introduction, helped me to date certain letters.

(f) I interviewed certain correspondents who helped retrospectively to sequence and date letters to themselves; especially significant help was given by Diane Meyer, John Crawford, and Harvey Shapiro.

(g) If only a year date was possible to infer, *such letters are printed at either the beginning or the end of a given year*, depending on whether internal evidence pointed in one of those two directions. If there is some doubt, a question mark is added to the year, e.g., [1971?].

It was the aim of this edition to date as accurately as possible every letter by Oppen included here.

Textual Issues

A letter by Oppen usually had double spaces between paragraphs as well as an irregular indication of a left margin, almost always far larger than the normal "5 space tab." Closure of sentences was often suspended, and dashes were typed with space around them. Some unconventional, emphatic dashes were invented of up to nine hyphens in sequence. Parentheses and quotation marks opened and often did not close. Oppen underlined and capitalized for emphasis, but very often elided titles of works and of journals into lowercase letters, without italicization or quotation marks.[8] Sometimes words in a sentence were framed by surrounding them with white space. Any letter by Oppen generally had plenty of open space. In a letter to Dan Gerber [June 22, 1971], explicitly, if briefly, about the poetics of letters, Oppen speaks about the use of expressive space in his letters to be "something about breaking the words, the sentences, the locutions *open* to make some room for ourselves   Here among the subatomic fragments." In 1969, Oppen wrote, of Armand Schwerner: "A number of experimental poems, largely experiments in the isolation of words, a exploration, depend on space and the organization of the page which cannot be displayed in brief quotation but achieve in the book a remarkably pure lyricism of word and silence and of skepticism."[9]

For the kinds of textual issues which these statements on notation suggest, I have taken a posture of compromised editorial humility, not seeking to normalize or to conventionalize Oppen's presentation. On the other hand, in print, it is not possible, or even always desirable, to approximate a facsimile of the text. Therefore, the following ground rules seemed to walk the difficult line between normalization and respect.

(1) Closure has rarely been provided in any situation normally calling for such, if it was not present in Oppen's letter. Periods have not been added at the end of the sentences I could, if I were playing grammarian, define. Parentheses have not been closed when left open by Oppen. "Close quote" quotation marks have been added only if confusion in reading threatens to become acute; I thereupon provide some punctuation in square brackets; e.g., [']. But the gain in the constant exfoliation of thought to thought and the record of mergings and associations are all appropriate to the rhythms of the letters. By this tactic of noninterference, Oppen's deeply imbedded syntactic, structural, and philosophic rejection of closure, finality, or absolutes is respected in its textual manifestation. One other striking rejection of closure occurs in Oppen's ubiquitous postscripts, which often become longer than the letter.

(2) No mark of punctuation, with one exception, has been normalized.[10] Oppen's surprising and witty notational system has been retained. In the case of parentheses one may see ((((((((((or even (((((opening thoughts and afterthoughts. None of these exfoliating parentheses has been closed unless Oppen closed it/them; obviously, the petal- or wave-like signs on the page have been retained. In the case of hyphens and dashes all have been given as Oppen generally typed them, and have been notated in ways consistent with his typing when I transcribed autograph letters. Normally, Oppen used space to set off a dash; this has been retained, and, when rendered in the text, all "normal" dashes have been regularized into Oppen's usual procedure. There is also a long dash— anywhere from three to eight or nine hyphens joined—these make an interior code of extension and connection throughout letters. These more extensive dashes of varying lengths mark pulse and notate a startled interior listening, but have been regularized on the text page.

(3) These letters are characterized by a large amount of unconventional space between individual words, between paragraphs, and in indentation of paragraphs. This space has been a very vexing issue because while as a critic and poet (and letter recipient) I found it fascinating and justifiable, as an editor I was forced to see that its retention would have

been problematic for the collection.[11] After trying the presentation of the page in a way much closer to facsimile, I discovered how much this would compromise the number of letters I could include, and just how homemade it looked. Feeling that, in the final analysis, it was Oppen's words that were of value more than his "silences" (however interdependent these arguably are; see his note to himself, 1966), I made a very simple decision by a very painful route. All Oppen letters are presented indented with generous spacing for every paragraph. This is meant to symbolize the irregular "tabbing" which is characteristic of Oppen, by which he offers the possibility of a new "margin" beginning anywhere on the page. This edition will give a more than normally spaced indentation, but one normalized to the printed page.[12] The irregular local spaces between words were sometimes dropped because of typesetting requirements. Oppen most often double-spaced between paragraphs, except when he was writing a more formal, or business, letter. The floating paragraph on a canvas of white has not been retained.

Oppen used space between words as a form of punctuation with openness. Those local spaces have been given approximately as written so that the isolation of words or phrases has been consistently respected. The principle, thus, of space is that the more local space (within sentences and paragraphs) has been retained, but the spaces surrounding paragraphs and indenting them have been standardized.

Other Editorial Corrections

In the case of spelling, I have retained Oppen's versions as much as possible.[13] When there was an obvious misspelling of any kind (*too* for *to*, or the spelling of any proper noun), I have corrected it. When typographical errors occurred, I have corrected them, except in the rare cases when the missing letter(s) could plausibly indicate a joshing tone, a colloquialism, or a dialect. All proper nouns have been capitalized, although a few of the errors in this practice by Oppen are worth noting: that lowercase "art" in such forms as "San Francisco Museum of art"; "New York Museum of Modern art" bear some weight, as, does the occasional use of "jew" for "Jew."

When Oppen used quotation marks, he often varied, for no apparent reason, between double and single form, even around the same phrase. Therefore all of Oppen's quotation marks have been normalized to singles; all editorial quotation marks are doubles. All close quotation marks are given in standard American usage, that is, outside commas and periods. This last constitutes a complete and thoroughgoing correction of Oppen's habits. The other correction in quotation marks has to do with the way they can hang at some distance from their citation. I have corrected the gap between punctuation and statement for quotation marks and semicolons, but have left the gap where periods were concerned.

The ends of lines are always "wrapped around." I have not tried to replicate Oppen's "line breaks" at the right margin, although occasionally these seemed to me interestingly expressive; this sense of prose "line breaks" was especially true for autograph letters late in his life.

Oppen very rarely used square brackets; the one or two uses (e.g., in a letter to Harvey Shapiro, Fall 1975) have always been normalized to parentheses, so that I could retain square brackets as the exclusive sign of editorial interpolation.

Oppen's Citations and Allusions

I have noted the sources of Oppen's literary and cultural allusions in most cases. When he cites from his own work or alludes to it, I intrude [CP]—*The Collected Poems of George Oppen*—with a page number in square brackets. His final book, *Primitive*, is of course [P]. Whenever I find a line in a letter that seems to go into a poem in a slightly altered form, I note [cf. CP]. Sometimes Oppen will misquote; an interesting example is a difference in emphasis between his memory of Zukofsky's "An Objective" and what Zukofsky actually said. I have tried to track down all such allusions, and put the original in a note. Under no circumstances would I change Oppen's remembered word to comply with technical accuracy, because the nature of the misremembering could be pertinent.

Acknowledgments

George and Mary Oppen originally agreed to this collection in 1980; my great joy is to acknowledge that trust. Their friendship, sustained over more than twenty years, has saturated a good deal of my life and work. Linda Oppen Mourelatos assisted in countless ways with information, verification of my readings of autograph materials, repeated proofreading of my drafts. This was all accomplished with unstinting generosity and perceptiveness. The deep support and interest of June Oppen Degnan and other family members—Diane Meyer, Eve Haight, Alexander P. D. Mourelatos, Aubrey Degnan-Sutter, the late Panthea Perry—were central to the project.

The papers of the Oppen family were purchased by The Archive for New Poetry in 1983 and catalogued and photocopied by 1988. The Archive has been a very hospitable and useful place to work; its collections are superb, and the staff unflaggingly welcomed their sporadic East Coast visitor. Among the helpful were Stephen Rodefer and John Granger, former and current curators of the collection, Lillian Gutierrez, Geoffrey Wexler, Jackie Dooley, and most especially Lynda Claassen, Director of The Mandeville Department of Special Collections. Bradley Westbrook catalogued the collection of the George Oppen Papers and was of great help. The assistance of Michael Davidson, Professor of Literature and former Curator of the Archive, I shall put in a special category of thanks—for hospitality, friendship, and informed hopes for the project as a whole, and as well for a thoroughgoing reading of my introduction. Marjorie Perloff, and anonymous readers, as well as Joanne Ferguson of Duke University Press, each in distinctive ways, contributed to the ultimate appearance of these letters as a book.

The academic leave which I was awarded by Temple University in 1987–88 contributed immeasurably to my ability to finish this work. Temple University not only supported me with this Study Leave, but also had awarded me a Faculty Summer Research Fellowship (1985) and a Grant-in-Aid of Research (1983), which were applied to this work. I am very grateful for the institutional support I have had for this and other of my scholarly projects. Temple University also awarded me a Research Assistant for 1986–87; Heather Thomas's contact with correspondents and biographical research contributed decisively to the pool of information both for my biobibliographic section and for annotations. I would like to thank her for being an enthusiastic partner in that phase of my work. In addition, two National Endowment for the Humanities Travel to Collections Grants, in 1985 (deferred to 1986) and 1988 (deferred to 1989), facilitated two trips to The Archive for New Poetry at La Jolla.

A number of people gave special help at key moments. Eliot Weinberger helped immeasurably at the beginning of the project by developing a mailing list of possible Oppen correspondents, and at the end by casting a skilled editorial eye on my introduction. Certain of my colleagues and friends submitted to bibliographic quizzes which helped me annotate the letters: among these are Gabrielle Bernhard Jackson, Bruce Comans, Marion Faber, Tom Jackson, Steven Lehmen, Marjorie Murphy, Judith Lowder Newton, Daniel O'Hara, Daniel P. Tompkins, Nigel Wheale, the late Kathleen Zsamar, and always, with tact and resourcefulness, Linda Oppen Mourelatos. Shirley Kaufman and Rachel Back did specific tasks in Israel. Bill Ryan and Steve Hanneford each gave vital bits of word-processing information—however simple it may have seemed to them. Lois Peterson, the former, and Minda Hart, the current InterLibrary Loan officer at Swarthmore College Library, allowed me to exercise my borrowing privileges to the utmost. Steven Sowards, the Humanities Librarian at Swarthmore College, gave explicit help. Eleanor Bennett, Administrator of the Swarthmore College History Department, allowed me to use computer and Xeroxing facilities as a "51st State." Oppen's military record was interpreted for me through the courtesy of Joseph M. Logan, Retirement Service Officer, Fort Dix, New Jersey. Finally, I am grateful to the Freedom of Information Act for opening the (however narrowly interpreted) possibilities of using FBI files for scholarly research.

Without the patience and forbearance of all the correspondents of Oppen, this edition would not have been possible. The correspondents whom I contacted offered their patient assistance, endured queries and probings for facts and dates, and were disinterestedly helpful. They provided, over the years, close to half the pool of letters with which I worked to make this selection. Often their Oppen letters have come to me with eloquent reminiscences of, and testaments to, Oppen's generosity, integrity, and presence. This collection is in large measure a tribute to the nature of those individual relationships. They are Anne-Marie Albiach, Charles Amirkhanian, David Antin, Paul Auster, Anthony Barnett, Anita Barrows, Philip Booth, William Bronk, Jane Cooper, Cid Corman, Ed Cox, John Crawford, Robert Creeley, Michael Cuddihy, Shirley Kaufman Daleski, Donald Davie, L. S. Dembo, Robert J. Bertholf for the Estate of Robert Duncan, Theodore Enslin, Serge Fauchereau, Kathleen Fraser, Theresa Fulton and her executor David Eisendrath, Dan Gerber, Maria Gitin, Eli Goldblatt, Linda Gregg, Jonathan Griffin, Michael Hamburger, Charles Hanzlicek, Michael Heller, Milton Hindus, Eric Homberger, Miriam Humboldt Schwartz for Charles Humboldt, David Ignatow, Frances Jaffer, George Johnston, Robert Kelly, Hugh Kenner, Elizabeth Kray, her executor, Vladimir Ussachevsky, and assistant Kathleen Norris, James Laughlin, S. R. Lavin, Denise Levertov, Philip Levine, Mark Linenthal, Jane Lippe-Fine, David McAleavey, Tom McGrath, Gerard Malanga, Jack Marshall, John Martin, Diane Meyer, Eric Mottram, Alexander P. D. Mourelatos, Linda Mourelatos, Edward Mycue, Aleksandar Nejgebauer, Audrey Nicholson, Geoffrey O'Brien, Michael O'Brien, Sharon Olds, Max Pepper, Allen Planz, J. H. Prynne, Carl Rakosi, Naomi Replansky, Carol Tinker for the Estate of Kenneth Rexroth, Zivia Syrkin Wurtele for the Estate of Charles Reznikoff, Martin J. Rosenblum, Jerome Rothenberg, Claude Royet-Journoud, Anthony Rudolf, Steven J. Schneider, Philip Schultz, Ethel Schwabacher through her literary executors Christopher Schwabacher and Brenda S. Webster, Armand Schwerner, Hugh Seidman, Harvey Shapiro, Tom Sharp, Charles Simic, Mary Ellen Solt, Gilbert Sorrentino, Sherman Stein, Tony Stoneburner, John Taggart, Charles Tomlinson, Robert Vas Dias, Diane Wakoski, Sarah Appleton Weber, Brenda S. Webster, James Weil, Eliot Weinberger, Henry Weinfield, J. D. Whitney, Frederic Will, John Wilson, Douglas Worth, and Julian Zimet.

Others in charge of specific archives of—or pockets of—information assisted with, in certain cases, detailed responses to queries. I should like to thank Randall Babtkis and Brian Mertens of the Academy of American Poets; Professor L. S. Dembo of the University of Wisconsin-Madison; James Laughlin, Publisher of New Directions; Frances Phillips for The Poetry Center at San Francisco State University; and Carol Law and Charles Amirkhanian for their assistance with Oppen photographs.

The librarians in charge of special collections deserve thanks for their searches, and their attention to my project: Robert J. Bertholf, Curator, The Poetry/Rare Books Collection, SUNY-Buffalo; Bob Buckeye, Starr Library, Middlebury College; Richard Schimmelpfeng and the late George F.

Butterick, Curator, Literary Archives, Homer Babbidge Library, The University of Connecticut; Carolyn A. Davis, Manuscripts Librarian, The George Arents Research Library, Syracuse University; Susan Ehlert, University of Wisconsin Rare Book Department; Elizabeth Ann Falsey, Manuscript Department, Houghton Library, Harvard University; Loss Pequeño Glazier, Curator, American Literature Collection, University of Southern California; Cathy Henderson, Research Librarian, Harry Ransom Humanities Research Center, The University of Texas at Austin; Robert A. Hull, Manuscripts Department, Alderman Library, University of Virginia; Charles W. Mann, Chief, Rare Books and Special Collections, Pennsylvania State University; Seyed M. Moosavi, Research Associate, Harry Ransom Humanities Research Center, The University of Texas at Austin; Timothy D. Murray, Curator of Manuscripts, Special Collections, Washington University in St. Louis; Roger Myers, University Library, The University of Arizona; Dan Rylance, Department of Special Collections, The University of North Dakota; Christa Sammons, The Beinecke Rare Book and Manuscript Library, Yale University; David Schoonover, former Curator, The Beinecke Rare Book and Manuscript Library, Yale University; Alice Schreyer, Special Collections, University of Delaware; Jonathan Walters, Manuscript Assistant, and Saundra Taylor, Curator of Manuscripts, The Lilly Library, Indiana University; Frank Walker, Fales Library, New York University; Jonathan Walters, Manuscript Assistant, Special Collections, The University of Chicago Library; and Patricia C. Willis, Curator of American Literature, Beinecke Library, Yale University.

In addition, I would like formally to acknowledge the permission granted by the following collections for the publication of materials by George Oppen. The primary source was The University of California–San Diego for the George Oppen papers, and the collections of June Oppen Degnan, Linda Oppen Mourelatos, Charles Reznikoff, Jerome Rothenberg, and John Taggart; originals housed in the Archive for New Poetry, Mandeville Department of Special Collections, UCSD Library. Oppen letter to Elizabeth Kray by permission of the Academy of American Poets; Oppen letters courtesy of The University of Arizona Library, Diane Wakoski Papers; National Archives of Canada, George Johnston Papers, MG 31, D 95, volume 7, Correspondence: George Oppen; letter to John Taggart copyright ©1990 by The University of Connecticut Library; letters to Carl Rakosi by permission of the Houghton Library, Harvard University; Starr Library, Middlebury College (papers of Paul Auster, S. R. Lavin, Cid Corman); quotation from a previously unpublished letter by William Carlos Williams is used by permission of New Directions Publishing Corporation, agents for William Eric Williams and Paul H. Williams; The Fales Library, New York University (John Taggart); letters to Robert Duncan and Robert Kelly, reprinted with the permission of The Poetry/Rare Books Collection, University Libraries, SUNY at Buffalo; Arents Research Library, Syracuse University (John Taggart); Oppen to L. Zukofsky, F. Will, and the editor of *Contempo*, by permission of Harry Ransom Humanities Research Center, University of Texas at Austin; letters by George Oppen to Donald Davie, William Carlos Williams, Ezra Pound, The Yale Collection of American Literature, Beinecke Rare Book and Manuscript Library, Yale University; Robert W. Creeley Papers, Special Collections, Washington University, St. Louis; Gilbert Sorrentino Papers, University of Delaware Library, Newark; Robert Vas Dias Papers (no. 9842), Manuscripts Division, Special Collections Department, University of Virginia Library; letter to Martin Rosenblum with the permission of Special Collections Department, Murphy Library, University of Wisconsin at La Crosse. The Department of Rare Books, Memorial Library of the University of Wisconsin at Madison, contained Carl Rakosi documents of use. Citation from an interview and reading by George Oppen as recorded on May 22, 1973, for BBC Radio 3 on a program produced by George MacBeth, copyright © by The British Broadcasting Corporation.

1931–1934

[From 1929, George and Mary Oppen traveled in France; in 1930 they took up residence in Le Beausset, in the Var. Upon Oppen's coming of age, in 1929, they had received an income. Between 1929 and 1930, Oppen wrote *Discrete Series*.[1] Also in 1930, Louis Zukofsky had edited the "Objectivists' Issue" of *Poetry Magazine*, which was published in February 1931. In October 1931, Oppen, as publisher, and Zukofsky, as editor, began To Publishers.[2] Zukofsky received a salary of $100 per month for his work. Not only did To Publishers print William Carlos Williams's *A Novelette and Other Prose* and Ezra Pound's *How to Read*, but there were plans to publish Pound's complete prose, to be called *Prolegomena*. By fall 1932, however, Oppen ended To Publishers because of distribution problems, differences with Pound's politics, and, as he says here, his own financial problems.[3] In 1933, the Oppens returned to the United States deeply affected by having seen Jewish refugees from Hitler; the Depression also moved them. In October 1933 The Objectivist Press, a writers' cooperative, was formed.[4] Oppen's first book, *Discrete Series*, was published in March 1934. The preface by Ezra Pound and the review in *Poetry* by William Carlos Williams became talismanic documents for Oppen's future literary career. Around 1934, the Oppens had a thirty-six-foot sloop, the *Galley Bird*, built in Freeport, Long Island.]

1932

To William Carlos Williams
[after January 24, 1932]   TLs with AL postscript   Beinecke Library

Dear Williams:

I enjoyed the "trouble" very much, out of admiration for the book, So don't, as they say, mention it.[5]

I was fairly pleased with the looks of the book myself, aside from one or two obviously regrettable faults (the printer regularly acts contrary to instructions at the last moment, and is careless intermittently). The price, which we were forced to raise constantly before publication, makes a difference of course. If the books were to sell for 20¢ as we'd originally planned, they would look "neat." "Lushness" was always entirely out of the question; they could, I'm afraid, be better without being de luxe nor obscuring the pressing almost to journalistic nature of the text. That is, without seeming bibliophile's items.

The round characters I thought were good with the text-- in fact, I like it better yet in typescript (which means also that the type should have been more widely spaced, which we couldn't afford). I'm enclosing the first page of the Ms. in which the thing is most marked so that you can see what I mean.

However, Pound and others seem to feel that the publications should look more professional, I think it is, so forthcoming books will be different. If we've experimented at your expense it was absolutely unforeseen.

Thanks for the book, which hasn't arrived yet-- your letter arrived just now.

I was very pleased--naturally-- with what you say of my work. And that "they will not think it aesthetic, but--": is "they" the public (what the poems do lack, I think, is the dimension of reading-- the direction in which one reads; that is to say, they do not and are not really intended to create an environment, so that if reading is to "fill time"--enuf to matter-- I can see that they are not very desirable). Or does "they" mean co-editors? in which case you mean that you can let me know-- or they will let me know if Contact can use the work.[6] If you will understand that I appreciate your letter, I'd nevertheless like to ask you to tell me more definitely if you might use the poems. Not necessarily if you will, but if you might. Which is what you write-- that you might-- but without in the least feeling that you are over-tactful for what would be peculiarly foolish reasons, I think that because your letter was also to thank me (for nothing, as I said), you might almost be forced to a considerable indefiniteness in refusal. And I'd really like to send the poems elsewhere if you will not be able to use them.

"If you *might*" because I'd prefer them to be in Contact. If you simply wish time to decide I certainly don't mind.[7]

Sincerely
George Oppen

meanwhile the enclosed-- unfinished when the others were sent. [enclosure unavailable]

To Ezra Pound
[August? 1932]   TLs   Beinecke Library

Dear Pound:
    There is no possibility of continuing To "under present conditions."[8]
    It seems that very few people can afford a business. That's as good a resolution of the system as any. When Macmillan et al. go broke we'll probably be able to re-establish To.[9]
    I'll have Darantière return your Ms. Registered.

                                                            Oppen

To William Carlos Williams
November 22, [1932][10]   TLs   Beinecke Library

Dear Williams:
    I think everyone has felt what you say of Louis.   His immediate environment--the space most people fill by gesture--he fills some other way, or else it *is* a vacuum. But-- he's usually brilliant about things he should know nothing about.   Perhaps it's seeing clearly rather than doing anything which is experience, since (you mentioned "even when we're in the position of the two figures from the whore house at Pompeii") there's usually some created situation-- imitation rape or something else-- even in that position.
    Tho I'm not in Majorca, I'm not sure the world goes to Hell-- in spite of that "pummice."   There's now seldom anything quite [like a?] chastity-belt, or quite [like?] an army on the rape: there's no reason why machines shouldn't sometime be controlled at least as well.   Or, they're controlled about as land was under feudalism. Being broke is not worse than leprosy-- nor is even being a serious writer. That sort of thing compensates for the intellectual difficulties-- what I really have in mind is that there is no place to return to with any improvement. And I don't suppose you'd meant there was.

(The times a'wri', according to the drunks on Majorca. And maybe I'm swopped up on something or other)

Louis thinks of coming to France next year, I believe. He could get along here on the money he has.   No answer, but it's less silly than half-starving.

I'm sorry you can't continue Contact.[11] Yes, please do return my Ms's; I think I've lost my copies of most of them. I'm sorry I can't send a U.S. stamp-- there's no way of buying one.

Yours
G Oppen

To Ezra Pound
February 9, [1934]   TLs with AL additions   Beinecke Library

Dear Pound:

I might have answered your letter at more leisure--[12]

"Yessir, a longer preface would overbalance. Section 1 dealing with wh'll find me shockingly modern will probably never reach those it's addressed to. But I'm glad to have it along on the chance.   Some little egg might ---. ¶ 2 does me heart good (deals with originality-in-doing-nothing and the tracing of derivations). I think I told you about the New Yorker who'd been converted he told me to Functionalism: whereby he so admired the skyscrapers he wanted to build one on the Arizona desert for a monument.

The book'll be named Discrete Series. Tricky, but I want a name out of statistics for "Party Aboard" ["Party on Shipboard," CP 8] and some others particularly, and the term describes my hon. intentions pretty accurately.[13]

"The glass of windows and a family laundry"-- Yes, I mean laundry on a line. Are there any installed tubs in these parts?   Not too good a poem-- put it in because it emphasizes the discreteness of the series-- since when I write straight description (there should be a better word for it) it has the same tone as the more argumentative woiks.   And goes into the book just there [CP 8].

OPPEN

Not so discrete, therefore not, in the other sense, which, I see.   'Laundry' 's not the word--[14]

George and Mary, circa 1946–49. *Photo courtesy of the late Panthea Perry.*

To Ezra Pound
March 10, [1934] TLs Beinecke Library

Dear Pound:

Sending you 2 copies of Discrete Series. Send more if you want em.

Poem with this-- sorry I didn't get it in to replace Civil war photo [CP 9].

Preceded by mounted police,
A band--
The corner-stone laid

The crowd on the civic pavement
See a new stone in turned ground.

Pre-war lit. Suppose you hear of the Gertrude Stein-Thomas. "which is a fact," but certainly quite a coincidence; and the cellophane underwear I understand she herself doesn't wear. Tho someone was talking about her "salon." And that it's been snowing pretty steadily for a month, creating almost "enuf" work.[15]

Williams Poems selling pretty well-- tho Williams and Zuk. had somehow managed to hope it'd sell better.[16]

(suppose you hear from Zuk himself.   AND from Williams
                              AND from
                              Oppen

[In 1931, Oppen corresponded with Pound; in 1932, Oppen corresponded with the editors of *Contempo*; and in 1934, he corresponded with Charles Reznikoff.]

1958

[Both Mary and George Oppen worked with a therapist for six weeks in the early spring. Oppen had his "Rust in Copper" dream which precipitated his return to writing, the dream offered the encoded conviction that he "did not want to rust"—and, as "copper," he would not rust. In May 1958, he wrote "Blood from the Stone." On July 7, the Oppens applied for a passport, and on August 26, for the first time in years, the Oppens were able to get passports; their right had been terminated because of their political affiliations. Linda had entered Sarah Lawrence College in September; the Oppens traveled to the United States in November, visiting their daughter and the Zukofskys.]

To Louis Zukofsky
[August 7?, 1958]   TLTs   Humanities Research Center,
University of Texas, Austin

Dear Louis:
    Good to hear from you. A long time. My life -- only partly apropos of hearing from you -- seems more consistent looking back than I had expected.
    First because, like you, I'm alive, although whole forests of pines such as you mention have died and plumb disappeared on the California coast. It is a pretty remarkable thing to outlast even the places of one's childhood, and I feel it must have taken quite some doing for myself. Took, clearly, a world built by my own generation, however badly.
    I think we did the only possible thing for fifteen years or more, although it would be an indefensible primitiveness today. I remember your praying mantis on the subway. I'm not even sure we'll get to stay out of the subway from here on in.
    I've asked many people to look up Reznikoff and you, with messages. None did. I found pieces of Rezi's poems and yours going through

my head during the whole war. Old men eating food all through Europe: girders still themselves where nothing else was. The sonnet in "The" -- your mother's shoes.[1]

My regards -- and Mary's -- to your wife, and Paul, and others. It would be very nice to see you whenever it's possible.

> Regards
> George

To Louis Zukofsky
[August 25?, 1958]   TLTs   Humanities Research Center,
University of Texas, Austin

Dear Louis:
> They went hunting lions,
> But a fly annoyed them

The difficult question for me would be in that area anytime, I think, rather than in the question of credulity. You were tempted to the Bulge, surely, quite without credulity. The rhetorical game of explaining away man-eating flies is a bad one, however. No doubt of it. It would seem that a tragic number of people went to their executions without quite recognizing the event as a negative feature of the regime.

I have seen some of your poems, yes.   I am that rare and rainbow bird what reads poetry --- on a sparse diet.   The quote above is Naomi Replansky -- a book called Ring Song -- a New Yorker, I think.[2] [Allen] Ginsberg and maybe some companions seemed to me to be happening at least more or less in the present. Tho I think the basic attitude behind the content and the lack of form is a matter of emotional impotence. Or inadequacy. The failure of an emotion that can motivate a life.

I just add, however, that the 'young generation' seems to me neither beat nor quiet. It is possible that I meet a special selection. They seem to me simply the healthiest in U.S. history.

I am very glad that you see Rezi.   To whom my most serious regards.   I would like very much to see any of his new work.

Linda, our daughter, will be in Sarah Lawrence [College] this coming term. I'd like to give her your address -- and Rezi's if you would like to be visited. (An exceedingly nice smallish adult I assure you)

> Regards
> George

June visited since my last letter, and reported on you -- all three.   Said you were nice. Which is true. Said you were shy. Which I doubt.

To Linda Oppen Mourelatos
Friday [Fall 1958][3]   TL with AL postscript   UCSD 33, 1, 14

Linda Dear: rather itchingly frustrating to write when we'll be talking to each other so soon. You've taken very good care of us in the matter of rooms. We continue to get printed stuff from Sarah Lawrence which refers to us as New Parents -- they feel we never really were parents before we got in on these things.
[one paragraph cut]
    You wrote: 'you'd write very differently if you wrote poems now.' Rough quotation. I send proof that it's not altogether so. (somewhat to my horror)
    The poem should be titled in the accent of Greta Garbo whom we all used to admire so: Not Zen But Now
    (The first stanza is pretty much the Zen 'Void' -- that we're objects like any little object in the universe, or maybe don't exist at all since only for a time. And the rest says we have a sort of permanence. It says, but WE don't tell DAISIES, it says; they wouldn't believe us if we did ---
    poem about you in a way, to celebrate my becoming a new parent, so it's only fair to send it to you
    You sound very fine on the telephone.
    Do you write in long hand because it's nicer? It is really, but mine's illegible.
    A difficulty about poetry or any such thing within a family is that one naturally expects that one's father or one's mother would say something clearer, more complete, closer to you and more treasurable than, say, a puritan stranger like Emily Dickinson. Can't always. Proving indirectly that conversation is not really an art. [cut; talk of mutual friends]
    I'll be so glad to talk to you and to see you   One crib to the right or to the left -- the slightest error in that hospital --- and we'd have had the wrong child. A good head of hair is very important.
    But we've always been lucky. We have the right child.
    (Now It Can Be Told Dept: One of your many early compliments to me was your version of America. You always sang it

'And crown our good
With Fatherhood --'

solemnly singing your own sentiments at second grade functions.
[poem, enclosed:]

Not strangers nor their sons.
Old as they come, really,
No one ahead
To fall from space from light
Which is the only space or light
(People will remember
"Me"?)

Sparrow on the cobbled street
Little sparrow round and sweet,
Chaucer's bird.
                    But we,
Our times -- our father's times.

Or if a leaf
Sparkles
In some wood?
O we love leaves, but we speak
To each other: "our times."

Our daughter, our daughter, no child but our child.

To Linda Oppen Mourelatos
[November 1, 1958]   TL   UCSD 33, 1, 13

Linner:
        The Stones   (? Anne's parents) visited. We treated them good. Very
nice people: very liberal -- disturbed about segregation, Dulles foreign
policy, etc. And not just if you ask: it's on their minds. Gentle people.
He's very patriotic to Chicago - - in what seemed to me a healthy way. A
little opposed to S. Lawrence for that reason.
        We were talking about Jack London, Mary and I. He is so very typical
of California once -- of a kind of Bohemia of old.   Not unlike the position
of Kerouac, in a way -- a proletarian among the bohemians. But a prole-

tarian when a proletarian was likely to be able to build a raft, sail a boat, handle horses -- unlike say Mac Blair.[4]

What's good about him is that he was a pulp writer -- also what's bad about him. Stone's slight anti-N.Y. feeling made me think of him, and of Sandburg, Dreiser, Anderson and the other mid-westerners of course.

I feel a little as if I were [in] London or something like it when I'm in N.Y. In relation either to Sarahs [Sarah Lawrence?] or Zuks.

And, somewhat like this, I was thinking the other day that tho I don't (naturally) object to abstract pictures, I am terribly bored by the pictures of abstract artists. (Why this letter? but we love you.

Dear linnerpinner Oppen:

(Con't)

I mean I don't like the artist to be abstract -- all the art I really remember is like Williams, Reznikoff, Rembrandt-- you know who and where and what the artist is

and, what picture of mine (how very very nice of you to ask) shall I bring.[5] (sure it won't be a fire hazard)   The adolescent with books under his arm is the best carved but what a subject!!   The small one of a carpenter? The one who's sort of built himself into a trap -- the stained wood. The tree is too big -- the Carlos too big. Probably the carpenter, no? Sad tho he is. Or which do you want. Linnerpinner darling, just say the wordee.

-----and I guess you'll just up and call on anyone we say, too, as if I had vapor lock again. And maybe I have in a way.[6] Anyway it's nice to have you. It's so nice I don't know how to say.

Love.

To Linda Oppen Mourelatos
[November 5, 1958]   TLTs   UCSD 33, 1, 13

Linda Dear

Home home in the rain.   Where the dear little buffalo play. And to the rest of your letters.

Alice, I love you too. And thank god for people like Casals.[7] And George loves Mr Wagner, let every fence proclaim. But that river never did wind somewhere safe to sea, did it.[8] Not Wagner's fault, and not really Twain's maybe: but it ended a little shockingly I always felt with the ap-

Oppen wood carvings done in Mexico, 1951–53. Mary Oppen was the model for the heads. *Photos © Charles Amirkhanian.*

pearance of Tom Sawyer out of nowhere but a previous best seller playing cops and robbers to demonstrate that boys will be boys

And those little American towns were not really funny, nor the whippings and the bitter widow woman. I just never liked Tom Sawyer. But what wonderful wonderful things there are in Huck Finn, and how the river ties them all together and carries them through the heart of America[. . . .][9]

[brief cut]

A wonderful report on the Z's. I used to walk Louis [Zukofsky] to the subway. We would talk a while at the entrance and Louis would get to feeling that I had a very long walk back. So he would walk me back.   Progress was slow in those days.   I am so glad you saw about the bohemians thru Katherine Mansfield, because all that time you were getting born. We were making space around ourselves to get a look around: no doubt we swung a lot of dead cats in it to test its extent.

I'm a gonna look for Howells Pete in the Benjamin Franklin.[10]

Louis hides some behind his wife I guess -- as you say like Seguieros.[11] Also Williams and most others. But the handwriting seems to me offensively irrelevant: I naturally don't care if it's extravagant. Russel Wright is probably very nice: Rezi we'll see together if you want.[12] I'm sure he's nice. He and Louis never really liked each other very much. His specialness is mostly an extreme (and of course forced or just a little bitter) modesty. A little bitter, but also his honesty as a poet   Which is what he didn't quite like about Louis.

When we visited, he would always rush out and buy a very big -- an enormous bottle of cream soda. He knew where to get them. It was his symbol of unstinted hospitality without violating total modesty. He knew everything about New York -- including where to buy cream soda -- but the way a woodman knows about the woods. In the first place, he walked everywhere. So the wild things followed their own trails through subways and overpasses and he caught glimpses of them as he walked. He knew where the milk horse stopped, and where the grocer gathered his eggs. And for all I know, saw the marks of the stenographer's heels in the early morning. And where to find simples, in which category he might just possibly have included us sometimes. Who else do you suppose drank his cream soda! He addressed a milk horse once in a poem: "Horse, how are your cousins, the centaur and the unicorn?" And he noticed in one of those filthy vacant lots "a girder, still itself among the rubble"   And an old man "eating with reverence food"[13]

-- a half dozen or so little things that I almost can't bear to think about. One is your "it's bue" -- for blue -- at the nursery school --- that's not sad, just makes me cry -- and another is the story about the note found on the sidewalk under an orphanage window "To Whoever finds This:
I love you."
And another is 'He heard' in tiny print at the end of Sick thrice.[14]
Yes the bath room scene is wonderful with Zooey.[15] They're special people -- wonderfully special people, looking at the world with the stoical amazement of children and hugging their own good sense to each other. But Franny seemed to me not special, but a terribly moving and clear account of what has happened to many young people sick sick sick of the smart alecs.
[cut a paragraph and a half about a number of friends]
I'll send you [Selma's] letter. And Louis' note, and some other letter I had in mind: I'll think of it. O yes, a very fine letter from June. Written in answer to my accusing her of oversimplifying things but the letter's clear enough by itself, and very intelligent.
To whoever gets this in the mail: We love you
And we couldn't be righter.

Dad

To Linda Oppen Mourelatos
[November? 1958]   TL   UCSD 33, 1, 13

Linda Dear
A long and rambling and very likely pointless letter I think I'm embarking on, and full of modifications and hesitations and other difficulties. And since I don't intend to re-write it (after all) it may come out a pretty bad mess. But doubtless no worse than a lot of my conversation.
I was started off by thinking of the Sick Sick Sick --- so clearly a guy of left convictions, like Walt Kelly -- who has less courage of course -- and the other Walt, the one on Pete's record, and Naomi Replansky and even those of the so-called beatniks who have any conviction or any passion[16]   And the guy who wrote Franny too [Salinger] --- certainly not a conservative. It seems to me a fact that those who have any real prestige or following among intellectuals all base themselves on left assumptions. Toynbee the historian might be an exception --- but he really dates from some years ago, when there really was a wave of conservatism. The real

drive for the fame of Eliot and Pound comes from then too perhaps --- at any rate it is certainly not for their political or religious views that they are read. The younger men can be 'withdrawn' and all that -- but if Ginsberg for instance when he did mention Sacco and Vanzetti had indicated solidarity with those who executed them I don't think people would have stood for it.   None of this was true even in the famous thirties. It is something which has happened steadily --- well, not steadily, but increasingly through the thirties to now. Even the reactionary politicians, though they're pretty well in the saddle, I think have almost no support from intellectuals at all. And the record of the scientists even in Germany is startling.

We tend to sort of come together -- though without really a program.   We know our mistakes --- others made mistakes too.   Those who supported Truman in 1948, for instance. Since the Korean War was surely avoidable at least should feel some responsibility for the loss of a terrible number of lives. They tend to do less soul-searching than we because they make fairly sure to share their errors with a very large number of others.

Don't know why I got into that.   The change is not only a matter of intellectuals either. The U S is capitalist, and capitalist means that industry is run simply for the profit of the owners. But every one knows that if the big steel companies or the auto companies decided for tricky reasons that it would be a good thing for profits to close down for a year, it would simply not be permitted.   The underlying assumptions of practically the whole population are something like socialist assumptions.

And more than that: much more than that. How many of us -- outside of the nuts -- don't know that we can only have the roots of our existence -- regardless of where we might live temporarily -- in a country in which the common people have one way or another won most of their rights. Even only in that part of the country where the common people have won a good deal: consider the southern U S.

The countries where that has not happened are such antediluvian kingdoms as Saudi Arabia --- there could be no room in such a country for us.

Well, but that is the classstruggle-- the famous CCClassSSStruggle. And I don't know what's the end of the class struggle -- what its final product is. In some countries I think surely it will be communism -- as it has been in some already. Where the people have been too long delayed in gaining rights -- where the ruling class is too guilty to dare make concessions. But in the US?   I don't know.   I sort of half imagine. Or I imagine rather clearly, but without any huge enthusiasm.

I should imagine that in any really terrible economic emergency we would pretty much start where the New Deal left off --- managers, administrators, social workers, engineers being called to Washington -- even drafted -- something like a war emergency. Disregard of private ownership of big industry where necessary ----- an enforced assumption that the welfare of the mass of the people was the primary concern of government, though probably with no theorizing about 'Working Class rule' --- and no such thing in actuality, either.

And yet this isn't too realistic a picture either. Or at least is far from a terminal point in the 'class struggle'   Because there would still be many opposing alternatives -- including war as an alternative to economic breakdown.   I am more or less assuming the increasingly obvious impossibility of war because of the newly discovered perishability of the planet.

I don't mean that it would all be arranged so smoothly and calmly and by the powers that be.   But I cannot imagine anything even remotely like the Russian model in the U.S.   Neither can I imagine that history will just sort of end with the present best of all possible worlds.

well, I didn't promise much. It would be more fruitful to talk, than to write.

[In the years between 1934 and 1958, RBD has found one extant letter, a [December 14, 1946] letter from Compton, California, to GO's niece Panthea Perry (then Ley) in which he talks about Linda, at six years old, as a "full blooded horse child" who was given the responsibility of breaking in some three-year-old Shetlands by a nearby stable. In 1958, Oppen also corresponded with June Oppen Degnan.]

1959

[In 1959, Oppen was "so pre-occupied with poetry at the moment that I have nothing else to write [letters] about"; this in a letter to his daughter.¹ During the year, he corresponded with three publishers—his sister June Degnan, for *San Francisco Review*, James Laughlin for New Directions, and Henry Rago, for *Poetry*—offering work. In May, the Oppens drove to New York City; in June and July, they traveled back to Mexico with the three Zukofskys. In the fall, having given up their Mexico City place (Oxtopulco #10), the Oppens lived in Acapulco for a few months; they then decided to return permanently to the United States.]

To June Oppen Degnan
[January 14, 1959]   TLTs   UCSD 16, 1, 2 and *Ironwood* 26

Jan something -- around the 14th

Dear June:

An absurd time to write a letter, since you'll be getting it a month or so from now. But I seem to be doing it.

[RBD cut information about a car]

Both Louis and Rezi mention that you asked for work. You'll be doing something also for S F Review. They could use a little life -- somebody's VOICE, my God.²

I've been writing steadily -- I guess some 8 hours a day, trying to get thru a back log of things I've wanted to say. But I write terribly slowly -- a world's record, I believe. And what I'm trying to do I find very difficult. At the same time, it seems pointless any longer to say less.

I wrote Louis referring to a discussion we had of various poets -- 'as for my preoccupation with metaphysics, I realise that the host will also insist that "it doesn't matter" if the soup is spilt in his lap. But he speaks in a combination of despair and good manners.' Or words to that effect.³ I didn't go on to make this point, but I think we have to recognize that people have been confronted with the idea of chain-reaction, the destruction of the world-- as a possible thought at least --: I mean that such thoughts are actually present in their minds. They are thinking about 'Eschatology' -- and the absurdity of the word -- even assuming I've spelt it right -- indicates how long the Philosophers have considered it part of their exclusive professional domain.

--- it is just naturally on all of our minds -- To such an extent that it makes most of the poetry seem silly.   And if 'the novel is dead' it is in large part for this reason -- not a matter of 'finding new forms.'   A happy ending: alright, the reader is happily married too -- but what then? I don't mean he's only politically worried -- he's more like politically hopeless -- he's metaphysically worried. And me too. I can't just write images and perception of a world which might just sort of cease.

If the novel is dead it seems likely to me that people just can't bear narrative, with its implication of the incomprehensibility of time, of the non-existence of what's past, and such.

There are a lot of difficulties. In the first place people simply demand to know whether you're a professional philosopher, or physicist. Just can't help that. People have written about love who are not professional psychologists. There's a difference here, no doubt, but we will just have to overlook it. Noone can help thinking *something*, -- once the subject is raised. And experience so far has not indicated that it will help him much to be a professional philosopher -- tho it may be fatal not to be. I don't mean naturally that I'm trying to elaborate a philosophy in a poem: I mean that these thoughts are part of one's feeling about everything -- it can't just be kept out, except by the purest of artiness -- by leaning on a literary tradition.

-- and there is the problem of form, damn the word. I'm not sure I haven't just a habit of form, rather than a conviction. The form of the old poems that I wrote. And it chokes on this sort of content. I've managed -- but I think I do need a new form, a new tone. And the search for a new form would throw us right back to where I started -- a new form is 'incomprehensible'   I hate to go through that again.

And, moreover, I would still define poetry as I did then

(I thought of a

PREFACE

My heart leaps up when I behold!

A grain of sand in the world,
An hour in eternity[4])

still would be pretty much my poetic credo.   So the form sticks -- the open-end form. And how to add an answer to the question, 'well, what if we cease to exist' or something of the sort. And who doesn't think that?

Next question: 'You writing for posterity, Fella?'

Next suggestion: Be a sport, if not a mutation.

Selma kept trying to force my book [*Discrete Series*] on me. I couldn't face it. Finally borrowed it and I thought some of the poems were very good, and none of them shameful.

I was really kind of moved to see I'd written a statement, and a very clear one, of what I was going in search of when I quit writing -- the Party on Ship-Board [CP 8]

I envied Williams then and I do now -- tho the similarity is really no wheres near as great as Pound hints [in *Discrete Series* preface] -- and hardly a 'poetic' similarity at all. But I envied and envy him for his ability to just go on, to talk along, without becoming strained or mannered -- it's the Americanism of the guy -- he doesn't sound like a cocktail party however loosely he runs on. And Rezi has the solid Hebrew voice behind him. But I have got to loosen up somehow -- and not by a disarming title such as HOWL because after all if you think it's silly and insincere to write a poem under the circumstances, you just don't write a poem.

Impossible not to suspect -- about some of these, not really Howl -- that a very short piece just can't be published unless it looks like verse.

We'll see. I do my best.

Love

George

To June Oppen Degnan
[before February 9, 1959]   TL with AL additions   UCSD 16, 1, 2

Just received the Loom. Looks wonderful, at a glance. Thanks.
Further on conviction:

> We move above the moving tree
> In light upon the figured leaf
> And hear upon the sodden floor
> Below, the boarhound and the boar
> Pursue their pattern as before

From Eliot's Burnt Norton.[5] Now, I know positively that I've not written anything that good. I know just as positively that I've not written anything as bad as 'my Puerto Rican Grandfather,' and such. I could not be positive. To write poetry means to correct and to re-write, which would require a perfectly firm conviction of what's good and what's bad, what's better and what's worse.   No use arguing with me. And as for being a great genius -- it's quite an order. There really isn't one even in every two or three hundred years, if you mean what I mean. To be a good poet is quite a thing by itself. To be a good poet is to add *something*. Add something to --- well, how long has human life existed?   Anyway, it's quite a thing. Great genius aside.

My poems begin to show the pattern of what I have to add. I am certain it's something. It's just one thing. Not enormous. You defined it wonderfully. As you see, it is not Shakespeare. If one had somehow lived before and after Shakespeare, he would surely feel that Shakespeare had added more than a language: had created a full half of human speech (alright; exaggerated. Some thing a little like that)   And almost created sight: compare even Chaucer. That's not me.   Don't have to be a great genius. After all, I'm just Buddy.[6]   Quite surprising as it is.

There's perhaps something peculiarly undemocratic about art, tho the fact bothers me very much. One really knows, after all, that a popular vote would give first place to Eddie Guest of the Face on the Barroom floor, so that one really disregards majority opinion to a degree one really doesn't in any other area. It's a peculiar situation

(By the way;   the above quote from Eliot   :   I stopped it abruptly just before the last line which is

But reconciled among the stars.

You see: poetry does criticize itself. A false statement makes bad verse. Even an Eliot can't smooth it. It's this which makes possible some kind of rational criticism, which saves one from pure whim, pure 'taste'

(Read that passage -- it's interesting. Dazzlingly beautiful, and startling how hopeless the 'but' is --

Alright -- I'll use another sheet of paper and clear that up. I mean: read (re-read) Burnt Norton. And particularly that strophe, just for this point. I have a funny feeling about these things in Eliot. Even in the Rock, which is just one violent effort to force these meanings into poetry.[7] I have no respect at all for the 'opinions'; not, if it came to a show down, even tolerance. But something approaching admiration or fellow-feeling for his attempt to force these damn things into his poetry in order to do his duty -- Maybe I admire myself more however for knowing what is one thing and what is the other and what are the levels of truth ---that is to say, for simply not attempting to write communist verse. That is, to any statement already determined before the verse. Poetry has to be protean; the meaning must begin there. With the perception. Eliot of course is consistent; he would not agree. He thinks of himself as deliberately finding the 'objective correlative' to substantiate a body of thought which he accepts. It is true, any orthodoxy would have to accept that. The Party Line writer is accepting nothing worse. Or even the liberal, the moralistic writer, the improving writer. Say, for instance, Julian [Zimet] so far. The modern temper reacts to a liberal statement as intolerable soap-boxing, and is remarkably tolerant to Yeats' Theosophy, Eliot's Catholicism, Pound's fascism. The reasons are strange[:]   one's partly that liberalism; progressivism at least, seems both hackneyed and insincere, being what everyone says he believes, and what no one really feels. ? ? I don't know -- I'm just running along on the typewriter --- but pro-democratic is not what we really feel most of the time, with the roads clogged with everyone in the whole country driving a car, everyone on earth playing three radios - - - - - Yeats, Pound, Eliot, reactionary to the point of insanity or freakishness at the least -- It's no joke.   And not a reactionary conspiracy: most of the critics are socially liberal . . . I think we would all like Sandburg to be a better poet than that crew. He just so obviously is not.

-- add Joyce, Proust, Lawrence for that matter.   Leaves Rezi and Williams. Both of them basically democratic, in spite of Rezi's nationalism, and Williams' sense of aristocracy -- his simple, asinine H. L. Menckenism once in a while. But when it's good it's really almost classically American-democratic.

----- AND being democratic has got to be absolutely non-dogmatic, a-political, unsystematic: whereas system, dogmatism and all the rest is found tolerable in Yeats Pound Eliot.

Just returns us to what I say: you've got to find your own way and do your own thinking. All of this is the past, and begins to show the obvious inconsistencies that are always so easily visible in the past. A poem has got to be written into the future. I don't mean something about the admiration of posterity (from where I sit, posterity looks like a bunch of damn kids) but simply that it's something that is not the past.

Have to write one's perceptions, not argue one's beliefs. And be overwhelmingly happy if they turn out not to be altogether unconscionable.

For in that really is the only hope: original virtue. Better be -- people will not much longer accept any ethic, any ethic at all, out of sentiment or superstition.

To June Oppen Degnan
[February 9, 1959] TLTs UCSD 16, 1, 1

Dear June
        Your letter more than fascinating. I'd agree I think to about every-thing you say. A few demurrers, maybe. Anyway, I have the intention -- I think -- of writing a very long letter back, to see - well, to see what I say.
        Certainly you're right to begin with: one writes just simply out of desire to get it *down*. Posterity, austerity, prosperity, and aid to the blind is probably not operating at the time that you're writing   .
        Well, as for poetry --- and if this is reasonably coherent, I may go as far as to mail it.   :
        After all, it is only understandable emotionally. Not a matter of in-tellectual high-jinks. Possibly one doesn't notice the fact in familiar poetry. But even the simplest poems of the easiest writers - for example

        Break, break break on thy cold grey stones, O sea

has no possible connection with the next line

        But ah! the difference to me.

except the emotion we associate with a breaking sea in grey winter weather.[8]
        Or "My love is like a red, red rose -- nonsense unless we have a reaction to roses.[9]

        Sunset and evening star
        And one clear call for me[10]

The sunset, much less the star, has nothing in logic to do with it. Obviously the 'call' might come at any time of day. But We know his feeling about evening -- the end of the day -- and the high dim light of the star, etc. I'm taking the most obvious poems that occur to me. But they are obvious largely because we don't have to *notice* our emotional response to those images -- it's literarily well established what our responses should be or are supposed to be. So the poems present no difficulty. There's no great difference between them and poetry considered difficult otherwise, as a rule. A matter of familiarity.

It is difficult to say anything very specific by comparison to a rose, today, because the sentiment has been generalized to include too much. People surely do have reactions to things in their lives, but I think they are upset and distracted if you ask them to realize not how they feel about a rose, but how they feel waiting for an elevator [CP 3].

And - a small thing, but operative -- people have mostly learned to read 'way beyond the speed of speech. And read new poems that way. Which makes hash of them. If they read a Robt Burns poem, the melody is so familiar that they can hardly avoid sort of singing it to themselves -- and so get the point.

All fairly coherent so far.

Rezi wrote

Among the heaps of brick and plaster lies
A girder, still itself among the rubbish.[11]

Likely he could mull along and tell you what he had in mind. But how other than with this image could he put into your mind so clearly the miracle of existence -- the existence of things. It is only because the image hits so clear and sudden that the poem means what it means. I don't know that he could make it any clearer by talking about it.

I write stacks and stacks of notes -- literally stacks of paper -- and mull them over, and sometimes wonder what I meant, and switch them around -- and so on.

[Here seven pages have been cut by RBD which gloss two Oppen poems: "To Date" ("Blood from the Stone") and "Time of the Missile," and which begin to discuss the issue of GO's possible success—a topic of interest to JOD.]

One really had to admit that there is no very absolute judgment of poetry -- either contemporary or later.   Shaw dislikes Shakespeare -- and it is not just one of his vaudeville acts -- he has an intense and puritanical dislike of the whole man, of the man who eats, screws, despairs, loves and uses his eye-sight -- and I don't doubt that he found Shakespeare just about the worst possible writer. And Wells has every reason to feel the contempt he indicates for Homer. And Wells, who is after all not an inconsiderable writer, also thought Henry James very poor stuff. His opinion should be pretty authoritative -- if you accept it, neither Homer nor James amounts to anything at all. You really have to decide for yourself.

I think that Rezi has written the most beautiful and profound poetry in my lifetime. He has absolutely no following at all. I doubt if enough young people know him who are now growing up to become editors, critics, anthologists know him to make him available to posterity's judgment. He is deceptively simple: no one can prove that he's real smart by implying that he understands Rezi. Pound's sense of identification with the Renaissance has more thrill to most people at the moment (and with medieval Provence and ancient China) than Rezi's identification with the Bible. People don't want that at the moment. And even the growing response to orientalism will probably not help him -- he comes by his oriental quality too honestly -- by way of Jewishness. That spoils it for people. Lacks exoticism.

Naomi Replansky has written some good poetry -- very much better than Levertov, who is not bad, and is directly comparable -- and who is getting considerable attention. Partly because Replansky is probably meaningful only to people of some left background. Partly because she happens to write in a conventional form, which cuts her off from the arty -- and with an intensity of emotion which is not at all what is wanted by the bigger reading public.

Beckett reminds people of abstract art for which people are known to have paid as much as a hundred thousand dollars, and makes no demands whatever on anyone's self-awareness. And such --- As for me: I say the poetry's good. And could prove it, in a way. It says things which have not been said, and says it from the whole man -- from the inside out -- from the actual experiences of life. But --- I'm putting an immense burden in the poems, and there are gritty spots. Almost everyone has despaired of philosophizing by now, and doesn't like it -- and here in addition they can see a flaw -- The Black Mountain Review admires my work -- my early work! But read what they print -- read any of the youngish crop of poets -- what very different lives they have led from mine. In fact, they have not led lives at all compared to mine. I've been writing as hard and fast as I can of the Infantry, skilled workers, row boats, people in trailer camps, the unemployed movement in the thirties, a family, marital love, children, the old codgers of Southern California, the H Bomb,--

What in god's name will they make of it? And why will they like it? I have twenty five years of life to write out, though, and that is what

I'm going to do. I cannot cannot write -- as I started off by saying in the first new poem -- about 'a world I never made' as every young poet that I know of is. I suspect I identify myself to them as the enemy the moment I accept some responsibility for the way things are --

or: I'm thinking with some courage, and writing with some courage about a life which has had some courage, and which will end at least with the courage to acknowledge that I have had ancestors and will have descendents. If someone wants that, who reads poetry -- then he'll be pleased.

We think of 'the public' or of 'the critics' or of 'posterity' as if somehow their judgment had absolute truth. But those are individuals -- think of any individual you know, and you realize at once how subjective and even accidental his judgment must be.

The early poems just have to stand as is -- Some of them come up against the limit of my understanding at the time, and sort of break to pieces. Those that stay solidly within what I had grasped seem to me good. But I am starting now as if from scratch to write of things I knew nothing about when I was twenty.   I just have to say it as best I can.

Now Shakespeare --- Time has proven Shakespeare great. But from soon after Shakespeare's death until some time about the nineteenth century, Shakespeare was not considered so very great a writer. More or less the Romantics who re-discovered him. And Romanticism --even with the extension given it by symbolists and others, may have pretty nearly had its day

Maybe someday Pope will again be considered the really great Englishman. -- For a while.

Nice to write along like this. Be still nicer if you do make a visit.

I really don't want to go traveling right now. I am banging this silly typewriter every day.

(You know; your letter has in one place roughly this argument: Since one dies anyway, why not try to make a success -- even with a detective novel?   The word 'success' doesn't follow, does it, except on the assumption that all the successes are gorgeously happy.   'Since one dies anyway, why not try to be happy?'   seems to me unanswerable -- only, as I keep saying, 'happiness' has to be defined realistically and empirically; not on some 'common sense' assumption which in practice has been continually proven untrue.

A statement to -- whoever will believe it:[12]
Whenever the mind rises, even a little, it is flooded with happiness. I know

of no other happiness, either in ours or in the simplest and most idyllic societies. A Polynesian, before the arrival of the Europeans, sits in the warm shade under a palm and he thinks -- I don't know what he might think; I don't know Polynesian thought. Let us suppose he thinks, like a Greek, 'the sun is a molten mass.' And he is filled in that moment with the most intense excitement and happiness. I don't know of any other kind of happiness, nor have I ever seen it.

To James Laughlin
March 7, 1959 (dated)   TLs   James Laughlin

Dear Mr Laughlin:
    You may remember -- my sister June, who gives me your address, believes that you will -- that I had several poems a little more than twenty years ago in the first number of (I'm quite sure) your first publication.[13] That must have been in 1933 or 1934, about the time that I printed a book of poems through the Objectivist Press. My first appearance in print must have coincided pretty closely with the first appearance of your imprint.
    I have some twenty or twenty five poems written in these last six months, after that gap of twenty years. I wonder if you would be interested in considering them for New Directions. Hardly for the neatness of coincidence, or the pure sense of old times, but it is true that I have some feeling of an historic spiral in emerging from the fifties in so nearly the curve in which we all found ourselves flung out of the twenties. -- And turning to some of the same people.
    I don't really mean to enter a claim of bending history with these lyrics.   But would you be interested in seeing the poems?
                                                    Sincerely
                                                    George Oppen

To Julian Zimet
[late April or May 1959]   TLs   Julian Zimet

Dear Julian:
    It is an act of friendship. And invaluable criticism. I am answering at once, I suppose in order to say *that* at once, tho I might discuss a little

Mary, Julian Zimet, and George, Acapulco, Mexico, circa 1956.

better after longer thought. You'll forgive a little incoherence, tho --- although your lucidity deserves a better answer.[14]

(I was at one time half afraid that you were over-impressed by the international intelligentsia. If by any chance you were, and if putting your mind to a friend's poetry has proven once again that intelligence and sensitivity is the only thing in the world that's useful - - - - I will accept your thanks.

But I'm not trying to stand things upside down --- the primary debt's from me to you for the criticism.

On Generation of drivers: you feel it breaks. Certainly not untrue
-- I thought it a sort of lyric leap, but perhaps I'm wrong.[15] I notice you
accept a lot of leaps without cavil, so you accept the principle. So you
may be right. The poem's sort of written tho, for better or worse. I just
meant: These young, as described --- who in God's name can be their
fathers. How could it be the old codgers described? An honest question.
And who do they -- these young -- love. And a definition of love 'An
entity of two and which they love.'

To aid the memory: [Here Oppen copied the final seven lines of the
poem, from "Half private...," without the final question mark, and replaced
the dash after "find it" with a comma.]

However. Such as it is.   Imperfect, as you say.

Man's Time. This is much harder to talk about. This is a metaphysic, I'm afraid. This and the Missile [CP 49], and the To Date. On the
missile you really tease me a little, tho gently, And I realize that everyone
has agreed to the absurdity of Angels on the head of a pin --- most of all
the philosophers, with the agreement of Wittgenstein, and the logical Pos-
itivists before him, and their fathers before them.[16] I'm a hold out. I'm
sorry -- I cannot really think twenty minutes about anything without coming to a metaphysical agony in the back of my mind. The man's time is
the least clear -- I'll undoubtedly write the same poem a number of times;
this was the best I could do at the moment.   I notice you got it emotionally.
Your paraphrase is really a sort of loyal defense of your friend against the
charge of being an old fashioned metaphysician. Loyal, but alas - - It says,
or tries to say: The universe is stone, but we are not.   The universe's
time is some kind of elapsed time, whatever that may be, but our time is
historical time, and the difference between one generation and a next, and
we *make* that time. We are not really such 'Strangers' even if we are afraid
'in a world we never made --- speaking of the historical, and not the astronomical world.   Our times are really a lot like us, and we are really a
lot like our times, and it's surely clear if we think how much our fathers
were like their times. 'No stranger, nor a stranger's son'   The bird is like
a bird of Chaucer's time -- but we and our times are different from Chaucer's.

    -- the poem is a poem of hatred of the 'Stone universe' and of love
for ourselves and Linda -- and all we have made of the universe by looking
at it.   I'm afraid that goes to real metaphysics in the Missile. Says among
other things that we didn't make the atom we are made of, but all the rest
is subjective. I believe it -- and it matters to me.   Have to say it.   That's
why it opens with the lyric of praise for vision --- about which you write

so beautifully in appreciation.   And the rest you say -- I told June, who was impatient for me to become famous, and wrote me some recipes, that I couldn't guarantee fame or the taste of posterity even: that I had to write what I think about. And I said, If someone is interested in that -- it is wonderful company. You are indeed.

You suggest it isn't really the missile --- that it could have been said at any time that 'This is the way the world ends' etc. Sure you're right. I didn't really mean to disguise it as a political or topical poem --- I just meant that I thought these things must be in everyone's mind with the threat of the missile right there.   I did go on to say that we can never be free of this immediate fear ---- Suppose we do make an agreement on atomic weapons --- do we really then feel assured that it 'will never be broken?'

--but I see your point. Perhaps   I should change the name. But the rest -- the laughing at me a little --- I can't help it. As I said.

Julian: there were only some fifteen years that political loyalties prevented me from writing poetry. After that I had to wait for Linda to grow up.   Yes: the poem says that I don't like to die.   Poppa couldn't say it: Buddy says it.   Go lean on someone else.

'I don't know how to make them go away and bring back the hand for holding, the leaping heart and its attendent rainbow, but if you're going to cry havoc in a small voice.[...]'[17] Tho you are saying 'I thought you were more of a man than that,' no scout master ever spoke so eloquently to me. If he had, I would have said with love and apology:

I will cry havoc in a small voice.

Sir.

yes --- there are two paragraphs in your comment on this. The second takes me to task, but the first is, as I said, wonderful company. Really all the hand holding I expected. I don't understand; you really think we should never say it? You think it unmanly to admit? Or braver to pretend that it doesn't exist -- the stone universe and its own stone chain reaction that might really - - - (And come to think of it, that's why I have to keep the name of the missile-- the poem describes something like despair because destruction by the missile would indeed be total defeat and meaninglessness in the future perfect.)

I'm protesting at length because all of the poems are about this same thing. As whose are not? The shorter lyrics are simply what the opening of the Missile is -- 'The eye sees' Poems about the human vision which creates the human universe and the blue eyes, and Man's Time and the living historical rowboat on the sea, and all the rest of it. And the opening of the Missile -- about the ship at the pier (you like it, and acknowledge it as accurate evocation)   but it is --- O, I do blush, me da peña --- talking about 'being'[18]

To Date.[19] Yes, I will have to work on it in view of your criticism. I had to get it written before I could start on the others, for some reason. Part one: 'That's me too. That's the way it was, in the good times.' (I'm quoting your letter) 'I remember some others, but never mind that, I'll settle for the remembered joy.'

Well, you mean it's not quite the whole truth -- even of 'Home.' In defense: I said only that was our ground. Which is surely an autobiographical fact. And echoed in that second of happiness in the war. It's also not the whole poem -- so really and definitely I did not say that was my ·whole life -- birds lighting down.   I only said that was what happiness is, when it is. But still, it is maybe less than true. And saccharine. As a novelist you would do it better? The 'opening scene' would have overtones? Well, you probably would. I don't know if I can. It is hard to write everything at once, or to interweave everything at once --- without making use of a sort of poetic portentousness which is easy enuf. But which I would hate to introduce into my own home! Better we should even hit with things. Or fail to Share.

'In every street . . . what they did then is still their lives'[20] ['](That verse is 'incomplete' -- you write. 'I don't know how to read it. Sad? Defiant?   etc. . . . to some extent the doubt extends over the rest of the action. .'

O my. How did I get to fiddling around like that? To my shame, this will sound like an Auden explanation.   I meant: These people in the crowds -- what they did then, in the thirties, is still the most important thing in their lives. And the philosophy they acted on is still the only philosophy it is possible to live by --- that one man adds something to the life of another. Of course, I needed to make that a totally forthright statement. Shades of Auden --- me, the unaudenized and diselioted! I'll rewrite it.

I had already put the word 'monstrous' back in the war section. I had omitted it in one version because I am haunted by the feeling that I have read that cadence and construction somewhere else. I can't remember where.[21]

The last section -- unmanly metaphysics again, but by no means despair, like the thought of the missile. Ends by saying we cut out a piece for life.

yes, Nature, stone nature and the empty space must be the mother from which we were born since the others are deserted too outside a closed door of nothingness and therefore presumably our brothers[22]

On Infantry you offered to hold my hand.   So O.K. you may file a formal declaration that you're holding my hand on that basis and not for metaphysical comfort. Not Last Things, but penultimate. It doesn't matter. I just said: the only thing in the universe that matters to me are the people I love and the things that are filled by their lives and nourish their lives.

I said the rest of it is just stone, and the enemy. And death, which is a victory of stone. And the mud, and the terrible ground. The half-life ground.

(Sidereal -- sorry.   I wasn't being learned. As how could I?   Familiar word to me as an old salt. Sidereal time means star time, to distinguish it from local time, which is what we conduct our affairs by, and purely a human invention. A matter which turns up in navigation.)

Love, thanks, best wishes.

George

(Reading over, I'm not too sure of the tone of the letter (Again!) I mean: I love you dearly. More than that. We are I mean an entity, and which I love.

O yes: the Biblical Tree - -[23]

I'm really somehow delighted that you didn't like that poem, tho I thought I was terrible proud of it. And thot it maybe a sort of shield against the slings and arrows of Botteghe. What happened was that I wanted to write a modern sonnet, to show I could. You say 'it sits rocking a little placidly on the front porch' which is to say that I succeeded a little too well in one aspect at least. You also say, really, that it's pretty much of a lie. Which I'm afraid is true. You report trying to convince yourself that that's the way it was with Mom and Dad. That does it! I'll just scrap the poem.

as the kids may not say -- you are an absolutely super super-ego.

You object to the reversed sentence in 'carrying in its frightful danger the brick body'?   I wasn't being 'poetic'   The sentence as I have it, says 'carrying IT.' Which is really what gives the image of the brick its impact when you get to it. Anyway, I'll always think so.

once more (I'll just give up trying to end this letter for a while)   You remember just before you left for Europe puzzling over why I liked 'Things' and mechanisms. You looked at me pretty suspiciously there. Said you'd never known a decent person who liked such things. Well, I like cars and such. I like them when they're handled beautifully. I like the things that people have wrested out of the idiot stone. The universe --- it should excuse me, but I don't like it. When I first wrote that poem Man's Time, I called it (Just for myself) Not Zen but Now. I am not proud of the pun, I just am telling you that I write the extreme of Nonzen Verse.

Don't leer.

Yep, that's me. Havoc in a small voice. Or Scat!   All the poems are about the same thing. The shorter poems are shorter fragments of what I want to say, the longer poems are longer fragments. I have only the one thing worth the effort of verse to me, or needing it. Which perhaps discloses that I'm not Shakespeare --- so, the secret's out. But that is what I write. About you, me[,] Mary, our adult child and everything we touch enough --- stone universe, but we are not.

So, if the nothing place reclaims our own atomic structure to itself   I WILL NOT LIKE IT. And unlike God in your story, I will give a damn.

alright, will have given a damn. Syntax again.

I am kidding about the blushing -- really quite un-abashed. I do not see how it is possible to pretend to be 'Beyond metaphysics'   What's your love for anyone, or mine?   Why cry over a baby, or your hand tremble if you pet a squirrel? [JZ had a pet squirrel] What are any of us worked up about --- if not metaphysics! My whole life is a fight against death. Yours hasn't?   And death's around us in the dead matter we came out of. Go ahead; blush like a peony.

I wrote of our meeting, Mary and I:

You stepping in
The old car, sat down close,
So close I turned and met your eyes.
Junked long ago -- steel,
Steel and Iron on its rubber tires
All that night was ours!

That was the first victory in my life over the stone. Or the steel and iron.

And friendship, Julian.   All my love.   Blood from the stone.

George.

To Charles Reznikoff
[before December 15, 1959]   TLs   UCSD 9, 4, 4

Dear Rezi:
        Your book arrived yesterday morning. I am grateful for it. I am just
overwhelmed and staggered by the verse. You observed once or twice in
the Automat -- with distress -- that I was about to express admiration.
Nevertheless, I don't know of any contemporary verse as moving as yours.
Which was to be my point in the Automat. I think the sound perhaps is
more skillful, the poems more consistently whole than in the early work
and the underlying implication more solid, more complete. It is strange to
hear the same voice again, and the poem form after it ends.
        The Eschatology of the religious poems seems to me sometimes not
vouched for by experience, and in fact the scraps of paper, the parks, the
bushes and back yards seem to attest something quite different. But even
to as simple an H. G. Wellsian atheist as myself such things as The Ha-
nukkah and particularly the staggering opening will stand against any
attitude. The lines beginning 'penniless, penniless' render Eliot simply
absurd. The critics would have made these things famous if they were
Christian: there is no statement in literature near them.
        I don't mean to violate the tile of the Automat, or to challenge the
size of the buildings in your city. I mean to speak with restraint.[24]

Thanks for the book.

George

We plan to come to NY some time after Xmas in search of an apartment.
Is it possible to find two rooms, three if possible, for as little as sixty
dollars? In any district. If we can do that we will keep this place in Acapulco too -- which would be an idyllic way to go about things. The place
here is reasonable -- in fact it's just a little under sixty a month -- so we
could manage that. If New Yorkers any longer will even discuss such small
sums.

[In 1959, Oppen also corresponded with Linda Oppen and Henry Rago.]

1960

[On January 25, 1960, Oppen's older sister, Elizabeth Frances Hughes (Libby), died at age fifty-four. In January 1960, the Oppens returned to the United States with trailer, boat, and all belongings. After living for about six months at the Hotel Dauphin (Broadway and 67th Street) and at the Standish Arms Hotel (169 Columbia Heights in Brooklyn), they sublet an apartment at 196 Columbia Heights; Oppen rented a room under the Brooklyn Bridge as his work space.]

To June Oppen Degnan
[after January 25, 1960]   TLTs   UCSD 16, 1, 2

June dearest
    Your letter. It establishes forever -- Mary just said -- that it was that child.   Which is true.
    I think Libby must have felt of the pills simply that she would not wake up. Which is what she wanted.   It was her life.   No one can say that she had to grow old.   It was her life.   Very much her life.   This happened a long time ago; from the beginning.
    I should have seen Elsie's letter long ago. No horrors either, June. Just a woman who had had a nervous breakdown, and could not understand -- no one then understood.   'We've been happy - - I love you -- I worry about the children and school and their clothes -- it seems -- since I did this and don't know why -- that I am not fitted for the business of life'[1]
    That's all she said.   All that she could.   Just, if only people then could have known - !   They just needed to know.
    Your letter is somehow blindingly full of life. For which, thanks. And for which all of these people need you very much.

Michael [Hughes] is fine. Of course he must have Libby's picture. And whatever he wants. The picture of me: I think Linda may want it, sometimes at least. Do you want it meanwhile, or could you keep it for us?

June dear, I'm cantankerous and stuff. We love you very much.

George

To June Oppen Degnan
[May 16, 1960]   TLTs   UCSD 16, 1, 2

Dear June:

Here we sit in our window, watching New York Harbor, which we have neglected too long. The traffic is most confused; it will take us some time to bring order out of this tidal chaos. It is pleasant, tho responsible work. We are amazingly native to Brooklyn Heights; we surprise no-one; we talk with the greatest freedom to anyone who sidles over. I find myself in conversations so thoughtful that I just don't believe it.

[RBD cut one paragraph]

--Brooklyn is a much under-rated borough.

Walked thru Red Hook the other day, watching the young women shopping and pushing baby carriages about -- wondering how many of them were the babies that got parked with Grandma when we sat down in front of the relief bureau --

-- they wouldn't remember. Only odd-balls remember anything. A strange guy running a book shop here I talked to. I said I'd been around here twenty years ago. He says, yes, I remember you; I used to run a book store on Myrtle Ave (which is still the worst of the slum area, a Negro area) I didn't believe him, of course, till he went on to say, without a word from me -- 'I guess I'm what you'd call a sort of a Socialist.' If he felt I'd find that information relevant, I guess he does remember me.

[RBD cut a one-paragraph anecdote about a boy and his girlfriend told by the bookstore owner]

And an Egyptian ship, the Cleopatra, docked right below us-- and the seamen promptly picketed her. Tied her up for two weeks. On the grounds that the Egyptian Gov. blacklists U.S. ships that trade with Israel. Handed out a magnificent leaflet about it.[2] A great borough. Martin's mama [cut, above] would be too long a story, a very Brooklyn story.

Louis [Zukofsky] has published the whole of 'A' -- or the whole so far. Printed in Japan for 600 dollars!!   Very nice job. Thru the good offices of Cid Corman, who is there.[3] I had known only the first 7 parts, tho I'd known them very well. I found them very much more moving, and very much simpler, than I had remembered.   I've bought you a copy -- which I'll send. Just read -- just let the music, meaning poetic music not actually sound, take care of it.   I think you'll agree. There are voices, people moving all thru it and a young man in N Y sort of wrapped in music.

The verse in any case has an extraordinary perfection. And startling because it seems always to be undertaking the impossible. Two very poor essays in the book -- one by Williams, one by Louis. Shouldn't have been included. People are injured by non-recognition perhaps -- I think Van Gogh was, I am sure Joyce was.   Maybe even Rezi, in limiting his experience and range. I don't know what Rezi would have been if the world had invited him in. Possibly less than he is -- because that has happened too. The faults of a man with only his own judgment to go by are certainly less suffusing -- they leave what he has. Presto's [Gregorio Prestopino] success, degree of success, keeps polishing him down to nothing in particular. What he really has I think is only in the Harlem series -- of which John Hubley (Mc Boing-Boing Hubley) has made a short; 'Harlem Wednesday' -- if you get a chance to see it.

Also 'Moonbird,['] Hubley's picture, you should see if it's around. Most wonderful.

Jehane Biltry-Salinger-Carlson (of the anthology 'Score') I think ran into trouble with her Mexican printer. I wrote to ask for my Ms back: some because it's good, and I want to get it printed; some because I don't think it represents me too well. I doubt if the thing will ever get out, I doubt if it will get distributed at all. I wrote that you'd offered help -- she seems to feel that she doesn't need help.   I had also offered help on the printing in Mexico; which she was quite sure she didn't need. Implied she was an old Mexico hand.   She is now.

I don't know where to send the stuff now. I looked at Paris Review --- which doesn't seem to amount to anything. Or likely to accept anything like my work.   Some of the Univ publications maybe -- I don't know. Probably something will turn up, or someone will write and ask. Poetry printing another batch. With an enthusiastic letter to me. I should get in touch with Laughlin again is what I should do. I admitted to Linda that I am the oldest promising young poet in America. A mean trick to play on my friends and supporters, including Linda.

Fourth Ave bookstore, where I thot I might pick up a copy, told me they had just sold a copy of Discrete Series for ten dollars, and an Objectivist Anthology for twenty. I told him I was maybe writing another book, maybe his grandson can make a buck on it.

-- I hope that 'colonel' Abel appeals his case on the grounds that the US Government has declared spying is not illegal. Neither immoral nor illegal, the man said. I wish this whole business were a comic opera;   it'd be easy to walk out of the theatre.[4]

-- and the students seem to have taken off. How come? I see students on the subway making a point of carrying leaflets as ostentatiously as possible -- a form of public announcement.

I've got almost nothing new written, since Acapulco. I've got to get settled. My head seems to buzz. I can't hear myself.   But the room's nice, everything's nice, things'll get going. We're not used to only two rooms; it's hard to control appointments, etc.   I don't doubt it'll be alright. Nice to be in the same country with Linda.

Love
George

To the William Carlos Williams family
[Summer 1960?][5]   TLs   Beinecke Library, Yale University

Dear Bill and Flo:

That visit was a great pleasure to us. It seemed a short time since 1930-odd.

You asked to see some of my work, which request is of course a kindness. Don't feel obligated to get it read -- certainly you don't owe me an elaborate comment. There are a lot of demands on your time, and on Flo's reading voice.

I was thinking during that visit that we have all of us defended our humanity pretty valiantly. I've thought from the beginning that we must make poetry out of the clarity of the human vision -- or just let the whole thing go.

With all our regards,
George
(Mary)

(I agree on the American language. It's true you've said it before: it's worth saying again. Surely there'll be poetry in this country only insofar as that lesson is learned. People who are afraid to talk won't produce much poetry. Tho Whitman has been no use to me. Perhaps arriving after you I didn't need him. I always feel that that deluge and soup of words is a screen for the uncertainty of his own identity.)

To June Oppen Degnan
[1960?]   TLTs AL postscripts   UCSD 16, 1, 2

June Dear :
      A proposal:
      I got Rezi's work - the whole of it. I've been overwhelmed by it again. I realize tho that the work is, as they say, uneven -- that is simply that he is printing at his own expense, for his own satisfaction, and just includes everything he has written. No reason he shouldn't. But it has undoubtedly done him harm. Rezi's work, when it doesn't come off is a real belly flop -- he doesn't fake things or try to retrieve himself with a 'great' line. The effect can be very un-climactic. But the best of the poems -- probably some fifty poems or more- are simple, clear and clean and overwhelmingly moving. And poetry which is absolutely unique. I can't believe that these poems in a Selected collection would not get recognition.[6]
      You know by now a good deal about distribution. And price, which is important. Could it be printed at such a price as to return the investment with a sale of say one thousand? -- i.e. a price of five thousand?
      Would you want to try this?   I don't really believe that good work is forever unsalable, or that critics are infected with incurable something or other. And there is no better poetry in English. Should be possible to sell, tho of course it would be one of those things of a dribble of sales over a period of years. Would surely be interesting to try.   Tell me if you're interested: we could try it together. 50/50 financially --- but!   you would have to do the financial work, in fact the whole work. Well, just say. Not a matter of justice.   Or even of laziness: I would make such a mess of the

office work that I'd have to do it alone, --I mean, I'd have to have only my own money involved if I were doing the selling or accounting.

I'd like very much to do it with you.

Love
George

You just phoned. It's bad about your back --Get well. Please.

G

[written on margin] *Only* if we can sell it --after all, he's able to *print* it himself.

To Cid Corman
[August 3, 1960]   TLTs   Special Collections, Middlebury College Library

Dear Cid Corman:

Of course your letter was a courtesy. But I have not been able to be sure, reading your note very carefully, that you are not feeling that the poems need to swing a little on some very generalized excitement.[7] Surely noise would not solve anything, and surely you are not saying so. But I don't know if you might not have in mind something like Olson's concept of 'projective.'[8] I think that what there is to that concept was said more accurately some time ago by Zukofsky in speaking of sincerity and of objectification.

In any case, I believe you are thinking more positively than I am of a sort of solidity of surface.   I think of form as immediacy, as the possibility of being grasped. I look for the thinnest possible surface.--   at times, no doubt, too thin : a hole, a lapse.   It is that you mean by 'a slackening of language'   There is no point in defending lapses--   but that is, of all risks the one I plan to live with.   I am much more afraid of a solid mass of words.

It is possible that what I concern myself with is not the whole range of literature.   Tho I must say I tend to feel that it is.   I think that poetry, if we are to bother with it, must be made of the clarity of the perceptions, of emotion as the ability to perceive.   The problem of diction seems to me that the poem must contain its words entirely.   Where it fails ---

yes of course it fails.   I have a belief that some of the poems, as they complete themselves, heal the diction. Where that happens it seems to me very good. And I am involved with things; with 'the light of things'

I mean to say that I take the point of some of your comments. Not, however, 'desultory feeling' -- I don't think so. Nor 'a certain dearth of impulse.' I think that is a mis-reading of the poems.

Thanks for the letter. And best wishes

George Oppen

To Cid Corman
[August 8, 1960]
TLTs   Special Collections, Middlebury College Library

Cid:

No, no question of my losing patience. I once heard a tourist in Mexico, discovering that the bus driver spoke English, yell to his wife 'The man TALKS!' Nice if he had recognized Spanish as a language, but I can understand his excitement. It's an event when any poetry is not met by silence;   surely pleasant to discuss my own.

I don't know how to discuss whether or not the poems remain 'below the threshold of operation.' How can it be argued? 'Some of my friends tell me I should be in Hollywood?' Or a Gallup Poll? A market survey? But it is true the question troubles me, and always has. Of necessity, one writes first of all to those who read poetry. It is a small particle to split. Leaving what nucleus of what atom? The absence of any sense of audience seems to me a serious problem. The 'frisco' movement (of which you are not a part, in that sense) does more or less know its audience. Some of the good qualities, I think, as well as some of the worst derive from that situation.

So I am the 'alienated artist'? But I cannot really denounce you as an undesirable alien. You declare yourself a *landsman.* Simply a fellow countryman to whom I am not a hero. Which I regret.

Which also leaves the threshold -- the problem of the threshold -- open. I don't know any rigorous solution. But I repeat -- it was the purpose of this letter to say -- no question of my 'losing patience.' It has been pleasant to hear from you.

George Oppen

(I have not seen Origin. I have seen some of your work. True that it does not seek noise or excitement. I was puzzled by your opinion. Searching for a reason perhaps I had in mind your geographic rather than your poetic position.)

To Cid Corman
[August 18, 1960]   TLs   Special Collections, Middlebury College Library

Dear Cid

Yes; there is no question of dismissing your criticism. Taking things more or less at random, as to order -- this is for the time being little more than an acknowledgement --

1. That 'abruptly' is weakening is unquestionably and flatly true.   'alien' is open to question. The form, as you say, must carry it. I am open to the temptation -- or in final despair, driven to inject a word [CP 23].

2. 'A kind of total non-contingency'   I think you mean as your basic comment, but the meaning of the word wavers on me. A lack of relation to a specific moment, occurrence? to the way it happened?   That could be a valid objection often, and has troubled me. I think it is what you mean.

3. 'The push from stanza to stanza is uneven.'   Well, a hole between the words. Where it seems failure, shabbiness, it is a failure of control. As you mean. But I am saying it is a delicate judgment -- I am not sure I agree in this case. I'll look at it again.

'Retirement' was not meant as pathos.[9] I continue to think that at this point we fail to communicate. It may be lack of clarity in the poems;   lack of basic clarity. Or you suffer less than I do from a type of metaphysical vertigo.   I cannot know. My concern with the things, the materials in the poems are that they *are*.   I have to be rather stubborn about this, whether or not the fault of communication is entirely mine -- if I am to write for any purpose of my own at all. I am afraid of irrelevant virtues in the poems.

'Travelogue[']' was not meant to mean more than you report. Re-reading I think it is just not there. Assuredly not inescapable.   I meant -- if this further incoherence helps --the experience of finding oneself native: and of finding oneself native only to the past in a continually 'savage' present.   The explanation hardly helps. I have written something of the sort in other poems, and settled in this one for what I think is a brilliance of light -- which might carry the meaning. I am speaking obviously of approximation, of compromise, or of something less than clarity.

There remains a point you return to. 'Desultory,' 'not somehow sharp enough for me,' a 'dearth of motive.' I tell myself, 'a failure of craft, evidently.' What I want of the poem is that it contain space, that it remain at rest to contain space, the space of meaning; that the form give not '*heightened* emotion' but grasp-ability. Forgive that 'graspability.' I am writing very hurriedly, and want to acknowledge the relevance of your remarks and to state my reserve on this

Regards

George Oppen

[In 1960, Oppen also corresponded with Linda Oppen.]

1961

[In the early part of 1961, Oppen worked intensively with Reznikoff in selecting *By the Waters of Manhattan*. On May 7 the Oppens sailed for England and traveled with June Oppen Degnan in England, Italy, and France, including Lascaux. In November, the Oppens moved to 364 Henry Street, Brooklyn, their permanent address until the end of 1966. On December 29, 1961, FBI agents interviewed Oppen at this apartment.]

To June Oppen Degnan
[after February 3, 1961]   TLs   UCSD 16, 1, 3

Dear June:
    I'll be interested to see your selection from Rezi. Hope you don't miss The English in Virginia, which is different from any other, of course, but I think very good. And of course such short poems as the old man 'eating with reverence food' and the short poem in inscriptions about the shoe lace -- 'as if in the machine of which it is a part /   something had gone wrong.'¹
    --I hope the encounter with Roy wasn't too bitter or hard to get thru.
    Very small things occur -- Linda introduced Rezi's work to some of the literary AND some of the not so literary people at S[arah] L[awrence] and reports by phone just extraordinary and amazed response --
    - I very strongly get a feeling that the time is most exceedingly ripe. People have perhaps been stewing up rather arty soups long enough.
    Jay [Laughlin] did ask Louis [Zukofsky] to do a translation of Catullus for him. Which was very knowing of Jay. Probably do very well.
    By the way, did he see my work? We discussed Rezi when I saw him at Paul's concert, and I didn't want to confuse things.
    -- Herald Tribune has a review of Paul [Zukofsky] that says he's a great musician, etc.   Times less favorable; says he's mechanical, tho perfect. Good sized audience turned out, in a blizzard.²

Rezi said -- gently and sweetly, and I think with quite a lot of emotion -- that he had turned out the books himself these many years, which was what he could do. And that whatever is done with it now, whatever is made of it, he will be glad of. Certainly I was moved: he was speaking of a life time's work that certainly has some imperfect lines, but not one fake line, not one word inflated.   Almost fifty years of work, I think it is.[3]

I will mail Louis' book -- been too much blizzard to reach the post-office without snow-wading.

Jay (again) phoned to say that Buddhadeva Bose is in N.Y. At NYU. I'll phone him, and do my best. Probably I'll imply that I have more connection with SFR [*San Francisco Review*] than I have -- it's an impossible thing I have to say to him. 'I've fixed up your poem for you'!   As I see it, I'd better sound like a semi-editor. I will say 'I've been discussing your work with SFR editors'   That seems O.K.   I'd very much like to be able to use the poems.

Jay said he's old, ugly, very dark.   Looked at me thoughtfully and added, and Bengali.

Like Luther, I'm not Bengali. That will be a barrier between us.

I said to Linda when she phoned about the response to Rezi that it will take two and a half generations of Oppens to do it -- but Rezi will be very very famous one of these days.

Louis will get his recognition too, for that matter. The Olsons, Duncans, Creeleys etc. are this generation of poets -- how good they are is another question, but they are this generation.   And they all look to him, and acknowledge him.   So his 80th birthday will be a gala. 'The poets' -- and therefore the critics--   will be there. If Louis is.

love --

George

you'll write to Rezi? Just telling him what's doing. Since Jay had asked me to speak to Louis, I realized that I would have to speak to Rezi first, short of swearing Louis to secrecy and such cloak and daggering.

To Mary Ellen Solt
[February 15, 1961]   TLs with AL insert   Mary Ellen Solt

[brief note as the covering letter for this statement: "It's yours: quote or don't quote whatever you want."]

The ancestor of Objectivist Press was To Publishers, which produced Williams' Novelette and Other Prose and the Objectivist Anthology, edited by Louis Zukofsky and containing his essay as a preface. That was the first use of the word 'Objectivist.' The preface I think is still a useful statement.

Those books were paper backs, which were of course a common object in Europe, but not yet introduced to the U.S. 'trade.' The bookstores refused to handle them; most of them refused to handle the books even on consignment. We had not the money to conduct a campaign by mail or by advertisement. I don't remember how many of the books were sold: it amounted to a few dozen.

Only Zukofsky and my wife and I had been involved in To Publishers. It was Zukofsky who got together a meeting of Williams, Reznikoff, Zukofsky and myself at which the Objectivist Press was organized. We failed to agree on any very detailed statement of principles, and Reznikoff wrote the definition of the project that appears on the dust jackets of the books: 'an organization of writers who are publishing their own work and that of others whose work they think ought to be read.' Even at that, the phrase 'ought to be read' shows some signs of careful formulation, but we were aware of a basic agreement. At the least, we meant to base poetry on the clarity of human vision and of emotional grasp, which was not everywhere regarded as an important part of poetic equipment.

Ezra Pound, who had agreed to the use of this name as part of our Advisory Board, volunteered an introduction for my book of poems, obviously a kind and disinterested act. A month or so after the book appeared a young writer by the name of Bob Miller showed me a letter he had received from Pound. It began, approximately: 'Dear Miller, it is a pleasure to read the name Miller these days when too many names end in "Stein" or "Sky" ---.' That was about the end of 1933 or the beginning of 1934. I don't know if any group of people in the next few years seriously committed their lives, their fortunes, and their honor -- sacred honor, was it? -- to an organization based on an agreement concerning the use of words. But we had certainly published good work, and in fact only good work. But it should be clear that the theory of Objectivism -- and there was one -- was Zukofsky's. For the rest it was a matter of a group of writers who in varying degrees -- in sharply varying degrees -- approved each other's work. My own interest in the group was probably greatest. I was interested in getting my own work out, I was eager to contribute to

Williams' influence on poetry, I considered and consider Reznikoff the most important of living poets, and I considered it important to get Zukofsky out. It's unfortunate that we failed to accomplish that. Like the others I attached no particular value to the idea of a group, much less a school.

George Oppen

To Mary Ellen Solt
[February 16, 1961]   TLs   Mary Ellen Solt

Addenda:

I cut that pretty short on 'Objectivism' We were all very much concerned with poetic form, and form not merely as texture, but as the shape that makes a poem possible to grasp. (would we all have thought that a satisfactory way to put it?) 'Objectivist['] meant, not an objective viewpoint, but to objectify the poem, to make the poem an object. Meant form. Louis' essay discussed sincerity on the one hand and objectification on the other. And sincerity-- very brilliantly, it seems to me -- as the epic quality.

Tradition? I don't remember discussing it. But who would write poetry if a poem had never been written? Beyond that, the members of this group had a very strong sense of their own histories. Rezi's awareness of the Jewish past, Williams' sense of America and its roots, Louis' relation to Bach and other 'sources we tide from,' ----- I am sort of short-winded historically, but not blind. I remember my father and my grandfather: I think of my daughter. I'm aware that the subways are pretty old (did you notice) and that the Queen Mary is fairly new. The ground seems very old to me. I write about nothing else. But I thought of Eliot as a sort of enemy at the time; I don't remember discussing 'tradition.' If we had, Williams would have spoken as in The American Grain, Louis might have used the word in a more classic sense, Rezi might have thought we were all talking about the day before yesterday.

And I would have been. I was twenty-four.[4]

George

To June Oppen Degnan
[February–March 1961]   TLTs   UCSD 16, 1, 3

Dear June:

Rezi coming over tonight -- I'll give him your letter. All very nice.

Chas Humboldt, the marxist critic, was over last night. I read him some of Rezi.   Overwhelmed him.   The more remarkable because Humboldt is of the 'what-do-you-mean-by-Jewish' school of left wing. Small straws in a light breeze; but I've spent a life-time drawing a total blank in showing Rezi's poems to all sorts and conditions of men women and children.

--Jay's is a very good straightforward letter. Should be pleasant to work with.

(Humboldt I just remembered is the man for whom some years ago I produced the definition that pleased me so much and struck Humboldt as so asinine: 'A Jew is what you and I are.')[5]
[RBD cut two sentences]

I saw Bose. Got along with him alright. He's obviously going to agree to having the poem printed. I simply promised him top billing. But he is immune to any concept of form. He sees no reason for my changes.[6] Trying to explain to him what the word 'kissing' means to me, and why I omitted his line about 'miles of kissing' I made smacking noises at him in the hope that he would see what miles of kissing would involve. He didn't but I attracted considerable attention in the NYU Faculty Club where we met. The literary life is a little less dignified than I had once hoped it would be. But anyway, all our love.

(Bose invited me to India. Learn a little Bengali, lecture and translate. Salary apparently; that is 'Money should present no difficulty.' You know anyone who would like to try it?)

George

To Charles Reznikoff
[April 1961]   TLTs   UCSD 9, 4, 4

Dear Charles:

Thanks for the copy of your letter to June.

I know you were not really disturbed by my nautical violence or stormy haste with the poems.   Still, I say again, I had made and typed out (with Linda's help) a selection from your poems, spending two or three weeks on that. That was the Ms that [C. P.] Snow saw, by the way. And I had gone over June's selection very carefully, annotating it in case I would have to argue the matter with June. And, in a word, I knew the work pretty much by heart. I was not really swarming up and down the rigging with a yo ho ho and a bottle of Jamaica rum. I'm just insisting on the point once more in self-defense. Not that I really had any objection to your portrait of me. I am glad to be presented in this light to June who, I believe, thinks of me as rather Rabbinical. But I don't want you to think that I really treat the work cavalierly. I am as round-headed as they come.

Enclosed the postcard from Mary Ellen Solt.[7]

We'll see you in about two months. Best wishes and regards,

George

To Linda Oppen Mourelatos
[1961]   TL [from Paris]   UCSD 33, 1, 15

Lindy lindy dear:

Les see -- where were we? Anyway, we drove South thru England down the small roads, under the trees and all almost like walking across a lawn and reached a little resort on the channel near Christchurch absolutely full of very small sail boats; the big ones maybe 16 feet long. The channel, when there's no strong wind, is perfectly smooth, and the men stand on the edge of their lawns, dangling a fish hook in the ocean. The men who stayed home. But it did indeed look very much like home. Stayed in a little summer hotel run by nice people: the man had been captured by the Japanese, which had ruined him physically, and he and wife and son and daughter bought the hotel. Very lovely; flowers around and all. The son very pleasantly trying to start a small car: I said: it just so happens that my wife carries an ignition file in her purse . . . I believe, I said, I could start it for you.   And did.   No questions asked about the file; after all, Americans. But he owes a good deal to Mary's odd manicurial habits; he was reporting for army duty and believes he'd have been court martialed. And we walked among the boats, and discussed the sea from the beach with beach-people.
[Two paragraphs about getting to France on the boat, cut by RBD]

Saw Man Ray last night with June [Oppen Degnan, their traveling companion]. He's a one-time confrère of the greats. Still is, maybe.   You'll have seen his name at least, mostly for his photographs. He knows Al Lewin, Rezi's life long friend.[8] And his Man's wife. Both nice -- but the business of rootlessness. Or really, of silliness. Arrived in Bohemia, c. 1912, bringing nothing with them, or nothing they wished to mention, which was back on the East Side by the Waters of Manhattan. Explains now that his art is not intellectual but that that's a very intellectual way to be, and finds the point hard to make. We'll see them again, tho, and again spiritedly agree.

This letter may not be perfectly organized, which will surprise you. We landed in [Dieppe], antique and somewhat sad, not so much picturesque as backward -- I don't mean ass-backward, but backward in time. Tho now I think of it, there was an effect of seeing everything, buildings and all, from the back. Not sure they have a front. Unbelievably cumbrous and primitive dock machinery. And drove thru Normandy; huge cold farms of Normandy. Arrived at Rouen, that awful dump, and went into a depression. Two depressions, one for me and one for Mary. If you'd been there we'd have tried to sit on your lap like Babe.[9] Don't feel guilty or anything, but where the hell were you? It's poor, and stony and bitterly in a hurry and historically stupid, monumentally stupid -- I mean its monuments are stupid, including the Cathedral. And I had seen the town rubble: they were bulldozing paths thru the rubble. And of course the rubble was not just stone, you know. There were bodies in it. We damn near died. People bombed and putting the same mess back.[10] We finally remembered that Rouen was always a horrible place, and in fact Normandy was always a horrible place, and took off Southward. June wanted to see the caves of Lascaux, and we were interested too. Didn't remember until we got quite close, that that is Perigord. Straight out of Oz. Castles, little fields, friendly farmers and all. And the real source of the Renaissance in Literature you know -- in 1200! Dante's 'sweet new style' meant the style of the Provençal poets of the Langue d'Oc. The people hilariously unaware of it. In Perigaux I saw a newspaper or Chamber of Commerce leaflet printed partly in a strange language. I asked someone what it was, and he was quite chagrined I'd noticed it. Said that it was just their patoise. So I asked how you say 'oui' in their patoise, and he said 'oc.' Meaning it's the ancient Provençal of Eleanor of Aquitaine and Bertran de Born and Guillaume and such. Same about the caves: guy told us they amuse the children. They're interested in the stalactite caves and such, but not in the paleolithic paintings. Possibly for Catholic reasons. Lascaux is overwhelming. The pictures not in quite as good condition as they look in your (Skira?) book, but very

much more powerful. Very strange: these beautiful little valleys, these wonderful gentle people -- and magnificent cooks -- where human time goes back so far.
[RBD cut material about the car and closing]

To Linda Oppen Mourelatos
[1961]   TLTs [from Paris]   UCSD 33, 1, 15

Linner dear:
    Promised to go into the matter of Paris. Too pleasant to sound adult about: I feel rather like a child -- I probably don't understand much, but things seem to be going exactly as they should. And when I speak to strangers as if they understand me, I feel I must be getting much smarter than I used to be. As you said to Andy.
    We were one of them there generations alright -- The Pietà of Avignon, which we so loved, is now hanging in a little roomlet all its own in the Louvre. Obviously several thousand people discovered it at the same time we did. And etc. The lovers of Paris are still very nice to watch: they all feel so beautiful, whether or not their measurements are 59-18-20 or whatever.
[RBD cut one paragraph about a casual travel acquaintance]
    Got mistaken for a Marseilles-an again which represents the peak of my French accent. Never did I do better than that. But I realize now that the miracle of my linguistic triumphs during the war came from the fact that I was involved in long conversations that gave me an opportunity to get going. Confronted suddenly with the need for a remark of some kind, I tend to say Qué pasó with an upside down question mark when I should have said 'tention, hein with an exclamation point. Which makes one feel foolish, and robs one of confidence in one's protective devices.
    Forgot to tell you that there are billboards up advertising Perrier, which is more or less the Tehuacan water of France, reading

Pshitt!
C'est la qualité de Perrier

    Can't explain it. Either they mean it, or Pshitt to the French ear suggests the tempting sound of bubble-water. Also a lovely sign in a hotel bath room giving instructions for flushing the toilet and adding that one should call the clerk for 'qualquier anomolie quelle conque' [quelque anomalie]. Naturally I have been hoping to speak of anomalies quelle conque, and happily, during the terrible dinner with the Chevalier [friend of JOD], the waiter spilt gravy on me. Chevalier, tho he is native French, obviously had never heard anything quite like me remarking smoothly to the waiter, 'C'est bien sure une anomalie quelle conque!'

-- I search for further opportunities. I may have to spill gravy on a waiter. June was fine, and had a good time. Tho we'd have gone broke pretty quick sharing June's expenses.

We'll get in touch with the people whose names Joe [Starobin] gave us pretty soon. Got in a café conversation with a young-ish prof. of Philosophy from Hunter, but he turned out to be a prf. of Ph. in the school of business administration, and was as you might suppose. Ceased following me early in the conversation. But I went right ahead with the business of an ethic of self-sacrifice or not doing what you want, vs. the aesthetic (as I keep provocatively saying)-- problem of what do you want, what would be NICE. As per my poem about the lyric valuables ["From Disaster," CP 29]. The professor said, it's really quite complicated, er. So you see that our life continues to be the usual mixture of triumphs and defeats; victories and dire anomalies quelle conque.

I send a final version of that poem -- not for you to do anything with as literary executor, but because I like the poem [enclosed was "From a Photograph," CP 47]. Tho it's a terrible thing to say to one's daughter. Maybe that's why I want you to see it at least fairly well said.

The Louvre is overwhelming -- I began to think what it would be like if we really carried in our minds a sense of inheriting or some way possessing those riches of the past. I believe that's what Pound is attempting to feel, or I begin to look at his work that way. And to understand Bill Williams' recurrent sense of impoverishment in New Jersey.

-- don't know what this comes to. But we have a considerable feeling of well being to recognize that we *could* live in many different places and different ways.

xxxxxxxxxxx   Pop

To Linda Oppen Mourelatos
[1961]   TLTs [from Paris]   UCSD 33, 1, 15

Lindy Dear:
[four paragraphs and a hand-sketched map cut by RBD]
Some rather strange impressions about the art around. I don't know

just how to go into it -- as if artistic time had stood still for quite a while. We went pretty carefully thru the Museum of Contemporary Art, which has work from around 1935 to 1955 -- or mostly in that period. You know, it isn't anything at all. Looks desperate, and looks altogether beside the point. I even feel a little different about the New York school. At least it was not destroying anything. It moved into a vacuum, apparently.

The exception is, very surprisingly, a picture by Buffet. Which is in the same style as all his work, that thin, spikey, very stylish style. But this is a 'pietà' -- actually of the war -- and that style of his creates a picture of tragedy so wide spread that it has become mere shabbiness [cf. CP 240]. And it is an immensely effective and sincere picture. Dated 1946. But that is really the only picture which seems to have even relevance or any distinction at all. What moves vaguely around in my mind, and so often does, is the feeling of how 'historical' our lives seem to be: I mean how much we seem to do about what could be done at a given time. Or something like that: As I say, I don't know exactly how to get at what I want to say. I could say something about not feeling altogether the Captain of my Soul and such, except that what I feel is a considerable elation not to seem loose in the world.

--explore[d] Ménilmontant, which is a working class district of Paris. And by no means a terrible situation. One could live there perfectly happily; certainly very much better than in the working class districts of New York. The old people are in bad shape tho -- There is clearly not much medical care. As in the US, or more so, the young people can't be very easily distinguished from bourgeois. Cafés different, but pleasant. People sitting around. The really little kids look fine; playing very nicely. Impossible to see anywhere the kind of anger one sees in New York, or the effect of gangs in anything like that same way. Certainly no threat in walking around. Must be less overcrowded, for one thing. June says that all of France has recovered mostly in the last two or three years; that the sense of bitter impoverishment was very considerable up to a few years ago. Which is probably why we find it different than the Peppers [friends] and others reported.
[three short paragraphs cut by RBD]

As for being French -- Probably it would be a mistake. Tho a very pleasant life. It is not a way one can go. No use mooning about that: one might as well paint pictures of brooks and cows.
[several short, closing paragraphs cut by RBD]

We're approaching the point of having looked all one can look. We would need pretty soon to settle in Paris or to go home.   No room to work, etc.

To Naomi Replansky
October 8, 1961 (dated)   TLs   Naomi Replansky

Dear Miss Replansky:

I mentioned your Ring Song to Clarence Weinstock, and was pleased that he was able to give me your address. I'm not sure I have a reasonable pretext for writing you: it seems to me reasonable to tell the author if one admires her poems.[11]

The sense of an audience, I suppose, is pretty well absent for everyone these days. I've shown your poems to a number of poets, most of whom have not grasped the experience the poems report at all sharply. That they went hunting lions when a flea attacked them seems a general aphorism: the Invisible Man probably seems to have something to do with the alienated artist to those who have no awareness of the situation on which you are commenting.[12] This is an inevitable loss: the poems stand as poems. For myself -- I have no idea who reads a poem of mine, if anyone does, aside from half a dozen people or so who could hardly omit to. Presumably the audience of poetry consists of very young people: I don't mind, of course, but I wonder a little if the very young are really those who should be my sole confidants and confessors now that I get well into the fifties.

Anyway; you've addressed me, who am not young, and who scarcely have my head in the red morning. Your work seems to me very fine. The twist and turn against the Middle English form and sound, (which becomes almost dramatize[d] in the wonderful short poem concerning the cough ["The Independent Cough," 27]), is very moving and very masterful, and so distinctively and unmistakably a voice -- and a feminine voice.

I want at any rate to send regards and best wishes.

George Oppen

[In 1961, Oppen also corresponded with Cid Corman, Diane Meyer, and Henry Rago.]

1962

[In the month after January 23, Oppen wrote a review of McClure, Ginsberg, and Olson for *Poetry*; on February 23, he signed a contract with New
Directions/San Francisco Review for *The Materials*. From March to April,
Oppen apparently wrote his essay "The Mind's Own Place." In June, Linda
graduated from Sarah Lawrence College, and on June 12, she married Alexander Phoebus Dionysious Mourelatos, a graduate student in philosophy
at Yale University. In the fall, the Oppens made a brief trip to Florence and
Paris. *The Materials* (as well as Reznikoff's *By the Waters of Manhattan*)
appeared on September 28; there was a reception (on the 21st) for the two
authors at the Gotham Book Mart.]

To June Oppen Degnan
[January 1962]   TLs   UCSD 17, 4, 16

Dear June:

I sent the Ms. to Laughlin. As sent to you. Identical.

Should you two agree to print, I will be very pleased.   I am desperate right now to get this behind me, and get on.   The folders will do
tho: I will put them away, lock them away, and try to go *ahead*.   I mean,
not to re-write these same poems. These should have been written ten
years ago.[1]

I believe people are terrified. Those who aren't will be. Someone
said to me the other day 'Change the axioms.' And that was a writer of
high school science text books!   It is necessary to talk, to begin to talk. I
mean to be part of a conversation among honest people.

Of course we are afraid the children will overhear us. But someday
someone will overhear the children and face absolute despair. The physical
scientists will give us no peace. One imagines a new Nietzsche crying in
the market place: 'Newton is dead. Haven't you heard? Newton is dead.'
Narrative, which is everyone's art, and everyone's comfort, is wearing

out.   There is no fact more obvious than that every life ends badly.   Very badly.   Loneliness, desertion, irreparable physical injury.   Every ship sinks.   Every calamity the hero escapes he does not escape.   I mean to be part of a discussion among honest people.

----without inventing imaginary geometries. There is nothing in which I am less interested than in imaginary geometries.

And NOT 'derangement of the senses' which ends in mere prose-poem artiness.[2] ---We HAVE only our sight.[3]

———

I don't want to include poems from Discrete Series in that collection if it is printed. I don't want to disavow that first book, really, to pretend it had not been printed. A different matter to select from it when in twenty years I may have a selected poems.

53 plus 20 equals 73 years. I can do it. In the last twenty years I have suffered only from erosion. The tone and the method of those poems makes it impossible to interleave them with the new poems. They would require a group title -- 'Juvenilia,' or 'From Discrete Series' which I think would be proper only in a Selected Poems. And it would look rather desperate to follow such a title with four or five very short poems. I have at least one, possibly three new poems that could be included. So I need not admit to being so desperate for bulk, for number of pages.[4]   And I think the collection is good enough -- 'important' enough -- to be the size it turns out to be. It seems to me good: better than I had thought. Have to hear what Jay thinks.[5]

> With love,
> George

Title for the book: THE MATERIALS

To Ethel Schwabacher
[early 1962?]   TLTs   UCSD 16, 10, 21

Dear Ethel:

Concerning our phone conversation -- in which I expressed myself too hurriedly -- I meant this:

There seems to me no problem for an artist more difficult than that of separating the brute ego, the accidents of the ego, from the self which perceives. Maritan says something of the sort, and I agree.   Of [Arshile] Gorky's late work, the flowering, the atmosphere and the line, the line you describe so brilliantly and so accurately moving thru the picture without resistance, forming here and there clots -- almost without losing speed that become 'moments' in the picture world -- that is perception, surely.[6] But the horror, the phallic horror, is that not really his own affair, his own problem? Perhaps I see it wrongly. But if he had lived longer, if he had worked his way thru that, then would one not have written a book to say that he had done that, that he had worked his way thru it to a purer art? I cannot feel, looking at the pictures, that *that* is my affair.

I feel anything but competent in talking of pictures; I am reporting what I have felt so far. Perhaps we'll have a chance to discuss.

George

Ginsberg, who writes a great deal about sexual horror, seems to me to place it more accurately, to distinguish more clearly between the auto- biographical and the line near the end of Kaddish: 'the key is in the sun- light between the bars'[7]

Or is that just the difference between my response to poetry and my response to painting?   Which is quite possible.

To June Oppen Degnan
[mid-1962]   TLTs   UCSD 16, 1, 3; carbon 16, 1, 4

Dear June:
air conditioner arriving tomorrow. For which thanks.

I have had a little discussion of the essay[8] -- and am considering. Charles Humboldt, for whom I have considerable respect, tells me on the phone that he wants to discuss it with me, and says by way of a beginning that he doesn't think the 'first part' belongs in the essay.[9]   That would mean the discussion of Impressionism, and the story about Sargent and Renoir. He misses the point of course if that seems to him irrelevant. And Denise Lev[ertov]., -- and the thing is almost written *at* her, and at her latest poems, some of which are very bad -- see the Eichmann poem in her book, and the poem in Mass[achusetts] Review -- Denise says it was 'extremely hard' to follow.[10] And must find it harder than that. Of course, she may just not be in a position to permit herself to follow it: she is very determined to be (or become?) a good mother, to enter political (anti-bomb, at least) activity, etc etc-- The essay very nearly tells her to stop writing for a while --- if she must, just now, arrive at edifying conclusions. or comforting conclusions.

But -- I am reconsidering. I don't want to collect rejection slips on a piece like that. It is much too infuriating and demoralizing. There are several things I could do. One is, of course, to expand it to at least 10 thousand words.

First thing : did I not stress enough the relevance of Impressionism? Or must I warn the reader that I know Eliot is supposed to have sprung full blown from French Symbolism;   that I am aware of differing. Will I have to explain to young readers that the first shock of Eliot's 'damp souls of house-maids' and similar lines was not the rather perfunctory dismisal of house maids as people, but the fact that he saw them at all![11]   And who would have found Sweeney in French Symbolism?   But must I argue it all out? Very possibly I must

and the connections between the 'act of vision' and populism? The connection between 'the rejection of the art subject' and populism   ?? Whereas the stream of Symbolism is the stream that produces the purely subjective art which I am attacking as the 'derangement of the senses'   the 'art of the perfumer.'   May need expansion.

But chiefly I might need to stress and underline the pivot or fulcrum of the article thus:

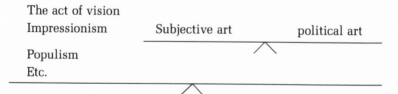

The act of vision
Impressionism   Subjective art   political art

Populism
Etc.

Those little fulcrum marks representing 'Vs.' or 'as against.' But I really do not want to make a knock down argument out of this thing. I had hoped to be permitted something like a discourse -- Gotta be at least 90?   Not that I'm impatient, but there's a risk of not making it.

A two or three weeks job to expand. And would be impossible not to distort everything in the course of a rigid argument. Don't know that I want to. I will listen to Charles H. tho before deciding.

Alternatives:

I could send the essay to Mas[sachusetts] Rev[iew].[12] They are 'published independently with the support and co-operation of Amherst College, Mt. Holyoke College, Smith College and the Univ. of Mass.' which sounds scholarly enough. The ivy-covered walls with rigour in their mortices. But I could send it with a little note saying that I am aware it is not system-building on the order of Mr Hegel.-- and just ask, do they want it?

or --- if Charles just does not follow,-- and Charles is an extremely intelligent man -- and if I don't want to write another four thousand words into it, perhaps I will make twenty or so copies on an office copying machine -- which I can borrow --- and just know that I have the thing down. And a few copies for the few people I'm sure will be interested.[13]

(Encounter [the magazine]:   on further thought -- the whole American viewpoint introduces one more distraction, and one more difficulty to the English reader.)

--just thinking about it.   Tell me what you think, meanwhile.

Heard myself on FM yesterday. Read some things well, and some very very badly. I believe I learned how to read. Certainly learned a great deal.

wid love

George

(Gilda [Kuhlman of New Directions] phoned in a state of indecisiveness. She wants to send the book to the printer -- do I want an autobiographical note. I said, write to you. She sort of demurred. I said alright, no note. Hope you don't dis-agree. I sort of prefer none. The back page indicates, titillatingly -- that I haven't been heard from since '33. An autobio. would have to state it definitely. With or without explanation? How with, in a short note?

--could say I was part of the Objectivists -- but that could really be worn pretty thin.   That I had an introduction from Pound in 33 [1934] is maybe enough, and the most to say

[written on left margin] (Did I tell you Mass Review is sending my poem to the 'Poets' Column' of the N.Y. Times? Lordy Lordy. How times and the N.Y. Times do change)

To Charles [Humboldt]
[mid-1962]   TLcTs   UCSD 16, 12, 1

Charles:

Thinking over our talk -- The fact seems to be that I just don't understand what you are saying.   If it's 'badly written' I'm stuck with it: my ear refuses to hear what should be changed, tho of course six months from now I may hear it perfectly clearly. And of course, I'm aware that it is a little idiosyncratic.

In the end, I thought you were saying 'who are you to be saying all this?' Which I do see is the question which every editor will want to ask me: the piece is probably not printable. I agree to that. Perhaps I became a little inebriated by the present atmosphere in which nearly anyone will read thru a piece of 'free verse' without overt signs of apoplexy, and began to imagine myself a prominent man of letters issuing bulletins from my desk. Still and all, I don't know what to issue from my desk if not bulletins, or where I can issue bulletins from if not from my desk. The thing I must do is to work this thing out in a somewhat new way -- to get printed what can be printed, and to mimeograph or Thermofax what won't be printed in order to send a copy to the half dozen people whom I want to read it.   I don't, after all, have to accept anyone's definition of What is a writer.

-- a simple matter of buying a thermofax. Amateurish as that may sound, is it not at least as reasonable as writing intelligent pieces for a newspaper -- the intelligent pieces aforesaid being addressed actually to not more than half a dozen people. *And then* not being able to say all of what you want to say: and in the end not thinking what you think per- haps.

But here is really the heart of the matter:

As for 'Whom am I to' etc -- I've remembered some of your lines and appreciated them as you know. Not some of the poems, but some of the lines. IF you want to write about the house you were born in, or about your relationships with people, the basic relationships of your life, or in fact about your life ---- well, who can stop you?   And if you don't want to, so don't. But where would literature come from if the demands which it seems to me you are making were met?   And if I don't speak for myself, who will;   and if not now, when? --[14] And what else would literature be, tho of course there is such a thing as a skill of writing which can be devoted to various purposes.

Or do I mis-understand you?

George

One more word: I talked to a man who is a professional writer in his own way -- a journalist -- who is by no means unintelligent and who told me that he was unable to understand your review of the Nuremberg movie.[15]   What do you intend to do about this?   What could you do about it?   And do you believe it is not really a demand not that you write more simply, but that you think differently?

I have always believed that I make sharper distinctions in these matters than you do, and that I am right to do so. If I were writing for the newspaper, and two or three people said something of this sort, I would just confine myself to simpler remarks in the newspaper, precisely as I would do if I were teaching a class and not being understood. And I would at the same time absolutely and un-hesitatingly dismiss his remarks as literary criticism.

Moreover -- apropos of something you were saying yesterday -- I don't see how I can think anything of Thomas Mann except whatever I do think. Whether or not I have 'a right to.'

Admitted I have some qualms now and then: this seems rather like 1920 romanticism. But to these rhetorical questions I ask -- in what is assuredly a peculiarly irritating style, and a bad habit of mine -- I can still see only one possible answer in each case.

The article is a statement of my opinion. If the word 'histrionic' seems to you pejorative -- well, so does it to me. And seems to me to follow from the word 'performance.'   'The image is encountered, not found' . . . ; it is a test of sincerity, a test of conviction, the 'rare poetic quality of truthfulness.'

seems to me a perfectly clear statement of a critical position and a sufficiently basic one.

Not using this phrase rhetorically or forensically: I do not understand what you want.

To William Carlos Williams
June 15, 1962 (dated)   TLs   Beinecke Library, Yale University

Dear Bill:

We returned from New Haven -- where we had been staying, by the way, for our daughter's wedding -- to find your book.   We were very moved that you had sent it to us.

--The work is so open and so frank and so solid! Like Auden, for whom I acquired a new respect, I have thought the Asphodel one of the beautiful poems of the language since I first saw it, as I have thought of so many of the poems.

Your poems have been for us from the beginning an opening of our times: not 'a monument' but, I think, a sort of permanent transparency. And we were truly moved that you had sent a copy.[16]

With our thanks,
George

To Max and Anita Pepper
[after June 12, 1962]   TLc   UCSD 16, 9, 10

Dear Max and Anita:

I don't know what we'd have done without you. Or worse, I'm afraid I do know.

Well, if I'd done that, I'd have been jailed, and not in a position to write you long letters. So you've brought this ill-return on yourself. Admitting that most of my disagreement with you, and certainly the form of it represented a desire to fight with somebody, I still find myself with an overwhelming desire to argue a couple of points.

If I am still seeking a substitute for murder, it will be good for me. If I have, as I think, more or less recovered from the extremes of rage, it may be interesting for all of us. At any rate I don't like to leave words like 'adolescent' in the air between us. What I risk is that it will still seem to you absurd and unnecessary even tho, as I write it, I am sure it will seem to me entirely lucid and an entirely reasonable concern. Well, I risk it.

Steve [Schneider]'s letter began by pointing out that one -- and I in particular, as he knew from my essay -- has a peculiar faith in small words, a feeling that they are in immediate touch with reality, with unthought and directly perceived reality. To say 'there is a tree' seems the very model of direct, down-to-earth statement. But, except for the number of letters in the words and the age of the words, it is precisely the same kind of statement as it is to say 'it is a monocotyledonous plant.' Even those simplest or at least commonest words -- 'tree' or 'table' or 'chair' -- so often appealed to as an escape from philosophic muddying-of-the-waters are classificatory words, are in fact 'taxonomy.'

Now I don't know if you'll prefer my way of saying it. Steve not unnaturally assumed that I would be willing to decipher his very compressed statement since he was arguing my essay. Also, he was being consistent. He, unlike me, has no particular faith in the little words. Alright, you may disagree. Anita [Pepper] will, I think: you may not. I objected to your review on these grounds: Steven would have been on your side. But in any case I do not think there is anything particularly adolescent in the statement.

Neither do I think that such considerations or pre-occupations are motivated only by the fear of death, as Anita implied. On the contrary, will you not agree that if we all lived forever, and were absolutely assured that we would live forever and in fact could not avoid living forever there would come a time, sooner or later, when one would cease to think of anything but such matters.   Say, after three thousand years, after five thousand years, after you had had your 2,457th child?   I think, on the contrary, it is the brevity of life which might reasonably be adduced as a reason for not worrying about such questions. To that argument I could counter only my historical optimism, my feeling for the future and for future generations, the belief that we might eventually come to terms somehow with the physical conditions of life . .

(as things stand, as the apparently absolute limits of knowledge stand, death is absolutely necessary. You may not like this statement. I only think it's true, not that it's pragmatically useful)

(and I want to make this distinction, tho I am not sure that I could establish it logically. And perhaps I should begin with a distinction between strategy and tactics, which I don't think you (youse: plural) really make either, and which perhaps I could handle. Maybe I'll get to it) -- you are both, by the way, the most consistently pragmatic thinkers I have ever met, I think. I don't know even know if you will entertain the idea of a statement which might be true although not socially useful. And I don't mean there is anything 'wrong' with such a position: certainly I don't know what 'Truth' is either. But if it is the difference between us I would like to get it said so that we can converse with some appreciation of each other's position.

But I could argue that position even on pragmatic grounds. I think it is a mistake, a pragmatic, a practical mistake, to think only tactically. I think recent history should prove it. I think I would agree-- I think I would agree again -- that in actual combat, in actual 'struggle' as the boys say -- perhaps all thinking and all art should be strategic at most. And perhaps in a final engagement, when very little freedom of maneuver is still possible, should be tactical only. As in Cuba at the moment. Or Cuba if Cuba is invaded in force. Maybe. But it is still a damned dangerous proposition, however tempting it may be, as surely we have learned.

I think the underlying question is something we touched on in conversation. I don't know which is the least irritating way to go at it: I'll put it in a question. DO you admire and enjoy any art -- any literature, say, in which the distinction is easier to make -- which actually presents new ideas, its own ideas, basic ideas or root ideas which have not already been presented in psychology, sociology, or political philosophy?

If I weren't afraid of being just too damn annoying I would underline that last sentence. In order to indicate that I would want you to answer -- if you are willing to play this game -- not abstractly but by thinking over the pieces of literature you like book by book, poem by poem, in order to see if actually there is any such work which you approve for its discovery, its intuition, and not for its agreement with propositions with which you already agree.

That would be the question. It would be the question of whether an artist like a scientist is supposed to be an outpost of new knowledge, or whether he is simply a man with an ability to say very eloquently what one wants said. The last is what is meant by 'the engineer of the human soul.' Which of course is the Soviet definition of the artist.

It was a question long ago -- before my time -- much debated. The decision went to 'the engineer of the human soul.' I agreed at the time, and as I said I might agree again. In a truly crucial moment. I don't know. But I do know that continued over a long period of time it leads simply to unrestrained and run-away lying, to a situation in which no one can even say what's pleasant and what's unpleasant, which he would LIKE, even, and what he would not like. Even pragmatically, and perhaps most of all pragmatically, I am against this test of art.

Perhaps what I would like is a truly democratic culture. Not a polemic nor a moralistic culture in the arts but a culture which permits one man to speak to another honestly and modestly and in freedom and to say what he thinks and what he feels, to express his doubts and his fears, his immoral as well as his moral impulses, to say what he thinks is true and what he thinks is false, and what he likes and what he does not like. What I am against is that we should all engage in the most vigorous and most polemic lying to each other for each other's benefit --- . Who could have the conceit, the self-confidence to believe that that is what we should do throughout all the rest of human history? [this paragraph has a line drawn around it in the left margin, with the autograph addition:] *Or simply:* 'Me too'

And a last question: the forms of 19th century art should last How long? a hundred years? a thousand years? forever?

--------alright: an ill return. Not really. Or not meant as that. Meant to complete a friendship --

--I'll admit that is a very funny remark. A drowning man gets pulled out of the water at considerable cost and discomfort to his rescuer. The moment he gets his feet on the dock he says, alright, obviously I owe you the deepest possible friendship. In order to make that possible, I will argue you round to my way of thinking. Now ----

But I DON'T really mean that. Not a matter of agreeing, but of establishing some differences of opinion as differences of opinion rather than as matters of maturity, as you were hinting, or of courage as I was hinting -- courage, or the absence of a rut.

Besides, I start such letters as this without deciding whether or not I will send them. The delay of decision makes it possible to write entirely freely. If I find that writing perfectly freely I seem not to have said, and therefore not to have thought, that anyone should be denied the right to exist, I usually send it. Seems only honest after sitting at a typewriter talking about a friend for an hour or two. So probably I'll send it.

or I'll send a short note saying, what is true, that you were both absolutely wonderful. And God knows what would have happened if Mary and I had been staying in a hotel room in New Haven.

with love, however argumentative,

[carbon; unsigned]

The point of that last being this:

I was saying to you -- or was it to Anita alone -- that I thought in part we were talking from different times of life. Moreover in that essay that Steve was commenting on, I wrote in one place the following:

Bertolt Brecht once wrote that there are times when it can be almost a crime to write of trees.[17] I happen to think that the statement is valid as he meant it. There are situations which cannot honorably be met by art, and surely no one need fiddle precisely at the moment that the house next door is burning. If one goes on to imagine a direct call for help, then surely to refuse it would be a kind of treason to one's neighbor. Or so I think. But bad fiddling could hardly help, and similarly the question can only be whether one intends, at a given time, to write poetry or not.[18]

[The next paragraph has been crossed out, but is interesting enough to retain.]

I would mean that -- tho I didn't say so -- not only of the writing of poetry but even of certain subjects of conversation and even of thought. With reservations, as expressed in the first parts of this endless letter. And to other situations than political. Some ideas are not politically useful, or useful to the childhood of a daughter. And in fact I wrote no poetry for 25 years. Don't know if I was right. But I was right not to write bad poetry --- poetry tied to a moral or a political (same thing) judgment. Or discuss it.-- I mean, I did not discuss poetry. I would grant you the same right.   Only, if it was justified for some years, first on one score, then on the other, I surely stuck to it too many years on either score. It was a mistake, and maybe a bad one. I don't know. But I was not in a learned profession nor in work as responsible as social work. I built tools and dies, houses, furniture. And before that the army -- where it made little difference what I thought -- and before that, as you know. Where that could have been the only decision. But I do not think that a psychologist nor a social worker can afford to lose touch with the thought of his or her own times; the thought, the aesthetics, the atmosphere. Nor in fact lose creative touch with it ----

dixit

But when any child has to understand? And in a learned profession or a socially responsible position--?

To Steven Schneider
[after August 2, 1962]   TLcTs with AL addition   UCSD 16, 10, 18

Dear Steve

    We find ourselves much preoccupied with Jules et Jim and related subjects --[19] Went wandering in the new or eastern wing of the Village as part of our investigation ---   Have lectured and been mildly lectured by Pete [Young] and others of the Young, who it is true stare as we might at a man who was drunk and violent as we roll up our artillery of psychology and sociology to confront a movie they liked, just sitting and looking at it ---- as they sit around and listen to music, as they hang objects in their rooms --.   Surely these young people make art a part of their lives in a sense we never did. It is possible that 'we' -- meaning a generation -- are secretly anti-art: perhaps we forgive it provided it is good. They prefer it anyway to non-art. It is pretty much what was called 'cool' for a while. That business of the cool, I think has opened the world of art, maybe for the first time, to people of something less than average intelligence --- I mean just to state this as a fact, if it is a fact: I have not a forensic climax in view. It is a popularization of art, compared to the years immediately before now. Of an art no longer moving counter to the stream? a suicidal art? . .

-- The new wave movies, the electronic music, or rather the music depending on hazard, the 'accidental' music, those of the paintings which are deliberately formless, the poetry which is automatic writing, more or less --- they may indeed display the truth, the meaningless river which flows with ourselves and our talk. And it may be that this is what art will become, the narrative of nothing, or of the inhuman event of humans. But I ponder simple brutal self defense: If it is that river, that meaningless river in which we are, it is nevertheless talk by which we are alive. If we want to continue to invent life for ourselves and for our children and for our friends it might be worth one's whole effort to find the alternative, some seed of an alternative, to this art. Of course none of this attacks the truth of the art, its validity; I speak of self defense, of an attempt, an utmost effort to make meaning, for who else, if it's worth asking again, has ever made meaning, or how else ---? I have a persistent fear that a culture, that all possible culture is being destroyed, and that people do not live without a culture. . I am not speaking, you will know -- of the suppression of an art or the disregard of an art, but of an attempt to get beyond it.

The risk of art, of course the risk of art. But there is no risk if *one intends death*. They are the people who face no risk and no hope, and they are not my fellows. We saw in the Village that they are not.

We happier relicts of an earlier day and a romantic art have been thinking about meeting you guys in Florence?? Be very nice to be in Florence together -- Last time we were there [1933] we had some impossible room with twenty foot ceilings and a courtyard, and we drank wonderful coffee in the cafe and ate microscopic cakes and saw dizzying pictures of a day, O of a very very early day --. And saw the Giottos, took horse-cabs about --

after all which, we could hire a car and drive to Paris together. Incidently, we would pass Le Beausset, where we lived. And Marseilles, which is a lively place for people who recognize the date, history and nationality of any sailing boat at a distance of five miles, and the probable condition and character of the crew.

Somewhere along the Rhône is a romanesque or rather early gothic tomb which we loved. Tho it was the first we had seen, so I don't know now --. And Lyon, which we can all dislike together, which will be companionable

What do you think?

Sent you another copy of the book. Tried this one by second class mail. Maybe will get there.[20]

George

-- I should say, but can't know what to say of the collapse of science. My father's generation took Newtonian optimism seriously, or took it for granted, and the youngish people, other than the social scientists, take the new physics seriously or take it for granted. I know we cannot disregard it, or simply leap over it by emotion and by rhetoric. But we speak of purpose: maybe it is reasonable to look to art, not to the philosophers - - - I take the emotions to be absolute: either the emotions or god --

There is a sentence of Yeats' by the way: 'Those who are concerned with truth have no pity.' And, misquoting the rest a little; therefore the threshold of sanctity is blood-stained, and haunted by murder.

[this section is autograph, and is then rewritten in type below] That art no longer presents a system, a belief, and cannot. Therefore the lumpen can and do enjoy art -- We have [mourned] the unpopularity of art -- But I think art will become unpopular enough -- And God help us --

------

and was I clear above? I am not objecting that people look at art. But that art can no longer present a system, a belief: therefore the lumpen can and do enjoy art. We have mourned so long that the artist is isolated -- What will happen when he is not?

Indeed, I think modern art will become popular. And god help us.

O well, o well; all the artist can do or should want to do is to say: 'me too.' and that he too acts because he acts.   Like Marvell.   Only what shall he act for. Surely more than pride.

To Louis Zukofsky
September 14, 1962 (dated)   TLc   ucsd 16, 11, 61

Dear Louis:

I see the first installment of your five essays in Kulchur, and astonished again -- or not astonished really -- by the relevance of these statements even after thirty years.²¹ When I phoned you -- a year or so ago, wasn't it? -- to suggest an attempt to get the Sinc and Objectification reprinted, I had in mind not so much that it might assist Rezi's book -- tho I have no doubt it will -- as that you should be given whatever credit a New Directions-SFR publication makes available for being the first and, so far as I know, the only writer to give relevant attention to Rezi. You received the suggestion by telling me that you were determined to do no more favors --. A reply which so infuriated me by the nervous energy it put into jumping into several imaginary directions that I said simply yes, of course. I reported the brevity of my reply to Mary as the first dirty trick I had ever played on you. In any case, I am glad to see that essay, as well as the others, in Kulchur. -- I would in more patient moments have found my way around whatever mulberry bushes were conjured up or hastily assembled out of odds and ends, and made the point sufficiently clear. However: irritations aside, the essays are admirable, and I am glad to see them again.

I happen to be certain that in whatever conversations took place between SFR and ND -- that is, between June [Oppen Degnan] and Jay Laughlin -- Jay held that my book should be printed eventually, but that a Collected or Selected Zuk - I don't know which he had in mind -- should be printed first. I have no idea why, holding that opinion, N D doesn't print Zuk on its own, but assume it to be problems of the budget. In any case, I offer you what information I have -- in fact, for the third or fourth time -- in the belief that it may be useful to you as well as reasonably pleasant to hear. I remember now that I carried to you at Jay's request the information that he personally would want to publish you before Rezi, whose book of course was undertaken long before mine was decided on, tho they appear simultaneously. That would appear to mean that June was not convinced to go in on the printing of Zuk. Now June has no lack of intelligence at all, or of perceptiveness, or of taste. She is putting a tremendous quantity of work into this venture, and obviously not with the intention of making money out of it. Or do you recognize that as an impossibility? I assure you that it is. But June is not really the little magazine publisher, is not typically the little magazine publisher, tho she happens to be connected with SFR. The publisher of the little magazine is someone who wishes to intervene in literature at the seed, the beginning, underground or damn near underground, somewhere, say, around Chelsea or North Beach. Such is not June, it happens. Her concern -- roughly stated -- is to make available to something which might be called The Public, writing which might benefit it if it is put before it in a manner to which it is accustomed. She has a much firmer vision of that public than I. This seems to me not only a permissible, but a cogent attitude. In the case of Rezi, at any rate, the poets and the aficionados of poetry have had their chance to become aware of him for half a century and, except for you, have done and said absolutely nothing about it. This is, by the way, the reason for the manner of presenting Rezi, the [C. P.] Snow introduction etc., which has startled me as much as, I am sure, it has startled you. But it would be a mistake to assume that June is wrong. It is extremely likely that she is not. Of course, we will see. But the attempt -- I agree with her -- is well worth making. And she is putting into the attempt a degree of skill and knowledge not usually presented as a free gift.

Alright: a poet's importance is not measured by the sale of his books -- Agreed? Nobody really thinks otherwise, or nobody who of his own volition ever speaks of poetry at all. Pound's blasts are stimulating to read and all that: they are our own little version of a football rally, and equally exhilarating in the same way. But assume that I needn't whoop it up here, Gideon's band or Sousa's band or the rest of it in order to say merely that a poet should, if possible, reach the people who could provide him with the knowledge of companionship. And who are always, one does believe, somewhat more numerous than the readers of the 'little' magazines.

But one does have to make a choice. The little magazines should present a poet as he sees himself. The 'big' publishers -- taking ND-SFR as big for the moment -- mediate between the writer and their conception -- by the correctness of which they live or expire -- of the available public. The smallest of the lit. magazines are simply subsidized: the larger ventures can not disregard completely the question of sales. No one wishes to contribute the sums which would be necessary, and which would be very large indeed. I hope I make that clear: I have the difficulty that it seems to me self-evident. A collected Zuk should be published as you've been publishing, without overhead to speak of, on volunteer labor, etc. A selected Zuk, it seems to me, would be an excellent thing for SFR-ND. I have no idea whether June and or Jay will think so. And what with one thing or another of the past, I am moved to point out that I can become neither rich nor famous nor lucky in love by intervening in any such affair. But if you are interested, say so, and discuss. What you think might be selected, etc. I feel really quite certain that a MS we agreed on would also be acceptable to ND-SFR. Tho, I repeat, they have not said so. We'll discuss it if you wish to.[22]

Regards to Celia and Paul

Charles Reznikoff, George, and June Oppen Degnan. Author's party, the
Gotham Book Mart, New York City, September 21, 1962. Degnan was
copublisher of *The Materials* and *By the Waters of Manhattan. Whitestone
Photo.*

To Ezra Pound
[September–October? 1962]   TLs   Beinecke Library, Yale University;
carbon UCSD 16, 9, 28

Dear Pound:
      You'll see that the back cover of this book [*The Materials*] quotes an
introduction you wrote for my poems many years ago. I was in fact
about twenty-one.
      I suppose if we should take to talking politics to each other I would

disagree even more actively than all those others who have disagreed, but there has been no one living during my life time who has been as generous or as pure as you toward literature and toward writers. Nor anyone less generously thanked.

I know of no one who does not owe you a debt.

George Oppen

To Ethel Schwabacher
[late fall 1962]   TLs   UCSD

Ethel dear

That was a fine evening   And we thank you for dragging us forth.[23]

By the following morning I saw this:

The play becomes clear, the conflict becomes clear as a raising of the question of the importance of a nation, the importance of a culture as against the simpler relationships and simpler emotions of father and child and mother and child, if one remembers the necessity of a sacrifice -- the 'practicality' of a sacrifice -- is as definite as -- say -- the sacrifice of a soldier who undertakes a suicidal mission   It could be seen as a plot identical to such a modern plot.

It is not, then, simply a play about madness, or fear or cowardly contrivance --- That Clytemnestra says at one moment: One must believe in the Gods because   if one did not, life would cease to have meaning -- is a part of the complexity of the classic times

which perhaps I tend to think of as simple.   Of course they were not.

I write all this down just because it occurred to me. And in fact kept me awake some of the night.

Thanks for the evening
George

((You see what I'm saying: the question of the play is the question of being numerous   )))) [CP 147, 151]

we've been thinking about it for a long time.   Because we cannot exist, however mothers may feel, without a sense of depth in the past and expectation in the future

To William Bronk
[December 21, 1962]   TLs with AL addition   UCSD 16, 3, 9

[above the salutation this is written] (only 'news' in this letter is in the
last two paragraphs, 2nd page. Better read them first)
Dear Bronk:
     I find this in my note book:

     It is probably tiresome
     To write of the writing
     Of poetry. But a friend
     Who saw the rooms of Keats and Shelley
     At the lake
     Saw 'they were just boys' rooms'
     And was moved
     By a simple matter. That there is nothing
     More to be
     Than that, that there are many things
     Less than that.

     So I have had in mind, like you, that one would not want to end
his life as a stuffed shirt, even if the opportunity should present itself.
     But tho any one of us might conceivabl[y] be scarred by success, I
think in the actual situation we have all been marred by neglect. I don't
know, it is hard to say. We are what we are, and can't look from outside
of it, a product of all that has happened. Vanity yes, but I doubt if that
has ever much threatened to distort my life or my writing, and I doubt it
of you. In fairness to ourselves, something other than vanity. It is in fact
remarkable that a poet survives as a poet, that a man can continue to write
carefully, lucidly, accurately, resisting the temptation to inflate---- what do
we have to edit out of our first drafts? ---- tho he receives no sign at all
that he is *heard*, that he is audible. It is that, rather than merely thwarted
vanity, that threatens his sanity and his scrupulousness, or subjects him
to idiot temptations. I know you know this.
     I seem, at the age of fifty-four, to be outliving some of the more
outrageous quirks of ---- what? of fate? of the market? As if justice,
strangely, did finally get done. Or perhaps I am becoming superstitious.
Charles Reznikoff's book, By the Waters of Manhattan, has been printed
with mine, as you probably know. I first encountered Reznikoff's work in
1929 -- that is, when I was twenty-one, and Reznikoff must have been

about thirty. I was perfectly certain that he was an important poet, and have remained certain of it.   Since then God knows who have been declared to be great -- there is no point now in trying to remember their names. Whereas Rezi has been continuing to print his books at his own expense for forty years until now.

I kept telling New Directions -- my sister June needed no convincing -- that Rezi had been disregarded, with no deliberate perversity on anyone's part for forty years quite simply as a consequence of the importance of his work. The publishers' readers and reviewers glance first of all at the work to see whether or not the writer is imitating the right people. They see of course that Rezi is not, and regard him as not hep, as a sort of hick. A Jewish hick. I was perfectly sure that he needed only to be presented *seriously*, with the full seriousness of a publisher, to make him visible. It was June who did that, who made the seriousness of the publisher clear. And did it very brilliantly, the C.P. Snow introduction included. Tho I was opposed to the introduction at the time. And in fact the reviews so far have been spectacular. A strange thing, and in a way infuriating. Why could no one -- except Zukofsky -- have said anything during these last forty years?   What in god's name do the 'critics' think they are *for*?   They are not criticising writers, but appraising the decisions of publishers' readers. And so are the givers-of-prizes.

But at any rate it has been done. So as I said, I am becoming superstitious. That anything at all ever gets into literature thru this weird machine that has to begin with a publisher's reader ----

June Degnan phones me from San Francisco to assure me of her complete agreement with my appraisal of your work.[24] To say also that she will not get round to writing you till she knows what her schedule will be. That will be some time. But I think I can really assure you that the book will be printed, and adequately handled. It will -- tho I am sorry for it -- undoubtedly be some time before it can be done. Perhaps a year. And of course anything can happen. God knows. And New Directions, the other half of the partnership, must be convinced ---- but really that part of it is not to be worried about;   I am sure they can be convinced. That isn't the worry, just the totally unpredictable slings and arrows of chance. But I think really you can be quite confident that the thing will eventually be done.

I have been instructed frequently that nothing should be said to a writer until the presses are actually waiting. They say it is too much for a writer's nerves. But I am unable to agree to that kind of secrecy involving a man's own work. And write to you therefore very freely and very frankly to keep you, as they say, 'posted.'

Sincerely,
George

[In 1962, Oppen also corresponded with Diane Meyer, Henry Rago, Jerome Rothenberg, and Peter Young.]

1963

[In January, Oppen worked with William Bronk's manuscript *The World, the Worldless* (1964) and, with Charles Reznikoff, began a book tour that culminated in a reading and book party in San Francisco.[1] The Oppens spent their first summer on Little Deer Island in Maine, bringing the twelve-foot sailboat which GO had built in Mexico. The assassination of John F. Kennedy in November was an event upon which Oppen wrote a number of reflections in both 1963 and 1964.]

To June Oppen Degnan
[after January 16?, 1963]   TLc with AL additions[2]   UCSD 17, 3, 10

June:

There are good poems here -- I had written down the names of some twelve poems on the first reading, but of not more than three poems which would have attracted my attention or would have caused me to remember Bronk's name if these had been the first poems of his that I had seen. Those three I believe I would have noticed -- the new painted house surely -- and I would have wanted to see more of him.

I had grown very depressed, tho, in reading thru the group. I was really questioning whether or not our enthusiasm had ever been justified. The thing that happens is that *effort* disappears in the weaker poems, they seem to *fall back* into this position--.   When I turned to the ms of the book, I was carried away again, I saw again that it was a tremendous book.   The order of poems, by the way, I thought very well arranged. The first and last poem add to the impact of the book by their position, and there is a fine modulation thru the book. I felt just no doubt of it at all. But I felt perfectly certain, again, that the collection could be injured by lowering the average of the work thru the addition of more poems less powerful than the very best in it. I don't know that I would take this position about every possible book: it is a special situation where every poem expresses the same philosophic position-- And, in fact, the same mood.

[cut 3 paragraphs about specific Bronk poems]

[p. 2] The purport of the poems, of course, is the solipsist position. (Agreed that this position has been fatal to a great deal of art.) The thing about these poems is that they put this statement forward with absolute concreteness, with absolute simplicity, with no mistiness at all: that they prove themselves by their concreteness, that they speak with overwhelming gentleness -- where they are best -- and compassion. I don't think I have ever before heard the statement in Not My Loneliness But Ours: once said, as it is here said, it seems inescapable. The loneliness not of the individual, but of the group. The poem moves quietly, patiently, as if with a scalpel, disclosing what is there. And the Skunk Cabbage I think among the most moving poems I have read. It is just a 'picture' of the plant, a picture of the tenderness in the flesh itself ----- there is no such poem elsewhere. It has nothing at all to do with Stevens and his little elegances; it is something else altogether. As is the Virgin and Child, with Music and Numbers. There is a double meaning of 'numbers' in the title, and indeed the music does sound through it -- Also very far beyond Stevens.

There are at least sixteen poems of this quality, I think. Now I don't know what will happen to the book in the reviews, but sixteen poems of such quality is a rare thing in anyone's book, they surely justify printing. The reviews ----? Clear in the first place that the weaker poems are open to attack. They appear to pound. Not very pleasantly. And some even interject an O or an Ah (in the collection I saw) to turn the poem on. And they show a lot of Stevens, not terribly good, that is not terribly elegant, Stevens. They can be attacked ---- Can't guarantee the reviews. But I don't know if anyone ever can. I think the best poems in the collection are as fine as anything written in --- a very long time; I mean a very long time.

I think what will happen is that most reviewers simply howl that all this stuff is too much for their little heads, that they were taught in Creative Writing not to philosophize, that it doesn't seem very cheerful -- etc etc. And that a few people will say that there's been nothing like this written, and a few people will not be able to get the book out of their heads. So I don't think it will die on the publisher's hands, tho I know it will not have a triumphant reception in the Poetry Clubs. I should think it would be a matter of a trickle of sales, but I am sure that the book will not die.

A poem must not mean but be.   Sure.   Still no law that a poet must be as stupid as MacLeish. A poet who is not stupid at all does provide a degree and quality of companionship not to be obtained from-- well, I won't name them all.

[p. 3] In spite of an impression around that modernism has made stupidity Literary, it seems to me that the poems which have really emerged are on Bronk's ground. As for instance Ginsberg's Kaddish -- as against Ginsberg merely Howling. Haven't most people noticed that by now?   Or Beckett. As against Dylan Thomas urging people not to go quiet. Who talks about Thomas? Nor will the new directions imaginably be the new dadaisms or the new derangement of the senses -- Or Deep Image-ists looking for inspiration in the belief that Somebody Up There Speaks English.

alright, alright. But we ought to think a little bit about NEW directions (been no objections to Rezi at all, with the single exception of Commonweal, and Commonweal's objection was on extremely special ground -- I speak delicately -- and Rezi's surface is if anything rather more conservative than Bronk's)

((suggesting possible end of silly season, as you wrote to Snow.

———

I am arguing for Bronk. I have no special urge to attack Rothenberg of the Deep Image. He may well come up with something, and [Robert] Kelly seems an even better bet. But meanwhile Bronk has come up with something -- -- constituting no less than proof that the symbolist is not the only possible direction ---

[p. 4] I would want to stress this very heavily:
1) Where Bronk, without fresh insight or fresh passion, 'puts into verse' again this point he wishes to make, the verse itself deteriorates to dreariness. It picks up cadences and worn out conventions of 'poeticness,' largely from Stevens and from Shakespeare. A reader or a reviewer not very conscientious could easily grow to dislike and even to despise the poet if no selection at all were exercised in putting the ms together.
2) I've had a great many opportunities to re-consider this selection: in two long letters to Bronk, in a whole day spent discussing with Bronk and hearing him read in Hudson's Falls, and in going thru the ms three or four times again now.   ---- It seems to me a very, very good selection of the work; it is a very fine book. I was glad to have this chance to re-assure myself. We have no reason to worry about it.

[The rest of the letter is devoted to a list of Bronk's poems "which might be submitted for magazine publication"]

To Denise Levertov
[after February 18, 1963]   TLs   UCSD 16, 6, 21

Dear Denise:

It slipped my mind when you phoned, but I had meant to thank you for reviewing The Materials, particularly as I know you had not wanted to give time to reviewing.[3]

I'd dispute, of course. I don't know about the romantic-antiromantic question: I had simply never thought about it. So that I am at any rate not involved in anti-romanticism. On the level that romance or anti-romance seem to me to exist at all, I am probably as romantic as possible. I think -- well, state it as romantically as one can, and I will agree. I think human life without emotional response, without love in fact, is unrelieved tragedy. Or if there is a more romantic formulation, I will probably accept it. But not as an eschatology, as a transcendental. Perhaps that is what you felt. And I do not look for the color of romance in others' poetry or in my own, but for the rare poetic quality of truthfulness [cf. CP 208].

As for the intent of the poems -- I don't know how to clarify it much, or to insist that I speak pretty simply, tho I believe I do. I am not trying to be complex, nor subtle, nor even gloomy.   I suffer doubts whether it might not be better simply to keep still. But what must be said about keeping still is -- that we abandon one another. Eventually.   And mendacity is not really the best policy [CP 132]. What we create by accepting a duty of joviality, or of either romantic or rationalist optimism, is the harshest and loneliest civilization, I think, which has ever existed. And I do think that poetry is a test of truth. A test, at least, of conviction. I think it has no other usefulness.[4]

This letter of thanks has become a letter of demurrer and of defense. But I do mean to thank you for writing the review.

-- I mean, I am arguing the attitude behind the review, or the attitude I take to be behind the review, but I note that you made the review as friendly as you well could in view of a considerable disagreement. Which I'd become aware of, aside from the review.

Like to urge you again to come look out our attic window sometime. That is, we could look out amicably in our several ways at 'the necessary city' [CP 45]

Regards
George

To Gilbert Sorrentino
[Spring? 1963]   TLs   University of Delaware Library

Dear Gilbert Sorrentino
I read your review -- in fact the series of reviews -- with a great deal of interest. Comment on the deep image seems to me magnificently cogent. And the review of Rezi -- tho all reviews have been favorable-- easily the most intelligent review of him.[5]

I write to say this, of course, and to send this last stanza of a poem -- to be printed elsewhere -- as discussion of the last sentence of your review:[6]

The small nouns
Crying faith
In this in which the wild deer
Startle, and stare out.
[CP 78]

The poem ["Psalm"], by the way, has an epigraph from Aquinas: 'Veritas sequitur esse rerum' -- and did you not reverse the order of Aquinas and Kant in your Chronicle? That 'Veritas sequitur' is central to Aquinas, who would surely have liked Sorrentino on the Deep Image.[7]

Would seem to be my only disagreement tho   --- I haven't read Spicer, but I will.

With regards
George Oppen

To Denise Levertov
[after April 13, 1963]   TLc   UCSD 16, 6, 21

Dear Denise:
The poem's lovely. Whereas when we talk in essays we talk at cross purposes. Which would seem to prove the uselessness of talking in essays.

Just once more; and then no more:

I was quoting myself [from "The Mind's Own Place"] when I wrote of things we would like to believe, etc.   I had written somewhere more fully that there are things we believe, or would like to believe, or think we believe, which 'will not substantiate themselves in the concrete materials of a poem.' But there are, there really are fruits in the world, and this is the experience of them, and therefore a part of the world really is as you say that it is, as you prove that it is:

> living in the orchard and being

> hungry, and plucking
> the fruit.[8]

That seems to me proof; that seems to me absolute proof. And therefore poetry -- to taste and to see, and thereby to know that it is true, to construct meanings that one knows to be true.

But I still think you are making no such demand on [Paul] Goodman -- which doesn't matter -- or of the statement, for example, that we are members of each other -- which, being in the poetry, does matter.[9] Tho I think too that we are members of each other: I believe that; . . or think I believe that . . . or would like to . . But what a poem it would be in which one saw that and tasted that!

But the 'middle generation' failed, I think -- precisely those you name -- not because I disagree with what they want to say, but because they abandoned the figures of perception for the figures of elocution, of assertion, of syntax.   Whether the voice is moving or not;   whether they are 'sincere' or not.

It is true I argue out of friendship, out of admiration. But the poem is lovely, and there is nothing to argue about. Even I see that.

With regards,
[carbon: unsigned]

To Charles Tomlinson
May 5, 1963 (dated)   TLs   Charles Tomlinson

Dear Charles Tomlinson:

'Happy that company who are intoxicated with each other's speech; who, through the fermentation of thought, are each other's wine.'[10]

Sa'ib of Isfahan, the translation by Edward Browne. Or; 'our language is our country' I'm not sure of the accuracy of that quotation.

I hadn't thought the Discrete series 'bad,' but I do think the poems require the help, the very great good will of the reader. Which you generously supply.[11] I had meant to carry the thinking and the form of these poems as far as I could without abandoning the figures of perception for the figures of elocution, or even of mere assertion, which I profoundly distrusted. There seemed at the time a tremendous difficulty of honesty; the whole weight of sincerity seemed to rest on one's own shoulders. As how should it not? But there was perhaps not a body of honest work, certainly not an accepted body of honest contemporary work, a sincere and public conversation in which to join. Not, perhaps I should add, that I take truthfulness to be a social virtue. I think very probably it is not. But I think it is poetic: I think really that nothing else is. The sentimentality of an old codger? -- but I was a mere fine broth of a codger at the time.

It's been pleasant to be invited to talk about oneself -- and to speak with such affection! I see I have rather sneakily accepted praise. But I am reminded, quite against my will, that the poems are, after all, fragmentary and sometimes strained.

As to the 'Objectivists' -- the word properly in quotes because the word has caused some confusion: it derived from an insistence on 'objectification,' on form, a matter worth mentioning in the wake of the Amy Lowells. Tho Zukofsky wrote also of 'sincerity' as the 'epic quality.'

As you suggest, no one's work altered, so far as I know, after the word was coined. It appeared in -- I think three -- essays that Zukofsky wrote. And of course those are simply Zukofsky's essays. I must have owed more to Zuk. than either Williams or Rezi could have: both Rezi and Wms being older than Zuk and I younger. I had seen Zuk's work in Exiles in, I think, 1928 -- being nineteen or twenty at the time -- and had set out to meet him. His conversation and criticism were important to me, were of great importance to me at the time. I don't remember therefore that the essays themselves came as anything new to me.

I noticed that Williams, in the autobiography, speaks of the first meeting of the Objectivists in an apartment on Columbia Heights.[12] That would have been our apartment, my wife's and mine. But what we discussed then was the undertaking to print books. The work of course already existed in ms. And the dust jackets of the books carried the explanation, written at that meeting by Reznikoff, that the objectivist press was an organization of writers who had joined together in order to print their own work and that of others which they thought ought to be read. It was about as much as could be said. We were of different backgrounds; led and have led different lives. As you say, we don't much sound alike. But the common factor I think is well defined in Zuk's essay. And surely I envy still Williams' language, Williams' radiance; Rezi's lucidness; and frequently Zukofsky's line-sense.

Those essays, by the way, are reprinted in Kulchur No. 7. I had not seen them for some twenty years. I can't judge their current interest, having known them so long. And the style is crabbed. But they seem to me sound statements.

An essay of mine, slightly referring to these things, will appear in Kulchur 10, incidently.

Not sure if you wanted all this, but I'll complete the history. The Objectivist Press derived from To Publishers;   paper-bound books printed by my wife and me in Toulon.   Printed the Objectivist Anthology --edited by Zukofsky -- and Williams' Novelette and Other Prose.

Commercially disastrous. Paper-backs were new to the U S, and encountered trouble with the U S Customs and the U S customs-- the men on the pier, and the men in the book stores. Both of whom said they were not books. The book stores simply would not stock them, or most would not. Thereafter that meeting on Columbia Heights, etc.

The poems of The Materials were written between 1958 and 1962. As I believe you surmised. Too long, too personal a story to undertake here: I kept nothing of the little I wrote for some twenty five years.[13] That matter of one's peers -- I have come to believe again, perhaps in more rather than less despair, that the only possible hope is in the conversation with one's peers. Or in thinking as if one were in contact with one's peers.

In England, a couple of years ago, I visited Tim Pember, a writer whose work I had seen, and I had been given his address. He showed me your work, among others. I was struck and delighted. Reason for my promptness in response to your first letter. I don't remember whether Pember indicated that you knew each other -- I have in any case lost his address, tho I could get it for you if you might want to see him on your return to England. He is teaching in a village not far from Winchester.

I'm sorry, since you will be in New York, that we'll be away in August -- unless near the end of August? You are welcome in Little Deer Island, Maine, if you could possibly make it. We could supply a room.[14]

With regards

George Oppen

To June Oppen Degnan
[May 1963]   TL with AL insert   UCSD 16, 1, 4 [no salutation]

Some notes:
'Wheelers and Dealers' is not an attack on you, tho I heard the phrase from you.[15] The poem means to acknowledge this abstract way of thought as perfectly contemporary, perhaps the only way for a clear intelligence to go, barring a fanatic stand. I don't expect you to be fanatic: there is nothing more 'in-groupy' -- more sectarian -- than that. In fact, you seem to have modernized us -- as we were proud of being 'modern' when we were 19, and amused by Pound, etc. who *thought* they were.

This set of poems -- from Psalm to Wheelers and Dealers, the order in which they were written --makes a rather desperate declaration of faith. It is true I can't convince myself that human society will survive long without some such stubborn faith -- but that is almost an open declaration of desperation.

Well, I don't know that we will survive. But I don't suggest you should be really grandmotherly.

————

I can draw a useful moral only for editorial purposes:
The modes that were once 'original' in literature, end today only in a stale symbolism, or some kind of surrealism, as you say. Meanwhile what is forming among artists sensitive to their own times is a metaphysical concern. (Metaphysics: a language that talks *about* physical fact. Physics describes it or thought it did)   We have come to the end -- we have *seen* the end of the assumptions of the generations of the immediate past.   It is that, and not some alleged stuffiness in the arts, which creates the cultural crisis. It is the poets who discuss the real crisis in whom a future generation would naturally be interested.

Item: The interest in Rilke, Kafka.   The appearance of Genet, Beckett, Miller . . .

Item: Who has not by now forgotten Dylan Thomas, Durrell, etc? End of prophecy.

————

Parenthetic: Meanwhile Bronk is greeted, interestingly enough, as Pound, Williams, Rezi were greeted thirty or more years ago with the feeling that there is something childish about his concerns. The proper concern of a mature artist is, of course, the concerns of his grandfathers. There seemed in the late twenties something childish about writing of red wheel barrows, rather than the more stately mansions of the soul.[16] Apparently there seems something childish now about writing of anything else.

Not to deny that many people will assert that they feel weary confronted by Bronk. But since Bronk's attitudes take off from Gödel, Heisenberg, Einstein, and theirs from Newtonian mechanics (d; 1727), their belief that they are in some way ahead of him is probably an illusion. In any case, how long can it last -- speaking of the 'two cultures'?

A version of Mayan Ground [CP 119] was printed in Thin Line [in 1962]. Of the 41 lines of the present poem, 20 are identical, or very nearly identical, with the poem in Thin Line. The poem as a whole, however, is drastically revised, and is almost twice the length of the original. I think it can be used. You'll find out the practice on this?

If it can be used, I have a group that I think very impressive:

Mayan Ground
To --
Rape of the Sabine Women
Bahamas
Wheelers and Dealers
Narrative[17]

As you see, I did my best to talk myself into something I know to be very, very foolish. I see there are some good names in Atlantic: I also see that the things they have were not written seriously, they were written for Atlantic. Randall Jarrell's, for instance, is obviously thrown hurriedly together from notes for a lecture to undergraduates, with all difficult points removed. Done, surely not for prestige, but for the check. To send them poetry seriously intended is absurd;   if it should appear it would be embarrassing, as embarrassing as launching into poetic discourse, say, to [Person's Name]. It is a very silly thing to do.

If you can get something approaching an invitation from the New Yorker, or from Encounter and if you want to work on this sort of thing --- alright;   You might remember, tho, that Poetry would presumably take the whole series, which would be an impressive thing; quite a display.

Poetry has only 6000 readers; but I doubt if 6000 of the N Yers' readers read the poetry, or if ten read it with attention.

However -- if you like.   And if you think it possible.

Please file this: it becomes our 'contract.')

'To --'   means, obviously in the first section, 'to a Lady Poet, to the Domestic Poet, the poet of the happy ending -- . By the end of the series it has come to be a sneaky way of saying 'to the universe.' And still, therefore, against the domestic poet. Suggests it really offers more hope, moreover; more basis for 'the good life.'[18]

Sec. 1. The question -- again -- of saying 'terrible things.' The question of whether one had better lie.

2. Could have been this (in phrases from Lu Chi)

> And thought stirs
> In 'the inch size heart'

> 'Homeless, nowhere to return'

3. So -- be modest.

4. The rather startling idiocy of feeling oneself the big shot, finding one's way 'among the foreign lights.'

5. It is a place.

> Nothing has entered it.
> Nothing has left it.

i.e.,   Absolute mystery. Alright. But we also forget, and the thing is really lost, is really gone. Poem says I regret it.

6. The river. Cause, the fascination of physical cause, of weight ----- as against the chaotic city. But the river, like other physical 'causes' is part of some circle ----- etc [No comment on section 7.]

8. Sense of well being -- because the world is a big thing.   And the sense that the *stage* is 'the diminished point.'   As against the romantics, maybe

9. Probably clear.

> including the point that we fear now, like the Indians, the disappearance of the people --

> [typed isolated on a separate page]   And her closets -- no real clothes. Just astounding earrings and perfumes and bright scarves and bikinis and dress up things . . . . She said she was 'afraid,' she said she was always afraid .

Letter from J.O.D. [cf. CP 122]

To June Oppen Degnan
[September 12 or 22, 1963]   TLTs   UCSD 16, 1, 4 and *Ironwood* 26

June, our very dear:

I won't bother you with revised versions [of "A Narrative," CP 132–40] hereafter. I promise. This only because it was written Monday morning after our long conversation -- re-written I mean -- And I would swear it is in this, the non-miracle, the incredible fact of reality.

Amazing how many of the poems derive from things we have said to each other -- the two sections of To --, and I no longer remember how many other things. I would like to be able to write about that candle of yours ---- I would not be able to, it is not my vision, tho it's a vision (it is de Beauvoir's, I think)   Humanity seems to me fairly precarious -- but the thing would still be there!   Or so I feel always;   even my vocabulary is affected by that conviction, that 'the Truth' is not a pronouncement but a thing.

Well, we talk. Which is a wonderful thing. You are not very metaphysical, and I am not very human. 'This activity, originating in the midst of men, moves in a direction away from them.'

Moves, therefore, as you correctly sense, towards death--   For all my violence, you are a great deal stronger, a great deal more durable than I.

For which I am glad.   Little Aub said, 'I knew you'd save me'

George

(Parmenides -- Alex's Parmenides -- worked this out, worked out this of which we talked: Existence one encounters as the existence of objects.[20] Yet it is difficult to say that an object exists. Even rocks grow by accretion, and diminish by erosion, so that if I say 'This rock' it is already not the same rock.   And yet surely there is 'is-ness.'   This constant changing, this constant flowing, ceasing-to-exist, of the object must consist of the mixing and separating of primordial elements which are themselves indestructible, and it is these elements -- whatever they may be -- whose existence constitutes is-ness. . . . a sort of atomic theory by metaphysical necessity.

But Being was for him not that is-ness, but a 'sphere' in his poem -- what I was calling the possibility of existence, the laws that would have to obtain for anything that did come into existence, an indestructible fact ---

----- I don't know if this sort of thing is a useful way to speak of it.

It seems like argumentation or puzzle solving. Whereas the point is something else, the point is the mind operating in a marvel which contains the mind ---- the point is the marvel, not this that one likes and that which one doesn't like, but the marvel, the Loved, the Loved and Not Loved -- [CP 76]. It can really not be thought about because it contains the thought, but it can be felt. It is what all art is about.

To Charles and Brenda Tomlinson
[September 1963]   TLs   Charles Tomlinson

Dear Charles and Brenda:
[One paragraph praises CT's poem "A Word in Edgeways," in *The Way of a World*; one paragraph talks of the possibility of a brief trip to England to see the Tomlinsons; one paragraph considers whether CT should send an essay on a San Francisco painter to the *San Francisco Review*.]
     I should not have bothered you about that poem [CP 3]. I regretted it at the time. But this was the contrivance:

     [sketch by GO of an elevator door with the two globes over it, one indicating up, the other, down]

So familiar at the time that I don't think anyone was puzzled at the time. Printed c 1930 in Poetry. The office building evoked by its lighting effects in those dim days, And its limited alternatives, the limited alternatives of a culture. And its quiet / stone floor [CP 3]. From there to 'thus' -- big business -- 'hides the parts' [CP 4].
     Don't for the love of Pete let this worry you further. Your version of the child and the ball --- up, down, up down --is a gift, and a good one. I accept. And the other is lost -- it so happens -- in the mists of architectural history. And cannot be restored to the consciousness of any reader without a red crayon. And a two-color print job, which is prohibitively expensive.
     -- Similar thing, Louis' saw horses ["A" 7]. Which I think was entirely clear at the time. The A's, the M's, the horses, the words, do dance, and only thru the verse -- all of which I think he meant as a programmatic statement for his verse. The primacy of music.
     I had heard of Louis delivering half hour diatribes about That Oppen to innocent visitors, one of whom, at least, made a silent and edgewise exit. Not, I hope, to you? But perhaps I had better say that Louis really has no grievance against me, nor has the world, or no greater grievance

than it has against anyone in these times of the population explosion. And Louis no greater grievance against me than against anyone who 'gets printed.' Awkward for me, tho.[21] And overwhelmingly ironic to discuss my position as 'a success.' I hesitated to go into it, fearing I might become an inveterate explainer on the terrain of myself, but hearing that I am less inveterate than some ---- Perhaps the effect of your poem has been more comforting than salutary after all. (and I doubt that I'll produce another book within quite a few years. Maybe that'll heal things)

'This earth, this throne of Kings, this England --' You mean the man was looking down at his rubber boots when he said that?

But Mary's from Oregon, a good deal wetter than anything you can show, and New York is the worst climate in the world. AND has no mushrooms.

> with regards to you both
> George

To June Oppen Degnan
[September 26, 1963]   TL   UCSD 16, 1, 4 and *Ironwood* 26

June dear:

Read the Jung all day, and far (by now) into the night, and find it a fascinating autobiography, a fascinating book, therefore. Story of a man's concern. I cannot think of it, tho, as touching at any time the ground of philosophy. This is not an objection to the book, but it would be an objection even to the concept of 'Jungianism' -- Jungianism would be for me the act of thinking about Jung, a very interesting man.[22]

Perhaps this is just to say that my mind runs on different problems. I do feel that the presumption of some process of evolution is quite strongly founded, and if it is true there really is no mystery about the existence of man. There seems to me in Jung a degree of mystery hunting of which the result, if not the purpose, is the avoidance of the rather awesome and mineral mystery. If we started with the existence of the universe, and man finding himself confronted by it, I think then we would be somewhere near the root of myth and symbol, and of dreams, and of concepts and of the incredible effort of the psyche to interpret and to understand.

The mystery for me begins where it begins for Aquinas: The individual encounters the world, and by that encounter with something which he recognizes as being outside himself, he becomes aware of himself as an individual, a *part* of reality. In that same intuition, he registers the existence of what is not himself, what is totally independent of him, can exist without him, as it must have existed before him, as it will exist after him, and is totally free of nothingness and death.   (which is, for Aquinas, the intuition of God.   It is at any rate the intuition of the indestructible)

Now, I could begin from there. But to make the psyche the very heart of the mystery makes possible the use of words and concepts which are almost nursery-words: heroes and stories, flying men and princes, as the heart of the mystery. I think these are parts of the culture built by men facing the inexplicable universe. And that we can understand them, and must understand them, because we live -- insofar as we are human -- in history. And I think it is true that Freud is almost contemptuous of history, and therefore at times grossly underestimates the human psyche. One can understand, thru Freud, a child who shows moods of sudden anger, but not Billie Kaplan's letter to me.[23] And one cannot and surely must not live his life with the purpose of becoming a Freudian graduate-cum-laude.

Whereas Jung can put some of the purpose of a life. 'The purpose of existence is that it addresses a question to me. Or conversely that I am a question put to existence which I must answer for my self, or accept the world's answer' (quoted from memory; I can't find the page right now). That's beautiful and useful, and clean outside of Freud, I agree. It is the kind of passion and dedication which makes the autobiography a very fine document. Tho it does not, for me, accept the question which is put by existence. Somewhere there occurred in Jung the (apparently) unexamined conviction, or insufficiently examined, that in man's unconscious is held the knowledge of everything in the universe, including a knowledge of the universe 'under the aspect of eternity.' I cannot believe, I cannot even suppose it to be so. I think perhaps it is the record of a man who worked with patients; who tried passionately to help the patients in his consulting room to find *in their minds* the answers to the problems that haunt us. But I think they cannot be found already implanted in the mind. They can be found, if they can be found at all, in our lives, in our encounter with the universe, in history, in the future of man, in the dialogue of art and this dialogue of philosophy. I think of the truth as emerging not in the atmosphere of mystery, but in the brightest light that can be obtained or can be borne: the tremendous pull of truth, the tremendous desire to know and to say I think is, as someone said -- I forget who -- because the truth

is all there is;   on the other hand, the truth is everything that there is ---
--- most terrible, most wonderful, most to be loved in the blazing daylight.

As to the immortality of the psyche -- surely I do not know.   I am
far from offended by Jung's thought and speculation concerning it. It is
true at least that in the universe 'there is something' -- i.e., something
absolutely unlike anything we know in physics or mechanics.   The universe could not have made itself. For science, all things explain each other,
but they do not explain themselves [CP 134].

To June Oppen Degnan
[October 31, 1963]   TLs   UCSD 16, 1, 4

June Dear --

So there you'll be by now [in Nassau]. Hope you're alright. Please
wire if you're not -- if you're lonely, if you're cold. --

That poetry reading preys on my mind. I looked up [John] Berryman's 'Songs' --. it is Stevens' Comedian as the Letter C -- Berryman's
Henry is precisely Stevens' Crispin, used in precisely the same way and
with very much the same tone -- it is the Comedian as the Letter C   vul-
garly jazzed up.   Like Rezi, I could wish I had never heard the word
poetry, or certainly never used it.   Impossible to understand these repu-
tations unless we are playing some deadly gallows joke on each other --
Well, we are not playing it, so that's all right. I wish there were really an
island, someplace, but of course there isn't. No man is an island; mankind
is incontinent. I picture the seas around Nassau as very beautiful as against
that fool performance.

Mary was talking to you about Lorine Niedecker. She came to N Y
for a few days in 1930 or so, and we met her. She must be 60 now;   a tiny
little person, very, very near sighted always.   She had graduated from
Wisconsin but was too timid to face almost any job.[24] She took a job scrubbing floors in a hospital near the run-down farm she had inherited, and
she is still living in that crumbling farm house and scrubbing floors.[25]
Someone in Scotland printed a tiny little book of her poems, which are
little barely audible poems, not without loveliness. This is one:

Remember my little granite pail?
The handle of it was blue.

Think what got away in my life!
Was enough to carry me through.

the book was reviewed here and there, and very sympathetically.
They printed more copies -- they had probably printed only a couple of
hundred. I saw a little poem of hers in Poetry: (quoting from memory,
but I'm sure at least of the last lines)

In one year, a book published,
And plumbing. Took a lifetime
To weep
A deep
     Trickle.[26]

My point being: better be anything than a big frog.   Big Frog Like
Berryman. Guess I wrote all this just to get to say that.

And yet poor Lorine, of course, too.   Surely people are not easily
or naturally happy, and therefore in spite of my moments of rage, we do
not need only to learn to let people alone.

and of course one doesn't really let people alone by writing poetry
at them. One says at least   *Listen* !   Which isn't bad advice.

I was so pleased by your telling me on the phone that I was too sad
about death. The poems are not really sad about death, but about limit-
edness. Not so much that one dies as, as Rezi proves with the phone book,
one *couldn't* live forever.[27] But I was glad you dissociated yourself so
clearly from 'all we have is time.' For one reason, because I have a continuation of the Guest Room which I thought you might take to be an attack
on you. It isn't, not an attack on anyone who thinks of -- well, understanding -- as the purpose of one's life. The poem uses the Nassau house, but
I was thinking of Seville and George and of San Mateo. The first part of
the poem too: 'the noise of wealth, the clamor of wealth' is the dinner
parties of San Mateo. The rest goes on -- and clears up San Mateo, a subject
I had to come to sometime.   It goes on to

         . . . . . the rich
Who are an *avant garde*
Near the limits of life.   Like theirs
My abilities

Are ridiculous,
To go perhaps unarmed

And unarmored, to return
Now to the old questions --
[cf. CP 90]

-- and then tells about leaving San Francisco. I'll bring it with
me.   Too long to copy.[28]

O well, June dear, love to you. We are all very wild, we are wild
with each other. But among my superstitions is more than half a belief
that few people die till they're ready to, and we surely are not.

George

(dedication)

To June

Who by some miracle of kindness
and of tact has been able to
give to me, in spite of myself,
those things which I needed to
survive.

To June Oppen Degnan
November 24, 1963 (dated)   TLTs   UCSD 16, 1, 4 and carbon 33, 1, 12

Dear June

Don't know if you get the newspapers. Or if you hear only Florida
stations?[29]

The New York Post implies almost openly that the role of the Texas
Police is not clear. James Reston calls for a presidential committee to investigate both the Texas Police and the FBI. Which makes clear a very full
understanding of the possibilities, tho he doesn't go into it. And it is
possible to discern an awareness on the part of the N Y Times, with careful
reading. Not of course the Journal American or the [New York Daily] News.
And [Lyndon] Johnson has ordered an FBI investigation of the police --

Not at any rate successfully a Reichstag fire, if it was in anyone's
mind that it might serve. Too many doubts have been expressed already.   But surely a frame, and a very classic one. It is almost impossible
that Oswald could have been the assassin at all. -- could have fired the
shot.

There is at least in 'everyone's' mind -- I suppose I mean the intellectuals -- that something very violent is going on, and that perhaps they are fools. We begin to remember again how much we really do care, how much we have at stake, how very endangered we are, how far we are from the belt-buckled semi-fascist population, and how close we are to each other.   The 'a-principled' Kennedy, the half-educated liberal-arts major, the academic Alan Dugan, the weak liberal, the disturbed radical --- Perhaps something like this might be felt. That it is -- simply -- again a period of crisis.

Seeing the photos of Jacqueline Kennedy with her children -- the silly Vassar make-up removed -- one realizes what a very beautiful young woman she is, and recognizes her strength and her honor. And the children stand quietly, and one remembers that such children understand speech and honor and it has been possible to tell them that they must behave honorably --.   And they stand quietly with their mother. Perhaps we will have to understand all this, and that perhaps all such people are endangered in the present world.[30]

I saw LeRoi Jones -- who has been feeling very left-rebellious -- at the [Lita] Hornick party. And told him something like this. And he agreed. The war-games of the Beats and the Academics look a little silly -- with the vandals outside, I told him. And we agreed.

I know, of course, that you do.

Love

George

[In 1963, Oppen also corresponded with William Kaplan, Elizabeth Kray, Norman Mailer, Diane Meyer, Panthea Perry, Henry Rago, and Steven Schneider.]

1964

[The Oppens went to Nassau in very late 1963, to a house rented by JOD on Hog Island; GO returned in mid-February, MO in early March.¹ On April 9, Oppen read, with David Ignatow, at the Guggenheim Museum, and soon after, took a freighter to England. The Oppens summered on Little Deer Island, and on October 9, Oppen delivered the complete manuscript of *This in Which* to New Directions.² The Oppens again went to Nassau from early December 1964 to about March 1, 1965, purchasing an O'Day eighteen-foot sailboat.]

To Diane Meyer
[1963 or 1964]   TL   UCSD 16, 7, 28

Andy
        Send you this carbon in apology   or is it defense --- it is defense --- of attacking Renée   That is, Renée as avatar of art, of pure art - - - -³
        Don't of course waste too much time on it, and it's no great revolution itself, but here it is
[statement enclosed as follows]
        If one is to move   to experience   further one needs a syntax, a new syntax   A new syntax is a new cadence of disclosure, a new cadence of logic, a new musical cadence   A new 'structure of space'   _____

        I imagine myself the tenth man on earth, and I say: Sometimes I feel like a motherless child   It is a tremendous moment, a great poem But I am not the tenth man on earth, much has been said and clearly one needs to say more, to say further.   I MEAN FOR *ONESELF*   One needs to say more, to say further than has been said   And clearly there *is* more
        or, of course, one dances, and it is dancing.   One dances because it is oneself that wants to dance   If one dances nicely it's nice   Not really different tho or in the end from the endless singing of the radios . . . . nevertheless if one dances nicely it's nice

Whereas if one makes a discovery, a move, one takes a chance ((we talk nostalgically, affected by the styles, but we, or I don't really mean it))

It is a minor point, that is it concerns only oneself if put this way, but there is no other adequate motive   One doesn't dance very long or very much for lesser motive

or very well, really   because one is not the tenth man on earth - - - there've been a lot of men   and women

To June Oppen Degnan
[late 1963–early 1964?]   TLc   UCSD 33, 1, 12

June:

I send these for you to read, and for safe keeping. There will no doubt be revisions, and one or two are little more than notes which I would not want to lose.

I put them together in a somewhat testamentary frame of mine, tho I am feeling rather well.   But will add:

If I should consider --or if I were considering -- a collected works, I would feel that all of the Materials could bear reprinting with the exception of Debt [CP 39]. I have a copy containing minor revisions of some of the poems.

Of Discrete Series, I would probably print the poem[s] on page 7, 8, 9, 11, 15, 17, 18, 19, 31, and possibly 33 because of a reference to it in a later poem.

Of these in this ms, there seems nothing which would do anyone any harm. But I would omit at least Red Hook [CP 124],   Memory at the 'Modern,' Bronx Zoo, Street [CP 109]. I believe I would print all the others.[4]

The book which seems to be forming I think of as having the title, This in Which. And a fly leaf saying, Veritas sequitur esse rerum. And another fly leaf saying, for June Degnan.

———

Tho I've said that Levithan [CP 68] is my defense not of the work, but of my role, still it is obvious that the poems arise from my own need to write them. I do not know that they are of use.   It is possible that they contribute only to the process which is stripping people of their defenses. I don't know and I don't know of any way in which it might be possible to get beyond what is said in them. And yet it is clear that the poems are not written in total isolation, and could not be. No one's been *happier*, in fact, than we.

If a writer manages to write, he does have some belief, some hope, in a way of life which he is creating or helping to create. There is no serious writer who is not concerned that there should be at least some editors and publishers who have broken altogether with the conception of literature as a part of the entertainment industry, and are able to regard literature as a process of thought. If you live to be very old, I think surely you will see a crisis of culture, I mean of our whole culture, a way of thinking and of feeling. In which case literature will exist, if it exists, as a process of thought. Surely I don't know, but perhaps some of it might serve. Not as revelation, but as part of a process of thought. I suppose there are small motives in writing -- but there is also this.

Overstatement?   and yet, where *but* in literature and in art?   Not, not surely in the simple merchandising of goods and of entertainment. There have been dedications to Jay Laughlin, with reason. And my flyleaf can well stand not as 'to my sister, June' but -- To June Degnan.

George

To Steven Schneider
[January? 1964]   TLcTs   UCSD 16, 10, 8

Steve:
Seems long since we've talked, and I miss you people, the two of you whom I feel I know best. Tho I've really known only one of you -- the Other One -- since infancy. I am dazed in the Bahamas; a series of guests have gone thru the house and me and we have sailed in most strange and exotic and biographical waters. I try not to push metaphors -- there is a temptation to tell you of ramshackle lumber piers extending into these blue and turquoise waters, and of ocean holes and 'rages.' And of tourist beaches and self conscious gents in Truman shirts on them, and godawful currents. And such. I've completed some longish poems begun earlier -- started some new work, but in a dazed manner -- What I want to do, really, is to copy out two or three poems to send you by way of conversation. A terrible

habit, but I am too confused or too clear to be able to bring myself to write out an account of events.

The 'Guest Room' [CP 87–90], taken as an account of the visit, would be wildly unfair to June. It was written before coming here this trip -- written in anticipation. Turned out supernaturally prophetic; we lived thru this damn thing and all the issues raised in it.   Moreover, the poem to begin with was primarily an account of the family home, or 'family home' or in fact 'family' 'home' in San Mateo, Calif, c. 1924 where I reached the bottom of what I know of despair so far --.   But the poem does tell of our first and violent fight with this house, during which a great deal happened to the three of us[5]

very strangely, we fought thru the issues of that poem in fact and in detail, fighting thru the family attitudes and Jung and the fear of death and some Eastern mysticisms -- we seem to be a threesome, incredibly enough.   We have some feeling -- I write this with hesitation, and it is not the right phrase -- but the sense more or less of having established the ground of a family, an extended family, of Aub and Dick and Andy and Linda and Alex and some grand-nieces and a grand nephew who were not consulted at any stage of the affair --   an absurdly loamy phrase as a description of Mary and me and June and as the ground of all these young people who are certainly not us -- but something of the sort.   Well, I'll copy the poems.

Mary and I kept thinking of you and Toby [Armour, then SS's wife] and Marymicaela (MM [their child]) as we fought and talked, and felt as if you were here, or should have been. The poems may seem to pose as the hero of all this, but the fact is that June was truly amazing.

tell me about MM and Toby and finances (business?) and New Hampshire and whatever else.   The floor and the windows of that house in New Hampshire looking out on the meadow keep leaping into my mind.   And the Jaguar, which sort of shook us -- only metaphorically -- as if in preparation for these events.   I'm becoming very superstitious. As if this unlikely train I caught on April 24, 1908 were -- not exactly 'going somewhere' -- but covering a great deal of ground. With no assistance from me whatever.

with love
George

[cut postscript pleasantries]

To Armand Schwerner
August 5, 1964 (dated)[6]   TLs   Armand Schwerner

Dear Armand Schwerner:
    I find on reading the poem carefully, that I am moved to discuss --
tho I find myself also hesitant. The poem is a marvel, which is perhaps
all that's worth saying, certainly all that needs saying. In fact I thought
that the sentence in your declaration on the book should have read 'The
business of the poet is to see so intensely that the door opens and he --.'
That is, it occurred to me that the sentence should end there. If one imagines a door opening, can one then specify what he - or oneself -- shall do
thereafter or what he -- or oneself -- shall see?   And still I want to discuss
the work, tho with all possible hesitation and respect.
    As one reader = one vote, then; I am not sure the poem does not
lose something in the first movement -- even justified as prologue --and
elsewhere where the tenses and occasions seem to me unclear;   where the
poem seems to seek escape into atmosphere and preamble.   Amble.   The
whole man is probably holiest, as you hold; but not ambling?   or pream-
bling?   I know the words holy and whole (and, I think, hale) are cognates,
not mere puns, but the point would be also I think in the wholeness of
the verse, a wholeness even in the syntax, a haleness in the verse.   ---
tentative, as promised. There are a great many people would disagree.
But I am sure I would prefer the whole section on Wordsworth and his
trees removed [sec. Vc]. The problem of the identity of mixtures has really
been so carefully discussed at least beginning with the pre-Socratic logical
atom. And -- the point is -- Wordsworth would have known that.   So it
seems an historical shallowness, and historical over-simplification. To the
effect of the innocence of our grandfathers. And -- no other reservations.   The search for particle within particle till they run thru the fingers,
and the turn to the attempt to find reality in the flotsam-objects of the
beaches, and the stumbling suddenly on the 'reality' in another sense of
the Mexican rope: the mind -- the 'basket case' -- to whom it is shameful
not to be a man -- the breath which refuses to dissolve into the common
atmosphere -- all magnificent. If here and there you argue medically --
argue as to what would be healthy -- well, it is indeed rather Talmudic
argument, and it is the tension and the drama of the poem
    (an afterthought on the Wordsworth objection: a friend -- a friend?
-- told me, apropos of my declared faith in 'the small words': George, the

word tree is just taxonomy. Which seems to me harder to deal with than the 'zillions')

    All that parenthetical.   I think the poem very fine work.

                with regards,

                  George Oppen

To June Oppen Degnan
[August 9, 1964]   TLTs   UCSD 16, 1, 5

Dear June:

    Your phrase, the creative *now* -- is a name of what I've known for a long time now that I must manage.   The phrase becomes one of the seed phrases.   First one -- what -- one 'grows roots' as they say, but we really want to say 'shares roots'

    and meanwhile, the 'creative now' -- the tip leaf which is oneself growing into 'new space.'   frightening, and not frightening, not as frightening as if one weren't.

    I think I divide my time differently from most people.   And perhaps not particularly wisely. I did only the one thing for twenty years. And now I want desperately to get my own work done.   I talk about other things, and I think about other things, including Goldwater. But the fact is that if the White Citizen's Council or Chinese invaders burned this house down, I would pick up my typewriter and my note book and move elsewhere, if I could.[7]   I feel lucky to hear the echoes of Synanon [a therapeutic rehabilitation program for substance abuse] from you and to know it's there, and that it is indeed a part of the creative new [sic], and that we have --- I don't know;   if we can say it, that we have somebody there.

    We'd be most lucky, most impossibly lucky if some of your friends come to Nassau -- as tho everything nowadays will get brought to us. I just don't know, I don't know why the world or how the world decided to be so idiotically good to us lately. It has, so far as I know, no reason at all.

                love

                George

To Charles Tomlinson
[August 31, 1964]   TLs   Charles Tomlinson

Dear Charles:

Your analysis of Wakoski is very cogent, surely correct.[8] But I was interested in a sort of authenticity, the very hand of *that* girl. Of Zeno: 'I know only / that arrows do not always / reach their mark'[9]

Schwerner has sent me a long poem ["Prologue in Six Parts"] -- which quotes me at length, and is in fact a meditation around my Narrative [CP 132–40] and other work I read. Impatient with me sometimes, but he thinks that I, like Akiba of the Haggadah came out a sane man. Most flattering, surely. And it is a very beautiful poem, very far beyond the work in his book --. I can hardly go around forcing it on peoples' attention. For a sane man, it's a bit awkward. But he seems to be a poet generating more than enough force and originality to arrive on his own feet. I'm pleased about the Zuk --. I feel quite a lot of anger about Zuk, as you must have noticed, but I continue to owe him a good deal --- Pleased that he'll be printed. And still and again angry that he wishes to be printed so portentously.

Enclosed the poem ["The Forms of Love"].

Regards to all --- and thanks to Justine [a daughter of CT] for the very nice 'Old Fashioned girl Holding a Lap Dog'

George

To William Bronk
[September 2, 1964]   TLs   UCSD 16, 3, 10

Dear Bill:

June sent me the four new poems to read -- And I am grateful to her and to you.   I am impressed as always by all of them, and thought the Lock on the Feeder one of your major poems.[10]

I would want to dispute a bit --- I read that poem as ending at 'or moving water have failed to bring us to.' It would seem to me so absolutely conclusive, so absolutely beautiful. Whereas surely something a little professorial happens right away to get the thing underway again; 'We know all this, colon' . . It is not that I don't feel the statement of the rest of the poem, this proliferation of the egos and I's which refuse to be quite reflexive. But it can be said otherwise. June pointed out to me how many of the comments on your work said 'absolutely original,' and I think that *must* be felt of them; there must be no possible impression of a statement having been *put* into verse particularly in a prosody which quite often relies on iambics. I do think a poem must be no less than magic, and surely the stone revealing itself is magic and absolutely conclusive. A very powerful poem.

Hope you'll accept this as dialogue, Bill. I do not consider my work superior to yours ---- I suppose I think I know *some* things.

and of course you'll pay no more attention than you wish to. But I hope you'll try reading the poem with that line as its last.

I explained my critical methods to someone lately. I said that when I read a poem and am unable to speak for several minutes thereafter, and read the poem twenty times and find that I cannot control my voice ---- I regard it as a good poem. I was describing my encounter with your work and with Reznikoff, Langland, Wyatt, Keats, Rilke, etc -- not so broad an etc. either. My student-questioner -- I mean a student at NYU -- wanted to know how I could be so positive in my opinions.

Therefore with regards,

George

I apologize and return to the charge. Which may explain my friend-less state:

I thought your original ms -- not the book -- marred by those iam-bics. I think you consent far too easily to spell out your meaning in iambic recitative. Which I regard as cheating, as making it 'sound like' po-etry. Which I assure you we can all do. How could it be difficult? But it required a more complex and a more integral and a more conclusive music to justify the 'Lady, sing to this baby, even so.'[11]

That is to say, as twenty other poets have said by now: at your best -- who's better?

George

Bill:

A post script --- I've just been asked to talk to a Columbia class in Modern Poetry this Thursday. What they do is study a text -- I demurred against going thru Prufrock with them, on the grounds that there are enough essays on the subject, and will use Virgin and Child with Music and Numbers. I'll read two or three other poems from the World, the

Wordless to give them the hang of you ---. All of which should considerably improve a class in Modern Literature.

I wish I had mimeographed copies of the poem, but I'll read twice or three times, and that should do. The request falls rather handily so soon before publication date --- and I'll enjoy very much doing it.

Since Ned somehow got me excruciatingly all over that dust jacket [of Bronk's book], I'd better make a clean breast of the fact that you are not unknown to me.

Should be a very good discussion, and much to the benefit of Columbia.   I'll let you know how it goes.[12]

regards again
George

To Aubrey Degnan-Sutter
[approx. October 1964][13]   TLs   UCSD 33, 1, 8

Aub:

Mary says you phoned -- in evangelical mood. I answer by letter not for formality nor even for emphasis, but only because I spend so much time at a desk, and do have to change the subject occasionally, so that it is easier to write than to phone. And here are the things I would say, duly numbered:[14]

1. One gets rather well occupied by the time one is 56, and there is simply not time for major excursions.   I mean -- I really don't have time.

2. I fight automatically and fiercely against derangement of the senses, and have been consciously doing so since I was nineteen. As witnessed by the first poem in Discrete Series, by the fly leaf of The Materials, and will be again on the fly leaf of This in Which:

' . . the third path, the arduous path of appearance.'

3. That covers some forty years; a considerable momentum. We're committed, Mary and I, as artists, and therefore very seriously, to the common, the un-doped, the un-staged, the plain and ordinary daylight. Whatever we see now, we'll see that way -- or fight to do so.

4. I believe we can't be astonished by any hallucination whatever. Whereas we are totally astonished by daylight, by any brick in a brick wall we focus on [cf. CP 162].

5. And astonishment -- which is a form of stubbornness -- is the core of our lives.

I speak only for us. It's O K. Not for us. Eventually not for you either. Bon Voyage, and keep us in sight, waving avuncular and auntly handkerchiefs on the pier and talking to each other about old times.

And really, really do not get hooked; i.e., don't try narcotics at all. But I'm sure you know that. And don't escalate marijuana. It's serious; we can give you horrendous reports from the Mexican hospitals, if you need them. We saw.

George

To Linda and Alex Mourelatos
[September 30, 1964]   TLTs   UCSD 33, 1, 16[15]

Dear Lindy and Alex:

I just finished the Warren Report -- or the Summary -- as no doubt you have too. I thought it altogether conclusive; I feel sure that this is what happened; If Europe and Latin America never does believe it, I won't be surprised, but I am sure that this is precisely what happened. And I thought this report far beyond anything I know in literature -- surely beyond anything I know of in prose: overwhelming, haunting, inescapable,   I don't think it can ever be altogether out of one's mind again.

Chapter VI is perhaps the most startling, because we do have a literary precedent for it: it is Bloomsday. It follows with startling closeness, which is a tribute to Joyce, but this is far beyond anything in Ulysses.   Like Bloom, [Jack] Ruby mixes into a thousand affairs he doesn't quite know anything about, and yet manages to know something about -- he 'sets up' several interviews, he speculates inconclusively about the billboard in the exact equivalent of Bloom in the museum; perhaps it's the shabbiness of his business and his relation to his 'dancers' -- not that he has a relationship, but the character of that relationship -- which serves as the equivalent of the bar of soap in Bloom's pocket all that day in which he is trying to be one of The Boys. And Ruby shocked, weeping every now and then, wandering about the city and phoning distant friends almost in a daze, terribly moved, frightened, also hands out cards everywhere he goes for his striptease show, as Bloom all that day is actually selling advertising space. And his mind, like Bloom's turning over slightly inconclusive, slightly inadequate ideas and schemes; quick-minded and some-

how inadequate. More than adequately quick-minded, but too 'different';
too mixed, or differently mixed --

The river flows thru Bloom's day,   But everything comes together
on Ruby's head in that newspaper office -- all the things he has been
dealing with most of his life, and also all the things he has forgotten or
half forgotten and which he is altogether incapable of expressing to himself.   He begins to talk about the right wing pamphlet and immediately
after hears the announcement of the assassination. And thereafter the man
he is talking to is preoccupied by telephone calls cancelling advertise-
ments.   Like Bloom talking to Stephen, Ruby cannot understand his final
act. Because, as he said, a Zero, a Nothing had caused this event, someone
must act, he thought.   And from somewhere in his background he thought
that a Jew, a Jewish man, a man 'of the Jewish faith -- and it is so stupid
.. and I never use the term --' must act.   Some old man back in Chicago
might have said, In the sight of the lord, tho not like me, in the King James
translation. As absurd, as incomprehensible as any act 'in the sight of the
Lord' [cf. CP 73–74].

Bloom in Nightown is of course Ruby's carousel club. The two
things echo against each other. And it is the Carousel Club which is authentic. I have never read anything -- Ulysses or anything else -- which
seems to me as staggering as this account. Partly that one knows it actually
happened;   impossible to know how one would read it without that
knowledge.   But it is possible to see at every moment, in every sentence,
how superbly it is written.

Oswald seems simpler, more familiar, even tragically familiar. Stephen Daedalus had a great difference;   Stephen was actually great. Whereas
Oswald needed to be great, absolutely needed to be great, and had no
possibility at any time of being so.

-- it is true that it is not possible to understand, not possible to
understand politically, certainly, how Oswald could have wanted to shoot
Kennedy. That he wanted to perform an historic act is clear, of course.   But
he wanted to perform an act which would identify him as a theoretician,
a man of principle and of understanding, and a man who had served 'his
side' -- This is what the Europeans know, as they would know.   But I think
one must accept that it did happen.   Perhaps he was altogether desperate.
Everything had collapsed for him, both the Russians and the Cubans had
refused him, his wife had refused him ------ Well, no use in this: he
seems surely to have done it. He has no possibility at all of being

great;   And that is the story's terribly tragic ending. It matters very little what precisely he did.   Maybe he just pulled down the sky on himself.

--but there's never been any account of events like this, and I am overwhelmed by it.   Perhaps you felt differently: tell us how you feel.

with love,
George

(the parallel is more than a literary curiosity for us: Ulysses is so deep in our lives. It was the first modern literature we read, it was our education.   And it was the beginning of our lives together

---I guess it was Lindy's grandfather.

But we read it in a pirated copy in a pornographic magazine; the Two World's Monthly. And this is the Report of the President's Commission.   It was all true --

To Diane Meyer
[October 1964]   TLs[16]   UCSD 16, 7, 29

Andy Dear:

Herewith the first two pages of This in Which -- Revised.   The 'Wisdom' is roughly done -- I am much tempted to leave it so   Last flare of Romanticism?   I'd be interested to hear what you think

The book will open with these two poems.[17]   Followed by Philai, followed by Psalm. Which makes a prelude, a statement of the metaphysical vision and the anthropocentric -- the 'social' as they would say.

Not so easy for me as for [T. S.] Eliot --- whose metaphysical standpoint is faith and whose anthropocentric standpoint is the Age of Faith. And therefore I haven't, I'm afraid, written a Wasteland, haven't written a decisive expression of a period.   I meant not to try in this book. I mean to try in the next [Of Being Numerous]. Probably can't - - - My god, you should see me in this patched-up work room talking like this!

George

[In 1964, Oppen also corresponded with David Antin, William Brown, John Crawford, David Ignatow, Betty Kray, James Laughlin, Naomi Replansky, Nina Schneider, Harvey Shapiro, Robert Sward, James Weil, and Leonard Wolf.]

1965

[From early December 1964 until March 1965, the Oppens were in Nassau with June Oppen Degnan. Leaving in early spring, they drove their eigh-teen-foot sailboat and JOD's amphibious Triumph from Miami to New York, berthing their boat at Daytop on Staten Island. In early summer, they visited Madison, Wisconsin, to see Linda and Alex, who spent academic year 1964 to 1965 at the Institute for Research in the Humanities. The Mourelatos family then moved to Austin, Texas, in August, where Alex had been appointed in the Department of Philosophy. In Maine over the summer, at Flossie Powers's farmhouse, Oppen worked on the manuscript of "Another Language of New York"—a long sequence poem. He was ex-panding a poem forthcoming in *This in Which*; the completed poem was to be titled "Of Being Numerous." He circulated the expanded and ex-tended version of this work among some correspondents between August 1965 and early 1966. On October 18 *This in Which* appeared, copublished by New Directions and San Francisco Review.]

To June Oppen Degnan
[1964–65][1]   TLs   UCSD 16, 1, 5

June:
    I didn't manage to define it too well when challenged. What can one do in an Hungarian restaurant? But here:
    To recognize the new, the 'new generation':
    not by the dew on them. On the contrary, where there are the clearest and sharpest marks of trampling, of devastation, destitution, the rawest wounds, is the head of the army column [cf. CP 166].
    The law of human entropy -- the arrow of time -- is: those who hold fewer beliefs have come later.
    The 'cults' are less than religion, require fewer beliefs if any at all. That is why they come later.

The 'religious revival' of the moment is primarily the loss of faith in rationalism --- it is nearer maximum entropy.

I don't know that one would want it to be so. Just that one doesn't like to ride horseback facing the tail of the horse.

Moreover I can't answer the question: 'at whose behest does the mind think?' [CP 84].

George

To Diane Wakoski
[February–March 1965]   TLcTs   UCSD 16, 11, 21

Dear Diane:

Hardware arrives the day we leave --- We are committed to driving an amphibian car from Miami to N Y with a boat in tow, so we won't arrive for a while. We'll phone when we do --²

Of the Hardware, Mary said to some rather painful visitors who gingerly examined this example of what they had almost feared might be going on -- Mary said;   there are beginnings, something might happen, whereas the New Yorker and Esquire are a dead end, and a crushing weight, a destructive weight.

With which I agree.

It seems to me these dreams are more becoming to the Young Ladies than to the men, The men are continually in danger of arriving at something like the line, duly printed, I regret to report, with fancy typological [typographical?] effects and all:

'dreams are real'

whereas the intransigent fury of DW and Carol Bergé seems at the least newer, sharper -- to be something. A root of poetry.

and yet I would say: 'I, I I I I, find me, find my navel, so that it will exist, find my nipples, so they will exist, find every hair of my belly, find . . .'   It is a root of poetry, it is indeed, well, I don't know. But just, I think, the necessity of getting further. . Because it seems to me still the pitfall that has trapped every woman poet who has written in English: I am good (or I am bad); find me [cf. CP 158].

Not that one doesn't respond.   One wants to find, one wants very much to find, but one also feels a trifle foolish if not positively guilty;   one thinks of the big business men with their 'girls' and so writes thus cantankerously.   I think the poem is good; and Carol Bergé's also.   See you in -- two weeks??

George

To Diane Meyer
[Spring 1965]   TLTs   UCSD 16, 7, 29

Andy dear:

I couldn't be more pleased by anyone's good opinion than by [Bob] Callagy's -- particularly as I try to get again to humanity as a single thing, as something like a sea which is a constant weight in its bed --- the last quoted from Discrete Series.   So I've tried before [CP 8].

--and I didn't send you a version I thought shameful. Tho I knew I'd do some more work. And did a little beyond the last version I sent -- Putting into an early part of the poem *amor fati* -- giving the Latin because it means it's been known a long time -- the love of fate.[3] Which becomes the center of the poem, its meaning. And it's finished, I'll not fiddle further -- tho when I come to print it finally I might omit 14 and 16 -- which may be distracting, tho I like them.   Alright?   I wouldn't have sent a version that caused me acute shame.   It was you I meant to torture, not me. I was demonstrating the grubbier aspects of making something. Because I think the last refuge of scoundrelly women is that they wish to feel beautiful while they make something.

I was just showing you. But what was I showing you? An uncle in unnatural childbirth.

Buddy

To June Oppen Degnan
[April 22, 1965]   TLTs   UCSD 16, 1, 5

June Dear:

I'm glad of the good words about Rezi. Tho the praise of L[ouis] Untermeyer is an unreliable compliment.   Otherwise what news, what news? As for the *News* -- if I should abandon all resolve to be realistic -- if I should say what I think we *should* do -- I think the people should march on Washington and arrest the president. And I think they should do so immediately -- tomorrow. I find I am more devoted to democracy than I had known. I find I am absolutely opposed to secret actions, carried out in pursuit of secret policies and strategies by secret means. These secret procedures seem to me unlimitedly perilous. I doubt the ADA delegation would convince me of anything other than this. 'Seduced' is indeed the word;   these secret snugglings are very seductive.

I mean of course that 99 percent of the people should agree with me, and then they should act in the most rapid possible way to stop all action in Vietnam pending public discussion.[4] Whereas, on the contrary, they are going to get used to this war. The power of the fait accompli. And it is indeed -- and horrifyingly -- impossible to attempt a stand of moral indignation, or to talk of atrocity [cf. CP 160]. I am not actually able to say that I am opposed to dropping burning gasoline on people from helicopters. It is by now a method of war, and will be used until something more terrifying is developed. So talk of atrocities at Nuremberg was a disgusting sanctimoniousness. But we *have* managed to establish some limitation of the savagery which we may exercise against our own citizens. It could be tempting to a majority of the people at certain times to agree to the arrest of trade unionists on the grounds that if the country were at war, the ability of workers to strike could imperil . . . and a slightly more elaborate argument could justify the arrest of members of the League of Women Shoppers and the P T A. The doctrine which solved this problem holds that the state may not arrest or execute any citizen unless they present a fairly clear and present danger to other people's real or imagined interests.

It might be possible to apply that principle to international affairs: to hold that it is unjustifiable to pour burning gasoline on children unless it is quite clear that it is to our immediate interests to do so. And that, having regard to human fallibility, it is impermissible to do so on the strength of an argument which purports to demonstrate that it might, under circumstances to be expected in the future, or that in the considered opinion of two or three -- possibly deranged -- men, it would, in the future ---- and also in view of partisan politics . . . I think we could, actually, hold to the doctrine of clear and present danger, tho I don't think we could manage a more thrilling moral position.

Nothing very absolute. It is in fact sickening. But surely it is a sane minimum -- it is hardly decent, but it is more or less sane. There might be a gain even in confronting this dead end of principle; if we should begin honestly to converse -- as against the present tenor of editorials and election campaigns --- I believe we would reject the worst excesses.   And I would settle, naturally, for avoiding the worst excesses.

--- Possible for individuals who know each other and love each other to make a decent life. And that's as far as we've got.   Therefore with love,

George

To Steven Schneider
[received April 29, 1965]   TLs   Steven Schneider; draft UCSD 16, 10, 16

Dear Steve:

It's been a joy to have the Bonnefoy.[5]

Will I have a chance to return it to you, will we see you soon? Or shall I mail it?

---- I find myself over this innocent note rehearsing the discussion of ethics again. I will feel better pleased with myself, tho you will feel no better pleased with me, if I add this final effort:

I think an ethical statement is an expression of the will. Erotic man. Chromosomes or as you like.[6]

'You *should* have a desire in regard to the world, in regard to mankind' ---- an expression of my will in regard to that man.

Whether my will, which defines the good, is good -- You know, I don't know. But, what I feel is wrong with the ethic of posture is that, put less pleasantly, it is an ethic of striking poses. And the Artist, the Dashing Bull Fighter, the Strong silent man of the west are all aridites, I cannot think of any which is not. And arid lives.

--still not argument: willful expression.

I consider the statement 'Man must be treated as an end' etc: I consider how I feel about it, there is nothing else for me to consider. I am not consciously telling my chromosomes like a rosary, but who knows [cf. CP 184]?

with argumentative regards --- warm regards, warmly argumentative

George

To Diane Meyer
[April–May? 1965]   TLs   UCSD 16, 7, 29

Andy dear --

you phoned -- and I got to trying to remember if I'd ever acknowledged Eve's poems ? Not sure if I did or not. They're wonderful, of
course. Funny thing is that aside from being wonderful remarks, they are
also poems, complete little things . .⁷

Eve? Eve? she got a belly-button? I mean, she was once firmly
attached to something, namely you?

odd experience. Women do have peculiar experiences.

I'm finding it difficult to write poetry -- An eerie feeling writing
poetry with the war going on. I don't know if I can. A lot of resistance, a
lot of doubt, too much as things stand to induce people to throw away a
few million lives of young men - - - - I suppose there'll be an 'incident.' HAVE people recognized the amount of lying that's been done?
enough to just not believe it? Maybe not.

In which case we'll go thru the worst part of history. Quite possibly
we just will. Tho it is possible we will not. The doubt is very overt, it has
never been more so. --- People have never been so close to a refusal, the American Legion 'patriotism' has never been so near to the disreputable . . Meanwhile burning gasoline;   it is 'eerie' also to talk about 'politics' We sit in
this little room -- it's really like a light-house -- it's really unbelievable.

There's really a contradiction -- Of course I know it has roots in our
whole history and in the talk on the streets as far back as I can remember,
and still there's a contradiction. Impossible not to wonder if a disgruntled
CIA high command asked a vice president how he'd like to be president
.. It *is* a thing like that, a kind of mad clown, nothing that was even
respectable intended this, there's obviously insane talk about dominoes
and face   I don't think it can be continued, I think it will be stopped.
But I don't even KNOW how many people have been burned alive, how
many half-burned children.   Well --. Seems it can be done.

To John Crawford
[June 1965]   TLTs with AL addition   John Crawford; photocopy
UCSD 16, 3, 46

Dear John:
Sequel:⁸
I might have acknowledged Creeley's examination of the line

There is going to be (a war)   as brilliant teaching -- and Olson's [']that which seems to exist in itself we call meaning[']   is a good statement of the thing --[9]

--is that not more relevant, by the way, to your discussion of Polanyi than the tertium quid -- which seems nothing more than Hegel and Marx. That which exists of itself can not be explained   it cannot be analyzed, it is the object of contemplative thought, it is known by 'indwelling.'   The Given.   'things explain each other / Not themselves' [CP 134]

--- the conclusion of diction -- predication as a direct function of the terms he chooses -- is excellent and cuts under a great deal of talk.   But I would like to get to the first moment, the crucial moment in which one has not yet found terms and has, for the moment, stopped the noise in one's head ----- that moment which is held before the mind which searches for terms -------- Does it not happen?   I too am not positively moored to Whorf.

(In fact I do not agree at all, do you?   You mention Gestalt. Remember Kafka's and Koehler's Apes?)   Presumably no noise in the ape's head at all.

enclosed a copy of A Language.

George

To Lita Hornick
[Summer 1965]   TLc   UCSD 16, 6, 14

Dear Lita:

I'd like to suggest to you that if Kulchur prints such things as Felix Pollack's attack on Denise Levertov, the magazine will become an instrument for the blackmail of editors.[10] I would like most seriously to suggest to you that it is within the province of an editor to prevent that use of a magazine. Moreover I think that kind of attack on a woman poet -- deliberately speaking of shit, menstruation, wet dreams, falsies -- is obviously injurious to poetry, to the freedom of poetry, an attempt to destroy a poet, tho of course it will not do so.

I recognize that this is very much in the tone of a letter to a local newspaper; I mean it in approximately that spirit. I think the piece is unforgivable, not so much to have written -- it is common to be very angry at editors who refuse a poem -- as to have printed. I think really, really,

really, whatever one's debt to the poor, the unknown, the furious, I think one need not print such things. And I write to tell you so.

With regards, tho, of course,

[carbon copy unsigned]

To David Antin
[August 1965]   TLs   David Antin

Dear David:

Not really a matter of whether I like New York vs. What's-to-like?[11]

'I cannot altogether disengage myself'   'many men more capable than I'   'they know by now as I know'   'they will come to the end of an era first of all peoples' [CP 157, 161, 156]   etc.:   I think it is only at this point that one confronts anything at all except Cummings-esque self-congratulation. I would make something like that my objection to 'a nation of idiots.'   'To see what really was going on' -- quoted from the first poem of Discrete Series; in quotes in the poem [cf. CP 3, 177].   It comes from Henry James.

The viewpoint from 'the islands' is simpler, but 'most difficult.' It presents a dead end, the shipwreck of the singular. In the face of which we seem to have chosen from the beginning the 'meaning of being numerous' [CP 151].   And is not the 'nation of idiots' also too much imagination, in this case bravura-theatrical?   Or even a sort of permission to go ahead with the wars and the War for the sake of the affluent society of scholarships and little magazines?   Which in any case -- the going-ahead -- is what is going to be done, I realize, and if I object to over-simplification it is only out of intellectual pride and the desire to know what, really, is going on.

There is a section of the poem which acknowledges -- two sections -- that we will not be able to go back and begin over.   Several sections question whether there is a way forward which is out. The problem of the will, the Redemption of the will, which requires the doctrine of Grace. We do not have that theological structure. That line of poetic thought, that genetic line of poets have only cummings with a small c, as against Grace with a capital G.   Won't do.

We'll be in Brooklyn Sept 1st, and will phone.   regards

George

To Rachel Blau DuPlessis
[August 16, 1965]   TLs   R. B. DuPlessis

Dear Rachel Blau

Academic? I don't know. It does rather decently avoid argument and the essayist's raw ego.[12]   A paragraph on page six, if I read it correctly, required some rather sharp knocking about to avoid saying 'Williams thinks so and so, whereas I --' But the academic appears as a discipline, even perhaps a decency, not as the generative force. Surely nothing wrong. Tho it's nice of you to apologize. It could well be embittering that you should be staggeringly intelligent at whatever inconsiderable age you are, and the apology is helpful to one's feelings.

I thought the thing got underway, really, on page four or thereabouts with 'the poem is a set of connections.' And beyond there I jotted down several dozen admiring notes and startled quotations -- Williams 'forging the artistic distance' is perfectly realized, and basic --

are you not over-patient with Jarrell?[13] Surely it is 'possible to re-spond' to the letters not because they were copied out on a typewriter, but because they were written. But in any case your 'seems in some way to have preceded it' (the poetry) is magnificent, like the sudden illumination of a poem.

The 'wandering among women . . . the position that he takes toward all events --' 'Those kinetic forces, dispersal, metamorphosis, and con-nection'   which gets to one center of the poem, as you meant it to.

--- are not those connections, or some of them, a weakness in Wil-liams? A simplicism, a too limited, too insistent response, a preoccupa-tion?   Even beyond that, the essay comes very close to demonstrating that it is the metaphorical nature of the poem --! ----   which limits it.   For the cataract of the Falls, the 'root' of the falls, preceded history. The metaphor occurred too quickly after all --

To place Williams in relation to the Eliot of the quartets, one would have to encounter this -- and I think poets must encounter this in any case. For the fact is that the myth vs. the singular ----- is not the problem. For the problem is beneath the myth, and even beneath the singular ---- which I agree is more profound. Obviously.   It's what happens.[14]

'Dispersal, metamorphosis, and connection.'   Yes, what the poem is built on. Not what I would speak of, not what I would have said in the poem --- I would have said: 'thought leaps on us in that sea --' [cf. CP 140]

There it is: my raw, my contentious, my non-academic ego.   I'd have written a lousy essay on Williams.

[The second page is cut]

All regards,
George

To John Crawford
[September 1965]   TLs   John Crawford; photocopy UCSD 16, 3, 47

Dear John:

Your comments brilliant -- and valuable.[15] As 'exercise' in a way, tho you dis-allow that: as demonstration at least. A standard of reading, an augury of the classes you will teach. It augurs, augers, gimlets, well.   A calm light of clarity which has no coarseness, no crudeness in it --.   An intelligence.

I would defend the line you challenge -- tho with some qualms, centering around the word 'once': a vulgarized historical sense perhaps in the vagueness of the 'once.' I'll reconsider sometime when my ear is fresh again.[16] But meanwhile:

One will finally say god
Or one will be unable to say anything

as you say, ontologic. In Augustine somewhere something approximately like this: 'It is impossible to know anything which we do not know from its roots'

Then: Tho they said God once and behaved worse than we.

(non-viable 'God,' I agree: hoped the capital would agree to that.) But stressing that indeed I speak of the ontological not the ethical problem. The assumption behind it the common one: that history, probably from the archaic, certainly from the medieval to the present is a history of increasing agnosticism. I think that is true. And ineluctable -- 'Merely the length of time that has passed' -- and will continue in spite of anyone's will. And that this is a process into philosophical crisis.

Not into ethical crisis in the sense that we behave worse and worse.   As: the crusades, the institutions of slavery, of drawing and quartering, public crucifixion, the oubliettes -- as commonly adduced.   We possess a *greater* sensitivity to the ethic of 'identification,' and this point is important to the poem. Doubt, rather than faith, is the motivation of an ethic of pity. The one ethic left to us --- or, or?? If one wishes to think, and if one wishes to think about a city, here he must begin.

The next section however acknowledges the relation of ontology to ethic [CP 160]. Atrocity becoming ordinary -- worldly -- despite the secular ethic, despite our fear of the disappearance of an ethic which is not based on an ontology and an eschatology. This is the meaning of 'crisis.'

Admitting again the validity of the question concerning 'once' --- as you indicate, in no clear historical context.

A number of revisions in the ms since sending you a copy. There are now 34 sections, and some alterations, send you a copy sometime

The 'difference of voice' you hear correctly, and pick example with precision.[17]

But I told myself not that I was more rigorously saying only what I meant but that I was saying more fully, even when less essentially, and even at sacrifice of 'perfection.' Not to hide one's tracks. Why I have started teasing myself again about . . . I grow old. . I grow old . . . . Shall I wear my trousers? . .[18]

[the rest of the letter is cut]

To John Crawford
[September 1965]   TLs   John Crawford; TLc ucsd 16, 3, 42

O sure John, that's alright. More than alright. 'With humility, but pointedly' -- beautifully said. As at 18 I might -- I wish I had -- have written 'with humility but pointedly' a renunciation of the poets I had loved. Keats, and -- more modestly -- Stevenson of the Child's Garden of Verses and -- more modestly -- Walter de la Mare;   'with humility' for I love them still. But had to look about me.

And still 'Street lamps shine on the parked cars' [CP 166] =

> The rain is raining all around
> It falls on you and me,
> It falls on the umbrellas here
> And on the ships at sea[19]

read on Riverside Drive at the age of 9 from a handbook given me by my sister Libby. Been trying to say all my life what I recognized then. And I think -- by way of a claim to concreteness and having used my own eyes, that the universe is not an abstraction, it cannot be abstracted from anything, it exists of itself in a pure state, it cannot be derived by abstracting from anything. And that, I think, is the point. As for 'lying to one's hands,' spontaneity, whatnot --- I don't know. No opinion. However one works, however one happens to work. No holds barred. Not, for me, a high dive: can't be done by starting in a certain way. More nearly a wrestling match. or just to remember that any carpenter can build a table. That you can do so also is a surprise only to your friends and instructors who know or think they know that you are not a carpenter. And it's your own piece of paper.

I am not, in that sense, a friend. I know you're a carpenter. Pleased, in a friendly manner: Not, like a friend, astonished.

Regards and best wishes,
George

To David Antin
[October 1965]   TLs   David Antin

Dear Dave:

Well, since David Ig[natow] is being honest, how could I desert him   ?

Again, to be as unpleasant as possible, I could speak from Age -- De Senectootle:

David as well as I -- And Reznikoff, and Williams, and other long-lived persons, arrived on the scene when obviously the way to write, the manner that defined poetry, was the manner of Sara Teasdale or the John Hall Wheelock or something called Joseph Auslander or etc. etc.   We did not -- none of [us] did -- agree. Nor later to the obvious modernity and 'rightness' of the [Richard] Eberharts, the [Karl] Shapiros and the other greatest poets of their time, nor to Dylan Thomas and and and Our error was clear to almost everyone --

One avoids that swamp by no prescience, but simply by asking oneself what one does know and what one doesn't know, what really is important and what is not --- Important in one's life.   An awful thing to say, I realize; but it is what makes your Vietnam poem, it is precisely how you proceeded, and it is the only way   ----[20]

In the manner which is now 'what's going on' is a great deal as ephemeral as 'th' optic orb,' that unblinking eye. . . . the manner, and all that relies on the manner, is ephemeral precisely because it is the going manner . . . . . is the manner which -- obviously -- defines 'the poetic ---'²¹

      Yes, the village explainer

              us old farts are trying to warn everyone . . .

                       George

(Merely to sound like one's generation -- how nice it sounds, how nice it always sounded -- at the time

It CAN'T be that easy!²²

To Rachel Blau DuPlessis
[October 4, 1965]   TLs   R. B. DuPlessis

Rachel, thanks for the promptness, the special delivery -- and for the letter itself. A living mechanism in that young woman, the *life* of the mind   !²³

    I'll comment on the comments -- tho life may diminish with comments on comments

    on 7, I don't agree really. I need that, and need it as flat as it is to establish that half of the burden of the poem which is hardest to establish ---- the concepts evolved from the fact of being numerous, without which we are marooned, shipwrecked ------ it is in fact unthinkable without them [CP 151].

    To establish that flatly; to establish the stance of the poem, which is not satirical . .

    and as a solid base for the leap to amor fati, which is the first line of the next section and which, if I have given it validity, is I think the major achievement of the poem.

    all other questions raised ponderable at the least :

    The additions to 2.   Unquestionably 'busy argument' as you say; included as temporary notes to myself in that copy. I've intended to re-work it.   Trying not to lose too much.

    on the three lines of 'we will finally say god --' I am being peculiar about it I know. I seem to want the weak cadence. But acknowledge that I will sometime have to get rid at least of the word 'once,' which is a sort of vulgar historical sense.

    The chorus (androgynous) enters with;

'Find me' [CP 158]

etc.   I think it's valid. It may echo faintly thru the poem

A project:

Discrete Series -- a series in which each term is empirically justified rather than derived from the preceding term. Which is what the expression means to a mathematician, as I gather you know.

(I thought too late -- 30 years too late -- that the flyleaf should have carried the inscription   14,   28,   32,   42   which is a discrete series: the names of the stations on the east side subway.

The Materials: to restate the themes: solidly

This in Which means what it means in the Psalm [CP 78]. But contains some private amusements in that it means also the achievement of form;   that the materials in achieving solidity, form, appear in the light of the miraculous. Or so I mean them to. -- And I don't mean to write the same book again.

Another language [the poem CP 94–101] ----- is imperfect.   Has to be, tho I don't mean it's not my fault. But to begin: a looser, a more commodious language, to make possible at least one more book --

Eliot somewhere speaks of a point -- or simply says that there is a point at which the poetry no longer matters. It's true and, as he knows, not true. There is a point at which one reaches what one meant to reach, the thing that the poetry was for. One gets there, and can throw the rest away. At that moment nothing that went before matters. Neither the prosody nor the images ------ neither entertainment nor sermons.

'advanced guard' means that, if it means anything that matters

whereas the elaboration of technology is *always* academic, even if the Academy is not doing that at the moment.

Again: thanks for the letter, and the train trip to New Rochelle.

with love,

George

There's nothing very complex, nothing requiring tremendous aesthetic argument: we need courage, not 'audacity' -- Pound's word -- but plain courage.   To say what it's like out there . . . .   out here.

———

Write me again when you are a Doctor, have flunked out, collapsed, have run away, or are otherwise free

———

To Rachel Blau DuPlessis
[October 21, 1965]   TLs with enclosure   R. B. DuPlessis

Rachel:
    Another letter.   To teach you, in character of Father William ("You
are old Father William, the young man said, and your hair it is turning
quite white, and yet you persistently stand on your head; Pray, do you
consider it right?")   not to ask questions.[24]

George

Notes on Prosody?

There are certain things, appearances, around which the understanding
gathers. They hold the meanings which make it possible to live, they are
one's sense of reality and the possibility of meaning. They are there, in
the mind, always. One can sit down anytime and sink into them -- can
work at them, they come into the mind, they fill the mind --- anytime.   One tries to pierce them ----
    The process by which sometimes a line appears, I cannot trace. It
happens. Given a line, one has a place to stand, and goes further --
    It is impossible to make a mistake without knowing it, impossible
not to know that one has just smashed something. Unearned words are,
in that context, simply ridiculous --.   tho it is possible to be carried astray
little by little, to find oneself, quite simply, trying to deceive people, to be
'making a poem.' One can always go back, the thing is there and doesn't
alter. One's awareness of the world, one's concern with existence -- they
were not already in words --- And the poem is not built out of words, one
cannot make a poem by sticking words into it, it is the poem which makes
the words and contains their meaning. One cannot reach out for *roses* and
elephants and *essences* and put them in the poem ------ the ground under
the elephant, the air around him, one would have to know very precisely
one's distance from the elephant or step deliberately too close, close
enough to frighten oneself.
    When the man writing is frightened by a word, he may have started.
    when a vowel or a consonant or a cadence cannot be altered without
making a hole in the poem, the prosody is O K.
    Unwilling to construct a systematic aesthetics, still must add that
we 'engender in beauty.'   I don't want to try here to explore that.   Would
we discover our faith in Goodness, the Good, or simply the emotional

component? Possible to discuss 'prosody' at this level. But How To Write a Poem ended, as it should, with the letters O K.

This is my post-post-graduate present.

George

To James Laughlin
[November 1965]²⁵   TLc   UCSD 17, 5, 10

J:

I find I want to say what is said in the reviews in the back of the book section: 'I couldn't put it down.' It's true - - - Perfectly clearly another man, a clear personality, a way of speech.²⁶

These might give the heart of the work:

The City (page 17 [14]). Its bitterness a little familiar by now, but it has a quality of its own - - It could be the city seen by a seaman, it is *placed* as if from seaward. As in the goat (Second section) and the section [stanza, section 1] beginning 'what are the facts.' I would say seamanlike, sailorly. Or workmanlike.

The Creator (page 10 [7]) with the beauty and energy of an Alba in strange surroundings,   Summer Scene (26), the 'squirrel's tail flying from a handlebar' [32] which becomes a paradigm of his speech because it is a symbol, a flag.   And equally the three trees graceful as a neo-classic picture of nymphs   with no connection to the small

> poor louse
> crawling in the bark ridge
> for his life²⁷

I thought this a very fine poem. But - - - the matter of the last several lines! I don't know what to say, I don't know why, in half a dozen poems, he does this.   The last lines of Address of Oneself (30)   and The Woman (8 [6]) - - those last three lines are intolerable - - - or the Man at Work (12 [9])   This is officious and I would not deliberately undertake to patronize this work - - - But these seem to me lines lame beyond belief - - - Well, less than half a dozen poems. All, for some reason, in the first third of the collection.

Early American chronicle (57 [52]) among the very fine poems, Flora and the Ogre (85 [70]) - - all these possess a profound and northern rhetoric. Extracts from a Private Life, first section (87 [72])   displays most

clearly some debt to Pound.   I don't in the least mean that Pound's existence explains Rakosi's.   No one will manage to think *that*.   Nor does
Stevens', tho there is a reaction to Stevens, and an essential relation in
that the very body of the poetry is a rich, imaginative and supple rhetoric.
Rakosi understandably includes a (mocking) Homage to Wallace Stevens
(90 [74]) which is crystal clear as to what he owes and what he does
not.   The poem begins:

> *Clear me with this master music.*
>
> . . .
>
> *this drama sets the clock[s] of epigram[.]*
> and the line: *Stamping her wronged head on an old medallion*
>
> (wonderful in context, if not here)   And
>
> *She heard a subway of demotic voices*
> *scoffing at all unmusical dispassion[s]*

not entirely or not only a mocking parody of Sunday Morn-
ing.   Rakosi's clarity as well as richness, his scrupulousness, has often
the tone of Stevens.   (Not the final depth of Stevens)

The poems are most beautiful when most literary - - strangely, to
me strangely;   they speak at such times from great depth. And a depth
which is his own. There is a firm, formal wealth in his line-sense - - - the
work will probably become no part of the Berkeley-Black Mountain-Village
canon for the time being.   Tho one could think that Duncan at times owed
something to it - - of course, he cannot.   And one could wish that Olson
did.

I've been citing poems as a sort of quick guide to the ms. But it may
be that the poems gain in the wealth of context.

O, surely the work is well worth printing! I should think June
[Oppen Degnan] might like it - - for the qualities here indicated and for
its clarity.[28] Which I also value.   I think, almost as fundamentally as June
does, that clarity is becoming a moral issue.

[In 1965, Oppen also corresponded with David Ignatow, Elizabeth Kray,
Linda Oppen Mourelatos, Panthea Perry, Robert Sward, Charles Tomlinson,
James Weil, J. D. Whitney, and Julian Zimet.]

1966

[Early in 1966, Oppen finished "Of Being Numerous," and in February went on an antiwar demonstration to Washington. Oppen introduced Diane Wakoski and William Bronk (April 14), Harvey Shapiro and Theodore Enslin (November 17); both readings were held at the Guggenheim Museum. May 31 marked the final FBI report on Oppen; it concerned his and Mary's travel plans. The Oppens went to France and Belgium for a month between early June and early July. The end of the summer they spent on Little Deer Island. Oppen read at St. Mark's in New York in October. *Discrete Series* was republished in a facsimile edition of Mother/Asphodel Press in Cleveland sometime in the fall. At the end of 1966, they decided to move from New York to San Francisco.]

To John Crawford
[January 1966]   TLs   John Crawford; photocopy UCSD 16, 3, 47

Dear John:
        The dream - - -   I can report of myself: I think I have had only two decisive dreams in my life. One I acted on ten or fifteen years later, or acted as the dream should have taught me to do, but without thinking of the dream - - That is, I had told myself something I was unwilling to hear.   And that dream I think cracked me rather badly: it was a nightmare, I felt it as a nightmare, and I was not able to get out of it, to get out of it as a nightmare for a week or two weeks - - I mean I think it very nearly killed me.   It was in war time, which made it harder - - - - - - and perhaps, under the circumstances, harder to accept - -* [* goes to the end of this three-page letter with this note] In brief: I dreamed that I shouldn't be trying to kill people, hero or no hero.   Or not as part of an army.   And it damn near killed me.   But I still don't know if it's "true"   I know it was what I thought.   But there's a limit to my superstition: I don't know that I know absolutes, and can't imagine knowing absolute values, even in dreams.   I am sure, in fact, I don't.

The other, tho I took two years to understand it - - - I reacted at once as you did.   With elation, in fact hilarity. I was driving somewhere the following morning, and found myself swerving the car from one side of the road to the other - - -- deliberately - - and howling with laughter, actually swaying from side to side on the seat, howling with laughter and swerving the car from side to side of an empty road - -. And it was one of those startlingly witty dreams; I was laughing at a small thing in the dream, and one which was not really very funny.   An excuse for elation, a false excuse for a real elation. I guess I knew I knew, or knew I would. The dream said in its imagery that I was not going to rust - - - - but it was not until two years later that I sat down with a piece of paper for the first time in twenty years and thought my way into a poem - - - - [1]

---

as for superstition, I am more superstitious - - prescience, destiny and the rest - - than it would be reasonable to confess without need.   And not, I really think, because I want to be superstitious - - - It has been born [sic] in on me, and the alternatives, moreover, are all implausibilities   Outrageous and absolute implausibilities, and I don't find it too difficult to be rather constantly aware that I don't know - -

- - the word God seems to me to have no function other than to justify the pronoun he in place of it - - - carrying with it implications which - - I don't mind that they are unexamined presuppositions, but they seem to me so petty and so childish that - - the word blasphemous occurs to me .. I did discover permanence in that other poem. I am of course not the first to have done so, but I did it for myself. It seems to me   what matters. I don't really care one way or the other about small occult occurrences - - occultations? - -. I sort of think what I sort of think on sort of evidence, without feeling that it touches any root of things.

I have declared my faith in 'the small nouns' [CP 78].   That they are the names of things.   And all that goes with that!   The leaves' shadows!   Thereupon the sun is nine hundred million miles - -   is it? - - away, and it is burning and light rays are .. and straight lines .. and the leaves are ten feet above the ground ... and the light from nine hundred million ... and   and   I sort of believe all that, or anyway something about the word.[2]   And I suspect that I will seem to future generations a touching, or perhaps only amusing model of natural faith and piety - - - my days bound duly each to each.

———

I've realized from your 'Letter' [a long poem by Crawford] that you've had to work your way thru a right-wing mystique, working your way out of son-hood as primary .. Not easy. You must, like all intellectuals, know a great many Jews, in fact I am myself quite a number of Jews, despite my lack of Yiddish and all - - If you should ever come a cropper, which you won't - - will you ever think, as you must have thought, coming to in that field: What am I *doing* 'way out here!   ?

- - - I usually talk rather a lot, rather a silly lot about Jewishness, and it seems to me that I never have to you   ?   Another grounds for superstition??   or just that I try not to talk like a damn fool to you. Probably the latter. In any case, to make up for it I'll take you to Flatbush Ave sometime and give you LESSONS in anti-Semitism - - - -   Terrible scars, terrible mars: the least attractive qualities in the world are those which are a consequence of failure and those which lead to success. The least pleasant conditions of matter are on the one hand death and on the other indestructibility. - - I'll show you Flatbush Ave.

but you'll not get over it.

You and the analyst are fine. The analyst's 'this may have been a perversely healthy thing to happen' is good, and a model of theological discretion, unlike this letter. Your 'Nothing perverse about it' is great!

And yes - - 'we all just barely make it.'

George

- - - - naturally I don't know what your dream meant.   You'll know in a short while - - say, fifty years.   Meanwhile partial explanations, which is what you'll have to get along on, can be useful. . . I really *know* that they can.

To Steven Schneider
[January 1966]   TLs with AL postscript   S. Schneider

Dear Steve:

I guess this is it - -   Doubt that I can carry it further.[3] It's been a harrowing work for me, partly for the difficulty, a difficulty I suppose of courage or of honesty in permitting the imperfect to appear imperfect, and the difficulty of distinguishing that decency from the indecency of permitting mere sloppy work, a different kind of faking - - .   Imperfect, but I think it has to be.

The long quotes in the first section [CP 147] are Mary, verbatim, telling me about Bonnefoy; the next words, beyond what I've quoted, were 'that's what Douve is about'[4]

It also contains so many of the issues - - well, the issues that are issues between us: it'll be a considerable tribute at least to my possible lucidity if you like it at all.   - - - -   And perhaps you will agree-- as you need only agree, I think, to accept the poem - - that this attempt must be made: and maybe it's made honestly. I'll be much interested in whatever you have to say.

Other quotes from here and there. The magnificent 'He who will not work' is from Kierkegaard: the context of the entire poem alters his meaning somewhat, but the elisions indicated by dots do not - - - It's what he was saying [CP 158].

'I'll be much interested in what you have to say' I see I wrote, writing like an ass in the middle of the night.   I mean, the poem after all is about friendship, in part.

George

a problem sometimes of syntactical delicacy   ?   One occasionally finds himself within a subject -- -- or a predicate

To June Oppen Degnan
[January or just after, 1966]   TLs   UCSD 17, 5, 10

Dear June:

I suspect you may have froze?   Which I would regret.   But the TV did say 10 degrees in Miami - - -. Unless you crawled into Dick's shirts with the tarantulas, which would have been the best move.

They're really pretty great, the Oliphants,   IF unfrozen.

Basil Bunting appears in the Jan Poetry with a long poem - - truly a magnificent poem.   Unforgettable;   Creeley told you rightly.   No other literary news of moment that I know of[5]   As for THE news, it's been steadily agonizing, except Fulbright on the TV last night;   brilliant, mild, reasonable - - There's been nothing like it in public, I realized, for a very long while.[6] Well, so there've been two things.   Hardly related to each other, except that I'd been finding the poetry which is current impossible if not ridiculous to think about until the Bunting arrived   to make such undertaking seem ponderable again.[7]   I phoned Betty [Kray] concerning Bunting, with urgings. Betty's tired, really tired - - tired of poetry, which is understandable.   Don't know if she believed me; I tried to say that this is a different matter. I don't suppose we'd need more than a dozen poems if there were not so much bad poetry about: hate to return to Pound's forensics, but bad poetry is certainly the enemy of man.

A number of people taking care to declare themselves unassuaged by the Johnsonian peace offensive - - A veteran's demonstration on Washington, which I'll go to.

I think we must decide to live thru this - - the napalm and the rest.   Easy enough to throw oneself away with horror but I don't suppose that's really what we want to do.   To manage to live with it, to live thru it, if we get to, without however deceiving oneself.   To speak calmly and carefully of hell.   I have no great knack for it.

The problem is to be useful if one can be, to be calm, but to know what's true. Not to play Truth or Consequences, not to choose between truth and consequences even when one talks to oneself.   To try to write it down bluntly, I mean that the Vietnamese - - a great many of them - - are going to be burnt alive, and a great many subjected to various careful tortures - - - and we will, in a way, accept it, we will talk politics, and try to find Johnson and the CIA a way out in order not to be taken into a general war and the end of us.   But one begins to understand the Germans now, and I would much prefer not to.

The word is 'madness' alright.   One shies away from the word because this madness flows so smoothly from our definition of sanity: to get what one can.   It is really true that evolution has gone too far 'if life is a search / for advantage.'   And it would be very difficult to define life as something else.   The evolution of the mind, unlimited in one direction, and absolutely limited in all other directions - - I don't know, it is simply not viable without a conscious effort, a conscious invention on the part of the mass of the people which seems simply impossible

maybe the 'mass of the people' will surprise us again.   There is - - built-in, genetic - - a model in family relations, in family love, which is not, it almost never is, *merely* predacious.   It's there, it's not an impossibility.

Not quite an 'invention,' therefore.   Which really is impossible. But an extension?   If the 'mass of the people' do make such an extension of sentiment, will it have anything to do with what has been more or less formally said or written? A time-lag maybe: a century or so back. A man was saying to us the other day that perhaps Johnson would behave differently if he had sons rather than daughters. Naive in a small way: Johnson's sons, if he had any, need not be at the front. But you see the assumption he was making, and it was justified. People do want 'the world' - - the human world - - to continue. They have no particular reason to, but they do. Which provides the possibility of rational argument. It is just that, unfortunately, insanity possesses a tremendous pull, insanity is very infectious. But I wrote that last sentence as a generalization. Actually one encounters a great deal of resistance to the administration propaganda even in the street - - resistance or at least doubt. I don't think this last round of offers to all and everyone to decide what Vietnam should give Mr Johnson - - - well, it's certainly had some effect, but I don't think it's been overwhelming.[8]

Well, as I said, we should at least try to live thru it, which requires some self-control. The strange thing is that life is so nice, one doesn't encounter many mad dogs in the *street* - - - if only one were permitted to stay away from the rabid, if only they didn't become *President,* even. Half a dozen mad dogs in every block - - it wouldn't really matter if one could just handle the national convention and the electoral process in some way

by the way, life in the immediate environs is indeed very nice, not excluding the blizzard. Which was beautiful   and extremely exciting to the small fry of the block.   Honest-to-god snow drifts are new to the newest arrivals.

you, however, don't have steam heat??   And have froze???   answer if you can.

George

To Linda Oppen Mourelatos
[April 2, 1966] TLs ucsd 33, 1, 16

Linda darling:

I'd remembered the Brecht poem.   It's very moving and very serious - -. Charles Humboldt had found it so too;   we had talked of it very often, it came into his mind again and again. And now it is strange and moving that you find you have kept it all these years.[9] What it says has been very nearly the central problem - - maybe it has really been the only problem - - for us as a family.

Self-sacrifice!   one could almost say: you may sacrifice anything but yourself.

but of course one must be able to distinguish between oneself and a second helping of potatoes.   to keep a lithe figure, perhaps, and a certain liveliness of spirit to avoid such confusion - -

We have oscillated between the knowledge that we love only those whom we do really and actually love - - - - or, driven by horror or compassion, risking ourselves, that is, risking each other, each other meaning also you.   I had that dream - - I think I've told you.   It was a nightmare, I felt it as nightmare, the worst I have ever had, and I was not able to get out of it for a week or two weeks.   It was in war time, which made it harder to accept.   We've surely not solved it - - just oscillated. It cannot be solved as a question between two conflicting claims, they simply conflict sometimes.   What one owes to one's wife and child and friends even is to keep oneself as safe as possible - -   There's no way round it, one's nobilities, minor or not, are at their expense.   But just because it would be unbearable to find oneself alone in the universe, the social ethic has roots of great power.   It is why I become so angry at those who *depend* on the poor, the oppressed, for their ethical well-being, for their 'values,' as they so horribly say.   I wish, I wish the poor and the oppressed did not exist, and we could look only for what we do really value, 'the ground I stand on' as you wrote not long ago.   'The lyric valuables' I wrote in the Materials [CP 29]; or 'Behind their house, behind the back porch, are the little woods - -' [CP 172]   I've been agreeing with you - - the thing begins with the positive, with what one does want.   We must know what we really do value, what we really do want, nothing else will stand up

I am not sure this is very paternal, to say - - well, I *can* say, this is what we are all of us concerned with, and that may at least be companionable.   Which is maybe all we can offer, Lindy darling, and I suppose all we ever could, when one comes to think about it - -

A Catholic philosopher, name of Gilson, has a very nice sentence: 'Philosophers' - - and, he could have said, poets - - 'think about *things*.' With or without the italics, a very nice sentence.   I would teach it in 8th grade, with a shift of emphasis: Poets and Philosophers *think* about things.   And with the PhD diploma, I'd tell them: Poets and philosophers think about *things*.
[excision]

as a matter of fact, we're pretty good.   We've punched our way in and out of various paper bags, and acquired ourselves.   And we love you, which is a point to the good

Pop

To Charles Hanzlicek
May 30, 1966   TLs   Charles Hanzlicek

Dear Charles Hanzlicek
    Thanks for your very fine letter. [An explanation of, and citation of the poem "To C.T.," CP 142, is cut]
    I sat down to write the autobiographical note you ask, but - - well, a matter of so many years, to begin with - - and a matter to explain of a first book in 1934 and a second in 1962 - -. Too much.
    But no; no teaching.   Negative autobiography.[. . .]
    (Articles on my work?   A Pound introduction to Discrete Series, 1934- - in S F Public Library- - -   a number of reviews of Materials, but - - - reviews.   Thomas Merton including a section in a new book, apparently - -[10]   Not much bibliography)
    (Perhaps I could help with my own statement about my own work, approached a little more basically than in the opening of this letter:[11]
    I think that poetry which is of any value is *always* revelatory. Not that it reveals or could reveal Everything, but it must reveal something (I would like to say 'Something') and for the first time
    The confusion of 'must not mean but be' comes from this: it is a knowledge which is hard to hold, it is held in the poem, a meaning grasped again on re-reading - -
    One can seldom describe the meaning - - but sometimes one has stumbled on the statement made in another way.   As Parmenides' 'the Same is to think and to be' is Charles Reznikoff's   '. . the girder, still itself among the rubble'[12]
    Heidegger's statement that in the mood of boredom the existence of what-is is disclosed, is my Maude Blessingbourne, in Discrete Series, who in 'boredom' looks out the window and sees 'the world, weather-swept / with which one shares the century'[13] [CP 3, 177 and 186]

    I think this is the law of poetry, and the only law.

(I use two of the fragments - - tho one my own - - which have run thru my head almost constantly thruout my life)

George Oppen

[note to himself][14]
Wednesday, June 1, 1966 (dated)   TL UCSD 16, 1, 6 and 33, 1, 21

I slept in the afternoon yesterday, and had confused and elaborate dreams. When I woke - - after sleeping a long time - - I told Mary about them as best I could. I said I had dreamed several phrases which seemed to me very important, and immediately on waking I attempted to repeat them to myself, intending to write them down, and found they had dissolved or dispersed;   I was unable to pin down any single word or to form an impression of what they had been about - -

And I told Mary, then, the one thing I could remember out of what seemed to have been a long and complex dream.   Mary and I were in a large country house, preparing to leave by car - - I don't know what car - - and in fact entirely prepared but detained by various affairs of a rather large group of people in the house as if at a garden party, or guests at a summer residence - - it was definitely summer.   I don't remember ever having seen that house before, and yet it was a kind of house very familiar to me, a large, light wooden house, a very large sitting room, very lightly and casually furnished; I have an impression of chintz-covered wicker chairs, and a vague familiarity about the carpet, for which reason I didn't visualize it clearly, and probably French windows -- certainly not any other kind of window -- an openness. At one time in the dream -- the only section I was able to remember clearly - I was sitting in a chair near a group of people gathered around a small card-table at a sort of conference. The phone had rung, and I had answered -- there seemed to be a small telephone table at my left --and was listening with the receiver held between my chin and shoulder and I was taking notes either of the telephone conversation -- in which there were, for some reason, very long silence [sic] broken by short sentences in a rather low and rather rasping masculine voice -- I think I associated it with a gambler of some kind -- or I was taking notes on the decisions at the table -- I don't know which.   I was surprised that I could listen to two conversations at once, and pointed out to myself that the phone conversation contained those long silences. Explaining to myself that that made it possible.

I was writing notes on a sheaf of papers with odds and ends of typing, and notes and corrections in pen and ink -- which is precisely how the notes which I keep on my desk look.   I found it difficult to find room for what I was writing on these partly covered sheets, and tore off several pages from the very back of the sheaf -- which then seemed rather to be a 'tablet' -- expecting them to be blank paper.   They were not, and I said aloud:--with the feeling that I was saying something very funny --'NO books have any blank pages' -- I spoke with a pretence of ill-humor, which was the humorous effect.

I had been reading, the day before and perhaps that afternoon, Martin Heidegger's *Essays on Metaphysics: Identity and Difference*, Philosophical Library, N Y, tr by Kurt F Liedecker, borrowed from the Brooklyn Public Library by Mary. I had been reading the first essay, 19 pages long, without being able to understand it clearly.   Tho I was reading with great excitement and great effort.   Sometime during the afternoon, after I woke, or early evening I had written down from memory a note -- on a partly used sheet of paper -- which was a quotation from the essay.   Later, writing a letter to Fred Siegle, I typed those remarks into it, without acknowledgement or quotation marks.[15] In the note I had written for myself I had consciously changed the word 'incalculable' to 'infinite,' and in the letter I changed it back.   I did not send the letter for two reasons: first, because I realized that the paragraph was a plagiarism, and second because I had written the letter about some poems he had sent me without more than barely glancing at one of the poems.   I had realized that the procedure was absurd, and didn't know why I was writing the letter.   I knew I was envious of the phrase;   it occurred to me that where Heidegger had used the word substance, I would probably not have thought of it, and would have used the clumsy word 'matter.' And I wrote 'which is the subject of our planning' with the knowledge that it was my own phrase, an alteration of his, but derived from some other sentence in his essay.[16]

That night I sat up late, very carefully reading the essay, and after many hours felt I had understood it -- It was very difficult for me to grasp the extreme Idealist assumption on which it was based.   When I had grasped it, I turned it over and over in my mind for a long time, unable to accept the assumption, but convinced that a part of the statement was of crucial importance to me, of such importance as to alter the subjective conditions of my life, the conditions of my thinking, from that point in time. I got out a poem I had been working on and had been unable to finish adequately, and wrote into it -- in pen and ink, because Mary was sleeping -- the statement from my unsent letter, with slight alterations: the phrases which I took to be my own, and the phrases which were from Heidegger. -- Changing the 'incalculable' this time to 'unthinkable' -- in order to make the reference clear in the abbreviated form of the poem, which reference, in Heidegger and, now, in the poem, was simply the acceptance of the inevitable final death of mankind -- an actual acceptance, a dealing with it --

The poem, with these lines, seemed to me the most important I had written, at least the most important to me. When I came to bed, Mary was partly awake, and I told her a little of my excitement -- just that I was excited. But immediately on getting up in the morning, and before I had had coffee, I realized I had plagiarized a climax of the poem. I read the poem, and made slight changes in the phrases that were mine -- removing a line among other things --but feeling dis-heartened. I thought perhaps I could look up the original phrase and use it in quotation marks -- tho I didn't want to, since it was a climax of the poem. I glanced thru the essay without finding the passage. I then read the passage over and over; I made coffee and read the essay a number of times again -- without finding that passage! I have not been able to find it, tho the essay is only 19 pages long. I have not read anything else in the last week except a book of Auerbach's, which could not possibly have discussed any such subject

---- It seems necessarily true that I did not read those sentences. The essay does end, however, with these two paragraphs --- which seem, in the essay, a non-sequitur:

'Whatever and however we may attempt to think, we will think in the context of tradition.   Tradition preponderates if we are liberated from afterthinking into anticipatory thinking which is no longer a planning.

'Not until we turn our thoughts toward what had already been thought, shall we be employed for what has yet to be thought.'

(a note to the word 'afterthinking' -- a note by the translator -- reads 'or *reflection*.'

Nothing in this that does not permit one to speak of 'the unconscious mind.'[17] Only that it's hard for me to think of whatever mind that was as real unconscious   !

--and that is not what I was thinking that morning -- the word had not occurred to me.   As I started hunting thru the essay the third or fourth time, I didn't know if I was in the real world or not --

I had written that statement in 1959 -- In Time of the Missile.   But had said it rather weakly.   The statement in Heidegger is rather veiled and just for that reason the mind pierces it with terribly shocking suddenness

-- not the simple statement of fact, which he takes for granted, but the realization that he means to incorporate it into a philosophy ---

Reacting with shock to what he had written, my mind went on and said the rest, and I thought that he had said it   ?   But the name of the essay is Identity and Difference

a thought which has not been greatly simplified by the event.

To John Crawford
[Summer 1966]   TLs with AL inserts   John Crawford; photocopy UCSD
16, 3, 47

Dear John- -

Sorry to be so long in answering - - I answered at once, and realized sometime later that I had not been at the typewriter while doing so.   It really occurred to me at this precise moment that I had never really typed that out - -

I'd talked about the problem of the 'I' in feminine poetry.[18]   EVER solved?   That we know of, *ever*?

Well, to reach outward far enough to produce the pure beauty of

The moon is down, and the Pleiades
And I am alone

or that realler distance - - a New England distance perhaps, and surely a feminine distance;   [feminine] meaning here something like 'domestic': which gives it such impact

. . . and then

I could not see to see.[19]

But except Emily Dickinson: *anyone*, really?[20]
But if it is to be solved, it will be solved maybe by distance, by

some sense of the distances and the realities around the 'I' - - and, actually, Jo's abstractions are very good, don't you agree?

Truth was the trouble

is really fine, no?   and 'a circle world' (of childhood)   and 'I am not afraid to see what is left of you - - - - without furniture, in effect, and that whole context. There's courage in those lines and *freedom*

Freedom of thought, freedom of style, freedom of emotion which is openness to experience.

and I am trying to be as accurate as I can, as correct as I can, in the matter of where the chance of poetry lies, but it is true that I tend to think first of what will lead to a life, where the constructing or the acceptance of a life lies.

I am not trying to say that I don't think Jo can be a poet - - I think probably she can - - - but the fact is I don't primarily care.   I think of her as a person and I don't think it of terrible importance that she should be a poet. We get so obsessed. That part of 'being a poet' which resembles being a weight-lifter or a jockey or a driver of racing cars is   a disease.   That part of poetry which is a realizing, a revealing of the world --- O, that's something else, and is more often than not unconnected with print.   Or even with typescript.

I mean to say: Jo seems very lovely, and she says a number of very lovely things. And I hope to god she does not sit at a desk and mail innumerable envelopes to innumerable little magazines, but makes a life.

and makes verse of it when, as and if she wants to.   No reason to think she won't do so very well.

Her stubbornness, which often shows as faults in the poems, is the best sign of all.

Well; you see what I am saying as far as *Poetry*, pure advice on poetry, is concerned --- and I suppose that's the only field in which I might be imagined to possess competence: I am saying; let her not polish or inflect or twist to style, but let her take time.   Let these things in her mind sink down and merge and differentiate and take on colours and --- let her take time, let her become who she is in her own world, which, of course, she will create.   Not only the child's world which,   it is true, is circular: bounded by adults.

Well, you asked.   I keep starting a new paragraph to talk, as requested, about *Poetry*, confronted by the evidence of a very lovely young

woman I find it hard to stick to that point, if it is a point at all
[RBD cut four paragraphs]

George

To Serge Fauchereau
[June 19, 1966]   TLs with AL insert   Serge Fauchereau[21]

Dear M. Fauchereau:
Your letter reaches me only after some delay -- ironically for the reason that I am in France.   In Paris, tho, unfortunately, not Surgères, and your letter was forwarded from New York.
I will answer as best I can: the conditions of travel make typing a little difficult --
To Publishers was established with my wife and I as publishers -- the status of Publisher somewhat modified by our age, which was 21 -- and Louis Zukofsky as editor.   Our first publication was the Objectivist Anthology, edited by Zukofsky [1932];   it was not the product at least of any formal discussion and certainly not of any formal decision or affiliation among the contributors. Attitudes toward the introduction undoubtedly varied, but not, I think, in any case to the degree of basic opposition to the position put forward.
Several dozen commentators and reviewers have by now written on the assumption that the word 'Objectivist' indicated the contributors' objective attitude to reality. It meant, of course, the poets' recognition of the necessity of form, the objectification of the poem. The point may seem rather obvious today, but it was not an unimportant stance as against the liquidation of poetry into the sentimentalism of the American so-called Imagists of the late twenties and early nineteen-thirties.
The Introduction to that anthology spoke of Objectification in that sense, and spoke also of the quality of sincerity.   No one of course will object to sincerity, but there is a question of definition -- I am almost tempted to say, of the sincerity of the definition.   I think it is still true that the weakest work even of the best of the young poets occurs where the poet attempts to drive his mind in pursuit of emotion for its own sake, in pursuit of excitement in the conviction that all that is not excitement is insincere.   I would hold that the mere autonomy of the mind or the emotions is mendacity, that all that is not truth or the effort to achieve truth is adulteration. I believe that a poem, if it is indeed poetry, is always

revelatory;   it is perhaps the inability even to imagine the possibility of a new conception which has created the all-but infinite reduplication of confusion on the order of 'a poem must not mean, but be.'* [starred sentence inserted here by RBD] *(it is true I speak of a Realist poetry: Realist in that it is concerned with a fact which it did not create)   and this is essentially a continuing agreement with what was said in the name of 'Objectivism,' tho my manner of stating it undoubtedly is not identical with the manner in which every other member of the group -- if it was a group -- would state it;   The Objectivist Press, which was the successor to To Publishers, carried on the dust jackets of the books this statement: 'The Objectivist Press is an organization of poets publishing their own work and that of others which they think ought to be read.'   And that may be as much as could accurately be said toward a definition of the group.

You ask of Pound's interest: certainly his kindness and help were unstinted. And his Active Anthology (Faber and Faber, 1936 [1933]) printed Bunting, Zukofsky, Rakosi and Oppen -- all in the Objectivist Anthology. And Pound's (and Eliot's) insistence on -- I was going to say, insistence on the necessity of form, but I am tempted to say simply Pound's and Eliot's literacy was certainly an influence on the writing of the introduction to the Anthology, and probably on the writing of most of the poets included.

As to the current interest in the Objectivists: they were rather wiped out, weren't they?   by the generation of the Academics. The Academics having now disappeared without a trace, we seem rather to have been stumbled on by the young poets who must have wondered what if anything could have been going on between themselves, that is, between their appearance and Pound, Williams, Eliot and Stevens, who are at least three generations before them.

My Discrete Series will be off-set by Asphodel Press, and should appear soon. I will send you a copy; the original is of course long out of print. You'll judge for yourself; I think you'll easily discern a thirty-year difference but I believe you will also be aware of a continuity.

And, as to continuity: it remains my opinion that Reznikoff, Rakosi, Zukofsky, Bunting of Briggflats are the most considerable poets of my own generation.

With regards and best wishes -- I will be glad to write further if I can be of help —

George Oppen

I will call for mail at American Express for the last time on July 10th -- Address after that date, 364 Henry St, Brooklyn. It would be pleasant to see you while we are here, but that would be impossible perhaps?   I don't know the distance to Surgères, and because I am answering hurriedly I have not yet looked it up on a map.

One hopes this letter is decipherable: I can do better on a type-writer having what for me is a 'standard' keyboard.

To Serge Fauchereau
[July 25, 1966]   TLs   Serge Fauchereau

Dear Mr Fauchereu:

I am mailing today my Discrete Series (having located an original copy) and The Materials, together with Reznikoff's Waters of Manhattan - - to make sure you get one.   It is true, as you say, that James Laughlin will gladly send you a copy, but I send this to make sure that there will not be a delay, and in an attempt to make up for my inability to send several other things at this moment. The exodus from New York in summer is almost equivalent to the exodus from Paris, and Loquitur and the Zuk essays may have to wait till September.[22]

Rexroth did appear in the Objectivist Anthology, of course.   But I believe that may have been Zukofsky's initiative rather than his; I think certainly he would not feel any identification with the matter now.[23]

I do indeed know that my poems are difficult to translate. The line sense, the line breaks, and the syntax are intended to control the order of disclosure upon which the poem depends - - And the tone, the intention, is often conveyed, of course, by the prosody. I had often reflected that the poems might hardly be translatable - - I think your translations an excel-lent job. A few queries:

La Construction du gratte-ciel --- My word, the *Building*, has a more direct reference to the action; it has also some sense of 'the creation,' it is a word that might be used of the 'building of one's life.' It gains something in this way, and has even a very slight unexpectedness in reference to a sky-scraper because of the non-Latin root, the homeliness of the word. The individual workman is clearer. It is likely that French hardly possesses these snobberies and reverse snobberies: would 'bâtiment' produce any-thing comparable [CP 131]?

c'est le travail du poète - - of course my 'business of the poet' cannot be made French. My French is far too rudimentary for me to know if 'the affair of the poet' will go literally into French - - Or 'the undertaking'? The implication of an *attempt* is present in the phrase 'the business of the poet' [CP 131]

Et de les exprimer   a lot lost.   Difficult, I realize. But 'to speak out   meaning, to exhaust, to say all that can be, and to speak   out-wards   Can it be done [CP 131]?

You note the difficulty about culture - - - the word is unexpected in English in that context - - Perhaps the French no more so [CP 131]?

Il peut y avoir   alright   and you skillfully produce an echo of rhyme not far from my sharp rhyme on 'brick' [CP 99]

Un dimanche bien tranquil - - - necessary to sacrifice *so* quiet of a Sunday which, it seems to me, gives duration both in its sound and the strain of the meaning [CP 99]

Marie-Anne   impossible I'm afraid for the French version to read 'Mary-Anne'   I would like it to be possible;   it would control the cadence, which is important there.

J'espère
Leur sens et leur saveur

Two things on this [CP 97]. My French accent is very bad, so that I cannot reliably hear cadences, and your judgment in moving the line break is probably correct. But the line break as I have it produces the suggestion of a meaning which is modified finally, but still present

I hope, to meaning
And to sense

If it can be done   ?   And, the possessive 'leur' seems to me a mistake.   The question is not of the meaning of a specific word, but of restoring *words* to meaning   as, I do not think one could speak of restoring language to *its* meaning, but to meaning.

Again;   the translations are excellent. And these suggestions are made for your consideration only.

With all regards
George Oppen

'Le charpentier sur les poutrelles - - - [CP 131]
Would this man call himself a charpentier?   the men who worked on the Tour Eiffel for instance?

Is it as strange to the French ear as it is to mine to hear of a charpentier assembling steel   ?

one last query: Can the line divisions of the English not be followed in the translation in [CP 97]

Possible
D'utiliser
Les mots pourvu qu'on les traits
En enemies.
                        ?

To John Crawford
[Summer 1966]   TLs   John Crawford; photocopy UCSD 16, 3, 48

Dear John: 'a matter of wanting to take the most powerful risk for the given unit of time' is magnificently - - and ambitiously said.[24] And the obverse touched [Cid] Corman.   Sensitive and often delicate, as you recognize, his materials are exotic, but they are often corrupt.

And this is a cruel thing to say of Corman for it is NOT what he wants, he has wanted purity.   But materials far from one's origin (no pun) can be corrupt. Everything which is not earned is corrupt- -

Fragmentation: an attempt to hide in the things one meant, really, to climb out of   ?

- - those materials so easily handled - - it is not that they are pure.   They are so easily handled *because* they are corrupt.

Those materials which force themselves upon one, those materials which crash into one's life from atomic space and the historical space which is one's own --- they can be crushing -- one can most certainly fail -- but they are not corrupt.

The academic - - sure, sure, we all know.   It's been adequately discussed. But one wants to know, to know while he is still young, and there is no more powerful emotion than the desire to know --.   'At whose behest does the mind think?' Powerful and autonomous, autistic   ?   (it is true that academia does sometimes present the Lineaments of Satisfied Desire.   Not quite as imagined. Rather as at the terminus of a competition - - Or the middle of it?   I imagine watching a long distance runner thru field glasses in the middle of his race, and see a picture of the Lineaments of Satisfied Desire with - - not a vengeance, but a victim. . . no doubt it can happen. Won't happen to you.   That is the one thing I will undertake positively to guarantee of you - -.

and yet I sympathize very closely with what I take to be Corman's position. Words cannot be wholly transparent.   And this is the 'heart-lessness' of words.[25]

In despair, so many turn to 'the machine of words' and arrive, if anywhere, at the Hermetic.   forgetting *that* had already failed before it had begun, whether thrice-greatly or Blavatskian.   'For neither can that be said to be found which is believed but remains unknown'

which is from Augustine, and should warn me to stop typing at random in the deep blue sea - -. More simply: the need to be able to shift focus, depth of focus, with precision, to control distance, real distance, I mean visual distance and audible distance and get at the crucial moments right on top of the thing, an inch from the thing; at that moment, no quotes, no references- - at that moment, something near transparence after all - -. [. . .][26]

But I mean to present at least this basis for work, as against the deliberate search for a mode *in advance*

which I feel positive is a mistake.

--to let one's hand be forced by what is MOST CENTRAL, and by nothing else.

to let go, to drop into the real bottom of his mind, into the con-sciousness which is always there.

It would follow - - at the end of a page of typing not really necessary in addressing you - - That one must not, at least, stake himself on becoming famous. No way to guarantee it, and in any case if he is serious it will be a long time to wait.   Now as always. I don't know why.

He must establish himself and his life, whatever himself means to him - - but he must not find himself living - - living entirely, I mean, living totally - - in a dream of impersonal fame, dreaming of himself as being anything but what he knows he is - - - I keep thinking of the word 'blas-phemous' lately, tho I'll not try to defend it.

I do recognize that there are people whose ability to write poetry depends on a kind of remoteness, a kind of not- existence, dislocation, distortion, arbitrariness - - But I simply don't happen to value that poetry much.   Is it belles-lettrism? - - I'm stating this attitude   to state a   taste, I state it only as a taste. And to a degree a romantic one. Which has its own penalties, the problems of Realism, and its own alienation, a very

drastic one. As against the 'machine of words' which resolves everything
- - - until one steps out the door.[27]

where it becomes like all machines a kind of poisonous frenzy, the
mind locked in its cage - -   Had I been class valetudinarian [sic]   (had
I had A's rather than F's) I would have said magnificently: . . to free the
mind into the present, into the things actually relevant to oneself, into
'creativeness' as they say, and thereby to free it   from the poisonous
frenzy of Brooklyn.

- - - and you see that I share some of Corman's position.   I think
only that what injured him was a failure of nerve, a failure of courage - -

(((it's clear that I argue too much)))

((((‘The identity’:   I happened on this in Péguy: ‘He who was once
a father is a father always’ - - I am not insisting on the fatherly relation to
the world, and trying NOT to refer to the fatherly quality in my arguing
too much - - - But you see the point   ?   the point of identity, the
mysteriously real

((((one is also always a son, god help us all or at least both.

George

To Charles Tomlinson
[August 16, 1966]   TLs   Charles Tomlinson

Dear Charles:

Venerable as one sees me now, he would little believe that I began
life as a simple infant in New Rochelle, N Y, in nineteen-O-eight.   The
story may well give hope and courage to younger men.[28]

Zuk was born, also in youthful circumstances, in New York City
(Manhattan) in 1904   Rezi also N Y   --1894, I think, but am not sure of
the precise year. Old times, old times, there were men in those days, but
we were not. We were infants.

Eliot's *Marina* in Objectivist [Anthology], O my daughter.   No Stevens, alas my son

I am horrified and covered with guilt to think of you typing other
men's poetry

-- if there remains time, I can write to N[ew] D[irections] (I have no
books here) to ask them to send you two copies of each paperback - -
clipped, it would surely make a good enough ms?

Let me know

I'm particularly pleased you like - - 'accept' - - the Mind's Own Place. Many people very huffy at the time. Not, they said, a matter of position - - I believe they thought it 'crude'

We've both written often by implication of courage, and I suspect we both know quite a lot about it. Not, of course, thru being fearless [cf. CP 127]. And therefore, as always, best regards,

George

To Serge Fauchereau
[October 14, 1966]   TLs   Serge Fauchereau

Dear Mr Fauchereau:

We could say -- surely I would say--:   The image for the sake of the poet, not for the sake of the reader. The image as a test of sincerity, as against (tho I may quote inaccurately here): 'The sun rose like a red-faced farmer leaning over a fence,' which last is a 'picture' intended for the delectation of the reader who may be imagined to admire the quaint-ness and ingenuity of the poet, but can scarcely have been a part of the poet's attempt to find himself in the world -- unless perhaps to find himself as a charming conversationalist.[29] That quotation, of course, does not rep-resent the best of Imagism: the weakness of Imagism has been this af-fectation and feminine self-love, the strength of Imagism its demand that one actually *look*. Its strength, in the poem, that the world stops, but lights up. That lucence, that emotional clarity, the objectivists wanted, and by that they are related to Imagism. But not the falsity of ingenuity, of the posed tableau, in which the poet also, by implication, poses. The image as a factor of a realistic art, a realist art in that the poem is concerned with a fact which it did not create.

As you well say, an American movement.   American -- when writ-ten by Americans -- as a consequence of the definition of poetry as 'in-eluctably the direction of historic and personal particulars' (Zukofsky).[30] These distinctions might well justify subsuming Bunting under Objectiv-ism -- a categorizing to which I am quite sure he would agree, tho I believe it is quite true that none of the poets who have regarded themselves to any degree as Objectivists have resembled each other in their surfaces, their manner, their lives or in their ultimate concerns as men.   I believe it to be rather sharply distinguished from most of the movements which have had their centers in Paris by this fact.

———

I think your translations admirable. There is a difficulty about the last part of O Western Wind [CP 53]. Difficult, as you know, for me to judge the French. In the English, the noun 'eyes' directly above 'across all my vision' gives immediacy to the poem -- gives reality to the poem. Would it be as effective in the French? The possessive would unquestionably weaken it for that usage. It would have to be your decision.

(No doubt you know the Middle English poem to which the title refers:

O Western wind, when will thou blow
The small rain down can rain.
Christ! if my love were in my arms
And I in my bed again

I take it that the first line is equivalent to: '. . when you will to blow' -- the older usage survives in 'Will you, won't you' 'willy-nilly' (which is Will I, nil I) And in fact in 'Will you?' tho the modern ear hears that probably as a simple future

I seem to be becoming scholastic, which is hardly my *forte*. You must forgive it; the typewriter ran away with me.

———

I too am unable to obtain the copies of Kulchur with the essays you wish. I'm sorry not to be able to send them.

and yes, I would very much like to see your translation

(Trailer people: the trailer would be *remorque* : but the poem refers to a trailer to live in, a house trailer in Americanese, which I think you would call a caravan [CP 35]? There remains a difficulty: there are in the U S a number of permanent or semi-permanent settlements of workers living in such trailers; the reference is to such colonies, not, obviously, to vacationers. Nor can one imply gypsies: the man is very much the old Yankee. Probably cannot be given precisely in the French.

'Shrinking in themselves' --- a sort of drawing back into themselves which is also a lessening --- If you imagine an apple shrinking. Or a man becoming old -- and attending to his own affairs with skills which were once public.

With many regards
George Oppen

To David Ignatow
[October 8, 1966] TLs David Ignatow

Dear David:

We enjoyed your visit. Therefore I'm writing the bread and butter note.

Did we give you bread and butter? Well, shelter.

-- as for your adventures, David, we are delighted. For the sake of life. We are fond of life. Is that what you were asking?

―――

Jim Weil, of Eliz[abeth], asked me to write a review of Enslin for Eliz. But Enslin has reviewed me, with praise, in Poetry AND in Eliz. It seems to me this is embarrassing -- even appallingly so. And yet it is ridiculous that he should be denied public praise for such reasons. Moreover I am sure that he is about to gain a general recognition, as I am sure you are also sure that he will, and it will rebound to one's credit to have been aware of him ---- Could and would you write the piece for Eliz? and if you do, just give Weil an account of this letter. Obviously your praise would be fully equivalent to mine, and would be approved by all concerned.

―――

Our seminar on Whitman: I should have said:

When we say that poetry must be at least as well written as prose, we don't mean that it should be 'the same.' And if I say, it should also be at least as important as prose, I don't mean it should be 'the same.' The flaw is occasionally in Whitman's spirit, as I think you would agree, despite what you said, and a flaw almost continuously in his intelligence.

(alright, alright: be calm. A rouser of a seminar, no doubt)

((a student where I once read asked me what my 'influences' were, and I started listing: Descartes, Bergson, Henry James, Hopper, the Flemish painters, Blake ---- that is, poets scattered among the others.   Accurate, I think;   probably for any of us

   (((and in honesty I should have added: The Child's Garden of Verses, the Oz Books, the Arthur stories   etc))))

          Regards

          George

[In 1966, Oppen also wrote to William Bronk, William Brown, Marvin Cox, Rachel Blau DuPlessis, Theodore Enslin, Elizabeth Kray, Walter Lowenfels, Gerard Malanga, Diane Meyer, Michael O'Brien, Panthea Perry, Donald Phelps, Gilbert Sorrentino, James Weil, a letter published in *Elizabeth* X (December 1966), and J. D. Whitney.]

1967

[Early in the year, having left for San Francisco in mid-February, the Oppens bought the Polk Street house. They gave a year's notice to the tenants. By the end of February they lived at 574 Chestnut Street in San Francisco, but incompatibility with the landlord, who thought, due to a visit from long-haired Charles Hanzlicek, that they were harboring hippies, compelled a shift to 2154 Mason Street. They kept the Henry Street apartment, and in both June and September returned to New York City for a few weeks; in between, they spent a foggy summer on Little Deer Island. At the end of 1967 (possibly in November) they moved in to 2811 Polk Street. During that year, Oppen read at SUNY-Buffalo (February 17), and on February 20, Oppen and Reznikoff read at The Poetry Center, at the YM-YWHA, New York City (Armand Schwerner introduced them). In the later fall, Oppen read at the California Institute of Technology, and on November 28, 1967, he met Hugh Kenner, a meeting to which he often alluded for its definition of the twenty-five-year silence. During this year, he began "Some San Francisco Poems," circulating drafts of "A Morality Play: Preface," which later changed almost totally.]

To Elizabeth Kray
[1966–1967?][1]   TLc   UCSD 16, 6, 13

Dear Betty
    You said -- I don't remember exactly, but roughly -- 'No one will speak clearly about Zuk.'
    I felt it as a just accusation, so here   (tho there is a danger that I have more time to write than you have to read.   But here, if you want it -- It isn't really hard to do)
    Louis edited the Obj. Anthology. I supported him while he did so because tho I knew very little at the time, I did know this: that he was

right. That he was almost miraculously faultless in his judgments. Pound, Williams, Marianne Moore were of course not unknown at the time, but consider who was NOT in the anthology. And Bunting, Rakosi, Reznikoff and me all absolutely unknown at the time. Even Lorine Niedecker, her tiny poems; but shining like good deeds as against the work that was in the standard anthologies --- As the young men now recognize.[2] One or two one- or two-line fragments from the work of friends: it is clear that they are adduced as indications of what poetry should be, or where it begins, the selection itself becomes instructive. Granting this, I think the anthology is faultless. In an unlikely time.

this fact, which is actually the record of his poetic program, of his life, deserves recognition -- I think it does.

AND; he retains his perspicuity, when he is being honest: I imagine that any young poet with whom he has corresponded owes him a debt of gratitude.

One comes now, with real difficulty, to his work. It is a matter of saying frankly what I think. I know you can judge the work for yourself, it is a matter of being frank about my own opinion:

There begin to appear reviews saying he is the greatest poet of his time. And even so skilled a talker as Creeley sounds lame in giving the specifics -- painfully lame. His admirers review him most reluctantly. His 'ear' -- there is no difficulty about that. An ear for 'music'? Surely sometimes. ALWAYS an amazing ear for tone, a totally unexpected tone, for 'juncture' as Creeley well said

AND stupidities. Stupidities in the work of such magnitude that one cannot mention them at all without seeming to reject the work altogether, which was not what one intended. And perhaps some factor of being over-awed. The Big Stupidity -- it works somewhat like the Big Lie. Quite as effective. And he knows that; I'll come to that later. He is not stupid. You said once 'An unconscious fraud' Well, as a matter of fact -- Not unconscious.

There is a story in his book It Was.[3] It is written in an attempt at an elegant 17th century style -- which happens to fail. The speaker, at the beginning of a day, is searching for a phrase. The story begins to describe the situation in which he lives; a little apartment in the Bronx. On some days he and his wife can hear the lions in the zoo. He has his neat little breakfasts, his neat little writing desk -- sometimes he sits under a tree in the park to write. His wife, on these occasions, brings him his lunch ---

-- suddenly he finds the phrase he has been looking for: 'It was good to me'

It is a man giving thanks for having achieved a priggish life, a genteel life. Consciously;   he knows what he is saying, and its poignancy Perhaps despair.   One could say cynicism. I don't want to speak brutally
I think it's clear enough.

Sometime about 1935 or the end of 34 more likely -- Louis, in friendship or partly in friendship and partly to demand to know whether my poetic practice was a conscious rebuke to him, attacked the bareness, the lack of defense of Discrete Series. In the end he was defining a tactics to me. I was startled, and finally said: Louis, you're tougher than I am.

this is partly a funny story about me -- the choice of the word tough.   I was staggered and shocked, and that word came out of my governessed childhood. I should have said 'calculating.' I thought of calculation, of ambition, as lower class, I suppose: I said 'tough.' Louis, a sensitive and physically fragile boy who had grown up in the slums -- the word tough meant something else to him. He turned white and was unable to speak. He said finally, you wouldn't use that word if you knew what it meant.

I really was young, younger than I had a right to be at twenty-odd. I thought he meant I had made an illiterate mistake in the meaning of the word, the root meaning perhaps. I couldn't imagine what it was, and was unable to answer. I realized a great many years later what he meant.

funny story. It also explains Louis. And his 'unconscious fraud'

This letter, written without having made notes etc, is wrongly organized. I should have begun with the first couple of paragraphs. I think he deserves recognition -- If Louis should ask me for five hundred dollars -- I don't know. Probably I would give it to him. I don't know

But the letter was not written to say this. I will surely not agree to anything again with Louis which is not stated clearly and openly. Enough of that.

On the contrary. The letter written because I felt an accusation and justified; one gets tied up in delicacies and impenetrable obscurities -- obscurities being, here, a polite word -- with Louis.   Whereas, I am terribly fond of frankness.

anyway: any significant obscurity, obfuscating, on my part herewith illuminated.

Regards
[carbon; unsigned]

Letters from 1967   **153**

To Ethel Schwabacher
[February 5, 1967]   TLs   Christopher Schwabacher

Ethel

  I noticed but responded slowly that you are disturbed if not angered by Rembrandt

  Heavy, insistent, terribly concerned with the real, the mystery not in the brown shadows but in the lit surfaces, the old woman cutting her nails in slant light!   Slant light!   the light also aslant on canvas of course which makes the canvas the world, as he wanted it to be. I recognize that the complexity of the internal is almost unlimited;   the fact, for me, should not hide that reality in which it exists.

  What one feels about a thing, and the thing. The second is the major fact thru which we will reach wherever we are going

  So that for me too Rembrandt is one of the truly important artists

  (just to say this)   with love and appreciation

               George

To Theresa Fulton
[February–March 1967]   TLs   Estate of Theresa Fulton

Theresa me darling:
'A herd of black Aachsen walk over the earth'

  what a dreadful thought.

  Yes, we miss you too. But entranced by San Francisco. A very strange city, so clean, and touristy, and sexy, a little neat financial center ----- Wooden houses, a strong wind, a truly startling light like no where else; if it were an historic city or a capital city, there would be a name for this light --- And some kind of consciousness of the sand beach at the western edge, the windward edge of the city;   a financial center which is very busy and is also a resort -- And full of very old memories for us.[4] But the information makes them dizzy or sea-sick, and they won't listen. I don't really blame them. The wires are not underground in this part of the city, they are still strung in the air on posts, a maze and mesh of electric wires; the city trembles with wooden, carpentered oldness, and yet they are all very stylish and sophisticated people and they don't want to think about this obvious antiqueness or, in fact, to see it. And then we come telling them: well now, sir, forty year ago I -------

  We keep that up, they'll all move to Piedmont.

The Barbary Coast corner of North Beach has become Topless Corner: Topless Girl Band, Topless girl wrestling, Topless shoeshine, Topless mother of eight, Topless Amateurs, Topless Mother and Daughter - - - - - - They know it's funny, tho.   Which helps.

We've fixed this place up: we're 'settled.'   I think. Difficult landlord, a Sicilian eighty-some years old, spent all his life in the Alaska fishing fleet -- a nice man --- But speaks almost no English;   speaks some Spanish, by luck: His wife speaks no English at all and is probably an authentic witch: He's taken to yelling at his wife in defense of us, and she is undoubtedly mixing evil brews somewhere to put various curses on us, I expect my hair or my ears will fall off any day now, unless the old hoxey has gone out of Sicilian spells --.   But the fact is the man really loves us: he comes to the door every day so far and yells Giorgio GIORGIO   Giorgio, you puta nails inna   Giorgio, I old man, Giorgio, I say you Giorgio ---

Be all right.   Of course, I won't get anything written, but he and I will have a nice time discussing these things in no language. We're beginning to feel the play would have ended if we didn't have these conversations.

Thanks for the mail   Hope it hasn't been too much trouble.   Been wonderful for us. First time we've gone away without trouble that way;   the Post Office always has got in a mess on forwardings. This time we just didn't tell em nothing. We've sent them a forwarding address now that we're settled here, and the mail forwarding for you should gradually, at least, taper off. We're very grateful, been wonderful to be getting mail.

send you some stamps to reimburse

Sorry you're not next door. See you in June however.

George

To Diane Wakoski
[after end February 1967][5]   TLs   University of Arizona; carbon UCSD 16, 11, 22

Dear Diane

'. . . I represented some valuable object which he set out to destroy so that he wouldn't want it any more   .'   It was, you know, very clear to an observer. And the mallet work that of a very small boy; it was strange to watch a small boy uninterrupted in such an endeavor -- Surely you know.

your voice, as in your poetry, seems to take place somewhere above or outside: a brilliant and beautiful poetry, it is not hospitable to proffered wisdom (if there is such a thing) and I find myself without a suitable role. I can only offer, with elderly awkwardness, our friendship

'The Romantic commitment' -- shouldn't there be, if there need be or is occasion for anything of the sort, not commitment but the simple word 'we,' the conviction 'we'?   Courageous, in its way, but not precisely romantic ? I think of you as so sharply outlined that -- again like the poems -- interior-ness takes on a kind of unreality, an eerie unreality, it becomes as eerie as 'real' things and a circle is completed

But you seem to me so sharply outlined that I believe you can think only of being alone or of dismantling yourself, being dismantled --

no wisdom meant, no wisdom intended, I am describing a sense of what you are in the world   How will it work out?   How do any of us work out

I imagine my turn to speak in a therapy group. I imagine saying

I am walking -- like a lemming -- Northward. Happens to be the direction in which I am walking, some quirk of personality, some tendency formed in childhood, some code in the genes, the D amned N o-torious P rogramming - - I happen to be walking northward. Very possibly the wrong direction, it may well be warmer in the south, there are better hotels East and West -- I seem however to be walking north. I just want to know what will happen, what it will mean, or perhaps only what I will feel, what I will think   What I'll find.   That's what I want to do and that is what I'm doing.   I don't want to be cured   I don't know that I want more money   I don't want another or better wife or another and better daughter   Not even another and better self   I don't want to be cleverer than I am or more powerful than I am or even more admirable than I am, tho I acknowledge I stink, I just want to know what will happen[6]

and I cannot cure myself of the conviction that you could say the same thing if you wanted -- well, just to say it   (with, perhaps, compass adjustment)

I suspect we'll meet at one of the poles.   Or even in Brooklyn. It'll be, as always, a pleasure

love

George

To Frederic Will
[between April 26 and May 13, 1967]   TLd   UCSD 16, 11, 44

Dear Frederic Will

Reading the Speculative Essays for several days.[7]   It is a luminous book, and profoundly moving in that it insists on the depth of our concern, I mean the depth of the things that concern us.   Us meaning us, just us, not 'the artist.' From that concern surely we must begin, unless we shall speak of the redemption of the will -- and how shall one speak of that? There is nothing that can will what the will shall will;   if there were, to sound like Fragmentary Greek for a moment, we would call it the will

therefore the human given.   I had not understood, had not 'seen' that moment in Oedipus: indeed I see it now. A debt to you. As if the tremendous stone monster had asked, Do you know who you are?

Of the Heidegger: thinking of the poets I know, I believe this may be the most immediately useful of the essays to get into poets' hands at this moment, the most likely to move things most sharply forward now.   Having no German at all, much less Heideggerian German, I am dependent on translations, therefore my knowledge of H. is sharply limited. But I have a superstition concerning my relation to H. The poem which happens to be printed as the first poem in Discrete Series -- my first book -- was written in 1929. That, I've learned, was the year in which H. was giving his Inauguration Speech in which he spoke of the mood of boredom (in the translation I have) which leads, again in the translation I have, to 'the knowledge of what-is.'   The poem -- I don't know if you have the book -- begins with 'the knowledge of boredom' and ends with 'the world, weather-swept, with which one shares the century.'   And boredom was an odd word to use. I am touched by superstition remembering my hesitation over that word and the sense of having been given it.   Followed by a much later event, involving a dream and all the trappings, in which I had dreamed quite literally of being given a phrase over a telephone and, the following morning wrote into a poem a quotation from a short essay of Heidegger's which I had been reading the night before.   When I checked the quotation -- Not there!   A strange morning: I remember reading that essay over and over, ten or more times in dizzy incredulity, because I had been absolutely sure that I had quoted the sentence word for word.

The sentence: Substance itself which has been the subject of all our planning/And by this we are carried into the incalculable [CP 195]

which, tho the sentence is not in Heidegger, is close to your emphasis: 'the earth steps forth in all its massiveness . .'[8]

You will inevitably see, in my shy or sly stories of myself above,
that I invite or even urge admiration. And yet I do not seriously believe
that what I have so far managed is of actual value unless I shall be able to
go further --- further or forward meaning toward wherever we are going . .
I am between books -- that is, I have completed a book and must attempt
a next step. And, tho I had thought it was clear to me, am confronted
by   What is it?   something like a failure of nerve, of simple nerve.   I
have persistently told creative writing classes that I have no reason to
suppose that poetry is good for people, and I say that -- as I imagine myself
-- with admirable brusque courage.   But actually . . . .   I don't know
that my courage is so intact, and certainly not so brusque.   Full of tentatives and hesitations, I have trouble writing you now as I would like to
. . I would very much like to talk, to listen and to talk.   I will try to manage
a trip to Iowa . . or hope that you will say you can manage a trip to N Y
sometime.[9] In any case, I promise myself that we will meet

                                                  and with all regards
                                                  [draft; no signature]

To Sherman Stein
[late spring 1967]   TLc   UCSD 16, 10, 46

The man-made universe arrived this morning: Year One.   Caught
me up and dissipated my attempt to pack for Maine. It is now well past
midnight, or in fact well into the morning of Day Two, Year One[10]

Don't know that I would say quite what William Brown said (is it
Bill Brown of the Uncles Sam Hotel? whom I know)   What's held me is
not so much that proof is beautiful, but the strangeness of two levels of
reality -- which perhaps attack each other?   They seem to attack each
other.   But I am grateful for your fine use of the word 'concrete' as against
the messes of late, what with 'abstract art,' and 'in mathematics all the
cards can be put on the table['] ... bright and concrete those glossy cards
as against the shadowy ambiguity of the table, tho of course that table was
once so well-worn by forthright philosophic or anti-philosophic use

Is it really a man-made world you have there?   once begun, it functions thru the autonomy of the mind?   Well, it does if the mind is a rather
alien presence, a presence within.   'A patient reports' that I have never

been more aware of a force, doctor, a tremendous and essentially alien force which indeed forces the mind - - - And I continue to have no idea where it comes from, where it originates.   A table or a white bear shows up: he seems to exist of himself and that is surprising enough. But one is *possessed*   by mathematics. The Greeks have a name for him or it?   the demonic universe of mathematics?

I'm not sure I'm joking about 'demonic.'   I think of you in demon or trick-or-treat mood.   As dangerous as poetry?   Perhaps more dangerous?   I don't know. The danger of terror in poetry, the danger of nothing-at-all in math   Of Ouroboros with his tail in his mouth, disappearing. Frightens me because I'm a poet?   or only because I'm not a mathematician

The numbers act of themselves. Attach them to the ends of threads or the tail of a cat, and they take off again in the same gambol

Mathematics creating itself   Is the serpent *coming out* of his own mouth? Perhaps that's what I should have said.   He doesn't disappear, he grows and displaces the empirical, or what one thought was the empirical: I don't know that I can live with him. But I agree the book is beautiful and I thank you for it in a more than (or will you feel it is less than) scholarly spirit

The language without an apparent effort, almost intimate, certainly witty -- so clear and so orderly as to do the reader's work for him. And it is what it says it is: the spirit (tho I said demon) of mathematics, the way of working, the motive communicated irresistibly ---- mathematics creating itself, alright. The strange unbounded voice of a Wittgenstein

———

Somebody -- I forget who, whereas you probably know -- pointed out that Descartes' cogito should not have begun with the word 'I,' since the word postulates what he had undertaken to prove.   And suggested, rather, something like: Is thinking,   therefore I am . .

I seem to be able to imagine a brain in a glass jar saying something like that. I was trying to ask myself what the 'I' would be. Not a consciousness OF the world; perhaps it would think of itself as the world's consciousness?

it's the attitude some of the Eastern mystics seek, and find in suppression of the senses, so they seem to agree.

That mind could formulate the number series: I agree; a man made universe. A universe of numbers: like other universes, infinite.   Sure,

I agree. I fought him down the days and down the nights, from Discrete Series on . . But I agree: I think I would say only that I am talking of history. Historically I think we began with substance, with things --- Would you agree? or would you feel the consideration is relevant? Not, of course, necessarily to math, but to my concern.

I wrote in a poem in the new book now with the printer:

Substance itself which has been the subject of all our planning
And by this we are carried into the incalculable
[CP 195]

It isn't that I mind the incalculable. Maybe there is (and surely there should be) a lift in that last line. Because the book is a pleasure   I gather we want to get there, wherever there may be

with thanks
[copy; no signature]

To Frederic Will
[after July 22, 1967]   TLs with AL inserts   Humanities Research Center, University of Texas-Austin

Dear Fred
'Consolation?'   (your word)   I don't know. Except that tho it's true life is tragically short it is not true that there is not a great deal of TIME in a life ---. And also, if it's consolation, me too. I've written some poems in the last months, but they are poems that would belong, if anywhere, to the last book. I think that I know how to begin, where to begin -- think I have begun -- and find I've repeated myself, repeated cadences even, without need, without conviction. Possible exception being the poem that grew from your use of the word 'piety.'[11] I seem to know what I mean to do, and seem to be myself; I would like to get the thing said, I would like rather to get it thought, to grasp it -- I look at things and they become large, like barns, I feel lost and yet they are not big enough --- merely a little clumsy, reminiscent and clumsy. If there were barns anywhere in my background it seems to me I would be writing at this moment about barns --   It occurs to me that many people have

which is absurd -- for me -- and means I am lost, I never knew any barns. I smell strangers and strange smells, strange men, Dreiser and Sher-

wood Anderson -- earlier Americans. I could describe the smell of a sun-
bonnet -- I surely have no reason to

among other things, I have talked too much, or to too many people
younger than I.   I am adrift . . . .

offered as consolation   (tho I don't suppose it will serve)   but not
as lament.   I had known for a very long time that I meant to get to Of
Being Numerous.   I was not sure I could do it at all, I still carry some
elation that I wrote it, that there was -- again -- time. Tho it ends with
retraction, question, fails, if that's failure, of a conclusion   I am not so
confident as I have sounded that I will write another book

Pleasant meanwhile that you speak of valuing my work. Vanity, in
age, becomes shocking. Your praise and my vanity have caused me to
pontificate too much here perhaps. And, if I remember rightly, in a previous
letter also. The fact is --- we, my wife, Mary, for that is her name as they
used to say in the children's stories -- are in Maine again for the summer.
A summer, it happens, of fog. No one here ever saw the like -- They say
so freely   (Randall Pert, a lobsterman, said with precisely enough emphasis on a clear day: 'it's good to see you')   We have groped our way all
over Penobscot Bay in an 18 foot open sail boat, sleeping under a sort of
tent made by stretching a waterproof over the boom, and cooking on an
alcohol stove.   Days at a time, and one day after another when visibility
had been little more than ten yards -- A strange world.   We have anchored
at night and left in the morning without being absolutely sure where we
had stayed. We set a compass course for a buoy or other such mark: if
we find it, we can usually work our way behind an island and anchor. If
we hear an island -- the surf on the island -- and can't see it, we anchor
for better or worse where we are --- One positive identification;   maybe
only one.   Paddled ashore on an island, tho we could see only a foggy
rock or two rising out of the water -- Paddled ashore in an inflatable canoe
we carry along -- climbed on the first rock and found a Geodetic Survey
bench-mark giving latitude and longitude and the name: Job Island.
Which was what we thought it was. Gave us confidence. Tho some of the
towns whose harbors we slept in were probably the towns we thought they
were

as for why the island was named Job in the first place -- But such
things happen to me.   Not worth worrying about

And, of course, some sunny days.   But I wanted to tell the story.
Luxurious camping, as a matter of fact. Tho unyachtsmanly.

We have no reason for it, certainly no claim, but Maine has always seemed some sort of home to us -- No reason for it.   Except that Jefferson was too southern[,] Washington sat a horse too well, Concord hopelessly genteel --- So here we are.   Well, for the Summer.

And of course if I can say, to find a way to say or see, why of course I will. And meanwhile here we are -- But I mean precisely the opposite of salvation thru flight. Or it means the opposite to me.   Tho I am for the moment in this letter disregarding economic questions, all economic questions -- obviously -- including questions of 'status' which are ultimately inescapable insofar as status is freedom, freedom from persecution, harassment, freedom from cops. And, to be frank, freedom from loneliness - - - And is existence, social existence   (Genet's *Balcony*)   adequate status being obtainable also by attaching oneself to a public event: as, the Beats, the Hippies, or even being young, which is rather public these days

--well, disregarding these things for the moment.   Tho there may be little left of this letter when one does return to them. But I have withdrawn any proffer of consolation or advice some paragraphs back in favor of giving an account merely of myself. No use to anyone, but perhaps more friendly

It may be true we think we're Adam and Eve.   Simply, we think we're on our own.   I don't mean only in the toy boat. What else is there to think? What to make of it?   I doubt I'll really tell anyone very much: the thing may be largely vanity after all. Still, the statement, what statement one can make, has value to me -- O, has tremendous value, overwhelming value, as you know. .

There are things for each of us around which meaning gathers . . The mission is to hold them, to be able to keep them in his mind, to try again and again to find the word, the syntax, the cadence of unfolding -- I don't mean to promise redemption of course. A matter of being able to say what one is and where one is. And what matters.

'Not the symbol but the scene' -- quoting myself again [CP 192]:   I don't think I've very often versified something I already knew.   Where I have it has shown, as it does for others, as sententiousness. And what could be the use of it anyway?   what could be the use of it to me?

still less to rebuke the times with its own clichés.

I write at length.   Perhaps in lieu of poetry?   But also because we took a rather rough time in San Francisco. Partly because we were ill;

Mary with pneumonia. I probably answered your letter inadequately. And mean here to make amends

Regards

George

(Your sense of 'the coming' -- Which is why I spoke of the will. This hippie generation again: what will happen, what is happening, is precisely what they resist.

Ridiculous to be persistently irrelevant, ridiculously to dis-regard a force which determines everything   Yet merely to connive with the times? or can we find a use, in some way of our own, for the word piety?   more modestly said: some use for the role of spectator

To June Oppen Degnan
[after August 5, 1967]   TLs   UCSD 16, 1, 6

June dear

I'd written the enclosed as a sort of note to myself, or the beginning of a note to myself   Send it in a way as answer to your letter[12]

the times will be hard in their own way.   Poetry better be pretty damn good or not at all: there is something disgusting about the inadequate --

Told you, I think: I will take my time.   Maybe a long time.

Somewhat appropriate story:

Sailed to Belfast. We'd remembered it from the Galleybird --c 1932 [1934–35?]. It's in the back of Penobscot Bay, opposite shore from ours. We'd remembered liking it in the 30's; the New England mixture of red brick small industry and waterfront and docks --.   Had an impression it was a famous town;   never heard it spoken of lately. Anyway, we sailed in. A long deep cove, more than 2 miles deep, and two or three miles wide at the entrance, gradually narrowing. As it narrowed we saw beautiful houses on the hills and were talking to each other about the narrowness of yachtsmen; not a yacht, anchored or moving, in sight. Sailed for the very back of the harbor, by a highway bridge, which, by the chart, is the town itself and the town landing. Mary steering: I was on the bow getting the anchor ready.   Saw, suddenly, ahead of us, not water but pure filth: Chicken feathers, industrial waste, oil mud sewage - - The wind and the tide behind us: Mary swung and pulled back out as far as we could -- a few yards, and we anchored and paddled ashore - - - - -[13]

Very strange, very terrible. Hard to describe. Later, we spoke to people here about Belfast, and heard of two local young men being killed there: beat up by gangs for no known reason. We eat in a café there, and felt something like that. Paddled back to the boat -- After sunset by then -- and the wind had failed totally. Got a fisherman in an outboard to tow us back toward the head of the harbor a few hundred yards - - Nice enough out there -- and we anchored. Heavy fog and light wind in the morning but we left anyway. Got clear of the harbor by our figuring at least --- we couldn't see much --; the wind turned lighter still and we knew there were strong tides around. Knew that is, that we had no idea where we were - - and simply anchored out there in the middle of wherever. Could still hear the industrial banging from Belfast and Searsport. And ships coming out and going in. We managed to keep them off with nothing but the little fish-horn --- the ships (kindly enough) signaling and signaling as they approached, ten or twenty yards of us and barely visible. . .   Several hours. Fog cleared about one in the afternoon, wind came up, located ourselves and sailed for [Castine] -- just the other side of the bay, which is only some four miles wide at that point -- and [Castine] is The town of yachts, summer visitors

Castine -- I meant Castine thruout above: Castine   (Camden too far for that matter)[14] but Castine one of THE towns of summer visitors and fanatic yachtsmen and summer camps for children, complete with boats, and very very beautiful.   On the dock, talked to a youngish man with handsome beard, beautiful row-boat, and airdale --- we eyed each other while conversing

He finally thought of the way to do things. Introduced the airdale: 'this is Pip -- Great Expectations.   O, I said, yes. My name's George Oppen.   O   says he   I'm Philip Booth. Glad you didn't write about North Penobscot because I've always meant to - -[15]

Two worlds, two worlds.   Yes but what the hell?

Booth's a descendent of Maine. Inherited house, picture of great great great (the three is precise) grandfather in the parlor. Extremely beautiful house. Wife, three daughters. Nice little boat   Teaches.   Gave us his last book, which I'd not read: About Maine.   Very nice touch; very good verse.   But again, again one wonders: a heritage to play with, almost an inherited Disneyland. The salty language -- not only Philip, but everyone: Not, she gets along alright in rough water, but: She's an able little craft. She's weatherly;   not, she goes fast against the wind. . . .

this of course a little naive; the poetry not naive   But still.

O well: two worlds.   One we don't live in;   one we can't live in.[16]

it was a very nice visit tho in Castine. Spent the night.   Much admired for an odd reason: the boat was so small. Or I guess Mary was admired. Obvious anyone could sail the boat: But who the hell could *sleep* on it!

love to you

George

[the enclosed note] The Categorical Imperative: 'People must be treated as an end, never as a means.' Kant's idealism. For me merely anthropological, a taboo understandable as one possible rule for the preservation of a society

But it is true one must be able to say what is absolutely wrong if one is to speak 'morally' as we use the word. Which means, approximately, to speak of purpose. How judge, how prefer one thing to another except as one might prefer chocolate to vanilla, pie to cake . .

(the 'practical' point being that a life-time of choices between chocolate and vanilla is, I should think, pretty damn depressing --- chaqu'un a son goo -- too depressing to bear,   people won't do it long)[17]

Since we live with the war, what can we mean if we moralize about Hippies, drug addicts, good and bad literature --- How can we know what we are talking about, or rather what we are talking *for*?

One sees that the Old Left was at no time totally without point, tho it deservedly or even fortunately collapsed. The continuation of the war is the collapse of the New Left. The proof that it is -- not paradoxically inhuman like the Old Left -- but, as we knew, ineffective, absolutely useless, therefore cynical, a game, a fashion, a form of self-display or of keeping oneself occupied or of asserting everyone else's failure and one's own innocence --

The left is at all times -- even when it is ineffective -- an attempt to take seriously the declared purposes of a society.   It is always a matter of radical methods, radical means, rather than radical thinking, radical philosophy: its collapse is therefore no joke for anyone

one can of course declare his own purposes, his own, that is to say, morality.   or can one?

of course one cannot. Or only within the situation of the 'vertical consciousness' of oneself and god. Which of course would permit everyone else to be wrong and lost;   there is still what 'is right.'   A simple matter requiring only an epiphany

in the absence of which one may prefer chocolate to vanilla, or, obviously: Money, praise, temperate climate, three hundred horsepower, twenty five rooms, hundred foot boats, electric everything -- a matter of taste, of each one's goo.   But why poetry?   or anything of the sort, unless as a choice between flavors?

The poetry, the four books, Discrete Series, Materials, This in Which, Numerous -- proposed the awareness of the world as purpose. Nothing else essentially.   Not, perhaps enough - -?   But the search for power is the attempt to hide the world from oneself;   it is fatal;   Johnson, the [Lyndon] Johnsons, fatal. They may in all literalness prove so

To Alexander Mourelatos
[after August 9, 1967]   TL   UCSD 16, 1, 21

Dear Alex
Your spontaneous translation -- 'Shines by night, wandering around the earth, with a light not its own'   seems to me to give the loneliness and the alien qualities in the scene, and surely the sense of the lost, which is perhaps too romantic a sense of error, but surely a sense of error -- and so the main things are done.[18] Its effectiveness of course would depend on the cadences preceding it: it could sound prosy and stretched. And I gather that because this line is famous, there will be a tendency for people to look at once for one's translation of this line - - - and it is true, that line as you spontaneously give it would have to be carefully set -- in fact it rather needs the sentence precisely as in your letter -- 'that the moon is something which shines by night, wandering around the earth, with a light not its own'

alright: try other versions. I'll give here the things I feel can and must be kept from the Greek line, and those which must be achieved by other means than the Greek:

Surely one must keep the meaning of error in the word wandering -- since we are dealing with Parmenides

We must keep some approximation of the length of the original and the major caesura and the tripartite structure.

We must keep the lift in the last part of the line, and the word *light* must be the last word of the line. Otherwise we have lost the meaning of the line.

We must certainly have -- and perhaps can hardly miss -- the foreignness of the wandering moon. And this must be the purpose of the pun: the foreignness of the light -- foreign to the moon -- is directly stated. We have it pretty well in the wandering of the moon, and again in the contrast, the alienness of the bright moon and the darkness -- the oxymoron --. And we must keep this.

We don't need the pun on *light* -- we might find it, but we cannot afford to fool with the word *light* --- It must be clear and pure.[19]

To stray, to be astray, is to be foreign -- Which is where Homer got it in the first place -- A wandering fellow: a foreigner. We need to keep that[20]

the tam-ti's ---- they will not be the same thing in English. Bright in the dark is tam ti ti tam: and sounds it. Does us no good. The fact is that it is distracting, and destructive
[the letter apparently ends here, or a page is missing]

To Alexander Mourelatos
[August 17, 1967]   TLs with AL insert   UCSD 16, 1, 21

Dear Alex:
You'll have by now the line I wrote the following morning. It's the line I like. It carries the sense of awe, even of eeriness, which I felt in the literal version, and it carries the meaning of the pun, tho as metaphor, not pun. One could say it uses the pun.

Of the other [APDM's] version:

I dislike the word 'roving' almost anywhere. A debased word. And it carries the suggestion of purpose; of adventure or search at least.   'Roving ambassador': imagine 'wandering ambassador.' Whereas wandering repeats the implication of error. And avoids the half-romantic journalese of 'roving,' replacing it with the double motion, double indeterminateness of the space over the earth --

'a light not its own' -- I'd keep the 'its' if there is no reason to alter it except that the word is used twice. No reason not to use it as often as one has use for it, it is not a word of which one is asking too much, like the presently common 'fabulous.' *Its* is a pretty firm word and should be able to stand up to any amount of use. And 'a' seems to break the connection where one needs it unbroken. We were speaking of the moon, then we speak of *its* light. All clear and continuous.   'a light' is actually rather obscure -- 'Astray over earth, bright in darkness, a light not its own, a wandering foreigner' -- the 'light not its own, a wandering foreigner'   recast [?] as an equation has value, as you say -- I agree. But the 'a' remains obscure, somewhat more than obscure, it fails to say what you want to say, really . . . I'd keep the 'its' even if the 'also' is dropped. In which case one has, still, the equation

The 'also' is a sly professorial joke. I am, you will see, secretly a sly professor. A reference to the pun   Tho it is rather neatly a statement of the meaning of the line: a statement that the pun is there. And I like the joke. But I always like jokes -- My liking this one proves nothing.

Glad you were able to talk to Elia [mother of APDM]. This is the 17th -- Linda should be along soon.   Sorry you won't be here ---- but of course I understand about the work.

our love

George

(I do think the Greek says *also* by using a pun: the word *phos* says 'foreign-light-and-also-foreigner.' Plus the joke a phosphorous joke.

To William Bronk
[September 13, 1967]   TLs with AL addition   UCSD 16, 3, 11

Dear Bill

Of your essay -- I will call it an essay, tho the experience is the experience of reading a poem --.

I thought, really, that it is at the top of page six, or perhaps in the course of page five that it gathers its full strength -- Or wherever one may place it. I am writing after a first reading -- a single reading and a couple of glancing-backs over it. I don't mean to cavil or deny you the space you need. Just reporting: I was caught on page five, and knew that my heart was pounding and that I was reading as fast as I could by the top of page six.

. . to the phrase almost at the end, almost the last words of the essay: 'and it is by our most drastic failures . .' Which I take to be your statement, your declaration. The sentence is very very beautiful indeed.[21]

We (and you rightly mock this use of 'we') but *we* meaning those-who-have-been-alive-at-any-moment, have existed in the area of nihilism for a very long time. I think we can be interested only to know what may possibly lie beyond nihilism. For us? For anyone.   For anyone who may be alive.

Something beyond nihilism is visible (is almost heroically visible) in the beauty of such a poem as the Lock on the Feeder, in the beauty of the final sections of your essay.[22]

I don't mean to ask you for comfort or to impose on you any duty of optimism or of faith -- Surely you know that.   I just mean: we who have read Gödel and Heisenberg, we who have read Nietzsche, we who have read Sartre, we who have read Beckett and Thomas Hardy and Kafka (and George Oppen)   ((and William Bronk's the world, the worldless)) -- I ask you to talk -- as you talk here --- to US.

Or do we mean to crack our heads in an attempt to tell these things to a general populace who will know them very well in a few years without our help -- who, in fact, know very well now. They are merely afraid, panicky, and don't wish to hear these things said aloud. They are far more desperate than we, whatever they may say --

If we shout at them, lecture them, is it not because we wish to converse?   if we wish to converse is it not because of some hope?   Is it true?   or are we bothering a loose tooth, picking at incurable sores

Mary and I use the name Sunnyside -- quite arbitrarily or whimsically really -- to mean OUR 'back home,' our Hudson's Falls. When I talk to these people we choose to call Sunnysiders I find myself angry, caught in anger, caught in more and more angrily attacking the absolutely meaningless or transparently false phrases they clutch to themselves, wrap themselves in . . There is some justification: one has to try to clear a little ground if one is to be able to converse with them at all. But I become more and more angry and in the end possibly merely cruel

But a book of poems is addressed to other people

Surely you have a problem of anger, Bill, as surely you know. The problem of anger is the problem of the sense of audience

These are matters we have disputed before. I've hoped to say it more clearly than I have before. And in fact I dispute with no intention of instructing you in any simple sense but   well, I will say it brashly: I dispute in the hope of demonstrating to you that there really are some intelligent people in the world and that we know, we know . . .

I'm not denigrating what you have done, in the essay, in the World, the Worldless, in the Lock on the Feeder --. I mean: What now? What further? What have we now to say to each other? to ourselves?

but after two pages of foolish typing I remember that the place to begin is

'If they seem for a time to succeed, they blind us as though they were real; and it is by our most drastic failures that we may perhaps catch glimpses of something real, something that is.'

No one will write a more beautiful sentence for quite a while

(as for dispute: there is a sentence of Hegel's:

'Disagreement indicates where the subject matter ceases, it is what the subject matter is not')

((and try not to think too much about the book --- succeeds, doesn't succeed, etc etc   The thing is to go on, to carry your own thought further, your own work further   There'll be enough readers following you eventually. You have to make your way, it happens, entirely outside the enthusiasms, the ready-made enthusiasms of any school, and it takes time. Quite a lot of time maybe

((I am known to almost a few people: I'll be 60 next year))

George

To Harvey Shapiro
[late 1967]   TLs   Harvey Shapiro

Dear Harvey

The poems are beautiful   Beyond Battlecry [*Battle Report*]. -- I mean to assert it because I am never sure of poems until a book's complete: maybe you have the same difficulty. So I assert.

the souls in the streets   ! And of course how else would we build anything

It's a very very beautiful poem[23]

The Kabbala   the cabal.   It seems to me still that when you touch Rabbi Nachman,   (in this case)   the poems plunge to such depths! from which you can say simply   My friend,   and one won't forget it.

-- We walk,   we walked up Tamalpais -- the final peak, which is almost a steeple. Wonderful   So high the ocean looked curved I thought   And pieces of fog went below us.

We also meet young poets   Disheartening so far   I wonder who I'm writing *at*   A crop of young 'poets' touched by the drop-out thing, the revolt against seriousness or against education at least   And of course I sympathize, it is a cruelty to demand that a whole generation go thru college to qualify for routine jobs, and I understand they must find some solution, must revolt,   and I understand that they do prefer rock and roll bands and the comic books ---- But they also want very much to patronize me as a fairly nice fellow for an old codger who's lost his taste for comic books and is more to be pitied than blamed

on the other hand such non young poets as Eliz[abeth] Bishop, a good deal more infuriating. But fury isn't debilitating: I have a feeling that being furious at E Bishop may be good for us   Or makes us young again

--so we have 'a literary set'?   well, maybe.   But only one literary friend

However: the walks! and just places. cafés Stores I think we haven't felt such excitement since we were first in Paris together on the great venture

we feel again also far from somewhere or other   I don't know, and I don't think we knew then, exactly where . . Some of it very familiar -- (our adolescence) ------ and ineffably distant

It's true: you're read but in some way neglected. I see it too   Don't know why

You know, I really am too, somewhat   compared, that is   to a great many, a countless number of other people who I think are not really admired more than I - - - And Rezi also. I think perhaps our work tends to put no edge on anyone else's axe

And if I get less neglected, one should consider that I do provide a little edge for some defensive axes A poet unrecognized for 40 years proves, you see, that others too . . . . . .   That's about it. ((I note some people extremely demonstrative about me, the carrying of my suit case and such, and meant to think about it sometime. Now I have. They see themselves old and bowed and recognized at last in Podunk

As for the constant readers   i. e.   the constantly reading aloud and in public   some at least -- a great many -- are rather energetic finaglers

We encounter also the despair of the young disguised as political indignation   We try not to think too much of the loss of individuals -- frequently too clear, terribly clear: individuals who are losing themselves --- try not to think too much about it and are cheered by the quality of so many young people into an historical optimism - - -

The fact is we enjoy San Francisco   A little disturbed, but that may even be a part of what I mean by enjoying it - - - The house works O K -- it's kind of a wild little place, the city is, tho it's also very polish[ed] -----

George

I get some work done.   Slowly, but I think I believe in it

[In 1967, Oppen also corresponded with Charles Amirkhanian, Philip Booth, Ron Caplan, John Crawford, Robert Creeley, Robert Duncan, Rachel Blau DuPlessis, Theodore Enslin, Clayton Eshleman, David Ignatow, James Laughlin, Jane Lippe, Diane Meyer, Linda Oppen Mourelatos, Panthea Perry, Armand Schwerner, John Taggart, Charles Tomlinson, and J. D. Whitney.]

1968

[In 1968, Oppen read at San Francisco State University (February 21), the University of Wisconsin (April), Stony Brook (September); on March 31 *Of Being Numerous* was published.¹ On April 25, Oppen was interviewed by L. S. Dembo of the University of Wisconsin. Spending some time in New York, at Henry Street before and then after Maine, the Oppens went to Maine from the very end of May to September 1. The summer was stormy. He spoke several times of the difficulty of "getting beyond" *Numerous*; by the end of the summer he had "made some progress" on new work.²]

To Diane Meyer
[1968?]³   TL   UCSD 16, 7, 29

Andy: of your letter 'I know I stopped painting again because I thought I was seeking to make things pretty, a sort of shabby aesthetic relief . .'

we both have some trouble about this.   Storm and Stress Romanticism?   or an earlier romanticism: someone or something should know without being told   -- well, not that: surely without being lured: that would be fair enough ---.   OR an underestimation of oneself, as the first man on Mars, or those at any rate in the first party failed to broadcast a word because they didn't want to bother people with their troubles and discomforts ---?   But one needn't be the first man on Mars -- and how could you be, come to think of it? -- but only like Montaigne the first man who is oneself

-- sorry about that generic 'man.' Particularly in this case. In poetry at least there is just no model and no tradition for a woman's poetry, unless the fragments of Sappho, which I can't judge, and Emily Dickinson. And not much more in painting.   God knows from what source or in what way women's art will come----

(and there's not a line of poetry written by a woman which is not a woman's -- either by being different from a man's or by being less good you know about Dickens and George Eliot's first book?   The book was signed George of course (some nerve!) and the secrecy of authorship most rigorously preserved. Dickens liked the book and sent a letter calmly beginning: 'Dear Madame')[4]

Anyway, about beauty   we both have some trouble. I begin almost every poem deliberately to write a bad poem -- and am forced to rewrite   It simply carries no meaning till I do.   The word beauty means the quality which makes the thing graspable?   which is to repeat again the old saws about 'order'?   In which case, beauty is the intelligible.   In which case, we want above all to *know*.

> And the discovery of fact bursts
> In a paroxysm of emotion
> Now as always
> [CP 150]

quoting, as is my wont, myself.

But, as for fear of shaking things deeper, letting them fall deeper right now -- then don't.   I respect nothing so much as fear. And I suppose the direction we mean by the metaphor of 'depth' is just that.

To John Crawford
[1968?][5] TLs   John Crawford; photocopy UCSD 16, 3, 48

John:

If, having been born with one inherited eye, which has since atrophied, one has made friends only with the totally blind, one must occasionally take on kingly functions, or the role of leadership   O.K.:

I'm not capable of making change correctly, but it is true I can discuss money in a vague way

IF YOU KNOW a moneyed woman, ask her. Questions concerning money challenge the virility of males, and they invariably lie

but I assume you would have sense enough to ask a moneyed woman if one were available, and you must be desperate indeed if you ask me

(((that cuteness should be retracted: the fact is that no one   it happens   no one else will tell you anything useful for your situation   Do NOT discuss the matter with business-men, and still less with academics and professionals who think they're dabbling successfully in finance on the side.)))

Alright:

1   It is true that Jay Laughlin was able to establish N[ew] D[irections] because he had some money (a great deal, in fact)   It is not true that N D is famous and respected because Jay Laughlin happened to have some money.   Clear?

2   if you're talking of several millions, it may be possible to 'buy' something in the sense you mean.   Certainly you would have to know how to do it - -

   ((([Friend's Name], whom we speak of sometimes, has   with his wife   about twenty million. Not hyperbole.   And, having wanted to enter the diplomatic service, or to become a writer of plays, and a number of other things, finally entered [a] business on a smallish scale...... And moreover [Friend] has a brilliant mind)))

3   If not several millions, then:

   $100,000 invested in the manner of a trust fund for a man who does not intend to become a financier, would provide an income of some six thousand a year --- One would not be 'rich'   Right?   One would not impress the holy hell even out of doormen and headwaiters.

   Neither would the proceeds of two hundred thousand.

4   It follows that one million would produce some 60,000 a year and might, if properly handled, impress the holy hell out of doormen and headwaiters   (not really: people on expense accounts would out-spend one three or four to one))

   and in any case it would not alter the nature of the universe for you if you invested it in a mutual fund or a trust fund and did your proper work

5   If, having some capital, you mean to become a financial manipulator, you might become very rich. And much more likely would go broke   You would certainly have to serve a real apprenticeship in the matter -- I mean a REAL apprenticeship, not a matter of reading the newspapers.

   and of course you don't intend to do this   You could certainly not ALSO do something else

   So, clear?   you can provide yourself with considerable security, ease, a lot of minor self-indulgence and a larger freedom of choices than most people have   You can also get a look at a lot of things, can move around freely   Which has some value   So put money in a mutual fund or a trust or something of the sort, and do your own proper work   And simmer down   It don't mean much

YOU CANNOT DABBLE IN BUSINESS OR FINANCE AND ALSO
BE A SCHOLAR OR A POET   or, for that matter, sane.

George

To William Bronk
[May 13, 1968]   TLs   UCSD 16, 3, 11

Dear Bill

It's good to hear from you. I'd been aware that we were out of
contact, and reminded myself from time to time to write, but hadn't realized that it's been as long as you indicate in your letter.

-- leaves so much to catch up with now, and I have by some ill-luck
developed an injury to a nerve in my left arm -- I've had to ration my
typing during the last month or so.[6] Some rather non-committal but
vaguely hopeful prognostications from an orthopedist: but I think perhaps
I shall have to learn to write legibly with pen and ink. I dread the discipline.

Quite aside from that little problem I have not done much work
of any importance, or perhaps none of importance, in the last year
Something is knocking about in my head, I have a strong impression that
I am thinking or feeling my way beyond *Numerous*,   but   --well, perhaps I have been writing the poems which for twenty-five years I neglected
to write, and have now caught up with myself. Whatever the reason, I
think it will take me a while now - - - I catch myself now and then trying
to versify something which could as well as not be written in prose.   Bad
sign, I imagine.   May take me a while.

Good to see 'a sample,' as you call it, of your work. Very moving
poems.   And I have in our book-case, and frequently re-read the magnificent Lock on the Feeder.[7] I was in Madison recently at the invitation of
Lawrence Dembo -- who is easily among the best of the youngish critics,
with several books to his credit. I had brought him a copy of The World,
the Worldless. He assured me at once that he had the book and admired
it. So, you see, things do get 'round: what has life does live. Somehow.

It's good news that Corman is publishing a collection of Bronk.

———

Seems a great deal going on in the world at the moment, doesn't
there?   The kids, the rioting kids!   Amazing! Of course they are 'revolting

only against doing the things we have already done for them['] --- What could we think of them if they didn't? They want to do something else.   Something that has not already been done. I don't mean they have found it, nor begun to. But this strange, world-wide 'rising' ---- revolt, despair, demand ---!   The life of the mind;   what is left for them is the life of the mind   But for how many?   for how many IS that a possible way of life?

surely I don't know.   And what else is left for them?[8]

On the principle of 'rationing,' which is the principle of my left elbow --- this will have to do for a while. Tho there's much to say. It would be very pleasant to see you if you should be in N Y ---

all regards

George

((A young friend 'phoned during the first hour of the Columbia sit-in. She talked for -- I think -- more than half an hour. Troubled by events and the difficulty of finding her role, her place.   She wanted to be among the *actives* --- and felt that she somehow was not and could not wholly be so ---- Talked, as I say, a long time. After she hung up I remembered that it was from one of her letters to me that I took the quotation in *Numerous*:

'Whether, as the intensity of seeing increases, one's distance from Them, the People, does not also increase' [CP 152]

Dramatic.   She had somehow foreseen it.[9]

To Alexander Mourelatos
[after June 2, 1968]   TLs   UCSD 33, 1, 11

Dear Alex

I don't know that your fine letter is 'academic' in any sense   If it is, it is not the current academicism of the lit. departments   And comes to me as fresh, as the response of a person

Your . . . 'I think . . . nothing could serve better than the images you articulate' is the heart of the matter, the only thing that really *need* be said, the one assurance I could need[10]

I can't just at this time go back over the poem to judge or re-judge, or rather, it would be bad for me to do so.   I am having trouble getting beyond it.   I find myself making cadences I don't need, making cadences

I've used before only because I did use them before ---- 'imitating myself,' unable to get clear -- or back into the world.   I won't try, therefore, to say 'I agree about this, I don't agree about that'   or even to decide - - but nothing that you say is irrelevant

I can see, for example that [sections] 18–19 might be felt to be over-clever   As statement, or as isolated statement, I suppose I would stand more firmly or more insistently on the formulation somewhere in Route: 'Strange for them also, strange to be man -- '[CP 196] 18–19 appear some-what as an outburst, an outburst of horror   The drop, the flat drop to the line / 'Is atrocious' / [CP 160] might carry the sense of arbitrariness, of deliberate arbitrariness, the need to make a stance somewhere   and is carried in spite of that almost at once to the recognition of the fly in the bottle, even the villainous bombardier in the bottle   (the image of course is also the image of the plastic bubble of the helicopter)   and to another inflection of the bright light of shipwreck which breaks thru the attempt to declare simply and spontaneously that the atrocious is the atro-cious

without retracting, you know.   It is atrocious.   Well ---- a poem is really about myself.   It is an instance of 'being in the world'   Yes: an admission of 'what is autonomous in us'   or 'in the genes'   :   it could even refer to Kant, you see;   the limits of judgment, the limits of pure reason - - I said, remember: 'All this is reportage' [CP 192 and 193]   An account of being in the world, to stick to H[eidegger].

(the vision of something like God --- I said: All this is reportage Reports not a proof but a vision.   But if it reported proof - - that too would be a most fascinating report of what happens in the world

The book stays pretty close to that realistic point.   Which has this oddity: it seems justified to call it a realistic or materialistic point, and quite as justifiable to refer to it as a metaphysical or even a religious point - - - - that would be the value of the poems, maybe, insofar as they have a value: simply the sense of 'size,' of the size of reality ---- something like that.   An opening.

I think of the phrase   'the fly in the bottle' as a quotation from you, not as a quotation from Wit[tgenstein]   because that was the moment when we understood each other [CP 160]   I remembered that W. had said it of course, but I don't know that I understood W. when I encountered the phrase, and certainly I didn't care so much if I understood him or not

so - - a quotation from you.   And, in the context of the poem, im-mediately the vision of the insane, poisonous Johnsonian flies

who are not us   Not the four of us   Whatever our differences,   we are not those insane flies   I have no way to say how grateful
I am, or how fortunate I feel

with love
George

To Diane Meyer
[July 1968]   TLs   UCSD 16, 7, 29

Andy dear
the rock islands, the pine trees the ocean and the little boat   it's
all true. Can't tell you how beautiful   We came here vaguely convalescent   Somehow lost our balance in New York in the last month or
two-- lost judgment. I was unable to write.   The cruises re-establish a
standard ----- one begins to know again how good a poem must be really
to exist in any considerable way in the face of the forest and rocks and
ocean
or how *decent* it must be in the face, if it has a face, of the little
boat
We're STILL learning how little the little boat is. We become more
and more like canoe-ing naturalists   We anchor in creeks, we paddle up
on beaches ---- Tho there also we are at sea, with the huge new sail that
Mary made towering over our boat-full of extra clothes and water-proofs
headed down the bay at piratical speeds
well   in sum: We sailed again to [Castine.] Again encountered Philip Booth, a poet   who invited us to come meet Robt Lowell   We
went.   There was Lowell, Philip etc., the official representatives of the
New England virtues. They were drinking cocktails
And there stood we in our dripping oil-skins in their pretty living-
room
HEAR, O ISRAEL!   (Shema Israel, or something like that   Wish
I could remember the spelling)   A great fisherman's cry.[11]
So have no fear: we do you honor.   Talk about the piratical: a
dirty old man and his beautiful wife!   With an uncle and aunt like that
out there in the world, how could one be unhappy?   You're a lucky girl.
And as for us --- My god, how lucky we are. Who one is and where
one is and who one loves.
And who loves one   Andy dear.

Even Eve, I guess   who is unbelievable.   She couldn't have written the 'I see a Flower in a Thorn Bush'   She couldn't know that, she
couldn't have found that way to do it, she couldn't have found that calm
title   I don't doubt she's been a woman and a man and a boy   And
probably a belly dancer or she's been a dish of jello, and that suggested
the plan.   With or without a dash of whipped cream?   I keep wondering.
I'm not sure she could do the whipped cream
[page 2 is cut]

To Jerome Rothenberg
[after September 16, 1968]   TLs   UCSD 10, 60, 14

Dear Jerry
        a further note:
        I'm sending you a facsimile of Discrete Series[12]   You may not have
seen the work.   A similarity particularly to some of the African and
Esquimaux[13]
        Not that I was familiar with that work, but thru a degree of simi-
larity of approach
        In the later books I've struggled to broaden the statement beyond
the nouns   Discrete series is not concerned with predicates.   I think
some distortion in the translations and the modern work you adduce as
having a similarity to the 'primitive' derives from a failure to recognize
the primary concern with postulation - - - The inability to use the syntax
or an equivalent of the syntax of the originals.
        ('Disagreement marks where the subject matter ends;   it is what the
subject matter is not' -- a remark by that primitive, Hegel)
        On Gassire's Lute: Not 'chilling'   only as concerns the poet, is
it?   The age of vanity, the age of Peoples, of the creation of history as the
need of people, the need of art and the purpose of art -- the age of the
Covenant.   It created Homer's song as well as Gassire's, it destroyed Athens as well as Wagadu
        and the last age, the age of dissention, of the individual   The
glory in each man and each woman, it cannot be destroyed --- the indestructible Wagadu ---- Unless or until each man and each woman is destroyed . . .
        Which is chilling.
        Or is that how you understood it?

And the other ages ?   The age of greed replacing 'glory' ...?
Might that have been concretely visible to him?

———

I'll send the Discrete Series.   I'd like you to have it
George

[on left margin] A further note: As for now, I rather think we need the
qualities of Adam and Eve rather than those of the shaman.

To Jerome Rothenberg
[after September 16, 1968]   TLs   UCSD 10, 60, 14

Jerry
I wrote hurriedly.   Too hurriedly.   I meant NOT to protest the 'noun
series'
I am for further reducing the mechanism of predicate   which
'marks where the subject matter ends'
And was further mumbling something or other as to whether we
can make use of ritual. I suspect we've become for good and all a loose
set of Adams and Eves and incapable of Shamanism.   For good and all.[14]
And adduced Discrete   (copy of facsimile herewith enclosed -- I no longer
possess originals) as my own attempt toward the primacy of subject as
against predicate   Which seems to me a path still toward the 'primitive'
whether or not in the sense of historical repetition   --Armand [Schwer-
ner]'s Tablets of course dis-embowel the nouns but is therefore the account
of tragedy ---
All parenthetical however. I began this correspondence simply to
thank you for the book, and that remains its purpose
George

To Julian Zimet
[November 15, 1968]   TLs   Julian Zimet; draft of p. 1 at USCD 16, 11, 60

Dear Julian
[RBD cut half a page of personal matters]
Ah yes, the Woiking class - - you mention: the proletarian who

was never there.   And yet I think that was the most important undertaking to fail at   at that moment.   It seems to me I know some essential things that Williams, Pound, Stevens never knew   I have a poem either in the Materials or This in Which   that says something of it: beginning   It is true I had meant to arrive / At an actuality / In the mere number of us / And record now / That I did not [CP 141].

------ or I was explaining, by request, 'the twenty-five year silence' to Hugh Kenner   critic and of the far right politically.   I rather enjoyed explaining baldly, but Kenner found it painful and interrupted to say: 'In brief, it took twenty-five years to write the next poem'

which perhaps is the correct explanation.

It took you twenty-five years to get married

If, on the other hand, the New Left is conducting a revolution, and it looks like it is, it would seem to be a revolution against the Woiking Class   !   and not a bad idea

((the S F Hippies, a couple or three years ago, closed off Haight Street ---- a mill-in or a stand-in or a mob-in but, whatever, very much in .   Under the slogan: The streets belong to people!

The Proletarian, trying to use the street to get home from work was much angered - - In every event of the new left, the Proletarian seems to have been most angered   which is, in the lovely phrase of that English friend of Smith's   the purpose of the exercise and an excellent idea   Or --- ?   I don't know.   But it's the idea of the moment.   And not without point

((((all this under the heading of News from the New World or the Old World

and best wishes, best regards

George

[In 1968, Oppen also corresponded with Ron Caplan, June Oppen Degnan, L. S. Dembo, Rachel Blau DuPlessis, Clayton Eshleman, Theresa Fulton, Eve Haight, Charles Hanzlicek, Michael Heller, David Ignatow, George Johnston, Elizabeth Kray, James Laughlin, Philip Levine, Jane Lippe, Jack Marshall, Aleksandar and Gordana Nejgebauer, Philip Schultz, Harvey Shapiro, John Taggart, Charles Tomlinson, Diane Wakoski, and Eliot Weinberger.]

1969

[After negotiations begun in January, Oppen signed a contract on March 2 for a collected poems with Fulcrum Press (England); the book was promised by May 1970. In March or April, Oppen sent a version of "Some San Francisco Poems" to his friend Harvey Shapiro; he had been sending sections to Linda Mourelatos since January 1969, or earlier.[1] On March 20, the chapbook *Alpine* was published by The Perishable Press, dedicated "To those who as poets and publishers have rescued a nation's literature."[2] On May 6, Oppen was awarded the Pulitzer Prize in Poetry for *Of Being Numerous*. In early June, emotion-laden, Oppen met Ezra Pound again in the offices of New Directions.[3] The Oppens spent the summer on Little Deer Island, Maine, and about two weeks in September in Brooklyn at the Brossert Hotel. In the autumn, Oppen had arranged for a number of poetry readings: October 22 at St. Mary's College (Moraga, California), October 29 at San Francisco State University, November 5 at the First Unitarian Church of San Francisco, November 14 at University of New Mexico, November 18 at Syracuse University, November 21 at Bard College, November 25 at the Guggenheim Museum, and February 4, 1970, at the University of California at Berkeley. Oppen canceled this reading tour on October 16 by a telegram sent to Elizabeth Kray (Academy of American Poets) and a multiple carbon mailing to many friends—what he called a "bad-form letter."[4]]

To Robert Duncan
[1969?]   TLs with AL addition   Poetry/Rare Books Collection, SUNY-Buffalo

Robert:
       lending you a selection of Heidegger   'early' and 'Late' periods, if it matters. Fourth class, of course, but in this mail. Let me know if it fails to reach you within a day or two[5]

- - I had bought, but am only now reading Bending the Bow   And am temporarily overwhelmed

beyond, it is very far beyond, what has been done   As you know

((coincidence in your use of the word IT   in the Introduction   Similar passage somewhere in my poem Route in Of Being Numerous -- with the (probably persistent) difference: I had added, 'All this is reportage'[6]

your book would have been already in the printer's hands when Numerous appeared -- a matter of a similarity of approach: I don't mean that I got further   I am inclined to think I did not   in general and in sum, that I did *not*

And in Materials, a poem *Narrative*, which reports an experience in war: it is a recognition of sky and earth, a rebirth of words in war that you speak of also in the introduction . . .   I write but cannot hope to live in what is written: I mean to find, not create, the handholds: And am troubled now to witness your leap, the leap also in the music   my dedication to 'realism,' to the proof in the image rather than the creation of image for the first time, I feel, challenged

and yet, finally, I feel we must *find*   We are native, hopelessly native . . Hopelessly *included*   .   But you'll find yourself closer to H[eidegger]'s *Dasein* than I am

(and I exaggerate differences of purposes: the marvel of *Tribal Memories* knows, among other things, what little I know)

(and of course your Passages 24:   *Orders*   :   the orders of things[7]

George

To Sherman Stein
[1969]   TLd with AL additions   UCSD 16, 10, 46

Dear Sherman

The Man Made Universe Revised will probably be the end of me, but that's an excision normal to revision and I am far from objecting to your title or preface -- Perhaps because of the beauty of 'the number of ambiguities he can tolerate,' or the radical nature of the ambiguities and their odd -- not odd but awesome -- clarity.[8]

whereas I think -- with no earned right to think about such things -- that it is as method that math has its importance. The Scholastics could have identified the philosophic position of the 'pure' mathematician simply (simply!) as Nominalism? But the method surely is brilliant and pure and cannot be disregarded ---- of course, I know. To object would be to object to the future which is useless beyond any other uselessness. And anyway, useless or not, I don't object

But I'm impressed, I think I confessed to you, by the numbers One and zero. They behave like no other numbers. I think they mean Is and Is Not, and like Moses, our revered and thunderstruck ancestor, I think they are Real.

As against the cloudy majesty of One --- the Whore of Babylon! Two's and three's, odds and evens, the whores of Babylon. Whooo -- the brilliant quirks, and the nakedness! But the wives, the children, the laws of virtue? And the law of literature, which is not to allow rhetoric to generate rhetoric, words to generate words -----

But I value the book. I don't know if I said so clearly enough. It is a part of my belated education and a joy to read - - its wit and the wit of its clarity are pure delight

> inscribe on our banners
>> Disjoint the sets!
>> We Are What Is.[9]

To Diane Meyer
[1969?]   TLd with AL   UCSD 16, 7, 29

Andy   yes, your sense of it, sense of the world.   We get born into the thing, we just find ourselves here and we are as we are --- How can I 'reply'?

I promise happiness sometimes in the poems, I suppose, merely by describing happiness   I've wondered if I speak honestly because I cannot promise luck, and I have been incredibly lucky ----- Luck goes just so far.   Either Mary or I soon must face the question whether any life can come out well alone.   Whether a life can end well   I try to face it [CP 220]

What you say frightens me   That you say it.   You 'want not to be obstructed by the apparatus of living'   And Elsie, my mother, wrote: 'I cannot face the business of living'[10] And I think she meant most of all the children.   That she couldn't left Libby in bad shape, but I cannot bring myself to say that we must live in order to deceive each other, even to deceive the children. And Linda grew up to discover that the world was not as snug as we pretended - - - -

But you say 'guilty,' and I think you are being faithful to someone or something, in refusing to accept process, in rejecting process, that something is happening!! Maybe we -- all of us -- people -- have come about as far as humans were ever fitted to go, had or have any possibility of going - - - Maybe not. The things that appear dimly from here are difficult even to name

I've tried in a way   I'll copy out a poem meant to begin a next book, which possibly I can't write[11]

'Mirrors' in that we merely confront now or begin to confront reality   But in the idea of a mirror is the sense that it gives something back. The title comes from Corinthians [1 Cor 3:15]   : 'If any man's work burn, he shall suffer loss; yet he himself shall be saved, but so as by fire'   I'll copy the poem.   Not easy to say again.

Is there comfort if I say Me too   Us Too   We know   Here we all are   This is what we are talking about always, and the children will not always be children and will talk of this

You know that Eve will. Andy, DO you feel guilty to move beyond Libby?   Or do you feel a final loss to move hopelessly beyond Libby

It is true a man will grab an oar. Any stick to beat a father with

What is the feminine   The love of standing still, of hugging to oneself   Of containing? It is not a feminine culture, it is very hard for women. Terribly, terribly hard[12]

To George Johnston
[after January 20, 1969]   TLs   The Public Archives of Canada

Dear George

I don't mean to hasten the cadence of correspondence. Answer this when and if the occasion arises. I reply thus promptly because I read and re-read your letter and as I sit down to work, I am still in the letter --

'. . . demands of honesty and courage and nerve often run out . . and the softening my family have done on my heart   I am soft about their hopes and involved in them'   And you go on to describe your boy and from there to a number of facts about the world   It is all one can say, all there is to say

You have a strange modesty, almost a timidity -- please do excuse this. I have to say it because I am embarrassed to say that I too value the Excursion and the Prelude and the Intimations of Immortality as tho I were giving you permission. Or is it, as you say, a matter of 'idiom,' a difference of idiom? I am sorry we were not able to talk at length. Among many things in your letter I would want to discuss some are, in effect, questions But I am filled at the moment with the beauty of the letter and cannot bring myself to begin chattering about myself by electric typewriter

-- which does chatter --

Just to say, at least, that I understand about 'nerve' and the children. I stopped writing   perhaps you know   for some twenty odd years.   To begin with, the catastrophe of human lives in the 'thirties which seemed to me to put poetry and the purposes of poetry in question ----- I wrote of that in a poem called Pro Nobis [CP 141]. But, later, that we had a daughter. And still hesitate over a line, thinking of my daughter reading it   tho she is twenty-seven and in no way weak. Of course a father should be invulnerable   But of course she would know by now in any case that he is not -- Of course it is true I mean to put these things in the public record   And in the public music. We know, we both know, there is, at least, no other possible safety for us. For any of us. For the children either

Well, I did chatter some after all   I still mean simply to say I understand what you write. I mean simply to say   Me too

George

To George Johnston
[after February 7, 1969]   TLs with AL additions   The Public Archives of Canada

Dear George

'natives of the rocks' you   write. And, 'the war, in a way, rescued me'   that is, rescued you back to the rocks, the open world.   I feel this too about the open world; more strongly than I feel anything else

A grand-niece of mine writes a little (?!) poem:

If I were as big as the world
        And I held your hand lovingly I would squish it

If I were as big as the world
        And I held your hand
                Without squishing it

You would know
        How much I love you[13]

———

    Well, we feel similar things: you, me, and my grand-niece. The Old English and the Old Icelandic: I cannot read either one, but ---- well, the Jorgenbook is on my mind more than on most people's (does one count that as Icelandic?):[14]   you'll have noted our feeling, Mary's and mine, for 'that other antiquity,' the Northern, the non-classic, and I read, for example, Langland in preference to Chaucer [Cf. CP 105]. The discovery of the Middle English (in the public library in N Y, circa 1928) was of major importance to me - - - - -. There are connections.[15]

    yours is a beautiful letter. And we all 'only just begin' to know what poetry is about   Or love.

                            all regards
                            George

    George: could you tell me the etymology of the name Søren? or is it Sören?)
    ((From Sår = wounded?))

To Harvey Shapiro
[early 1969]   TLs   Harvey Shapiro

Dear Harvey:
    'Epistle' in lieu of a letter   Typical of the course of my disease - - - - - -[16]
    Difficult again to believe in the importance of poetry. The army tightens up, some kids surely will be shot soon. Art becomes (again) more and more a struggle *against* the artworld, the art-attitudes . . and against little else . .
    Depressed. And in a way, not.   It is blazingly beautiful in and about San Francisco, a great deal more beautiful than perhaps the poem manages to say
    but I've been working over it all these months   And in fact, more: I had notes and scraps of it written on our exploratory trip last year[17]
    I don't know that it's 'finished'

———

We kept ourselves, until the last few weeks, like English house-maids, very much TO ourselves - - - wandering around the city, walking over the hills (mountains, really within the city): taking busses every-where --- all very lovely, very beautiful. Tho we become, maybe more and more rattled. Had started by seeing a number of very young poets, and some not so young but very bad poets who came 'round. Didn't work out very well. I was continually reminded of an account I read long ago of a doctor-anthropologist who was sent out to work among some North Amer-ican Indian tribe. He took great pains to overcome the hostility of the Shaman, and was finally able to invite him to an operation for gall stones he was going to perform. The Shaman was truly impressed. He generously said: You are better than I am. Then he said: where do you get your stones?   I get mine down by the river   .

an awkward situation   How does one tell the little poetry groups and grouplets that one isn't faking??

so, we pulled ourselves together.   Wrote Duncan (a highly dis-guised cry for help))   spent a couple of evenings together: liked the man very much[18]   Very very brilliant   Something of a performer -- merely out of nervousness, perhaps -- But the performance very brilliant, and a very touching guy in the little interstices of the performance -- and I was very very tired of doing the performing myself for the benefit of the unlikely young . .[19]

--Rexroth away at the moment, tho we know him   and he's in-teresting

The local Bourgeoisie -- the dry-goods store owners, or their des-cendents, all over the damn place niggling their way around whatever they think is arty - - - - Damn provincial bourgeoisie, hell on wheels   Plain idiocy.

Insulted a select few, and cleared the decks   still: we're a bit rattled in this little   city

Don't know about the poem. I don't, at this moment, know much. You think *Numerous* is as far as I'll get?   I wouldn't like to think so;   I wasn't planning it that way.

as you see, we miss you

Give my love and all to Armand [Schwerner], David [Ignatow], Allen [Planz] - - - - Edna [Shapiro] and the boys

George

To Harvey Shapiro
[after March 23, 1969]   TLs with AL addition   Harvey Shapiro; carbon
UCSD 16, 10, 29

Harvey
I dispute nothing in your letter   I don't dispute your refusal to defend the liberal position[20]

Drama 'is created by people freed of their blocks'   drama including eventually the drama of The Bomb, the drama of which it is capable. But, desperate, furious, disappointed, unhappy, unwilling to accept life as society presents it and its possibilities to them, they see modern liberalism as a program which permits people to live as quietly as they can, for as long as they can, to live as they have been living, to find meanings as individuals -- IF they can -- in quietness - - - and they say that they find nothing in it   The revolt   (why not?) of the stupid

Or do they assume they will be stopped. Do they see themselves really only as a protesting minority?   If they should see themselves as a majority would they not see themselves as Brown Shirts, as the lady [reported in HS's letter] saw them? But Brown Shirts free of the accusation of being pawns or dupes of Imperialism, and to shout Hitler! Hitler! solves nothing.   It is true that they force now a serious discussion of what it is that we do want --- or whether we want anything   (('DAMN IT ALL, ALL THIS OUR SOUTH STINKS PEACE'))[21]

I don't think we could last long as animals   Our spit, I'm afraid, is fatal only to each other. But the program of 'lasting long' is itself liberalism: longevity I think they would agree, is itself liberalism ---- It is not non-discussable. Obviously it is not

------ I meant to approach this again in the last of the S F poems 'we have come as far as is possible' who reflect light like mirrors etc.: meaning language and clarity of the mind   as against 'the' (or D H Lawrence's) blood [CP 228].

(((like you, I'm not sure the sequence is successful   I've revised drastically, but doubt its adequacy

Stuck. Stuck. Doubt any poem's adequacy 'all words, dead words by dead people' and their hatred of the poet [HS's letter]. But I myself can live only for 'dead words' or rather, for their transparency.   Not, surely, not for the opaque 'blood'

I don't on the other hand know how to fight humanity   So that if this is indeed a choice now being made ---------- That, I think, would be that

I value your letter   These are in effect notes on the letter   I send them as is

((The Living Theatre perhaps did say a good deal of it: Failure of the prophets and the Wonder-Workers. Followed by slaughter (possibly inadequate) tho this last doesn't seem to have occurred to them   Or maybe it did: they must have relished those scenes to have worked so hard on the mechanics.   Thereafter the reconstruction of man on the principles of John Locke, Marx, Freud   etc   Liberalism   The quiet sur-vival, which amounted to a jail cell for everyone   (all agreeing: 'yes, yes')   But finally set fire to the jail. Not a matter of 'escape' but simply of fire because a jail should be burnt   Whatever may happen   And that I think is true.   I do NOT know how to fight humanity

and then the construction of 'Humanity' -- a single figure, A monster   Well, it's been tried   We've SEEN it fail in our own lifetimes Because really each one has his own life -- the historical factor is IN his own life or it is nowhere   It is perhaps they, not we, who cannot see thru a word   As that Great Monster, all we can do is destroy, and all we can destroy is ourselves

possibly many want that. It could be this that gives such an unmis-takable air of silliness to the liberal defense ----- That is to say, one must say a little more than that, one must say what we want, what we hope ----

if, of course, we can   I'm not attempting to predict the debacle -- the New Left may be very largely a phenomena in Night Town -- But they do, as you said, nevertheless force this question on us   I think we have come to where we would have to say fairly clearly why we do not want the debacle --- if we do not

(I am aware of not wanting it.   and have tried a number of times to say - - - The opposition and 'the Blood' or the young bloods have rather an advantage   Need only shout, and indeed the blood responds -----

(((((as I said, just notes -- just, rather, rummaging

thanks for the letter

George

(It is on my mind that as literature they will overwhelm us all for a while)   They are, as you say, very loud. I think they will have a huge audi-ence

To Harvey Shapiro
[Spring 1969]   TLs   Harvey Shapiro

Harvey - - - -

Much preoccupied with your report of the living theatre   and
such. Innumerable imaginary letters to you.   Ending with a little lyric.   In
which   if I remember my letter to you correctly   I reverse myself[22]

A young man in imminent danger of being sent to Vietnam or some
other jungle does not, I suppose, consider it absolutely necessary that universities should function, or that industries should function, or that confer-
ences on education - - etc. - - - Neither does his girl

Shamefully easy for me to forget this.   Anyway, herewith the little
lyric

A Modern Incident

The culture
Of the draft-pool, an exotic poetry
Between speech and action

Between action and theatre
A pop culture
Of an elite
Engaged in revolt

Between act and environment,
Hedonist, a property of the young,
A popular song, a clean
Sweep

George

(will send the poem with quotation from you when I make a clean copy)[23]

To Rachel Blau DuPlessis
[March 14, 1969]   TLs[24]   R. B. DuPlessis

Rachel

I wrote you this some days ago in answer to your letter   Don't
know just what it's about or why, and didn't mail it

which seems wasteful. Want not waste not. (i.e.: *I* don't want
it   So here 'tis

'Sometimes . . . the whole business seems an evasion, my part in it
included'

people felt there was something wrong with the old left, and there
was.   They were not speaking for themselves, and therefore there was something essentially and deeply wrong with them   We could be drawn around
any 180 degree bend or into any perversity: the phrase was: We are petty-
bourgeois, and *therefore*   this seems wrong to us.   But the Proletarian . . . !   IF we were proletarians . . . !   Whereas so far the new left, despite
any lapse of logic has had unchallengeable authority in that its people spoke
for themselves   They said what they wanted - - -

((their difficulty however in this being their 'allies,'   the Blacks   Who
have nothing whatever to do with leftist ideas but are a wedge in the same
board, and may, with the new left, crack it   They are also the guerillas, I
think many are becoming truly guerillas

I totally mis-understood and mis-predicted to myself what would happen in the Vietnam war   I had not understood guerillas, tho once I had
known   I seem to have forgotten   I didn't understand what Mao was
saying   (tho I had always admired Mao and read most of his writing)   or what Che -- that mad bastard -- was saying ---- - -

I had understood during WW II, and told myself quite clearly. The U S
infantry had one anti-tank co in each regiment: three squads, each with a
truck, a fifty-seven mm anti-tank cannon, two bazookas, a BAR [Browning
automatic rifle] etc etc and fourteen men. It maybe   could stop a tank
Maybe, because the German tanks had a larger gun, because our gun had
a tremendous muzzleblast which would draw fire - - - - - and because we each
and every one valued his own life quite a bit. We had by no means found
our lives unbearable up to that time, we were pretty anxious to get home
safe,   we were pretty confident the war was going to be won, for that
matter   Unspoken, undiscussed, there simply was an understanding that
men would take great risks, but would not simply throw themselves under a
tank with a stick of dynamite as some of the Spanish republicans did --- and
by which method one man could stop a tank

some of the French maquis did comparable things ----- It means that
a guerilla equals something more than 14 very heavily armed men - -

But I had forgotten   Or not really: I had thought that people could
not stand against fire.   Once, they could not. The Japanese, I've been told,
could not, and I know the Germans could not   I thought that no one could.

Well, that's what guerillas are. I suppose they are people who would find life unbearable without victory   But one cannot PRETEND to be a guerilla   Or if one can, there is no reason one *should*   One has to have a reason for doing these things   'A man will give his life for his child'   I wrote that [CP 189]   It's simply true   A husband or a wife will also   if that's how they feel   But one mustn't pretend to have such motives where one doesn't, one mustn't pretend or even think he SHOULD be a guerilla if he is not   He should if he is: if he isn't, what does the should mean?   A fake ethic, a forced ethic, we cannot construct an ethic unless we know what we want and how much we want it

it is wrong to become a hero only for the sake of deceiving others as to what one wants and how much one wants it   It is the most drastic way of propagating misinformation

-- alright?

we do really need to know what we want

I do, tho, begin to think that this   the situation in this country truly is a revolutionary situation.   I find it impossible to avoid a tingle of the ridiculous in saying so --- what, after all, are we fighting about?   ----- But nevertheless, nevertheless: the center position, the liberal position becomes untenable ---- because the left will not make a compromise peace, because there is a cops' rebellion forming; the cops want to do their own dirty-work, not the Liberals' dirty work ---: people are being forced to move to the left or to the right and that IS a revolutionary situation: a situation in which the center canNOT hold, is necessarily a revolutionary situation ----

well, I think it is. A most strange revolution. Or not really: it turns out that such things as hunger are not the only conditions that can make life unfaceable

which, after all, we knew

I understand that this is not proof that the left will *win*   Tho as a matter of fact I think it will

I am not entirely sure I'll be pleased - - - There is some godawful horseshit on that side too   A manure which may nourish the soil, but which I would find hard to live with

Don't know why I wrote a semi-essay   I ascribe these things to my electric typewriter   I am slightly over-powered
[cut]

George

To L. S. Dembo
[May 8, 1969]   TLs   L. S. Dembo; carbon UCSD 16, 4, 7

Dear Lawrence:

I had read thru those interviews cursorily when I wrote you[25]   I
see now it is not a question of 'editing,' but of the very much more than
lawyerlike - - - - the required word here is 'skill' but I mean   beauty.

anywhere at all. But among others: the bottom of page 167 and
continuing on 168   I am sure I was just answering questions as you
asked them, with no consideration of where we were going. And question
by question, elicited answer by answer, I come to say simply   That's
right.   And have never said anything better

((I would like to have said, on page 170 -- or rather I wish that
between us we had said [re. Pound]:

      . . . . . and I know that I'm reading a great poet.
      Q   At least a poet capable of great lyricism
      A   Yes.   A great poet.   A great man.

I say it now to you.

———

Louis for some reason was playacting Wittgenstein, in Pound's
slang.

Well, Louis possesses his own kind of courage -- and needed it thru
twenty years of total neglect -- and his own dignity   Various other kinds
of courage and a more difficult dignity are demanded of a man who will
speak clearly in public.   I wish Louis had possessed them: he is the most
intelligent man I have known, and I miss him.

((. . but claims, with Bottomless conceit, that his Bottom has obli-
terated epistemology))[26]

The hidden ironic Reznikoff flashes in the delicious: 'I don't know
if [whether] it's fair to get off [on] the subject of flies right now'[27]

Rezi   a very very proud man, having learned thru much more
than twenty years of neglect, very nearly total neglect, the tactic of total
humbleness, was, by habit, now, and perhaps the weakness of age, merely
being too humble, too obedient --- He need only have said ; 'I have never
read Williams, Pound, Zuk, Rakosi or Oppen, and don't intend to do so'
- - He was trying to answer with   propriety   And it is, of course, his
absolutely own, his most singular conviction of propriety which makes

the originality and the daring of his poems so wonderful --. Like his descriptions of himself in business, in jobs, the propriety of the university
was too much for him: it superceded his own propriety, and defeated
him

- - - but when he apologizes for his temerity in getting off the subject
of flies -- apologizes for the impropriety - - Rezi's still there

'what a man loves is his heritage'   tho I may mis-quote[28]

I note that my syntax becomes bolloxed in the final 'Answer.' I
was attempting to express affection. And became embarrassed

George

To Harvey Shapiro
[May 1969]   TLs   Harvey Shapiro

Dear Harvey

Of course, thanks for phoning me

My ambivalence [to the Pulitzer Prize] deriving from: It is, in view
of the record, a questionable compliment. Which is alright, and very dignified to say.[29] On the other hand, I needed it very badly - - at sixty-one,
the self-confident unknown is awkward --- I mean *gauche*, a gaucherie, I
commit gaucheries at parties - - - -

But odd to need such a thing

Therefore a little ambivalent per telephone.   But many thanks for
the message

See you pretty soon.   It'll be nice indeed

((mewling and Pewliking in my nurse's arms - - - I picture myself
as a flustered infant

But maybe I get to lecture the public: on Harvey, David [Ignatow],
Naomi [Replansky], Bronk   Interrupting, even in S F, conversations
about Brautigan, Lenore Kandel,   McClure - - - - That'll be a good
thing

Regards and thanks
George

To June Oppen Degnan
[after May 6, 1969]   TLsc   UCSD 16, 1, 7

June

Been studying the fact of R E liking The Forms of Love   [CP 86]
and   (which was the other?)   And Athenaem's refusal   (I think I wish I
had known of it - I need all the information I can get)[30]   Studying all other
bits of information, clues, that come to me, and reading thru Numerous
in the fattest voice I can manage, and in various accents and intona-
tions - - -

I don't quite know what I've done in and thru this book (with the
slightly embarrassing help of a deceased newspaper publisher [i.e., Pulit-
zer])   Something. Something done far more directly in the teeth, the
orthodontures, of the poetic taste, the artistic sniggers and nervous ticks
of the moment than I knew

-- been trying on that level of gossip to understand, to analyze that
review of Strand   to analyze the formation and deformation of taste,
fighting a battle of taste --- I'm licking wounds I didn't know I had: trying
to take pride in valors I was unaware of having possessed - - Celebrating
a victory (possibly temporary?) over surrealists and symbolists I had
thought were dead   I stepped over those dead dogs as innocently as
Reznikoff, if I understand the events correctly: to be greeted on the other
side of their carcasses by the aforesaid deceased publisher - - - - - a gruesome
life.

(((A clue to my semi-consciousness in the oddity of having discussed ethics at such length with Dembo   Been wondering how I fell into
that   Tho I notice now, in my research into my own book, that I was
repeating what I had written in #5 and 6 -- and commenting on in #7 --
of Route [CP 187–190]

well,   thanks for the information -- not, in itself, different from
a number of facts that reached me, but acted as a final straw that brought
this clumsy camel face to face with the unblinking needle's eye

((I imagine the camel seeing that strait over his shoulder - - a nice
posture for a camel -- having just ambled thru it unaware - - - - - Maybe.
Limits to the power of a deceased publisher.

George

To George Johnston
[Summer 1969, before July 26, 1969]   TLs with AL inserts   The Public
Archives of Canada

Dear George:
        Been some time since   since one of us wrote, hasn't it   I was
re-reading one of your letters   and found a sentence I needed to steal
in it   You'd said something about 'what we must face and which will
not give up its secret' - - - - Well: this is Summer, and we're in Maine   Sailing a little boat (17 feet long)   very light, very fast ---- Boats have played
a very large part in my life beginning in childhood, or in fact in infancy,
and a large, tho intermittent part in our lives, Mary's and mine   We've
sailed fairly ponderous boats on fairly ponderous voyages, but this is a
cockleshell, slightly too large to be a rowboat, but very light, very fast,
slightly unstable but wide, comfortable, and we sit in or on the sea talking
and watching the charts   The front and back ends under the decking
stuffed tight with sleeping bags, extra clothing, charts, anchors ropes compass cooking equipment food life jackets extra sails ----
        . . . sailing out into the Gulf of Maine   toward Mount Desert Island
in a strong breeze. A larger boat would be snoring along with the wheel
lashed, but we are in slightly risky waters for a cockleshell and moreover
these are new waters to us and we watch the charts and the seas and the
squalls rather carefully   and meanwhile the tremendous round stone
mountains of Mount Desert Island sliding by in silence
        . . . and anchor in Bar Harbor in the sunlight among fishing boats
and the vacationers' doings   just off the beach and the old houses of the
towns . . .
        well, I was writing of this 'back home' in Little Deer Isle, and for
some reason re-read some of your letters, and found the lines I needed
        'for some reason': Possibly good reason, tho not conscious.   Bar
Harbor is not more than sixty miles north and east of Little Deer - - but
in that sixty miles the sea and the coast begin to take on the feel of very
far north and very far east in the Atlantic   Hardly Icelandic: but surely
Labradorian - - - - and I seem to have thought of you[31]
        for some reason the boat becomes very small, very precarious and
very cozy, very innocent ---- an approach to the Icelandic   In summer-
vacation terms, I suppose tho still there is that which must be faced and

can't in fact, give up its secret - - - - which is approximately what I wrote   speaking of the little boat at anchor in Bar Harbor:

Glass world

Glass heaven
Unable to part with its secret
[cf. CP 245]

and so thought to write you again.   A summer saga.

A summer saga. But difficulty with the poetry, difficulty with the summer: the war goes on, it would seem it cannot be stopped: there is a dirty secret somewhere, everyone by now having acknowledged that this war, at least, is a mistake but nobody, almost nobody in government, even the 'doves[,]' speak of getting out simply by getting out --- a dirty secret, a dirty little secret described, I think, by Marx

and denied by the neo-Keynsians. Who may turn out to be wrong about more than that   It looks, in this country, as if the collapse of the whole paper economy has already begun   People very close to panic. Everyone we speak to except the hot-shot operators   And they of course can only live in a paper economy   And are blind to everything in the world but paper anyway.

including the horror in Vietnam and elsewhere   A strange gap between the absurd and childish paper and the very real torture and death by fire --- But what will we do?   It looks extremely like the end of something, and sometimes one's hope is in that fact: I think maybe one's hope for man, really ---

No way out of this   but to end this   Seems true.   The young seem to me magnificent, but I am aware that it is largely that they are young   Must be admitted, however, that so far their courage has held, and perhaps ours will too   It is, as a matter of fact, all one needs - - Would you agree?   Or to put it differently, it is a good thing that the present mess is unable to sustain itself (tho what finally arrived on the moon were not men!)[32]

George

(You won't mind my writing letters that are actually notes for a letter, I hope - - and you can, I hope, manage the mis-typing)[33]

To Jane Cooper
[Summer 1969]   TLs with AL additions   Jane Cooper

Dear Jane

 a visitor last night.   After which I read the weathers of your book till morning   When Mary got up she asked about it, and I handed her the book open to the last poem which she read and said in quite a shaken voice: It's really lovely, that poem. Really fine, very fine.[34]

 It is indeed.   And others   In addition to those you mention, the poem for Sally, the poem to your mother from Notre Dame - - - - O, a great many, and I do not feel, as you seemed to feel, that there are any serious lapses   any lapses as whole poems[35]

 'How can I tell which one of us is absent'   :   the theme, the world of the poems, the vision of the poems

 I was puzzled by your asking about music. But now I feel   that music is the problem, the problem of the next book, the problem of the way on

 there seem to me cadences that trap you, as if an obligation   Whereas music! the passion of music, the passionate needs of the music itself, the nerve to put a full stop, the nerve to break off   Maybe I mean not courage but fear which must not be denied by the music: to respond to the wildness of the world, the wildness of time, the wildness, therefore, of oneself

 -- I don't mean that I haven't heard and felt the heart of your poems: speech and the saying of one's name that breaks the houses of silence   Really, the contrary: to use silence, not to be caught up in a cadence, obliged to a cadence   ?   Which would leave form, music, as that which makes the poem graspable, the music itself, and every note, for the sake also of the thing grasped   But above all, and most amply, the silences: the breaking of rhythmic obligations.

 (((I've been drawn, just in the act of typing, directly into this talk of the way forward, of what seems to me the way forward, as if you would understand fully just from my quoting Mary that the poems moved me very much, that I felt their delicate and illuminated and pure and open depths   I assure you I feel them.   This is just the haste of typing and trying to define my own sense of music and my sense of where the music of your poems may find new footholds

 are the poems sufficiently in the past and sufficiently solidly in print that it will not be an invasion of the poem if I exhibit tentative excisions, the excisions I would have considered if I had written the poem,   as the fastest way of saying what I mean   ?   it is certainly the fastest way of indicating what I mean, but only on the understanding that it is open, even to me, to every possible doubt, to revision of the revision - - - - it would show only the direction I mean to try to imagine::::

((I'll attach the pages)

I type out in full in the hope that at worst or at least the poem in my typing will seem totally alien, and will not touch your printed poem --- again, *your very beautiful poem*[36]

I plan to mail this without time to review my own suggestions   What I hope, for one thing, is that there may be something in the way the numbers heading the poems 'sound,' even tho they're not sounded

(((((and yes, I'm aware of being anti-Lowellian in all this

CERTAINLY the way to the next book is the way away from Lowell[37]

love,

George

(Wonderful echo of Eliz. Barrett in the poem for Sally, in the opening lines. Not sure if you registered it consciously:

'What was he doing, the great god Pan,
Down in the reeds by the river?'[38]

To Eve Haight
[August 20, 1969]   TLs   Eve Haight and *Ironwood* 26, 43.

Evie dear   I'm going to write this down because I said too many things and you might remember the wrong thing:

That disappointment when one re-reads a new poem - - - It happens to everyone. It's deceptive. Pay no attention to it

It's possible that a poem doesn't have to be 'perfect.' Anyway, there's no reason your poems should be perfect *now*

Moreover when someone new is just working his or her way into what is to be said, we don't know very clearly what 'perfect' would be

even you don't know.   or may know while you're writing the poem but not later

MUCH later   you'll know.   It'll be *you* who found out

((I'm planning to show you Robert Creeley's remark: 'The possible is more important than the perfect'))
> So doan you go and forget
> > and love from
> > UNKEL,
> > > the Great one

To L. S. Dembo
[October 16, 1969]   TLs   L. S. Dembo

Dear Larry:
1) arrived in S F soon   before my tenth birthday[39]
2) [arrival in NYC after the University of Oregon] Mary and I arrived N Y
- - - Probably 1928   Could not have been earlier, might have been very early 1929
3) ["When did you meet Zukofsky and Reznikoff and under what circumstances?"] 1928–1929: soon after arriving in N.Y. account of meeting with Zuk in your interview with me. Zuk knew Rezi   Introduced us? Gave us his address?? Showed us the poetry at any rate: we'd have   found him
4) ["When did To Publ. begin operations?"] Wms Novelette and Other Prose was To's first publication. Probably took three months to get it thru the press?   Would To's operations be dated from that time? Or from the time we left N Y to find the cheapest possible place to live, and a printer. Zuk would have started assembling mss at the same time   Well: I think we arrived in France in 1931   May have been 30   (I had become 21 (1929) and received a smallish inheritance   Smallish income
5) ["Were LZ and CR in on the To Publisher venture?"] Zuk edited.   Only he edited: he only edited   We supported Zuk (barely) during the life of To Publishers   Rezi not actively connected with To
6) Returned from France in '33
7) ["What role did you play on the Objectivist Press and for how long?"]   Account of forming Ob Press in Wms Autobiog. I saw the ms of the Autobiog in the [Beinecke] Rare Book Library in Yale: in its glass box, it is open to that page.   Longer account in the mss than in print   (((mention of my work in Wms Letter to Agee [to Nathanael West]   Also in Pound's letters[40]

Wms account, and the accounts in the Wisconsin interviews indicate, correctly, that each man simply emerged with his own book - - - No sales machinery if I remember - - - If there was, Rezi must have handled it

But Zuk, Rezi, Williams and I met each other at times -- not formally as Obj Pub, but there were discussions bearing on the matter --

But no plans: there really were no plans, nothing in the nature of a practical plan at all. We were a name: a name for the title-page, but also a name which indicated an area of poetry

8) ["Was the Obj Press continuous with To Publ. or was there a break in between?"] Let us take it that To Publishers ceased to exist when we left France.   Obj Press organized almost immediately on our return to N Y

9) ["Were you politically active while you were writing poetry?"]   No politics while writing

(I remember an attempt to describe in verse the first street-meeting we attended   Didn't preserve it -- (remember the phrase 'stitched each to each' - -)

10) Joined the C[ommunist] P[arty] in '35 I believe -- Possibly early '36

11) ["What were the circumstances of your military service during WW II?"]   More or less volunteered into WW2   i.e. Was working in Grumman Aircraft   Automatic deferment, my draft card carried that deferment --

Disillusioned with the C P   unable to do *nothing* about the war - - - I meant to enter it   But wanted to obtain qualification as a tool and die maker   Grumman using me in that capacity, but refusing the classification to avoid a pay raise   Without the draft board, or asking for deferment as father (or as somewhat overage, etc -- I went to Detroit and got a job as tool and die maker, which I held for some six months or more   Labor was 'frozen' of course, and one was drafted -- punitively -- for breaking the freeze in this manner   I knew of course that I would be

Served as transport Non-Com [Non-Commissioned Officer, or Sergeant] with the Anti-tank co: later as gunner.   103 Division: 411 Infantry Regiment.

Landed in the first 'wave' (tho there was no German resistance) at Marseilles: skirted Paris   (you will remember that story: Paris was left to the resistance and the French First army to take -- first saw action in the Vosges mountains (St. Pierre Le Haut) - - - wounded in Germany soon before V E Day   Hospital in Nancy - - -

88 mm shell landed in a fox-hole: Three of us were in that fox

hole

'The circumstances'[41]

———

Hurriedly written, Larry   Good enuf?
and best wishes   Glad you're writing the piece[42]
George

To Elizabeth Kray
[October 16?, 1969]   TLs   Academy of American Poets

Dear Betty
You'll be angry   and entirely right.   But I have to cancel this
tour   And forget it was ever offered[43]
It would seem I can't go into business as a famous man -- or half-
famous either.   I didn't know that about myself, or had forgotten
I don't know how to apologize: there is in fact no way
Betty, I'm sorry   I can no longer hear my own poetry, I will never
be able to write another line, I will never know myself again - - there is
no use starting on this track.   The books will have to fend for themselves   I
lack a public character: I am afraid I am incapable of it.
George

To [a selected list of people][44]
[October 16, 1969]   TLc   R. B. DuPlessis

[Handwritten salutation to each individual]
The carbon (the bad-form Letter) is a small part of the wreckage:
after two months of paper work arranging a tour, I sent telegrams
today cancelling all 'appearances.'   I do not now know how I came to
disregard the circumstance that I do not want to make a reading tour,
cannot in fact sustain it, and have no need to do it

'the arduous path of appearance'   [CP 70]   Rendered the more absurd during the month of anti-war demonstrations

I send these carbons to assist, as much as I can, in Betty Kray's explanations for the Academy

George

To Robert M. MacGregor [of New Directions]
[October 1969]   TLc   UCSD 16, 8, 16

Dear Bob:

-- an interminable mess of wiring colleges, writing to individuals, evasive apologies, cancelling reservations ---- sorry I forgot N D

No, not ill   Can't live or for that matter think, I discover, in the atmosphere of the poetry circuits   At 60 I cannot believe I have more than a couple of decades: I need them for myself

I think or hope the books will manage without me

Thanks for your concern

To John A. Ertola and other members of the Board of Supervisors,
San Francisco
November 2, 1969 (dated)   TLc   UCSD 16, 1, 7 and 16, 10, 3

Gentlemen:

I thank you for the honor which you have given me, though I receive it at a time when honors may mean little and that little for a very short time.[45] In this year which may present our last opportunity to withdraw from war I urge you to speak for the most crucial interests of the people of this city in asking that our young men be brought home out of Asia, out of Africa, out of Latin America, and that we may lead our lives as a sane people.

Sincerely,
George Oppen

To Alexander Mourelatos
[November 3, 1969]   TLs   UCSD 33, 1, 11

Dear Alex:

Zukofsky's *Bottom: On Shakespeare* is replete with Wittgenstein

I don't know if *Bottom* is included in the Norton Collected   But the Texas U library is probably strong on Zuk.[46]

Numerous -- or is it Route --- has the fly in the bottle, of course [CP 160]

Don't think off hand of citations   Auden once said that his crucial talent was the ability to know what to read next   He must surely some-time have read W. next

my talent is to know what never to have read, so I cannot give citations from Auden. Probably in there somewhere

W's *sense of language*   taken as the beauty of language, as a beau-tiful style   Not at all the beauty of despair, but the beauty of language, and I think it is a most beautiful language   would open up very difficult areas of discussion

and I don't think his work has been an 'influence' or a source in this respect   But may have been.

(that, I suppose, is precisely what your student suspects)

Little help from me.   But enthusiasm for the project

George

[During 1969, Oppen also corresponded with Anne-Marie Albiach, Philip and Margaret Booth, William Bronk, John Crawford, Theodore Enslin, Kathleen Fraser, Roger Guedalla, Michael Heller, David Ignatow, Stuart Montgomery (Fulcrum Press), Linda Oppen Mourelatos, Kathleen Norris (Academy of American Poets), Steven Schneider, Armand Schwerner, Charles and Brenda Tomlinson, Robert Vas Dias, and Diane Wakoski.]

1970

[In January, Oppen received proofs from Fulcrum and asked them to reset the final section; in early summer he received proofs again. The Oppens spent the summer from June 3 in Maine, on Little Deer Island. During the summer and fall, Mary Oppen began writing the poems later published in her *Poems and Transpositions* (Montemora, 1980).]

To George Johnston
[late 1969–early 1970]   TLs   The Public Archives of Canada

Dear George
        where did we leave off?   and which of us left off?   Been harrassed -- or harrassed myself.   The possibility of fame or 'fame' having been (perhaps) presented, had to adjust. After several foolish undertakings and idiocies, have been hiding - - From readings, etc. --- from, you might say, 'comparative literature'   read: competitive literature.
        I better remain slightly underground   Slightly (because we agree on this word) 'Northern.'   Troglodite
        ((((occurred to me that troglodyte should indeed be spelled with a 'y':   looked it up in the dictionary and my eye lit first not on that word but   *trioecious*: Bot. Having staminate, pistilate and hermaphroditic flowers on different plants
        Well: vague, as vague as any Sybilline utterance, but there's something about flowers, flowering, and something about alternatives to male competitiveness, something about the feminine, something about peace - - - and, well, - - - - - No use being superstitious
        No use not being either, of course   Anyway, I report the event.
        And, in brief, this is a report of my doings   Mostly to keep in touch
        ((our doings consist almost entirely of walking over the brown California hills and remembering our first year together))
                                    and to send regards
                                        George
((Continue to read in Gisli, and to find strength in it))

To Philip Levine
[late 1969–early 1970]   TLc   UCSD 16, 6, 23

Phil:

not sure whether I replied to your letter -- nothing I regard as pa-
thology, but I note with a certain dizzy feeling that I become markedly
elderly in my ways -- I no longer seem to keep track of mail --- or know
where anything *is* - - - - Well. A very odd thing to happen to a child.

But I was very much moved by the generosity of your letter. -- one
clause - - I didn't immediately understand - - I realized suddenly that I
must explain. I'd noticed in your poem which depicts me very happily
making myself a cup of coffee in your house: I'd recognized a mis-under-
standing in the poem, but the reference being to what I consider a minor
foible in myself, my 'stained hands'   Phil, my hands aren't stained: I
just never wash 'em adequately - - -[1]

brings us to autobiography:

-- born of a couple of rather millionaire lines -- in the generation of
my father, aunts, uncles becoming something on the order of the International Set, etc . . Disastrous, of course   My mother's suicide when I was
four,   an elder sister's suicide, my mother's sister, - - - -among the males
- - - - - commitments, deaths - - - I am in fact the only surviving male - - -.
'fully surviving,' right thru second cousins and such remotenesses[2]

--What happened is that Mary Colby and I walked off.   Ran off,
actually, being under-age at the moment of running.   A running of mi-
nors.   But We who were angry, we who saved our lives and loves - - no
dis-ownings, no fulminations   Stern children: not stern parents.   No
danger, ever, of our starving - -

(the story told in This In Which: 'The Forms of Love' [CP 86]
'parked in the fields / all night' That was Mary, 1927   The night of the
first day we'd met.   Some instinct, something Mary knew, tho how could
she know: she talked and talked of her three brothers: how they had
hoboed, jobs they had worked at, that she, Mary, had picked hops, had
picked cherries, that it wasn't hard, that . . .

I knew I was saved, There were such things as jobs, and I was
nobody but myself, we could do what we wanted, and I was saved -- I
hadn't expected to be.

well. that's how it was.   We lit out.   But a childhood of nurses,
butlers and what not - - (it's why I know how to sail) - - -and minor in-
heritances along the way, Phil, which is how Objectivist Press got founded

- - and finally a 'big' that is, a big enough inheritance, tho I have no older relatives who would have found it so - - -

AND,   I do not know if these last four books could have been written if I had worked to the age of retirement - - worked steadily in poverty - - I think they would not have, and I think, as you think, that it is a terrible thing to say.   We had help from the dead. Who wanted to die.

But the proletarian hero - - Not yet.   Or not me.   a *little*, a minor heroism, and a guardian angel - - Whose name I do not know, and my principles prohibit an attempt to guess - -

act of Providence.   Unearned.

To return: ----the unwashed hands: stigmata of rebellion.   There are some losses in rebellions)

(another small story: after the war.   We were in L A, I had been working in a tool and die jobbing shop, then started building tailor-made radios -- phonographs, and then with a partner building houses   Message that my father (in S F) was dying.   Hypochondriac family;   my father less ill than that, the meeting in his hospital room as equivocal, as difficult, as dangerous to me as all our meetings - - The nurse came into the room and asked me to wait outside a moment. I walked down the hall to a little waiting room and sat down. The floor-nurse on duty recognized me (I look like my father)   She said, I guess what a man cares most about in his life is his son.   I was startled, I was absolutely startled and absolutely unprepared.   My father's temperature was running fairly high, I realized that he must have talked of me. My face must have shown how startled and how unprepared I was. The nurse saw it, and she began to cry   God help us all.

———

Well, there it is.

Confession.   Some self-congratulation too.   Obviously.   Some cruelty on my part too - - - There it is.

--survival.   never a wholly admirable story.

To John Taggart
[after April 7, 1970]   TLs   The Fales Library, New York University

Dear John
the problem being   for you as for the rest of us   a syntax or some equivalent of a syntax sufficiently 'locked,'   sufficiently *simultaneous* ----

your work beautiful,   beautiful where finally the word, the single
word or what seems like a single word, does it

she dies, herself being
dead,   stiffly in the old manner.

Drums.[3]

(((but   as for the rest of us   the syntax of the construction
of an image can clog the poem at times?   )))) I think this is the problem
I'll get the relevant Origin of course   And will be very interested
to 'read you'   as fully as, for the moment, possible   'The moment'
being: that-which-is-in-print-at present[4]
Question as to Numerous????[5]   lengthy answers involved, possible
product of inaccurate memory too - - But in general: conceived as a process of thought, section by succeeding section: but very drastic revision,
rearrangement, re-writing (therefore)   involved: changes in the thinking
too --- something over a two-year process.   The first section written after
some third or so of the poem had been written down, and altered the
conception in my mind drastically --etc etc   Not much use in these   (probably inaccurate)   post not mortems but parturitions   Post Parturitions.[6]

regards
George

To Carl Rakosi
[Spring 1970]   Transcription by Rakosi   Houghton Library, Harvard
University; photocopies with annotations by CR at Rare Book Room,
Memorial Library, University of Wisconsin-Madison

Dear Carl R:
Your Leah in the latest Sumac: surely among the most delightful of
poems written---

protest of
Belial, your oaf, notwithstanding-----[7]

I thought it would be ungrateful not to drop you a line to say so- - -
though it is only a line   In fact, written most hurriedly on the eve of
departure for Maine
Best regards
(and neither do I mean to slight the other poems in Sumac   which

are, of course, another and contrasting matter   ((Yes: also found in 'the plain world'))   Interesting to think of this, these poems, as extension of your remarks in Madison[8]

>   and again: best wishes

>   '. . . . . .let us hug and romp
>   in the plain life
>   or I am lost!

despite the owl and the lizard and the beef it seems to me for the moment that this is all there is to say;   all one need say- - - -
Or I am lost

[no closing given on transcript]

To June Oppen Degnan
[July 1, 1970]   ALs   UCSD 16, 1, 7

June--
>   your letter arrives--
>   of course I agree: the Demo[cratic] Central Committee would be the best possible place to be: the most appropriate to you, and most surely the most useful
>   Good luck!

>   - - I was just now writing a note to myself, as follows:
>   The N.Y. poem (meaning of course *Numerous*) is intellectual and philosophic; The San Francisco Poems are atmospheric. I could not have written them differently. But I am fascinated by the thought of a 'philosophic' poem about a small and beautiful city
>   - - to be able to say what a small and sophisticated city *means*![9]

Not that I think I could.

(a young English poet, Anthony Barnett, sends me a magazine with some work of his in which he quotes me and which is written 'around' the S F poems -- -- says, e.g.

> The play begins with world
> Which might have been the word

The first line being a quote from *Morality Play: Preface*: the first of the S. F. poems.

His second line being good exegesis - - the story of Genesis (which includes the Adam and Eve which is the reference of my Morality Play) begins with the world - - or begins, to quote precisely:

> In the beginning was the Word
>   -- --

                                      and my poem ends:

> You will see the young couples
> Leaving again in rags

(hadn't meant to start a Review of myself: I was considering whether or not I had hinted something of the meaning of sophisticated small cities - - 'atmospherically' at least

------

Mary suddenly started writing poems in a notebook, one after the other - - Astounding purity, strength, self-confidence, simplicity - - well, what else?   (John Crawford having asked if he could print the Translations of St. John in his little mag [*West End*]. Mary started (I think) to write them out for him, and wrote these poems instead

- - no end in sight. The poems it seems will just keep calmly appearing - -[10]

The rest, as said, is sailing.   Punctuated - - punctured? comatized? - - by a storm these last two days. We came home on the first edge of it - - Something of a lollapalooza, to use the technical term

                          much love
                            George

[written in right margin] (Tired of typing - - tired of typing - - if this is difficult to read anywhere, don't bother. Just conversation.)

To June Oppen Degnan
[August 5, 1970]   TLs   UCSD 16, 1, 7

June dear ---   the Women: discussed for many years, and in the same terms by the old left   Nor do I disagree   All of it is true - - - -

There are forces other than the ideas of justice forcing this discussion   It is discussed not because it should happen but because it is happening   The special skills -- created by tradition in part, by tradition based on the disadvantages of women as militants, no doubt, that is to say, tradition created by force, but also perhaps having to do with special qualities of femininity - - - but however the skills appeared their value is decreasing   The polarity between men and women is decreasing   And with that,   the need of women for *a* man, the need of men for *a* woman is decreasing   The broadening of sexual mores also contributes to this - - - - or the reverse: both men and women risk sexual freedom as their need for monogamy declines - - -

this paragraph too long and too sententious, or too obvious, I mean: it is what is happening   It will most surely happen   I think of it -- in my way -- as 'good' in that it is a part of the process which is occurring, the process which is existence   Something is happening!   Time is not a flow of nothing,   it seems to me we must think of time as creative, as truly unrolling, as not already there to begin with --- A process   My word 'good' is - - - - what? Faith?   Impatience, the desire to *arrive*   ? that is, to know?   But this about women, about mommas, about wives, about the pretty girls, the pretty girls - - - - - it's happening   Probably it's 'good' ---

I don't know how to measure happiness   The issue is happiness, there is no other issue, or no other issue one has a right to think about for other people, to think about *politically,* but I don't know how to measure happiness

-- and for more than that the issue is happiness: the 'issue,' the question at issue for human life is the possibility or the impossibility of happiness   but how to measure???

-- and will women tend to measure a little differently from men, or men from women?   I don't know   But most certainly no such theory of sexual differences, even if one could arrive at a theory, would justify an attempt to define an individual woman to herself - - I am, obviously, talking of freedom.   I'm for it   Even furiously for it: of course I am.

(((to say that something is happening, to say that time is creative, that it is not the unrolling of a script already written, is to say 'freedom' (The physicists have their little ways, but time and space are not really the same thing ---)

and as for freedom for women: to say, which is really the way I think of it,   I'm for you   For Andy   For Mary,   Linda,   Aub, --------- And believe in them.

George

The pretty girls, the pretty girls,
Their hair hangs down with love
They did so love the silly men,
The silliest men,
Such as I was

––––––

(and men less and less willing to support a woman, less and less able and with less and less need to do so -- Another economic breakdown of a slave system)

––––––

––––––

Vive la similitude!

To Robert Creeley
[October 3, 1970]   TLs   Washington University Libraries

Dear Creeley:
        my sister a short while ago asking me to have lunch with Gene McCarthy, assuring me for the nth time that he wanted above all else in this world to converse with poets - - - I said, well, make it Duncan, Creeley, Oppen Following which it was discovered that you would be -- somewhere, somewhere in the East I think -- on the day McCarthy'd be here;   following which it was discovered that McCarthy['s]   plans might

be altered - - - Seemed to be getting too difficult   Also I remind myself
that I am in the phone book, and if McCarthy wanted . . . . . .

Did you know of these maneuverings?   thought you might like a
run-down

((nevertheless there's a nice story about McCarthy: being driven to
the airport by someone urging him to run again who said, as perora-
tion: We have no one but you! And McCarthy said, yes: Isn't it terrible.

which might be adequate reason for lunch   Had it been a little
easier[11]

However: no reason not to have dinner sometime   or other
visit   The Bobbies, Mary and I?   since you're not in the phone book
- - - - our phone is 415 (from Bolinas)   771   1615

we'd like to see you
George

To Philip Booth
October 10, 1970 (dated)   TLs   Philip Booth

Dear Philip:

My kindred -- from a distant land -- that distant land, the world
one slowly wakes to[12]

Always wakes to   And always slowly at each waking.   The sea
that makes us islands   The margins

So much poetry being written, being recited these days and so little   :   we are truly grateful to you

-- I've been shaken somehow or other this last year, Phil   which
is somehow or other, I suppose, responsible for our failing to get to Castine
again, tho I forget the details of that -- Bad weather once, I remember, and
we turned back - - But we've been doing odd things ---- the 'world' of
poetry: too much for our sense of who we are and who and whatever we
are not -- Little stability gained in being 62:   I'm afraid that's bad news.

But our regards   ALL our regards
George

((((McCarthy I see ACKNOWLEDGING A DEBT TO YOU (the caps
are an accident of my typing -- an accident involving my thumb)   the

prosodic debt obvious   and the poems are of course a bit loose   But the poem about the third act: one can remember that[13]

and a man 'running' as himself! that may become history, an upturn in our history

in which you and poetry --- My God, Poetry! -- have had a part

the poets lie too little - - - I am forever expecting them to be excluded from the Republic!   in which case there would, come to think of it, be nothing left at all

To Harvey Shapiro
[after November 1, 1970]   TLs   Harvey Shapiro

Dear Harvey

I've been thick-headed -- wrapped up in my bits and pieces   Didn't know it was important to you that we should talk   I'd have come thru N Y

will now if it's warranted   I would like to: this is not pure motherliness say what you think   Not too hard   or even too extravagant just to get on a plane

eager to see the book   Won't ask how you feel about it[14]   What I said seems to come out all right -- one could have improved the language a bit   But it does make some points about your work which need making   Beyond 'vitality,' beyond intervention   of course I should have said --

Hugh S   Well, it is very very impressive   The verse   One would say, if it were prose, a most impressive stylist[15]

-- a novelistic quality, finally: one remembers it as if one were remembering a novel -- the sound of the verse aside   And it is that confessional gadget makes it a 'novel'   one sees it, as a story of the young man in L A, coming to San Francisco, then to N Y   A story   Carrying that 'wound'

and --- I don't know   'story' never seems to me adequate   And the confessional pretty uncomfortable.   Remarkable that he can handle it

But I think surely the handling of verse is assurance he'll emerge to very considerable rank in his generation   I don't see how not

----(I thought, *your* influence replacing Zuk's   Then Mary reminded me you had written that you felt my influence in it   Well, certainly some debt to you   And, there is a quote from me ((that I know Vallejo St near Presidio (near Presidio Ave)   that it is in fact my adolescent background, or a part of it -- adds to the novelistic quality   'the poisoned needle in the upholstery' !   very good indeed   very novelistic, of course   Young poet: rich girl, etc

all regards -- all friendship

George

((my bits and pieces adhering finally in the S F Poems   Final version in the Fulcrum Collected, if that ever does come out   Now some ten months late   Been writing him threatening letters recently,   and may withdraw it[16]   Laughlin says don't: he admires Fulcrum's list - -

I don't know   Haven't thought about it much   Just afraid the *length* of the delay is becoming ludicrous

-- and, finally, -- last couple of months -- I'm able to write lines without absurd and self-destructive labor

I did want you to see the final version of the S F poems   and have been expecting the book.   Since that seems delayed beyond calculation   (tho last promised it will be out in Jan) [1971; actually published December 1972]   I'll send you my ms copy   via ground mail

I'd very much like to hear you on the subject

George

To Hugh Seidman
[after November 10, 1970]   TLs   Hugh Seidman

Hugh

Poisoned needle discovered in the upholstery: you should be safe from the Jet Set   Which grows old as horse-hair and the overstuffed -- ('videotapeempire' you write)

'to me, now, the problem is to bring the poems and life out of misery into joy . . . . . or are all poems joyful, almost in the mathematical sense . . . '[17]

yes, but too narrow, too close a focus   Louis' emphasis, not mine   Say Geometry?   a measuring of the world   Or between these alternatives, see A 12 toward the close   'What, Goddess' and the following lines

very beautiful, I think   Very moving   Very simple,   very honorable

And -- not irrelevant to praise of this kind -- 'whether purity is a cop out' - - - at times: no joke.

———

I forgot what I wrote you   Praise surely   Harvey [Shapiro] wrote to say I should see the book, and to ask what I thought of it   I wrote him that I was much impressed   And added that I feel the narrative structure as both a strength and a weakness   A technical strength, but a weakness

((The 'wound' and the travels producing, I think, the impression of narrative - - -

Given now greater depth by your remark quoted above

And yes, finally yes, one must find a way to live outside of or in-dependent (essentially) of -- one might say -- Comparative Literature

But indeed one must find a way to 'live,' meaning finances   Let me know if I can help on tours etc

Best regards
George

To Dan Gerber
[November 15, 1970]   TL   Dan Gerber

[no salutation]

HAVE you read Reznikoff   not Testimony, but The Waters of Manhattan   N D 1962!   and some of the poems date from 1918!!

and or would you?

the difficulty being that poets and poet-students are the audience of poetry   They read and praise work they can learn from, have learned from   There is nothing to be learned from Reznikoff

consummate art, consummate craftsmanship   And a man walking the streets of New York, his head -- his Jewish head -- full of history

specifics if need in Zuk's   Sincerity and Objectification - - - which I suppose is reprinted in the Collected Prose   No use repeating[18]

You've doubtless noted Hugh Seidman

this being not a Dream   of Ezra, but my duty as (supernumerary) member of the Committee of Correspondence)

[no closing signature]

To Dan Gerber
[November 27, 1970]   TLs   Dan Gerber

Dear Dan
        No -- don't misunderstand   I think of Rezi as a very great poet
        one cannot learn Fashion, the Night Town of poetry from Rezi   I
would not have urged you to read him had I supposed you wanted to learn
THAT   I knew you did not.
        but one learns that poetry can matter, and can matter very much
        as you so beautifully and whole-heartedly say.
        and I've just read Levertov's Relearning the Alphabet -- the final
section of the book -- the section under that title[19]   Read and reread all
afternoon and evening - - - Dazed, drunk, surely a great poem ---------- I
was dazed and drunk with the life of the poetry   Her poem *Matins*, a
poem recounting domestic details of a morning ends with a door   'Cold
air / came in at the street-door' -- it is as if she had walked out that door,
opened the door and gone forth ------

        Damn damn damn Harper and Row   Your editor is speaking, del-
icately, of the depression, the current economic depression. Your editor of
course guiltless   And a nice woman, sorrowing in the movies   ((the point
is that there ARE such editors these days and once there were not and it's
not a bad world that hath such editors in it
                        I await your book
        ((hope to see you here   We have a spare room -- two passable beds
in it   if you want to borrow the use of it
                                George

To Dan Gerber
[late December 1970]   TLs with AL addition   Dan Gerber

Dear Dan
        thanks for the E Knight   Yes, a beginning   Clean writing;   a
beginning   Not without an element of 'pulp' writing?   honorable cleaned
up   (or down)   Maybe the way to begin
        I think of the Sherwood Andersons and such (the Anderson of
Winesburg Ohio) Lost history;   perhaps not readable now, but also a

beginning   A lot of time has passed   The difference in this is impressive[20]

thanks again

George

the 'thee' could almost have been Anderson Or should have been   Couldn't have been   The leap made here without fuss   Confidence in one's readers

I am something of an historical optimist

there's a line in Anderson (one of the poems)

'we wanted to know if we were any good out there'

((out there   being, tho I can't prove it, nothing like a minor Woodstock or night club))[21]

a beginning   Toward breaking the Cannon   Escaping the Cannon

(which I here carelessly transformed into an artillery piece ----- having visited some universities[22]

((but K[night] taking a lot, and too easily from the 'Pop' poetry-- to call it that -- the poetry of life-style etc isn't he? The canon of Woodstock   the easy canon of Woodstock   Nevertheless - - something! I agree.

To Hugh Seidman
[December 29, 1970] TLs   Hugh Seidman

Dear Hugh

Louis' simplicities   Louis' ambivalences -- and from there to Selden Rodman ----- the letter ringing with overtones and undertones about which, or in the noise of which I would write all too long[23] and circular a letter   Without saying anything you'll not have thought about ----

--- young poet, Ross Feld, writes in a letter that arrived in the same mail with yours:

' we take advantage of the artificial to speak, to forget for a moment our humiliation'[24]

and even this too dignified   A tactic of survival, survival of the spirit for those unrecognized for forty years -- Like Louis   becoming more and more --- and never entirely separated from -- a tactic also of competition

　　But Selden Rodman　?　Are any of the men he supports actually popular?

　　an old joke:　The people in a capitalist democracy possess a purely formal and theoretic right to elect their government, whereas in the communist countries the government possesses an actual and effective right to elect the people

———

　　alright, alright.　All this too simple, I know　and too clever　But as for 'Your wife's here / and your boy

　　and below

　　'It's so simple

　　Telemachus rose from his bed

　　and dressed' --- the compassionate stately beauty of simple narrative[25]

　　simply, one can't do it very often　And if one does it very often it is not only inadequate, it is not true - - - -

　　But it IS true that the world of the little mags is a very silly world indeed and I can very well understand the need to　 to know more than that!

　　that is:　I find your letter very moving　 And haunting　 (Mary too--)

　　　　　　　　　　　　　　　　　　George

To Diane Meyer
[1970?]　TL　ucsd 16, 7, 29

Andy -- you spoke of depth, the 'third' dimension -- however you said it　I was startled　 Been thinking about it a little

　　I think I don't care at all about design, pattern across the paper, the canvas, or the poem's surface　 Or the rock rhythm going in a straight line across the time　*Across*　time　 I'm not sure I ever visualize anything but depth . . . Or a point, a detail so sharply defined that I'm shaken by the implication of space

Diane Meyer (Andy) and George, circa 1970.

like describing a wave in the middle of the sea
I notice the 'new' poems -- like the 'old' ones say it over and over:

'Scope, mere size, a kind of redemption
Exposed still and jagged on the San Francisco hills'
[CP 220]

and elsewhere:

'Archangel

of the tide
brimming

in the moon-streak

         comes in whose absence
earth crumbles'
[CP 222]

———

Don't know.   I'd like to try to think about this   What it means,
what we're talking about

I have a feeling that whatever this is, this is what we are always
talking about   Never quite understand each other

((and again, the [']ity's['] because they stand in the middle of distances, and the [']nesses['] because they fill the room like a wash of color
- - - across the paper

And I don't care about them, they annoy me like a distraction

((O, of course the ugliness of the 'hole in the wall'   my objection
is not to the hole but to the wall)[26]

[In 1970, Oppen also corresponded with John Bracker, Jane Cooper, John
Crawford, Rachel Blau DuPlessis, Theodore Enslin, Maria Gitin, Eve
Haight, Shirley Kaufman, Elizabeth Kray, Deirdre Montgomery, Stuart
Montgomery, Carl Rakosi, Charles Reznikoff, Charles Tomlinson, Robert
Vas Dias, Eliot Weinberger, and J. D. Whitney.]

1971

[In 1971, by mid-April, Oppen felt that *Seascape: Needle's Eye* was solidifying as a manuscript.[1] Oppen and Carl Rakosi met, May 12, at the Rakosi reading at San Francisco State University. The Oppens spent the summer in Maine. By the end of the year, Oppen had arranged for the publication of *Seascape: Needle's Eye* with Rain Press.]

To Diane Meyer
[1971?]   TL with AL addition   UCSD 16, 7, 29

Andy,   I guess you do alright from inside that peanut butter can   I, at least, couldn't have written that letter.   Perhaps I do learn from you.   I want so very much to hear about women;   the men are insane[2]
        I think, frankly, that women are dumb but men are insane. You will see I am a humanist
        I am being less wild than you think.   I am -- maybe not a humanist, but most certainly a peanutbuttercanist: I'll accept nothing at all, no thinking at all that doesn't bring them along   Our companions, our companions on the road, our less talented companions maybe, the peanut butter cans: but to disregard such things is just to spin arbitrary ideas
        Meanwhile, or at the moment -- to repeat -- I think nothing at all, or think to no purpose. You better believe it.   I tell jokes and spin stories for want of anything better to say.   IF   I had any purpose in mind in telling you about the women of the family it was not to say I think you are my Grandmother Op: I may have had in mind to tell you that you come from an astonishingly long line, thru Libby, of unregenerate, unmodified, uncontrolled females.   Astonishingly long.   I am just trying to make camp in it ---- as comfortably as possible in primitive conditions and, like Paul [Andy's son], I wear my hunting knife
        he and I will get somewhere!   You watch and see

To Carl Rakosi
[1971]   Transcription by Rakosi   Houghton Library

Dear Carl:
   there's no firmer verse than your best   Dazzling and absorbing
   --yes, a contradiction in my words   Nor my fault: your virtue.
   And yes, a friend of 35 years   Always thought so, for that matter.   Happily verified.
   (((((I was much impressed, almost most impressed, by the lines of
'IN THY SLEEP',.....which in the book happen to be the second page of
the poem[3]
   ---reading it: I feel the poem should have ended with the first
page....The poem seems absolutely immovable in that form[4]
   I just report this--   re-action on first reading)))))
   (((notice again that J Laughlin takes us as friends of 35 years: my
books mentioned on your back cover
   'on your back cover'   :   neighborly indeed
   Again: there's no finer verse   Dazzling
   (and this from an old friend   Old old friend
                              [transcription provides no
                              closing]

To Charles Tomlinson
[January 24, 1971]   TL   Charles Tomlinson

Dear Charles
   'I liked the street for its sordid /   fiction of a small town order'
has become the picture of Henry Street for me[5]   'The image':   is
not a picture, is it, it remains the words - - - - the size of the words, I was
going to say   I don't know if I can say the thing clearly   Obviously I
haven't done so   here.   But the words become Henry Street for me
   and I also remember you and Brenda silhouetted against the (also
grimy) harbor
   Odd paradises, we find   But we find 'em.
                    A sense of proportion?
   Odd strengths.   My talent for grimness   Your aristocracy of work-
ing-class roots -- an aristocracy of roots   The contrary of the finagler
From whence the cadences of your poetry.   - - - I've been wondering,

since you write of resistance to your work, whether (as a form of statecraft) you should not undertake a more stately statement, a more full dress statement of your position   Of your state, stance   of your dignity   Yes, I know it's stated in the poems.   But if 'the critics' are implying that it is old stuff ? ? ? 'the primary elements can only be named' It is so damned difficult to make these people, 'the critics,' recognize the blatant mysteries

this last is Mary's phrase, talking to me a few days ago - - that old jade, their appetites, are whetted (or is it supposed to be wetted) by eagles with umbrellas in their beaks and such and such and such[6]

To Sarah Appleton Weber
[late February 1971]   TLs   UCSD 16, 11, 26

Sally

Mary's been talking about the Theology of the Middle English lyrics -- and quoting -- And both of us much moved[7]

On the sheaf of poems   I'll take quite some time to read and think and re read   And to write you   I want to write you now, tho, briefly - - It will perhaps begin a colloquy which may carry us further than some critique of my own from my own room might do

I'd like to try a version -- a re-version   To save hours and hours of typing, maybe, in order to say what I think   And you will know at once if you agree at all to my purposes - -- Well, let's try it[8] [. . .]

I mean: the words will NOT make the poem: the poem must make, remake, restore the words   They must be earned, at the very least   They won't earn a poem for you

'radiance'

Silence itself   precious life   ecstasy of our dreams
. . . . .
BUT WE HAD ALL THESE WORDS BEFORE YOU WROTE THEM
DOWN   AGAIN.

I admire and like the clear, the open spots in your work very much
I mind the barriers you erect very, very much
Just, at the least, strike them out   Cross them out
In the resultant open air you'll find some poems   and you   and, I think, the children   And Joe

And the theology of lyrics

Love, if one loves, is not felt as virtue   I canNOT bear: 'we are aware of our distance from perfect love'   This is outside the province of comment on the verse. But - - - who will not feel it?

I think only one's song will save one, redeem one --- something we may call 'song'   But then one must trust it   Value it   Not, at the least, HATE   you know this

the 'song' is oneself   And the world   But if, then, one is afraid of oneself?

I think one needs courage   'Leave all you have behind'   were those the words?   leave all you thought you should have or be behind.   I said I believe in the benevolence of the real.   I do.

And I think therefore the Chestnut Tree still stands in the verse Still stands as poetry[9]

Eternity in an hour   or, rather, a moment   Surely not in a journal   Leave all you think you should have or be behind and the poem begins to glimmer, to form in the mind

we are sleeping

but I am awake
Let this be the place of our dreams

although I do not know how to write them down

'I pray to you for your laugh'

———

———

You won't think I write in anger or rejection or, my God, contempt.   I know how hard it is to earn a poem.[10]

written in some passion, however   Not because of the spots I think bad, but because of the spots I think beautiful
IT TAKES YEARS SOMETIMES TO FIND ONE LINE

———

George

What, what, what do they say in the colleges? ? ? ? ?

To Dan Gerber
[June 22, 1971]   TLs   Dan Gerber

Dan

a man who can spell dilsexia [sic] ain't got it   Or not *bad.*
otherwise, things as they were?

As for my letter-style: can't be done as $E = mc^2$ much as I admire
such things   The e the m the c -- the letters of the alphabet, we should
be able to handle   And Energy,   o certainly Energy, therefore -- my
god,   have I produced a scientific discovery? -- therefore no equals

no, not a discovery   That's the business of entropy isn't it   It's
been spoken of

Nevertheless, if I were not now self-conscious about the epistolary
style you praise and which I had considered merely high wide and possibly
handsome, I would say something about breaking the words, the sentences,
the locutions *open* to make some room for ourselves   Here among the
subatomic fragments

But I meant to write to say only: Departure   And from the slope
of Tamalpais which is as it should be[11]

George

To June Oppen Degnan
[Summer 1971?]   TLs   ucsd 33, 1, 12

June dear, I'll type this out.   The strain in conversation is pretty great
Fascism and repression have played a major part in our personal lives, and
tho I believe very firmly that one should be able to think and to re-think
anything, the discussion of Franco and Nixon   is quite a stretch --
my voice tends to get out of control.

I'll type it out:

Alfonso, under pressure, fled   (to Cannes?)   Elections in Spain installed a Republican government.   Franco, a Spanish general stationed in
North Africa was in command of Spanish troops and a large number of
colonial (Moorish) troops. With additional arms furnished by Germany
and Italy, he invaded Spain. The republic was blockaded from arms ship-
ments, they possessed no planes or anti-aircraft guns at all -- Franco continued to be supplied by Germany   The war was long, nevertheless, and
very murderous   You were pretty young: the bombing of Guernica made

less impact on you than on many people of our age   It is not yet forgotten tho

Franco -- a long war, but he won   Followed a considerable slaughter (which continues) (('mildly')) Ten thousand men   it is said   were shot on a single occasion soon after the war in the bull ring -- Garcia Lorca among them.

This surely is not what you want   Is it?   with your very strong sentiment against physical violence, surely this is NOT what you want   Or admire In American terms: a general now in Vietnam returns with American and Vietnamese troops - - - - -   ?

Let us stop talking about Franco

Nixon.   Yes, I see the point. But Nixon surely is forcing a fight on organized labor   The unions may not make a wage demand without government permission -- AND the efficiency clause is an invitation to lay-offs, the creation of an unemployed pool. Yes, one sees: the U S can compete in the world market -- and control internal inflation -- by reducing wages.   And controlling them.   yes, yes;   but it will not be a peaceful country!! It will NOT

(discouraging: obviously now it will be 'wise' for the Democrats to nominate something like Humphrey.   To nominate anyone better will only split the labor vote, which they can have if they nominate a Humphrey   That's what they'll do. I agree it's discouraging

and that I'm no use in these questions --except that I do know something, remember something, about Fascism and proto-Fascism . . . . and don't think you would like them.

George

To Stuart Montgomery / Fulcrum Press
September 1, 1971 (dated)   TLc   UCSD 16, 4, 43

Dear Stuart Montgomery:

I've been pre-occupied with new work and rather deliberately, tho with some feeling of inadequacy and guilt, put the matter of the [Fulcrum] Collected out of my mind.   It has nevertheless been a somewhat nagging preoccupation and I would like to get the matter cleared up You will have noticed that my last letter rather carefully discarded all possibilities of 'litigation' -- if any had ever existed -- and I believe there is no present reason why we cannot deal informally and frankly from here on

As follows:

If the Collected is due to appear in the near future, would you tell me the approximate date

If you don't wish to print the book, would you release it. I am quite sure there could be no difficulty with N[ew] D[irections] over this since they will see that my last letter makes any *date* of publication unenforceable

If you wish to print, but are in some way delayed and cannot state an approximate date, or must state a date rather distant, I would take the opportunity (very gladly) to alter the final section of the book, and to make a new contract with you

If you don't wish to print I will, of course, have the opportunity to make these revisions and to send the book elsewhere, which will be equally satisfactory to me

I am unable or perhaps unwilling to believe that the matter cannot be cleared up in this way, and I am eager to be released from this preoccupation

With regards

((please do reply promptly

To Michael Cuddihy
[October 1971]   TLs   Michael Cuddihy

Dear Michael

yes surely I see your point[12]

But

'crimson'   because the girl possesses her own blood   That is, the doubleness of 'crimson' in that syntax

and less obliquity for similar reasons. I like the poem well enough I'm using it in a collection But I am no means solemn about it   The poem faulty from the start in that the last line is 'revelatory' and wrongly.   'Arranged'

Depth, the possibility of learning from one's own poem -- no, the

fact of having learned -- all this that can be called *music*   is, one
hopes, in other poems

　　　But I think it is worth printing   If you also think so, print
it.   if not not   the revision made while putting together the collection: it stands rather differently in a larger collection   Do as you wish,
of course

　　　　　　　　　　　　　　　　　　George

To Harvey Shapiro
[1971 or early 1972]   TLs with AL postscript   Harvey Shapiro

Dear Harvey

　　　yes, fame,   yes, fame.   Can't bear much fame, can't bear much
neglect   Your very self injured by fame, the poems insulted and injured
by neglect   (to put a lot briefly; 'the poems' means in part to have spoken
and not been heard, to have said and not been heard)))))

　　　Nothing seen from prominence, too much seen in the ditch[13]

　　　((I have a longish poem about the years of non-writing and
such   I'll   I was going to say I'll copy it out, but it was in Sumac   Book
of Hours   You see it?   if not I'll send a copy[14]

　　　Negotiating with N D as to whether or not I can let Bill Henkin and
associates bring out a thirty page book: i.e.,   I want to know if N D will
be willing to reprint those poems in a longer book --- say, a year or two
years from now.   I have somewhere around 25 pages I would guess
Haven't made final selections.

　　　I was unsure of the work, very unsure   And the early versions very
faulty. Been slow.   Been almost unwilling.   Sense of helplessness now
and then   Acted upon, fusions of subject and object, being acted upon

　　and that has to do in some way, it would take a great deal of time to
work this out in typescript -- something to do with fame and neglect   'how public, like a frog' in either case   Or froggish in any
case, public or not.[15]

　　　yes and one doubts poetry. Not, for me, the fact that no 'ordinary'
person reads it -- I don't really think about that.   But one says so little
- - -- one knows so little   we know so little before and after we have read
George Oppen   We've *said* so little, compared to what's happened
[one paragraph cut about a visitor]

　　　seem to be typing worse than usual. I see I'll have to go over this letter with a pen   Somewhat discourages me from going further   And hard to talk of the question you raise: what one wants, to know what one wants, to move toward it - - - What is it? Fear of loss of oneself as one knows himself, is familiar with himself? ? 'Fusion of subject and object' where all is acted upon?   I don't know   I suppose fear's a great part of our lives   I don't know

George

[typing apology]

To Michael Heller
[after December 6, 1971]   TLs with AL addition   Michael Heller

Mike
        glad you've initiated this correspondence - - - your definition of the 'political' and much else. But difficult to reply adequately partly because I am doing a great deal of work, and partly because I am not   i.e., not sure what is getting accomplished - - in poor shape to pontificate, and not wishing to lose your admiration - -[16]
        Tried --nevertheless -- to re-write your quotation from Erich Heller:
        The type of mind necessary to the artist --- or simply the mind of interest -- is touched always by experience, by particulars;   cannot remain within dogma, no dogma but this   which is not dogma but another and overwhelming force which we speak of or speak of nothing
        something like that, maybe   in order not to speak of any kind of *correctness*   other than awe - -
        Or better said in your question -- deliberately un-answered, which is its point:
        'Is it a poetry that one writes   ?'
        my refusal of the word 'dogma' above is questionable: this is,   of course, the question one MUST not attempt to answer or think of answering, this is what's wrong with all the 'courses' is it not?   The question: 'is it a poetry that one writes?'   is the question not to answer
        Is it a *poetry* that one writes?   Don't answer
        Is it a poetry that one *writes*?   alright: one's typewriter and desk could answer this.
        and this can sustain discussion: the act of *writing*[17]

George

(and yet, you know, it is a poetry.   The proof is this: a syllable wrong, a consonant or a vowel, and it has not been said - - The ear tells one   One revises and revises again: if it CANNOT be made right, there is something wrong with what one has said, has thought to do - - The ear tells one   There are things that cannot be put in a lyric - - or to reverse the old saw: anything too damn silly to be sung can nevertheless be said   After a fashion .

wow,   O wow, as they say, I've told you everything!

(will be glad to meet John Perlman)

To Brenda Webster

[1971–72?]   TLs   Brenda Webster

Brenda

I think the essay has value[18]   The finding of specific Freudian-accepted, Freudian-recognized symbols in what is usually taken to be the typically 'adolescent' quality in poetry -- 'Impersonality and the denial of the physical'

The temptation to that impersonality, the temptation of impersonality would remain -- so that the terms of therapy are not altogether irrelevant in speaking of the poetic advance   Alright.

and this, I don't doubt, is the background to the later poetry [of Yeats].   (I don't doubt that it is a bit rare to write very great poetry in adolescence)   But the great, late poetry --- do you think it may be the beast   moving toward Jerusalem [slouching toward Bethlehem]   ?   or, quoting   (from distant memory) Eliot: 'a man does not write poetry after the age of 29 unless he develops an historical sense' -- or, a sense of history   I don't suppose there is a children's history: one would have to feel himself *there* among the adults - - - This is pretty much the process

My objection is not to anything in the essay, which is fine: but only to say that this is the root of the poetry, and of its force for us   The poetry must, of course, have a root, a source, other than   'cure' of what ailed one   ?   You do not, at moments, seem to assume a force, a root, other than 'cure' or the normal process of aging

((objection to the first sentence: *mystical* and *concrete* are not antonyms, nor even contrasts.   It happens that 'mystical' and '*common*-sensical' are very precise antonyms   I can see the difficulty of using the

word   My underlining probably is not sufficient to call attention to the
literal meaning   But the *common*   sense of these things brings us to -
- - - - history, destiny.

        -- a further step, then, in the discussion of poetry   Not individual
therapy but - - - a force, some force. The harp that hung on Tara's wall,   the
harp that hangs on everyone's wall, really --

        alright, alright: it does when they're old enough -- it does when they're
too damn old

George

[In 1971, Oppen also corresponded with Charles Amirkhanian, Jane Cooper,
John Crawford, L. S. Dembo, Kathleen Fraser, Gary Gach, Eve Haight, Linda
Oppen Mourelatos, Geoffrey O'Brien, Charles Reznikoff, Ethel Schwabacher,
Armand Schwerner, Hugh Seidman, A. C. Spectorsky (*Playboy* magazine),
Tony Stoneburner, and J. D. Whitney.]

1972

[In February, Oppen asked his lawyers to terminate the contract for the publication of *Seascape* with Rain Press; soon after, in March through May, he read proof of *Seascape: Needle's Eye* for Sumac Press (Dan Gerber, ed.).[1] On May 3, Oppen read at San Francisco State University.[2] The Oppens went to Maine early (by mid-May) and, after a stormy, windy summer, returned to San Francisco via Canada, taking a rail trip across the continent.[3] In a letter from early October, Oppen reported, "a few poems since Horizon Few, but they're steps. Gain a line at a time."[4] In November 1972, *Seascape: Needle's Eye* was published by Sumac Press, and on December 20, Fulcrum Press (England) published their long-delayed edition of Oppen's *Collected Poems*.]

To Shirley Kaufman
[1972?] TLc UCSD 16, 6, 4

Shirley:
        (once more: I am very glad to have heard cantor Reich, and thank you for it)[5]
        ((too consciously 'pretty' at moments tho? I wish you'd heard that minute of the Cantor on [Sunday,] Bloody Sunday -- it's a very great minute -- but I cannot overcome a claustrophobia finding myself (when Reich was not singing) as [at] a card-party, a soirée, an Old Grad's day among a collection of people who know the nature of god because their parents told them -- as Eckhart rightly said of the Christians, that god would not be god enough for a flea - - - that room holds something less than a flea's world, a cozy half-of-a-flea --
        no worse than a flea's no better, no different, not even two halves of the flea The same half No escape; I come close to panic Panic because unquestionably, consciously deep in my blood - - - (DO see Bergman's *The Touch* : if you had seen it or when you have seen it I could

say deep in my sexuality without seeming absurd, arbitrarily absurd)   deep
in whatever I have is that story you tell again or speak of in the Introduction
to Kovner's poem[6]   Indeed it is deep in my blood, and I know it. There
is never any time when I do not know it. - - - - I do not really like the fleas'
god as I may have indicated, I feel more furiously isolate at card-party-bingo-
church-picnic office parties Catholic Protestant or Jewish - - as I would perhaps feel more alone among gossiping dolphins than among the fleas themselves those without speech   Afraid I am one of the Jews' Jews, stiff-
necked persons in the singular, I'll come to no good end   Who however
does?

     ((those who'd find manhood or womanhood at Masters and Johnson
or God in the synagogues, temples churches, parish houses vicarages?

     ((sorry I got to writing cleverly just above: the story your introduc-
tion refers to, the story from which Kovner emerges is surely my blood[7]

     (It is an incredible story, an incredible story, and thru all the little
shtetl jokes, shtetl card-parties we know it to be true!

     I didn't want to protest --- you had resolved not to 'force' the work
on me, but of course I want to read it.   Sat up a while last night
reading the introduction   We'd been up since 5 am or so, and I read not
more than half   Very moved again by the -- I've been calling it 'the
story' -- Caught up in it again - - I see that I would need the Introduction,
I would not, for one thing, have caught the meaning of the Hebrew words
thru their references to the Talmud   I might have recognized the ladder,
surely would not by myself have understood the drunken man, or not fully
----- But also don't and could not understand the Introduction   without
the poem   Do send it please (do you have a xerox?)

Shirley: again thanks for the evening   I am not contending, you know:
found this on my mind, unable to start work, and so I wrote it out (thus
far: not very far

To Dan Gerber
[January 11, 1972]   TLs   Dan Gerber

Dear Dan
     the Kremlin's informal elegance -- or ranch-house stylishness --
always a delight.   But I would rather burrow for stones, roots   coals
     or black water

As you would.[8]

Discrete Series?   I still don't think it difficult: still a little troubled by the accusation

- - a place   a place at least to begin.   But place in another sense: place without the words, the wordless sphere in the mind -- Or rather the wordless sphere with things   including a word or so   in it . . . . That I still believe to be, as they say, Poem: the thing in the mind before the words   to be able to hold it even against the language - - -

anyway, they mean what the later poems mean.   More raggedly done   Best I could do

'the knowledge not of sorrow . . . but of the world weather-swept' (the first poem in the book) and perhaps the closed car, closed in glass - - I haven't looked at the book writing this but it seems to me these should carry - - On the whole, I respect their silences: if I'm saved the silences saved me [CP 3 and 6]

(and of course, who's saved?)

How'd I get into this?   haven't thought about the book   In a long time   My impression that I got some of the notes more or less right Where it goes wrong, the notes too 'low,' probably   Too low in the musical scale - - - - something like that.

really wanted to write about what one knows but could not have said before the poem.   Always the issue to me, this is.   It is what writing to one's peers means.

odd thing to say with me being so instructive (and / or defensive)

I ascribe it to the influence of the Kremlin

all our affection   OURS, note

George

To Alexander Mourelatos
[before February 14, 1972]   TLs   UCSD 33, 1, 11

Dear Alex

came across your fine letter   (from Heidelberg) on *Numerous*   And I don't know if I ever answered adequately. It is surely among the best letters I've received -- 'ours . . . ourselves' (as you quote) : i.e.   yours --- yourself --- with the depth of oneself   You speak of Heidegger 'after one cleans out the academic rust': well, there are other oxidations in the atmospheres, and your letter shines with freedom from 'poetic' rust

Robert Duncan and George, mid 1970s. *Photo © Charles Amirkhanian.*

I enjoy the precision of your sentence, after you quote 'the sea anemone dreamed of something / filtering the sea-water thru its body' [CP 186]   where you add: 'I suspect it would have interfered with its growth had it focussed its attention on the filtering process itself'

the implication of 'suspect'   Acknowledged, yes.   I move maybe too freely from metaphysical assertion to - - - - the statement of how one can live a life. Freely, but --- a matter of trusting the emotions   since one must   And the title *Route*   and the autobiographical base of all the poems I think sufficiently acknowledges this   ?

I am not objecting nor protesting: the sentence delights me   ((ambi- valence woven thruout the poem; and perhaps most *glaringly* in 'the bright light of shipwreck' which you also note.

as I said at the start of this letter, I am not sure I sufficiently ac- knowledged -- nor is this adequate response.   Our relations are a bit com- plex emotionally.

((I will, if you don't object, send a xerox of this letter to Dembo whose thirty-forty page (is it?) discussion of me is supposed to be about to appear in the Iowa [effaced] (or somewhere) Review)) - - - or I'll read his article first

It is, in fact, this I wanted to ask   Your permission anent your
letter

(((emotionally complex relations indeed, Alex: is it possible to
say at this point, Alex, that I wish very much to remain your friend

George

To Robert Duncan
[February 14, 1972]   TLs   Poetry/Rare Books at SUNY-Buffalo

Robert

I wrote these lines   some months ago:

.   . Wyatt's
Lyric and Rezi's running thru my mind   I cried
And cried and cried   I will not recover[9]

(the poem continues   and approaches your 'unbearable   nearness'
'Garcia Lorca stole,'   page 29[10]

Narrative world   Populous world in the Truth and Life [of Myth]
I listen to the wealth   in all of your work   But my childhood was
the sea - - because I looked, because I chose -- And I am incapable of
envying anyone

(I suspect we create nothing else, you and I at least, but I am sure
we create our childhoods)

and unexpectedly a landscape appears between our extremes[11]

George

To Jack Kessie, Managing Editor, *Playboy*
March 25, 1972 (dated)   TLc   UCSD 16, 9, 19

Dear Mr Kessie

Your letter inviting my comment on the Mao article in Playboy is
the second invitation Playboy has sent me.[12] I am flattered. I am also dizzied, slightly dizzied. Me Mao and Playboy and a million readers, would
it be? I have never become accustomed to the abrupt alterations, cosmetic
operations on the news and the nose for news - - - Is it a nose, now, or a
bandwagon?   Bandwagon, bandwagon, no longer the American Legion but

the CIA, a very big bandwagon, will we know hereafter whether we wake or whether we don't?

I don't know. But I'll offer the literary comments that are within my province.

The poem *Snow* is, I think, the poem you have in mind in remarking that translations of some of Mao's poetry were circulated in the West *circa* 1946 (exclusively in left-wing publications, by the way) The last lines of the version printed at that time, following the references to ancient hunters, warriors, and Emperors, and intended to describe the present worker and peasant, were

> *At last a cultured man*
> *Stands on Chinese soil*

Mr Engle and Hua Ling give these lines as:

> *For heroes,*
> *Now is the time.*

No doubt Paul Engle and Hua Ling feel they have justification for this translation, but the loss of poetry is considerable. These were fine lines. And in fact there are other wordings which MUST be errors (the cannon 'crying') But if these hurried versions are read and re-read with sufficient patience, the classic image does come through, and perhaps this is all that should be asked.   IF the reader is sufficiently patient, the piece as a whole -- poems and prose commentary -- gives some inkling of the way in which poetry (that is to say, depth of meaning) may be involved in a politics which is radical enough to ask a question of purpose, of desire, to raise the questions of our purposes, of our desires, and no doubt Playboy is to be applauded. Possibly the whole damn trundling bandwagon . . . .? Well, it's hard to say Maybe human voices will wake us before we drown[13]

To Eve Haight
[April 1972] TLs UCSD 16, 5, 1, excerpted in *Ironwood* 26

Eve:

on the new poems: these are difficult and important ideas to deal with Difficult to deal with as resolve, resolution;   very very difficult to deal with in the certainty and bright light of poetry   Another voice enters, the voice of a mentor: it is sometimes not very convincing, it is sometimes a strain --

(that poem with the fine first line comes close to saying

'A lion is now eating my left leg,
This is the first trying test of my womanhood'   !

I am not mocking you   These are very very difficult things to deal with, difficult resolves   I am NOT mocking   I am *NOT*   Keep these poems, you'll use them, you'll need them   Whether you should work on them, think about them, or whether you should simply write more - - - or whether you should write notes mostly in prose - - I think, in fact, the 'notes' should attempt poetry   But your own impulse on this will be right   But keep them

They are, frankly, extremely bad poetry - - you will notice that some-time, and so I tell you.   They are also reassuring.   It is important to be capable of extremely bad poetry, those who are not do not *move*   It is important not to be caught in one's own first graces, one's own first grace-fulness, not to be dedicated to one's grace   It's important that what's dif-ficult should be difficult   Difficulty, the refusal of things to work out, forces one deeper, that is, deep enough.   In time.

'Out there' among atomic things, atomic events -- a difficult poetry Don't rush

George

((('Historic sense':   the full weight of what has gone before, of what has been thought and said   The 'presence' of those people, who thought and said - - - it's called historic sense, it's called -- O my God, this is embar-rassing for me -- it's called 'education'

To L. S. Dembo
[April 24, 1972]   TLs[14]   L. S. Dembo, carbon UCSD 16, 4, 7

Larry:
       '. . .the propositions : God is what is eternal, the moral world order, or love and so forth . . . . In a proposition of this sort one begins with the word God   This by itself is a senseless sound . . . . only the predicate fills the name with content and meaning . . . . it is not clear why

they do not begin with the eternal, the moral world order, etc . . . without adding the senseless sound as well' . . . .

'the individual is the absolute form . . the immediate certainty of himself . . . . unconditioned being'

self-consciousness is 'the absolute'   self-consciousness is 'science'   *science* used for the word *philosophy*

Hegel   Preface to the phenomenology 11. 1(6)
This to justify my reading of Hegel

———

of course you are right about the Henry James: I wanted the phrase

BUT I   wanted James in the book -- secretly, superstitiously, I carved his initials on that sapling book   And how in the forest of the libraries did you find it!!!![15]

I argued, shortly after Discrete was printed, that James and not Hemingway was the useful model for 'proletarian' writers - - - - and realized, in the ensuing discussion, if one could call it a discussion, that I must stay away from left-wing 'cultural workers'

'to know what, really, was going on' [CP 3]
and the story in it.

———

((the nouns   the things and the nouns which are their names: they matter and they matter above all because of,   in view of   'the benevolence of the real'   and there are other lines of that sort of import   I am writing, or   what?   I am trying to write, is maybe the right phrase   about the benevolence of the real [CP 195]   Sometimes called salvation

this, more than the 'political' which makes the failure of the concept of 'humanity' maybe crucial -- maybe catastrophic . . . Maybe

there's also The Forms of Love [CP 86]. The lake was not, after all, a lake   But that lake was central to our lives, mine and Mary's: crucial, seminal   the forms are forms of love

not Idealism: just the limit of what one *knows* acknowledged, the inaccuracies of knowledge

VIRGIN, THE WORD
COMES BY THE ROAD[16]

or: words are a mode of being?   'I write for myself'   The words distort, but are our mode   If there's a benevolence, however, it is the real which is benevolent ---well, am I adding anything to your account?   maybe not   Virgin, the word - - - -; that too is an account of experience;   so it seems to me   The word comes down the road which is there

(((Mary Oppen now putting together a journal, a life-story   She shows me her mention of James   For her too James was of great importance   glad I carved his initials

———

but obviously this letter is nothing on earth but the pleasure of talking about oneself. I apologize, but will send it

(((I keep thinking a single word, any word, holds all of the actual   And then in typescript   they don't   But will send this.

George

To Diane Meyer
[early summer 1972]   TLs   UCSD 16, 7, 27

Andy Dear--

Early in the year for Maine   cold and windy on the sea, the wind still blowing thru my head in this farmhouse room - - -The boat in those squalls is like sailing a sparrow, a wind-blown sparrow [cf. CP 239]

-- wonderful.   storm-bound a lot of the time, we see more of the villages than we saw in other years.   And other villages, villages chosen for shelter, not romantic interest.   (but shelter's pretty romantic in its way)

strangely, strangely, we feel strange in being so far from you and family - - -

a funny kite-string connecting us to San Francisco ----- and us huddled in miniature shelters on a rocky coast, playing marvelous games --- [cf. CP 239]

We play with loneliness, I suppose: always have, suffering loneliness almost painlessly, there being two of us   But not without fear   Extremes of loneliness, in a way, metaphysical loneliness, there being two of us   And yet it is surely the breath or is it the ether of life to us - - - [cf. CP 239]

fingers too cold to work, toes better not thought about, and possibly

detached   we are ecstatically happy flopping about this rocky coast like
a bird gone nuts in the wind

and love to you   very much love

George

To Brenda Webster
[June 1972?]   TLs with AL insert   Brenda Webster

Brenda:

some thoughts, emotions, perceptions in the poems--   No indication in the verse that you had reason to put them into verse, into lines
of verse - - - unless that they were too short for prose

You have to have a reason   I can't supply a reason for you   (a
music) (a movement)   Find it.   (the reason, the music, the movement)

Don't put in any word you don't WANT   don't strike any key of
the typewriter that won't make a mark that is part of THAT poem   THAT
music   THAT movement and that meaning   (change or get rid of the
sense of audience)

(Put in nothing that isn't useful to YOU to have written down)))

George

[. . . eight-line deletion by Webster]

Don't put in anything you think some friend will admire -- They'll
admire -- as they admire amateur carpentry   'My, did you make that yourself!'   But if they saw it in Sears Roebuck they wouldn't admire it
much[17]

To Donald Davie
[before October 20, 1972]   TLs   Beinecke Library; draft at UCSD 16, 4, 5

Dear Donald

Oxford having asked, I sent the enclosed*[18]

If you resent it at all -- and certainly it is presumptuous -- OF
COURSE don't use it   (I myself think that three or might it be four people
I can influence will not be embittered against the work   :   I think every-
thing is to be gained by *placing* the question

There is a considerable distance between us which I could not bridge in a short sentence or two more gracefully.   I spent a day (and evening) reading and re-reading, there is much I will not forget   And yet the wit of form and the tone it creates is not -- you know: it is not what saved me, it is not what I can live by

(naive sentence, this   Naive, I think, because it is always what we mean tho poets elaborate political theory and moral dicta from the straw that saved them)

regards and best wishes
George

*Rather, on second thought, I will not reply to Oxford until I hear from you

[the enclosure states] I am not without resistance to Donald Davie's poetry and to its wit of form, and yet a poetry of wit unafraid in the moral landscape and perfectly carved

‘ .   .   .   insulated wire
Conducting trade, conducting fire'

has, as Davie writes, its truth[19]

To Donald Davie
[after October 21, 1972]   TLs   Beinecke Library; carbon UCSD 16, 4, 5

Dear Donald:

I wrote that I had read and re-read -- still shaken and confused when I wrote -- enthralled, which is *enslaved*, as you point out. And, yes, I would say enslaved or in danger, I felt that.

I think the poems wittier than the Dunciad, and wiser.   And richer, and cannot, cannot reconcile myself   cannot understand WHY this tone, this form and this tone. The tone moves brilliantly, using the form, fitting the form, defying the form, playing another tone in defiance of the form   and yet I cannot understand why   I cannot speak as you speak and cannot truly understand your speech -- it is to me an exoticism: the definition of oneself alien, alien to me.   Perhaps it is true, as you suggest, that I feel myself the American and the Jew - - - Semite, nomad, no islander, unable to feel myself included in that tone or ever possibly included.

Alien?   Alien?   Yet I, like James King and Burke and most other men do not *disagree*, or refuse the *amen* -- other than, well, as above, being someone else.   As to not *disagreeing*: I have written just ONE review, knowing myself to be a narrow man   That was a portmanteau review . I wrote it in order to say in Poetry (of Chicago) -- this was of course quite a few years ago -- that Ginsberg was an important poet   But it was a portmanteau review, and I said of a book of Olson's very much what you have written of him   (Olson answers in one of the poems, saying: 'I wanted to open mr Oppen to history' --- oddly, not far, perhaps, from what you might say of me?   tho Olson is so conscientiously American)[20]   So, my distance from you is not in these flat dimensions. You point out to me the *Trevenan* not only because it is among the finest and most moving of your poems, but because it may contain a warning for me, a warning against narrowness, fanaticism, 'public indignation,' or at least public and publicized non-conformity

> Burke and the Jacobins of one mind,
> One self-same ruinous frame, unless . .[21]

well, I Said I am a narrow man.   And essentially an un-educated man. Damn, O Damn, Donald, I do want your friendship   WE want your friendship.   I escaped some things by the skin of my teeth -- the skins of our teeth -- and they were not, by the way, the things one thinks of as 'Jewish.' They were in fact closer to the sense of self of the English Country family tho tinged, so early, by the oncoming jet-set

Granted: nothing good about this   (except the boats and the sea, which you feel too)

-- the skin of our teeth, that is, a narrow escape, and we are narrow. (Several million Zionists wish to tell me that, being Jewish, I am not quite American, and that being not quite Jewish -- with two passionately assimilationist generations behind me -- I am not quite either

about which I sometimes think that, being not quite American since I am a Jew, I am the MOST American -- and essentially an uneducated man.   It is true.

The skin of our teeth is pretty thin, however, damn O damn   as I said . . . .

(the poem 'after Pasternak' -- and, I suspect, quite remote from him -- speaks to me absolutely directly   And so does *Emigrant, to the Receding Shore*   beautiful, beautiful, within my typically narrow Pantheon of the essentially un-educated man

———

Idiotic, my notice of your work   I can see that.   I was, as you can deduce from this note, thrown into some disorder, or, rather, conflict of emotion and memory   I have honorably avoided the word Exile, a sense of exile   it is becoming difficult to do so --- .   But idiotic to speak of 'wit of the form,['] without saying more of wit and of the meanings and the attitude of wit, and its roots   of wit as our wits, including in-wit . . . .

If there is anything in these notes which can be used or made usable or useful or cogent --- I'd be very glad of your help

your 'despair' -- you sign yourself 'despairingly' -- meaning: if a poet makes so little of what you have found and written down, what will a hack reviewer make of it?[22]   I don't make so little -- tho I stop, I stop short.   But it is not Burke's battle for discipleship, tho it is a battle, I am embattled, somehow or somewhere, and narrow as the battler always is - - - -

Donald   thank you, beyond measure, for the openness of your letter

George

To Carl Rakosi
[after November 7, 1972]   TLc[23]   UCSD 16, 9, 35

Dear Carl

honored by the dedication of your fine poems[24]

but as to whether I would or would not 'sacrifice art for man' - - I don't know how to think in such terms   Never try to[25]

I've said sometimes -- and may have said to you? -- that if I imagine myself Chinese   (which is fairly easy) -- and imagine the Chinese Communist party to have said something honestly and decently   (which is impossible)   I would also imagine myself going along with the proposition that the ending of starvation in China is the most important matter at the moment - -

Not the slightest chance of their saying anything honestly. I believe they said something about The New Socialist Man at this juncture ---

the objection could be called aesthetic: it rises in the form of nausea   Might as well be left that way.

Or appeal to Job: If one conceives of deity   one conceives there must be some connection between said deity and a statement which is true   Conversely, the sloppiest, the filthiest, the most sanctimonious lying must be the devil himself   Prefer this formulation to any proposition as to whether one would or would not sacrifice man to art or versa

------

((none of this objection to the poems

Just re-stating my 'position'   i e, my weak stomach.   I would rather strain a camel or swallow a gnat   etc etc

------

all regards, and thank you for
the poems
[TLc: unsigned]

To Harvey Shapiro
[end 1972]   TLs   Harvey Shapiro

Harvey:

it'll end, I think, by your getting two copies of Needle's eye - - -
(Sumac tells me the mails are slow)

No real need to tell you this, is there?   I was thinking again of your -- disappointment may be the word, or some sense of estrangement - --
'out of poverty   [to begin again]'[26]

yes, it's been said: which is precisely why I needed the quote marks ---[27] and so took the phrasing (tho not the versification) from Simic   You'll see, tho, the acting of the quote-marks when you look again --

the rest - - - the poverty is a poverty of the time at one's disposal   Yes, I'm a little disappointed too - - Inevitably the chunks, lumps begin to dissolve - - a little

but in fact I always meant, sometime, to write this book.

((when I quit writing I was attempting a poem that began: [']twenty-first birthday / stitch taken without thread /   '   ('twenty-first['] because twenty third or fourth, whichever it was didn't go as smoothly)

Your remarks on my mind because the second prediction -- that the book will be more popular (if popularity can be measured with a micrometer) seems to be verified   or being verified --------

   -- well, we have two proofs of merit: Popularity and unpopularity   I could maybe be satisfied with either if t' other dear charmer were away.

————

   You become filial, damn it: you'll never forgive me for dying. If necessary, to teach you a lesson, by God, I'll do it!

————

meanwhile, regards
George

(wait'll you see the picture on the back cover   An old man by God   an old man   How the hell did that happen!

To Michael Heller
[before December 26, 1972]   TL   Michael Heller[28]

Mike

   thanks for your letter -- It's true that I have been puzzled by the minor impact of the books --

   They mean to say   *Being*   I had supposed my self to be speaking with dazzling clarity   The lumps, the chunks, that which one cannot not see   Being even in 'the predominance of objects['] [cf. CP 68] - - - -[29]

   [']Spiritual' or even the profound has come to mean belief in anything that one does not quite believe   ?

   suppose, instead of an 'instant archeology' that imagines a personification of things already known, one imagines the first objects to become *object* to living consciousness - - their force in that among sensations they emerged as *objects* ----- can we suppose, in the history of the Sacred, a greater moment   ?

   this is the ground the poems meant to stand on. And to speak from.

   I went to a rock to hide my face /   the rock cried out no hiding

place' the poet's rock-stubborn head: no   hiding place up there
. . . . .   I flattered myself.[30]

Needle's Eye: I think you say correctly, speak accurately of some
change in the language   the language 'rises' a little?   etherealizes a
little, so imminently confronted by one's temporality - - - even a camel
might peek thru at that point, a camel or an old gent - - -

'in nakedness   /   inseparable' [CP 209] I meant;   it coheres,   it coheres *of itself*

Death wish? No   Adventure?   No, no, not precisely: the
poem speaks several times of the 'common /   place' [e.g., CP 206]   -- one
would not wish alone to be denied *that* experience ---

I think or hope the poem to be beyond 'have you prepared your little
boat of death'   and such - -[31]

———

'their power in that among sensations they emerged as objects--'   To
reverse that process;   bored by objects to wish to convert them to symbols
of interior sensations, interior movements - - is boredom indeed!

if we still possessed the word 'is,' there would be no need to write
poems   One inch above, one inch below what has already been said -- the
world opens up.

[no closing]

To James Laughlin
[December 1972] TLs James Laughlin

Dear J
I thank you for the note on The Waste Land from Ur -- or from
Genesis   to the Acts of Ezra[32]

the spirit, in fact the intention of the work seems quite pointedly to
be the making of a claim for the pre-eminence of Eliot over Pound as
poet   I'm not able to approach that question, or the question put in that
way -- it seems too close to the conversation at the horse races -- but I was
surprised to note that the suggestions of the final paragraph -- that the
Cantos would benefit as poetry thru excision as drastic as Pound's editing
of the Waste Land -- emerges as obviously true

I suspect we all admit to ourselves -- or I will admit *for* myself that I read the Cantos in fragments   as fragments.   Despite the challenges of the scholars

again thanks
George

Christmas regards

[In 1972, Oppen also corresponded with Charles Amirkhanian, Philip and Margaret Booth, John Crawford, Michael Cuddihy, June Oppen Degnan, Kathleen Fraser, Elizabeth Kray, Jerome Rothenberg, Charles Simic, Tony Stoneburner, Robert Vas Dias, and Eliot Weinberger.]

1973

[On February 22, Oppen read at the San Francisco Museum of Modern Art as one of "Four Major American Poets" with Robert Duncan in person and films of Frank O'Hara and Charles Olson. On March 7, he read at University of California, San Diego. In May, the Oppens visited England to attend the "Modern American Poetry Conference," May 25–27, at the Polytechnic of Central London, one of four American poets so honored—among Robert Duncan, Jerome Rothenberg, and Ted Berrigan. While there, Oppen read at Gonville and Caius College, Cambridge, and made a BBC tape of a reading and brief interview with Charles Tomlinson. In June, having returned to the States, the Oppens attended the National Poetry Festival at Thomas Jefferson College, Allendale, Michigan.[1] They did not go to Maine in 1973.]

To Robert Duncan
[January? 1973]   TL with AL additions, probably a draft   UCSD 16, 4, 15

Robert
        Myth   [this?] narrative   a populous world   But consciousness itself -- self-consciousness in itself, by itself carries the conviction of actuality   As has been said   *Sum*   and all placed in question by this absolute but the wealth of distance. I cannot free myself from this vision, or want to   But I listen, of course I listen to you --- and to all this wealth, the wealth of the book[2]   of your books
                                                George

        ((my childhood -- infancy -- too   I cannot escape or forget tho I also wonder why I cannot   My childhood was the sea   the inescapable myth of the sea   we are also small in comparison to the sea - therefore we make our way thru every wrinkle and pore of its skin
        And I am for some reason incapable of envying anyone -- incapable, that is, of suicide

To Robert Duncan
[January? 1973]   TLs   Poetry/Rare Books   SUNY-Buffalo; draft UCSD 16, 4, 5

Robert:
       I wrote a note   too hurriedly, very hurriedly   I am troubled now trying to remember what I wrote, and whether the acknowledgement was adequate at all - -
       Deep in work, distracted by work, and touched by jealousy, perhaps, and by the claim made upon me --   The Life and Truth is a marvel, it is magnificent, it is a major experience, everything comes into it but   I wanted to say but the bare world
       (of the poets   surely of the Black Mountain   do you notice this characteristic: that nothing ever happened to them)
       I am bound by some things that happened   That they happened -- yes, it is a kind of stupidity, I register this as a kind of stupidity, I feel it is so   But in the non-happening is -- there is a quality of simple snobbery   One chooses, if one can call it choosing.   Is chosen   was chosen
       Yes: some self-defensiveness, some jealousy in this note   Jealousy not envy   Envy is suicide
       Contrary of envy, the word in my mind is above all ME -- a cornerstone   Contrary of envy despite 'what happened,' various poundings on that stone   Not chosen   Was chosen   Ora pro nobis
                                                                                        George

To Michael Heller
[after January 6, 1973]   TLs   Michael Heller

Dear Mike
       I wrote inadequately - - it's the worst of all apologies, but the fact is that I have seen very little of your work   Could you send me a bibliography of what I should read?[3]

————

       'the commonplace is at the moment lost'   Well, I'm glad I read that.   One can make a life out of that sentence.[4]

(and so I stole it   My defense is the defense of the thief who was downright hungry - - - - I enclose the poem in its present version[5]

((I have not been bothering with the mags. for some time, the poem (however revised) is unlikely to appear until a next book - - some years away--

--- your phrase as epigraph on the fly-leaf, and so it can be properly credited   Can I assume your permission?   (defining by implication the Good, the more than Socratic Good)

Your namesake's sentence also very fine[6] These things   these things that can sometimes be said   !   the direct feel of living   replacing the abstract 'soul.' And finds, thereby, the soul. The love of the world.   (could one imagine, as the first moment in the history of the sacred, not personification of the known, but the imagination of the first moment at which object become [sic] object: among sensations,   object - - -)

or the love of the world   But it must be added -- well, happiness - - A flaw, a perhaps non-traversable gap in my work - - the 'impossible' luck of happiness-

-- or is this otherwise -- that the mind rise into happiness - - - - Of itself, thru itself --

((the first poem in Horizon, a Phrase of Simone Weil's [CP 205]   But I don't know.   Different minds.))

------

again, thanks for your letter
George

To John Crawford
[after January 23, 1973]   TL with AL inserts   John Crawford; photocopy
UCSD 16, 3, 48

Dear John
I can't answer these questions as you ask them --- or it would require so many pages --- Write it as you see it   And sure, quote anything you want anytime[7]

a few   'replies' - - sort of typical replies they would be:

The 'Marxism' of Discrete Series is, was felt as, the struggle against the loss of the commonplace   So -- yes, I'd read W James it happens[8] but the fact's not relevant   Sh[erwood] Anderson   Montaigne   sailed a boat, the sun as 'the predominance of objects['] -- Read the Middle English lyrics as 'phenomenologist[']   Read Langland 'for truth telleth that love is a treacle that abateth sin' to me, - the line moved me tremendously -- meaning to me what I wrote so much later   : [']love in the genes -- if it fails . . . .' [CP 184][9]

some poems of Discrete written 1928   If you look at the anthologies of the time, you'll see it was avant garde alright   Primarily because I could not have expressed what I felt in the old forms   Perhaps I *had* some sense of historical movement - - Yes, I did. But I don't *live* in an avant-garde

Pound's ego system -- the specific system   everything for the opportunity of stupid masculine rhetoric (i.e. where he is lousy) *Not* where he is not lousy.

Chartres: [CP 56][10]   what the world   cried out above the mountain was I Am What IS   The marvel of the fact, the marvel of the real,   not the whole of Christian or Hebrew orthodoxy - -

(as for your point: what 'produces a cathedral' is a thousand men hauling stone and cracking stone for one man 'carving by hand'   H Adams's is a pretty book, but what do you suppose he knew about handling stone

and the 'comradeship['] of war- - -   I reject this interpretation of the poem very strongly[11]

touched on this comradeship in Narrative, was it?   the section mentioning the unemployed and the subway [CP 161]   But I am not going to say thank god for the poor, the suffering, they supply us with 'moral action' - - - - - -

can make a touch of Marxism out of this: Love is love of the future   Without which not.

(((((also see From a Phrase of Simone Weil's - - [CP 205]   which says,   each, finally, and when he can - - - - - each his own journey - -

This'll have to do, or I'll be rewriting the poems for you - - Say it as you see it

no one said that Numerous is 'simply an elaboration of Discrete' [Crawford's reading of Dembo's point]   But that I have thought, all my life, about those themes have lived all my life on those emotional responses to 'the world'

(((John: your marxism is too 'scholarly'   Marx's books are Marx's books, but the Marxist political parties are ways to relieve the suffering,   and simple ways they are,   or they are abominations--- are or will become so - - IF they are not, to get the dams built, to save the people - - -

Marxists who don't get the dams built will sure as hell be lynched in a 'People's Republic'   Which means nothing at all about a new Socialist Man or a new art or anything of the sort, it means getting the dams built---   and, no, I don't want people to be hungry
And then?

———

BUT JOHN, DESPITE THE TESTINESS ABOVE, I AM GRATEFUL TO YOU FOR THE RECOGNITION THAT FROM DISCRETE SERIES TO THE MARXISM WAS NOT A 'BREAK'------BY ANY MEANS

(and then, IF you want to, and I'm not sure you will want to,   the road to Numerous by no means entirely within the Marxism   And 'back to' many of the things in Discrete put aside for the sake of 'active' Marxism - - - Marxism in action.

I told you Hugh Kenner: 'in brief'   (when I was explaining the period of political activity)   'in brief, it took twenty five years to write the next poem.'

———

To Donald Davie
[before February 7, 1973]   TLs   Beinecke Library; carbon UCSD 16, 4, 5

Donald:

of the American and British   (that aspect of your book, that subject of the book on my mind at the moment, and I want to get this typed down   ):[12]

this *effectiveness* of the American poetry: is this a reflection of the more powerful nation   ('uneven development of Capitalism' which some of your remarks also refer to):   the sense, therefore, of the more powerful, the sense of what is important, where it's at, who matters - - - The sense of the --- if not triumphant attitudes, not even of the attitudes which have triumphed, still, the attitudes of the triumphant ---

the thoughts, attitudes, words, tho maybe the fringe words, of those who are 'ahead':   what happens internally to those who are 'ahead' -- meaning, nearer the end or the edge

Jingoism?   the jingoism, a part of the jingoism that has made of Russia and China a horror?   Yes, of course I hear the Jingoism.   A Marxist, a Leninist derived Jingoism.   (and it is true that I do not, as the most popular of American poets *do,*   believe that The Way is to be found in the pre-industrial   (just as you do not)

And our hearts do not leap up for such things, jet planes in the sky --- Only that it is 'we' who get a glimpse of the abyss, most recent news of the abyss, news from that most foreign country came - - - - 'We' therefore, the most talked of - - not without reason.

((thinking, as they say, on paper: a bit surprised at where I find myself   Or, rather,   don't)

((discovering a new, or new to me, power of Imperialism ?   Well, in fact I was aware of it, and I guess this is me)

Sat up all night with the Thomas Hardy   Some landmarks of strength and strengthening for me in it.   Landmarks, sea-marks also for many who need them   if they'll use them.

-- a picture of the countryside, the countryman, the actual person, the poet, most subtly, almost secretly evoked again and again ----   perhaps by pure lucidity

---

(two partial disagreements: As I see Overlooking the River Stour: the mineral world grows dark to him, but it contains the human, and the human habitation - - the 'alack' not quite repentence.

and, The Voice: the center of the poem, for me   the musical center also   is:

Even to the original air-blue gown

the hyphen is also a dash
as I read it.   and the swing word, the, in fact, beautiful word[13]

———   ———

because I am not only a fool, but an inveterate fool, I return to
this: -- to our painful correspondence, painful to both of us:
'Didacticism dressed to kill with the greatest taste, elegance and
wit'
           I wrote
A poetry of wit, unafraid in the moral landscape[14]
     and went on to the words 'conducting fire'   It was my words
you thought inadequate!   Not wit, not fire, not unafraid, not the moral
landscape,   but *dressed to kill* and taste and elegance   ?   yes, I hear
the word *kill*, but Bond Street not the moral landscape: I did you less
than justice   ?

———

     Well, I am indeed inveterate and repeat now for the Hardy: Wit,
Fire   Unafraid, the moral landscape.

                                              George

To Donald Davie
[before February 15, 1973]   TLs   Beinecke Library

Dear Donald:
     'Painful' in that I learn   or confront again and afresh these con-
flicting claims   I had never entirely dismissed them: the question of
being numerous, of being part of a human unity,   a human entity,   I
have tried to face
     There is a conflict in myself: I find myself in the poems: ie,   at
the level of poetry -- antinomian.   As I enter the poem, I find myself
antinomian[15]
     'art is not good for us' I said except that we would surely die without
it.

———

     No, I don't think I'm 'radical' in your sense.   My 'proofs' are all
images.   My proof is the image.   'The common place,'   'that which we
cannot NOT see,'   etc, I don't think I've proposed anything but that we
commit ourselves to that mystery since in fact I think we must, I think we

do - - 'Surely infiniteness is the most obvious thing in the world' the commonplace partly because it is common, still more because it is the major mystery. the most extensive miracle

All of these things make the Hardy book valuable to me   But I think Hardy was afraid, very afraid, as I am, (see note *)   too afraid to talk of other ways of seeing, of experiencing, confusion of the senses, etc, having once seen *this*   But I said I believe in the benevolence of the real   Not 'Pessimist.'   Possible to be somewhat frightened by being alive without regretting the fact that one is.

Again: 'painful': I guess I meant to say that since I said it   Perhaps its more literal meaning, as you suggest: scrupulous.   But I value the correspondence -- in fact, for that reason.

regards
George

[typing apology] ((I have understated this: I think the correspondence is of very great importance to me: the correspondence and the *Hardy*

* I would NOT describe your approach to poetry as 'trivial' (the word from your letter)   Yes, I might think of describing it as too brave

To Donald Davie
[after February 20, 1973]   TLs   Beinecke Library

Donald:

Of course the poems must exist somewhere *between* us   and in fact your essay also exists some where *between* us: your meaning and your meaning to me.[16]

- - No grievances; I have no grievances at all in this   I value the essay, and will study it carefully.

Yes, as you say [in DD letter of February 20, 1973, UCSD 16, 4, 5]: I am a very Hardyesque poet   (tho not *thru* Hardy, as a matter of autobiographical fact. I found it elsewhere)

-- I was trying to find a phrase for this 'Hardyesque' element, concern, and said to myself: [']Metaphysic of the moment, metaphysic of the instant - -'   *Meta* physic,   which does not deny historicity, as you say.

Again, thanks for the essay.   And regards to Doreen.

George

Yes, our elegances, yours and mine.   Oddly, we come to this, our 'elegances'   by which in fact we touch each other very deeply[17]

To Aleksandar Nejgebauer and family
[March 18, 1973]   TLs   Aleksandar Nejgebauer

Dear Sasha
  and Gordana
    and co.   :
      we are so very glad to hear from you.   (I don't know if you re-
member your political re-assurance to us: 'We Jugoslavs have a great
political virtue: we don't like to work'   We think of this every now and
then, and are so very happy   It is the most joyful political sentence that
we know.
      and surely holds the ["greatest" has been cut] hope for humanity,
us humans

——————

——————

      and your word   'Adventure'   I'm pleased with the word *adven-*
ture   I've said the marvel, I've said the miracle, but perhaps the word
adventure is the simplest   and will suffice[18] [cf. CP 255]
      I'll send you   a copy of an interview with me that covers the
Objectivist history sufficiently I think --. And Pound?
      We met Pound again in 1969.   Jay Laughlin and two or three other
people of New Directions in the room. Pound enters with Olga Rudge.   Pound
silent.   Olga and the rest chatter to cover the situation.   I didn't want to
chatter, and stood up to leave   Jay says to Pound: give George a copy of
your book. Pound says -- uninflected, low voice: How do I know he wants
it.   I walked over to Pound and held out my hand and said, I want
it.   I had stood close, so that Pound would not need to reach out.   But
Pound stood up, and that brought us touching, or nearly touching each
other.   Pound took hold of my hand,   and held on.   I began to weep
Pound began to weep   We cried all over each other - - by that time neither
of us could speak,   so I took the book, and left. I don't know, perhaps
neither of us knew what we were crying about - - - - or, of course, I do
know.   Every sincere or serious poet who ever met Pound has reason to

have loved him. I write this out simply for the sake of the facts, the historical facts.[19]

———

Mary and I were thirty when our daughter was born. - - We've been glad we weren't younger -- very glad.   We've seen, tho, among friends of ours, that it is physically and even temperamentally very very difficult to take care of an infant at forty - -

But we're 65, Mary and I   We've seen children of 45 year-old parents grow up -- at least into adolescence. We think it works out well, we've seen it work out well.   (a little danger of too much precocity: the child knows you're in a hurry   )?

———

We'll be in England, Cambridge Univ and London U thru May and June of this year   Any chance of encountering you?

and to the new baby: Welcome

and thanks for your letter

George

To Dan Gerber
[before March 31, 1973]   TLs   UCSD photocopy 16, 10, 54

Dan:

there may be a Michigan school   ?   an intended remoteness in the language, the furthest possible remove from artiness, another remoteness, the remoteness from the event of a man talking - - - the man, who is talking, not the event, the 'image'? Remote thru the very small steps of small syntax.

Do you have some such sense of the thing? A startling number of nuisance-words, or what would, for my purposes, be nuisance words in the poem. Copula, articles, when's and before's and after's and if's - - - - - - - all that.   To me: fine poems, fresh poems, *harrassed* - - - Absaloms entangled in second-growth - - -

Always possible to *arrange* cadence into the words, or *arrange* the words into cadence   :   whereas the *finding* of the word for the cadence, the music, can produce a strain like the strain of bombast - - a vernacular sense depends very much on arranging   to achieve the direction and the hold of the wanted cadence - - -

THERE MAY BE ABSENCE OF THE THING, a Michigan school -- I stress my ability to conceive of such a thing

with, in fact, pleasure. If this is the case, maybe look again at Sherwood Anderson

'we wanted to know if we were any good out there'

(the perfect cadence to   out there - - - - Perfectly vernacular, even boy-ish. (to fit the statement: but the cadence, the cadence produces the statement of 'out there' as a thing that exists, the line has more than a novelistic quality - - a novelistic sentiment, more than that.[20]

Even Sandburg   The famous fog on little cat's feet poem -- Sand-burg's destructive sentimentality   But note that the words of the poem fall absolutely evenly, each word at the same volume: the slightest pos-sible modulation of pitch from word to word - - - - which saves the poem perhaps - -

and this often in Sandburg: unbearable where he does not do this.   the fall of the words - - -, arrangement - -

I'm not sure I've ever been in Mich -- for a moment if ever. 'pass-ing thru. Have some sense of the openness,   some sense that one's lines might   insist on an openness, a movement from left-edge of the line to right edge, not a stasis or a standing-on - - -- - - any of this useful to you???? [one page cut by RBD; specific rewritings of Gerber poems, and ad-vice]

'I've thought, here --- imagined the fields of mid-continent and a mid-continent ----- dryness, vernacularity - - -

But:

Think of Blake's vision on the prairies (are they prairies)   Think of Rilke's music on the prairies

we want, really,   no less than that

HOMER   we want Homer   *Thalassa*   meaning prairie (are they prairies)

George

(((good poems   even very good   Not good enough)))

To John Taggart
[March 28, 1973]   TLs   UCSD 11, 17, 11

Dear John Taggart

L Z's presence acknowledged and all - - I'm sure the work will be valuable for you to have done

YOU'LL judge it   and that'll be it   But meaning of song, mean-ing in song - - - I think you do *well* to have explored this

let the poems sit a while   I mean to also   they gather mean-ings

But eventually, eventually in the writing the care, the care, the hours and hours to give the reader entrée into the poem - - - - this has been my quarrel with Louis, or still more Louis' quarrel with me: Louis' secre-tiveness is not to me admirable

but Louis would disagree   even tho he might accept my word *se-cretiveness*

George

((well, once, perhaps   The escape from the Romantics.   But secretive-ness now has become . . . . . . ?

NARCISSISM?

BUT NEVERTHELESS[21]

(and -- no question -- a great deal to be learned from L Z   Now that so many have learned from L Z perhaps I tend to speak of him carelessly too carelessly

To J. H. Prynne
[received April 15, 1973]   TLs   J. H. Prynne

Dear [J. H.] Prynne:

Your praise of Needle's Eye   'so far out in the visible that ap-pearance blinks, and is behind us'   at the moment that such praise turns my head, the marvel of what you say and that you can say it reminds me that there are other poets - - other than I

Crestfallen, I mean my crest falls in that blessed   (isn't it, after all?) ocean.

(once, at 16, I was escorted along the walks of Cambridge keeping my own council, of course, but wondering to myself if, to begin with, I might survive to be adult, and second if I would ever walk scholarly past those windows[22]

I thought the chances slight. And the need to walk musing and scholarly and at the same time to have been sent down as befitted a Romantic, O wind, I thought, if winter comes . .

a few months ago, or maybe it was a year or two, we lose track, I was leafing thru the Collected Works and started to read that poem to Mary.[23]

I couldn't say the last words: we were both weeping. I hadn't expected that   Neither of us had expected that

———

Your arrangements seem to me idyllic and wonderfully thoughtful.   But Mary'll enclose a note   Mary having taken over the tickets, the times, the --- Lord, these things seemed so simple when we were twenty.

again thanks
George

I have Aristeas and the Kitchen Poems: I did not have Into The Day   Newly arrived   And indeed I thank you for it.[24]   Can scarcely credit the existence of the final poem   from frenzy to the darker   by which the lost lives   The poem's centrality, and its incredible beauty

To Aleksandar and Gordana Nejgebauer
[May 30, 1973]   ALs[25]   Aleksandar Nejgebauer

Dear Sasha (+ Gordana:)
(I'm quite Marxist, indeed.

'The shipwreck of the singular' I wrote. We *cannot* live without the concept of humanity, the end of one's own life is by no means equivalent to the end of the world, we would not bother to live out our lives if it were - - - -

and yet we cannot escape this: that we *are* single. And face, therefore, shipwreck.

And yet this, this tragic fact, is the brilliance of one's life, it is 'the bright light of shipwreck' which discloses - - - - - - 'all.'

———

———

Delighted you're writing on me: will *much* enjoy seeing it

And cannot tell you how much we would like to go to Novi Mir [Yugoslavia] - - Can't.   We'll try to *sometime*, at least, surely will get there sometime.

Love,

George

To Michael Cuddihy

[late summer or early fall 1973]   TLs   Michael Cuddihy

Dear Michael:

we too immensely enjoyed the visits -- there is nothing so poetic   (among poets) as NOT to gossip about poetry - - - but to begin at the beginning

But one must be somebody   As you and Mary [Cuddihy] *are* to talk to each other: to talk in order to hear -- that's what there *is*.

———

The 'long poem':   I am troubled and unsure.   But have completed a series of seven poems - - already promised elsewhere: can't offer it to Ironwood, tho I would like to   But will send a Xerox with this, that you may read it - - - - -

(the Xerox is of my copy which is not 'clean'   May be legible, tho distracting (read as *typed*)

I had not been thinking of Job as I wrote: thunderstruck to discover how closely the poem followed Job's argument - -

-- and so I named it.[26]

(this the more startling in view of the number of quotes, so many, and none of them from Job   I'd made myself a list of the references, but seem to have lost it -- includes Hölderlin, Jabès, Bobrowski, Luther, Montaigne (Florus' trans)

Luther's is   'seeking a statement' etc.   *Middle Kingdom* from Mencius - - and others   Quotes from memory, which is my disreputable habit - -

-- well, it happened that way I didn't plan it. But this also perhaps justifies the name: 'to praise the paths of the living'

--I've confessed several times that I tend to think I'm the only poet the world's had - - perhaps I'm learning to know better

I write this out thus circuitously to circle back to the opening of this letter [here a circular mark links up to the first five lines of the letter]

(well, elsewhere a foolish letter: writing
'notes' on myself.   I mean those were
lovely afternoons in Mill Valley)

George

To Jerome Rothenberg
[after September 19, 1973]   TLs   UCSD 10, 60, 14

Dear Jerry:

I am, of course, glad to give permission for the re-printing of the poems of Discrete Series in the Anthology you're undertaking.   Copyright is in my name, you'll need no other 'permissions'[27]

————

Do give me as much space as possible between the poems. If you cannot give sufficient space to make clear that the poems are, indeed, discrete,   use dots. 'bullets' is the printer word?   But obviously they must not be too heavy and unsightly   The point is to arrive at some design solution which will make clear that the dots are not dots of omission.   A correspondence on this might be near-endless: and your design sense is as good as mine. But give as much space as possible: the poems could be seriously distorted by seeming to be paragraphs: 'pensées'

AND best regards, Jerry
George

To Diane Meyer[28]
[Fall 1973]   TLs   UCSD 16, 7, 29

Andy dear, you and books -- You don't know how to read   You look for heroes -- or for children. You look for triumphs over your enemies, and so you judge the writer according as he agrees or does not agree with what you thought before you read him - - -

Or even as he lives or doesn't live as you live -- It ain't scholarly.

(this is the one good thing about the academics: they're accustomed to hearing things they didn't already think   Their danger is that they become accustomed to hearing things they'll NEVER know   Or think

well -- it's one way of keeping your spirits up   Whereas I seem now to be keeping my spirits up by having a desk and a desk lamp and receiving mail - - and   and perhaps that's sillier

and very likely I'll have to get rid of that   Alright, alright.   But I wish you wouldn't go dogging the heels of writers   (or heels) who seem to triumph over your enemies   (Why shouldn't they?   it's their own piece of paper)   And you SHOULD be able to read someone like Simone Weil, tho she was neither pretty nor graceful - - - but vivid   (therefore profound)   when she describes her own experience of thought and of feeling - - - - yes, you're a pretty woman, alright, alright, don't be so god damn snobbish --- or -- what is it? It's something that you know is not enough. (High-school snobbery)

(but maybe that's a definition of snobbery.)

((you think the desk is becoming to me??   I don't know. I worry about it   O I do, I do! But neither is long hair becoming to me   or cowboy boots   what'll I do o what'll I do, Andy, what'll I do

(I'll hide my wing under my head, poor thing

(Simone W;   she is surely not being didactic: Authoritative.   But neither does she always seem to be using the writing as a means of thought   So that when she becomes brilliant, paradoxical, epigrammatic, it raises a question - - even of sincerity - - - I think *that's* the problem

(I think she knew it)

((it's the problem of 'Christian humility'   The problem of piety   And *indeed* she knew that   Knew it was her problem   She fought with it all her life   It is a moving and sometimes a tremendous story

'When we hit a nail with a hammer, the whole of the shock received by the large head of the nail passes into the point without any of it being lost, although it is only a point. If the hammer and the head of the nail were infinitely big it would be just the same. The point of the nail would transmit this infinite shock to the point to which it was applied.

'Affliction, which means physical pain, distress of soul and social degradation . . . . is a nail whose point is applied at the center of the soul, and whose head is all necessity spreading throughout space and time '

S W[29]

———

———

Suppose she had never said anything else   Suppose nothing else had ever been said by *anyone*   .   .   ? This would be a literature.

Literature could begin here.

To Eve Haight

[November 1973]   TLs   UCSD

great child: hard for me to write a letter just now; think I did too much showing off - - - 'readings' and such

also time moves too fast: I get flooded by memories. I think even our relationship changes a little, mine and Mary's -- or rather, it seems to be what it was at the beginning, almost what it was at the beginning, and my time-sense gets confused   There's us and us walking down the street   And *future* has a different meaning: it's hard to keep up with

as for you: 'and by God I can't write'   always that way, getting into the new thing - - even between books.   I've had a bad year that way

--don't yet know what you're doing   If one tries to force the writing, it's like flexing a muscle without knowing the purpose --- and so it seems mere showing-off, or you're not sure if it is or if it isn't and no way to find out

the way to do it is: make notes, jottings, scratch note book, however you want, but KEEP it --- Later it falls into place, later you know what you meant ---

———

Me and Mary: I don't know   Don't know how to say it. I'm overwhelmed by the impossible luck, I'm overwhelmed by the impossible Mary, a miracle's a miracle, they say, but it isn't; a miracle becomes the world, seems to me I didn't entirely recognize a miracle --- the recognition that I needed a miracle rather frightens me now - - -

------

[cut several sentences about EH's experience of France]
        -- we're not a stalwart branch to light on   but anytime, Birdie, anytime   Light anytime, and welcome

                                                George

To Michael Cuddihy
[late November–December 1973 or early 1974]
TLs with AL postscript   UCSD 16, 3, 52

Dear Michael:

        I think you were hurt by my suggestion of displaying the earlier versions of some of the poems -- or asking you to display them.   I really did not feel that I was treating Ironwood shabbily -- and would SURELY not want to do so --[30]

        want to remind you that I have done this frequently: as,   A Language of New York in This in Which became the long poem, Of Being Numerous, in the following book. Laughlin was far from feeling cheated over that (I of course inquired - - - He found nothing to object to, and I think he was right - - - well, a sort of openness in it --)

        But I don't mean to argue this point. I'm only concerned that you should not feel I was treating Ironwood in a cavalier manner . I was not.   Or didn't think I was

------

        (tho, yes, I was using Ironwood, in a sense.   I don't think in an unconscionable sense   The new poems were not easy for me ---- forcing myself into areas that raise for me - - - - Well: you'll understand.   This is a quotation from Kafka's note-books:

        'Hold fast! . . then you too will see the unchangeable dark distance out of which nothing can come except one day the chariot;   it rolls up, gets bigger and bigger, fills the whole world at the moment it reaches you - - and you sink into it like a child sinking into the upholstery of a carriage that drives thru storm and night'

———

———

-- and I could not handle papers neatly, or make final decisions very firmly

--but now, yes, some shabby thoughts.   I'm omitting here 'the three-page poem' [alluded to in a previous letter] (partly because it probably will go thru some changes - - and a few short poems.   This is   (shabbily) - - well, I have great need to see these poems in the context of my whole work -- I need very badly to convince Laughlin to do the collected   And - - he too I think will want unseen poems - - They almost MUST appear in that guise, for they are the beginning of what is, I suppose, a last step I seem capable of - -

a last step but, as you will see, -- also in those I send -- also a beginning or hardly a beginning.

with the exception of the Reznikoff Reading, I send you the major of the new poems

Michael: I hope you will not be disappointed with these.   I cannot -- by its nature -- treat the new poems in any 'firmer' or more authoritative manner.

> with our love
> George

(primary consideration in the selection I send is this: these poems will *not* be revised)

To Robert Duncan
[Winter 1973?][31]   TLs   UCSD 16, 4, 15

Robert, I write this because I've been sitting up most of the night reading and re-reading Caesar's Gate - - Beautiful beyond beauty, and so far from me, I've been rapt out of myself, I was thinking,   What have you come to tell me, Robert - -

there'll be bees with their heavy legs and furry bodies and their gold in my mind for the rest of my life[32] [cf. CP 233]

> George

To Robert Duncan
[Winter 1973?]   TLs   Poetry/Rare Books Collection SUNY-Buffalo

Robert:

did I ascribe a *Selva* to you that you never wrote?   I think I did

Haven't had time to look. Rather, reluctant to look: Those few lines of the Selva Oscura running in my mind as we've talked: I took it as your dithyramb - - -

even speculated about it as a part of your refusal of singleness of the poem - - Been up all night at Caesar's Gate: carried away, and aware of my alienness.   I would have seen a red thread thru any fabric, dominant, the red thread no doubt being my self - - - I've been aware of this before, and so thought of what I had come to think of as your dithyramb -

'is there a greeness to verity, an almost indecent freshness in being aware of what is at issue?' - - - from the beginning of my adult work I've been aware of this 'indecency,'   the need to call on my intransigence - - or, rather, my indecency.   As against Caesar's Gate I am alternatively shamed by my indecency,   and - - - - absolutely in need of it.   and in fact I exaggerate here: I could by simple decision burn my ships at the Bosporous   (was it Darius who did that?) - - - - The one connection between us in our work is that - - the one essential tie -- is this: that we do not know before we complete the poem. Neither of us write[s] what we already know, and of course that's the essential life of the poem.

-- so   I could easily burn the ships with the first lines of a poem.   And, I suppose, you could leave 'em be - - A decision.

Say to me   (in all the elegance of my fractured French): Hypocrite lecturer, mon frère.

————

(there is surely no *richer* document on the creation of poetry than the *Gate*.

George

[In 1973, in several letters, Oppen included comments about Jew, barbarian, late Roman, which are worth excerpting. Oppen said of "the Judaism of the poems: a very strange thing to happen" (UCSD 16, 12, 1). Some of these letters have been arbitrarily assigned to 1973. One might point to CP 246–47 and CP 250–51 as places where these thoughts also emerge.]

From a letter to Dan Gerber
[late fall 1973]   TLs   Dan Gerber

    the country's crumbling, the world's crumbling, and somehow it's clearing the air: Can't remember such clear air in my life time.
    Barbarian at the Gates!   Inside or outside?

From a letter to Anthony Rudolf
[five days after Yom Kippur 1973]   TLs   Anthony Rudolf

(five days ago the war against Israel began again ---I don't know,   our history is incredible: the non-Jewish world is somehow accustomed to it
    'Jew' means: those to whom these things happen

From a letter to Michael Cuddihy
[October 25, 1973]   TLs   Michael Cuddihy

((of the word Jew: racial revolution in the streets. A civil war for dignity in the streets   and I neither Roman nor Barbarian))

From a letter to Allan Planz
[fall 1973?]   TLc   UCSD 16, 9, 18

I feel a bit like the late Romans in Gaul ---- Ausonious, was it, writing to a friend in Spain - - - (odd to be neither Roman nor Barbarian as the walls are breached)   the poems have seen this landscape, this ground, this 'dialect of its downfall'[33]

From a letter to Shirley Kaufman
[1973?]   TLs   Shirley Kaufman

Incredible, incredible history of the Jews, our history, people cannot bear our presence   I hardly know how to blame them,   they would have to defend us   (and worship us?)   or hate and look down on us

Easier, obviously, to hate us   'obviously,' and yet I find it
incredible.

[In 1973, Oppen also corresponded with Paul Auster, Anita Barrows, William Bronk, Cid Corman, Beverly Dahlen (San Francisco State Poetry Center), Theodore Enslin, Serge Fauchereau, Kathleen Fraser, Maria and David Gitin, Eric Homberger, Elizabeth Kray, James Laughlin, Mark Linenthal, Lawrence Livingston, Diane McGrath, Tom McGrath, Robert M. MacGregor of New Directions, Gerard Malanga, Audrey Nicholson, Kathleen Norris (Academy of American Poets), Michael O'Brien, Panthea Perry, Allan Planz, Charles Reznikoff, Anthony Rudolf, Steven Schneider, Armand Schwerner, Harvey Shapiro, and Eliot Weinberger.]

1974

[On March 21, Oppen introduced Charles Reznikoff, who was reading at San Francisco State University. The Oppens summered in Maine on Eagle Island, in a "camp" on a cove.¹ In mid-September, Oppen read at Shippensberg State University in Pennsylvania. June Oppen Degnan gave Oppen all publishing rights which she still held to his second and third books. In October, Oppen was preparing his *Collected Poems* for New Directions and mentioned in a letter that he had "some new, rather long poems."²]

To Robert Duncan
[1974]   TLs   Poetry/Rare Books Collection, SUNY-Buffalo

[no salutation]
     'the Word comes to existence, and for the last time, as language[']
     (that from Heidegger)
     no way to thank you adequately for the *Preface*   (Maps)³
                           George

To Charles Reznikoff
[1974]   TLs   UCSD 9, 4, 4

Charles:
     a great pleasure to see again the poems that were not in the New Directions edition.   Nothing lost in the passage of time, they mean to me all that they meant when first I came upon them - - - forty-five years ago.⁴
     with thanks for the book   (thanks for all the books)
                           George

Mary, George, and Charles Reznikoff, probably March 1974. *Photo © Charles Amirkhanian.*

To Philip Levine
[1974]   TLsc with AL inserts   UCSD 16, 6, 23

Phil
        I'm glad you're doing some 'readings'   Tho you must be weary   But it's going to take some time to get recognition of the stature of this work
        (simple: they can't make a school of you.   *Nothing* they can do with you but write as perfectly and as profoundly   How are they going to do *that* (so they don't talk about these poems enough)
        Nothing like this is going to happen very often
        Phil I'm so happy to be a contemporary: happy to share the language.   Tho they climb only the stairway of lost breath, they lion come   It is astonishing how they lion come[5]
                - - - Mary and I reading the books all afternoon - - -
                                                George

((all of us, I suppose, in pursuance of our duties talk about poems that don't, in fact, matter   Need to be reassured now and then that a poem that's perfect will do   Will *do*   *Act.*

(never a merely novelistic quality in the poems   I think it is because the music is so strong   But I think that the novelistic   might be a danger?   danger of diminution??

the 'image is very broad in the poems -- broad in time   This is precisely what makes the poems so magnificent   surely I'm wrong headed in this paragraph above - - Almost surely.   He's a long long lion with his tail in the past and his teeth in the street-corner   so I'm just talking   Passing the time of day, you might say. Flabbergasted by the poems.

(a poem including if not questionable history, at least you, me, Zayda's and other matters we might know something about

A Pound of flesh.   And blood   Always: every line.

To Tony Stoneburner
[January 5, 1974]   TLs   Tony Stoneburner

Dear Tony Stoneburner

I am delighted by the etymology of exuberance

The etymology of exuberance   (no italics)

' . . . . the milky way, and all the Galaxies'   And by Carol Elizabeth becoming water-borne in her own way[6]

(of late years, I've become merely dazed, slightly dazed, by coincidence. *The day before* your letter arrived, I'd written down, almost like automatic writing, the name of the book I've been working on: Myth Of The Blaze. The Blaze being 'all the Galaxies,' the night-sky, Blake's Tyger.) [cf. CP 242–44]

and now with your letter,   it shines in my mind: the happiest of Christmasses

We plan, this coming Summer, to live on Eagle Island. --if it works out   We think they'll find a shack we can have   (it's the most beautiful of islands: farmland on the top of the hill)

we'll visit [Little Deer Island], if we may - - - and anchor off your porch.   Or perhaps we can, again, pluck you off a rock

We look forward to it

and best wishes
George

as for New Year's wishes - - one hesitates   'the world'   coming apart a
bit?
seems to be doing as well as could have been expected
I'll wish you, and us, a brave new world, a brave new year.

To David McAleavey
[after January 29 and before February 6, 1974]   TLs   David McAleavey

Dear David:

thanks for your letter   Its quality, and,   in view of its quality,
thanks for your praise.

for the rest - - - page upon page upon page of typing looms before
me as I tell myself that you deserve a full answer - - -   Sixty-five years of
autobiography, after all   -----[7]

and yes, yes, somewhat unexpected 'biography,' so that explanations
have been invented - - - -and I should set it straight and all that.

compression   Rather extreme: The Forms of Love [CP 86]. Mary
and I: first 'meeting.   yes, parked in the fields /   all night.   Mary talking, talking by some instinct about her three brothers,   how they had
hoboed, how they worked in lumber, how she had picked hops one summer
- - - - I swear I knew in three minutes that I was saved: I could work -
meaning, ordinary work, a job, and I was saved.   That is free.

I am sure Mary knew what she was telling me --

the background being, yes, that mine was a childhood nurse-
maided, butlered, chauffeured, etc - - - all this having made much confusion - - - - So that:

a persistent confusion also between To Publishers (Le Beausset, Var
[France]) and the Objectivist Press.

I did not pay for the Objectivist Press.   It was a collective, exactly
as stated on the books.

I did support To Publishers

I did not 'edit' To Publishers   (tho I've seen several accounts having
me do so   I did not, and my name is absent from the books and from all
notices in order that It should not . . . . O   , well.

To Publishers and therefore the Objectivist Anthology was edited
by Louis Zukofsky

financed by me.   we were all young at the time: Dawns on me now that no one conceived clearly that it was possible to have some money without having an unlimited amount - -

Slowly, slowly, the gossip and confusion of the time reaches me   Occasionally -- occasionally occasion for blushing.

the word was -- I hear now: multi-millionaire.   Whereas what was uppermost in our minds, Mary and I, was my escape from all that

and we were, in fact, budgeting ourselves meal by meal in order to print those books --

ON the other hand: to have any money at all in 1932   !!

yes.   You see.

———

Politics.   And do you really want another twenty pages?   Limit it to one point: I did not write 'Marxist' poetry.   I made a choice.   Stopped, for the crisis, writing.

yes, different levels of truth.

(or different levels of lying -- as you wish

I *have* discussed this a little. And the conflicts, contradictions unresolvable appear in the poems, as in the prose section of Route [CP 184–96]

———

(and in fact the whole of that poem AND of Being Numerous [CP 147–79]))

———

Objectivist Press, a collective, was set up when we were unable to continue To Publishers: less than ten books having been sold -- We had been budgeting on the assumption of loss, of course, but of some return of money in order to continue.

———

David: this'll have to do.   Can't, can't cover sixty five years of - - --

(it really is in the poems)

Best regards, best wishes

George Oppen

Tell 'em I am one person.   Only one.   But not less than one.

so that's the true story of George Oppen.

[letter continues on a third page]
Politics:
1. We were not, and did not think ourselves, small Lenins.   or big ones
2. (tho I was, acknowledgedly, the best of the soap-boxers: tended, comparatively, toward frankness
3. What we DID   was organize the unemployed (unemployed Council and Workers Alliance   (mentioned in one of the poems) [CP 31; possibly also 28]
4. Were of some use in the New York Milk Strike.   Chiefly Mary -- as to actual usefulness[8]
5. The War

((as to the Communists: insane,   yes   Or a necessary self-deception.

on the occasion of Chamberlain's famous umbrella visit to Czechoslovakia, the mayor of Utica   (liberal) ordered all the church bells rung in celebration of -- yes -- Peace. And some spontaneous ringing of bells about the town

There were perhaps ten Communists in the whole county. Those ten were the only people in the whole damn county who knew that with Chamberlain's action the war had already begun - - - -

there were, you may not credit this -- but there were -- [there] was no one to talk to that day but the Communists - - - - - - - -

well, we're in too deep for a letter shorter than you asked for,   add to this Of Being Numerous

and forgive, with all else, the typing

(enclosures at random: I send what comes easily to hand.[9]

To Jane Cooper
[February 12, 1974]   TLs   Jane Cooper

Dear Jane:

What an extraordinary thing it must have been to 'find' these poems   Such poems!   Such poems as these!

(what an extraordinary thing it was to *lose* them![10]

Kathleen Fraser delivers the poems with apologies: she kept them two weeks or more, reading and re-reading - - with reason!

(we didn't discuss them: -- other than what was implied in her apology -- She wanted us to come to them fresh)

The prose section: it will be challenged, I suppose. Unusual procedure. I myself don't think you should hesitate or even listen -- I don't suppose you will The re-embedding of the poems into your life . . . creates something like a marvel

———

———

[RBD cut specific, brief comments on Cooper's poems]

'It is a woman's poetry' ? !

God forgive me.

What startles me is that as the sense of women writers as women increases, as the 'movement' of women increases, it - - - - curves back?

That the predominance of psychological   insights, psychological prescription and resolve *increases* --

[']half what the kind nets swallow[']

(not strange?   'Their own' weapons?   And I'm reacting to that?)

the psychological home-making, making a home   ?

That startling (and frightening, for I feel lonely) avoidance of the metaphysical dimension   (avoidance of the single person, whose psyche would seem simply *given*

the metaphysical dimension, which is the thought of being alone: with nothing. Say: born on a planet the size of a table?)

consciousness, which has nothing to gain, which awaits nothing, which loves itself [CP 150]

permissible maybe to quote myself because it's mostly Aristotle anyway

And E Dickinson   Yes, there's   that I acknowledge   With joy

it is true (as in *Twins*, for a single example out of so many) the psychological insight and courage is a marvel, a marvel to me, and I feel clumsy -- yes.

and write clumsily here   Meaning to leave myself open,   open to attack

for I feel lonely

and write perhaps *irritably*   meaning to invite attack.

and because I am startled, which is to say lonely, all the more in that they are very fine poems

George

the 'metaphysical dimension' is what you said to me, summing up or pondering what I had said to you, discussing your poems in Maine:
    'All experience is valid'

George

((((I think you make too many resolves about *what* form,   *what* prosody. Any *way it CAN be done*

(and this is in fact simply to repeat what I've said   (rightly or wrongly) in these three pages

((whatever those words mean))

(May we keep the Xerox?)

To Frances Jaffer
[1974?]   TLs   Frances Jaffer

Frances

it comes to me   it dawns, it dawns.   The 'field-related' man, unless he is badly mis-placed, is the accountant, manager,   statistician   We'd despair of talking to each other   Don't much try.

But the field-related woman may well be speaking of an aura, an ambience, a color of life and lives   It is a typical situation.   And I gladly talk, in order to hear more of this than I myself would be so little able to do - -

And so many of the women I talk to and listen to happily could be described as 'field related' - - - - and very few of the men - - -

- - -and so I said, and have said before -- that women are usually absolutely unwilling to entertain the thought of the metaphysical - -[11]

It dawns, it dawns.   After all these years!   I talk to 'field-related' women and not to field-related men   And it is true that field-relatedness is the refusal to talk of metaphysics, the refusal   to think the idea of Nothingness (this from Henri Bergson), the absence of a field

———

((my poem beginning: the puzzle assembled / at last in the box-lid . . . . the puzzle is / complete now - - - [CP 24] describes the refusal to think outside a field, a set of rules, of definitions -- - - Whereupon 'it' becomes a complete puzzle.))   And, yes, I was thinking of a woman at the time I wrote it. ((Yes, I quote myself too often. It disturbs me.   I tell myself these are difficult times))   Hard (or frightening) to move further

G

(thanks for the conversation

To John Crawford
[Spring 1974]   TLs, with AL additions
John Crawford; photocopy UCSD 16, 3, 48

Dear John:
[. . .]¹²

((but here -- not for publication --:   Anti-semitism of the left: the little 'organizer' (and the big organizer) who says he wants to proletarianize himself but means he wants to be the only 'intellectual' in the place --- And, there is that minority, always and everywhere the most endangered -- BUT: they have this peculiarity: many (comparatively) have gone to college.   How to get rid of them? alas, we know how they have been 'got rid of'

((I 'explain' here.   But actually I cannot explain - - -
someone imagined the prayer: 'O God: choose someone else'
(anti-Semitism (nihilism) of the Jewish Communist: to die for any-thing but one's Jewishness holds the promise of not being forgotten
((the proletariat will not be exterminated))

To Philip Levine
[April 5, 1974]   TLs   Philip Levine

Phil:
I once heard a communist 'commissar,' more or less -- National Committee man -- say that to a young Black boy 'You have no right to be an artist'

could have said, this is no time . . . .

and there's a poem of Brecht's -- 'To Posterity' I think. 'even the cry for justice/ makes the voice grow harsh . . . . we who wanted most to be kind have not been able to be kind[']¹³

. . . possible to accept this But they've lied TOO much there seems almost no way back -- For them.

((or: it's a mistake to invite the hangman to dinner))

(but of course she was only speaking of becoming a doctor   And she said 'bitterness'   It's another story, yes. And think of the monstrous statue in N Y harbor: -- 'yearning to be free'   !

((maybe we should have a little statue about an inch high with that inscription on it: 'yearning to be free'   Sad little statue: no denying it
George

To James Laughlin
April 13, 1974 (dated)   TL with AL insert   UCSD 16, 8, 7

Dear J

not my age, but what caused it   :   the years
I feel imagistically young: narratively old.

———

the twenty-five years of 'silence':   I think (know) all those threads were there at our first meeting

almost oriental, Mary said   The tao, the way   A way.   Our way. - - - and masculine and feminine? we cared about Mary's ambience in that chicken coop -- to be able to go into the chicken coop -- not, surely not, in the suburbs.

'confessional': weakness is common   I've put in the moments of extreme weakness, extreme error   and guilt   Not the love-cars¹⁴

To James Laughlin
[after June 18, 1974]   TL   UCSD 16, 8, 7

Dear J:

First: to thank you for the happy evening in New York. There are times when I love that impossible city.

James Laughlin, publisher of New Directions, George, and Mary, Polk Street, San Francisco, 1974. *Photo Ann Resor Laughlin.*

-- and I am immensely indebted now for your patient and lucid letter concerning my proposal of a single volume of the poems 1929–1974　.　I must confess that I had not forseen or considered at all the considerations you raise, and I see must be considered. Or, rather, on my part, re-considered. I feel somewhat abashed, as well as grateful to you for your summary.

Your suggestion of printing the collection *only* in hardbound in order to secure a place in the libraries and to force some serious reviews, has great appeal to me -- and would fully meet my purposes. It seems to me that it is true that this would tend rather to increase the sales thru Lippincott of the individual books [volumes published before the collected poems]　than to decrease them - - and, in fact, this seems to me the ideal plan. It would give me what I badly need: a line drawn under the 45 years of work, a place to stand and from which to begin the step into what I hope, and have always hoped, I would be able, finally, to do.[15]

--- to do, yes, during the next twenty years. I was wrong to have

284 Selected Letters of George Oppen

used the words *collected* poems in speaking of this proposal: I had not
meant to suggest an early death. Let us speak of it simply as Poems:
1929–1974[16]

(tho in fact to become 66 is an extremely odd thing to happen to a
child. I agree, tho that a *Collected* should await the final oddity of expi-
ration)

If you will undertake the hardback edition of the work to date, it
will fulfill my needs, and I will be very pleased.

———

———

I am taken by surprise to hear the situation concerning Bronk and
Reznikoff. I too value this work very highly. Rezi's By the Waters of Manhattan I value more than I can easily say -- I feel that if no other poetry
existed, we could make do on this.   The situation seems ironic, difficult
to accept: Rezi's reputation is increasing daily: his reception in San Francisco was no less than an ovation: they would not let him stop. The situation with Bronk is more difficult: he permitted me to edit the ms for
N D, but I think he is still resentful of my omissions - -. And Elizabeth
Press, I feel, has printed a somewhat damaging amount of his lesser work
- - - - I do think, tho, that it might be possible to sell the N D volume to
Jim Weil, of Eliz Press, or possibly to Cid Corman, rather than 'remain-
dering'

To Martin Rosenblum
[early July 1974]   TLs with AL postscript   Murphy Library,
University of Wisconsin–La Crosse

Martin:

sorry I didn't see your piece on *Seascape*[17]   I'll look it up on return
to S F (sometime in Sept)   But doubt I need offer additional remarks on
the 'Objectivists'   You'll have seen the issue of Contemporary Literature
[10, 2] with Reznikoff, Rakosi, Zukofsky and Oppen speaking (rather var-
iously) of these matters

Undoubtedly the Objectivists differed from each other.   And drastically.   I believe I thought of these poets simply as the poets I found
revelatory. I have no memory at all of having felt myself to be arguing or
supporting a theoretical (technical) position - -

(and yet perhaps the word *revelatory* does define a common intention or effort - - - *all experience is valid* --- the revelatory experience of
one's own life . . . . . .

   it is this that was uppermost in my mind (age 20 or thereabout)

   ((but this similarity among 'objectivists' prohibited other similari-
ties))

all regards

   - - - (and this is the matter of form) the poet learns from the poem,
his poem: the poem's structure, image, language: he also does not write
what he already knows (the danger is that as the poem forms, the doors
close)

   ((Pound, in conversation, circa 1930: 'there's the question how intelligent a given poet *has* to be')

   tho Pound was not using the word in its etymological root: Intelligent, the ability to gather - - - - he needs to be intelligent, he needs to
be intelligent - - - but Pound even then talking of Mussolini and - - - -the
rest of it.

   Misuse of 'intelligent'   tho perhaps said for my comfort) [typ-
ing apology]

all regards
George

To Diane Meyer
[summer 1974]   ALs   ucsd 16, 7, 28

Andy Dear
   - - or, you could have said, the cushy men and their professional
wives.[18] I can easily imagine them hiding from you, or escaping in food

   - - winds and sun here, and the open air: I feel close to you at that
party, coming in from the open air

   wonderful, wonderful sailing, the sea and the islands beautiful, and
the little boat seems to love us

   Sailed to Castine and back the following day: a crystal clear north
wind, white houses sharply visible twelve miles away on shore ----

   [Four sentences omitted by RBD] I realize more and more that we
have under-rated Mary all these years -- I don't know how we came to do
that.   I suspect that the women's movement might explain that to us - -

delicately, firmly, tactfully, and gently. Mary so much at home on these islands, in these forests, these woods. We talk to the people on this island - - people we've seen every summer for ten years. Mary whispers their names to me as they approach and I forget them again before I can say hello. It's getting strange, it's becoming strange. But the difficulty -- fortunately -- is not that there's too little, but too much. So that it's not the worst that could happen

       -- love to you Andy dear -- and thanks for your letter

                                   George

To June Oppen Degnan
[August 5, 1974]   ALs   UCSD 17, 5, 10

Dear June:

    Your letter very, very beautiful.   And yet, and yet - - - we have resolved that a President may not be a crook - - or, rather, that a small crook may (perhaps) not be President. Is it a tremendous moral resolve?

    - - Tho there have been a few faint, rather frightened references to J. Edgar Hoover, and Helms, and Milton Eisenhower - - but still no apologies to the jailed, the exiled, the murdered of 40's & 50's and the draft resisters of the 60's - - - -

    But yes, alright, still *something*, still something. Maybe, perhaps, it begins to dawn on the populace that 'conservatism' means the right of the 'big' to do what they please. I rather fear that the fact that Nixon is a pickpocket has rather obscured this issue.

    However, and meanwhile: [Walter] Flowers of Alabama, and [Charles] Rangel of Brooklyn is fine poetry, and I'm happy.   Ben Jonson's names of his characters couldn't compete with *that*![19]

    I wish I were a song-writer. Or a speech-maker. Flowers of Alabama, and Rangel of Brooklyn, our country, right or wrong, and waving fields of grain. Gentlemen, I nominate Waving Fields of Grain (applause).   But Nixon, that frightful little man. My sadism is more than assuaged. Why won't he give up, it is terrible to watch - - - a mangled rat on television![20]

    - - and they did vote for him, they did vote for him, tho they knew since '48 that he was a crook - - - but perhaps 'they' have learned something from this: I think 'they' have. So, yes, I agree with you. Patriotism,

Prosperity, Keep America Strong, etc., meant: why not a crook? And now everyone begins to see why not. That is to say, we've been scared. And that's good. It's very, very good. And none too soon.

(We're an odd country - - we tend to be unanimous. Suddenly everybody thinks it's wrong to bug telephones)

- - odd time to be in Maine, in a way. Half the summer's gone so fast we can't believe it. This island [Eagle] wilder --- it's not quite the word, but at any rate more oceanic than Little Deer - - - we tend to sail a little less, I think, for whenever we look out in wonder we see that we're in the sea - - -

Two publishers in the most recent mail (one Black Sparrow, which might be a very good place to be published) have written to say they've heard that I wanted a Collected Poems published, & that they will accept the ms. sight unseen - - - which is pleasant. But I think J [Laughlin] and I take it that we've made an agreement

(Black Sparrow *has* taken Rezi's new poems. So that's OK.) ((probably you knew this))

George

To John Taggart
[September 27, 1974]   TLs   UCSD 11, 17, 11

Dear John
--stopped in Austin to see our daughter and son in law -- home I think some 36 hours   /   too rattled, aerially   rattled to be sure ---- but have read a bit of your thesis -- some twenty-odd pages.   Not much as a reading - - - but immense as tribute to my interest in you, John, in the midst of answering heaps upon heaps of mail - - -[21]

'there are things we believe or think we believe or want to believe which will not substantiate themselves in the concrete materials of the poem --[22]

this is why he must follow 'the law of technique'   ?   this *is* in fact the law of technique?

this is the law   AND the prophets,   the prophecy   ?

Are you seeing technique as producing sincerity - - I would think in this sense: that attention to technique will force a change or even reversal in the poem - - there is no reason to versify what one already knows ----- but indeed your formulation may mean that one THINKS he knows - -

(the rectangles of your pure Crystals an instance of this searching light   a framing light[23]

and the margins beyond which perhaps the words destroy, distort - -

(it is not only the heavenly light, the pure light: there is terror in which 'words magic fails'

––––––

(I see that I really do not have time to write this note: too much to do   at the moment.   But wanted to acknowledge receipt and thanks   A marvelous gift

George

((apropos Louis: sincerity demands that one has BEEN there   ?   SOMEwhere ?   or? - - - - there rises the image of the spiderweb on the dead tree

Ariadne [Arachne?]   ;   the spider,   the guide

((and for one more contradiction: no denying the brilliance all but unbelievable of Louis' work

(you are of course correct: the philosophic background of Zuk, Oppen, Rezi (not Rakosi) is what 'the man in the street'   (who presumably has been run over)   regards as common sense - - 'Realist' (not, of course, in the Medieval sense   (tho perhaps the medieval angels on the head of a pin are there, the mathematic problem: one over zero if one should search for that antique echo - - most pronounced --and perhaps it could be said in all seriousness--- of Rezi

But Louis of course also touched by a Poetic Positivism - - I suspect its source simply the beauty of Wittgenstein's speech, language, it is a kind of seduction

(a touch of promiscuity: there are no philosophic virgins *intacta* these days   From the intricacies of Louis, the web   I regard myself (with possibly antique pride) as somewhat more nearly virginal in this respect - - Louis led astray in the 20's?   that era of flaming youth   (an odd picture of Louis: I acknowledge it.

but with this guilt, this guilty conscience   ? --- the long poem resolves itself in domesticity   'This is your house/   your wife's here, and your boy'

those beautiful lines.   Which make my joking tasteless

---- and yet these lines -- like all beautiful lines -- put poetry itself in question

tho these lines are Louis' thanksgiving to the muse[24]

as is, of course, *It Was*   I realize you cannot say this to the philosophy department

———

I thank you for the Study [typing apology]

George

[Written by Oppen on the back of the envelope]

(Z much interested in G. S. [Gertrude Stein] circa 1928–30 (in many conversations)   Have you noted Stein's debt to Lawrence Sterne?)

To John Taggart
[September 30, 1974]   TLs with AL postscript   UCSD 11, 17, 11

Dear John:

I have of course -- as you have too -- some reserves about a doctoral thesis which must seem to absorb the poem into itself, into the thesis   For the poem is of course not that, the poem is the moving edge, whereas the doctorate knows no time and the substance cannot live.   But you know this as well as I . . . . and indeed *the thesis frozen in its chains as it must be on a spinning planet* becomes,   in its heroism, - - I don't know.   a poetry?   a poetry seeking to be born   The ghost that haunts us   . A ghost is haunting the doctorate . . . ?

It is of course magnificently done   Its   own rigor pointing to a fragmentation of our rigors in the rigor of the whole, the moving edge.   'And one is I' [CP 247]

One is indeed I - - - me - - - and I have been much moved reading you

George

(forgive the hurried typing: my minor fragmentations

((in Louis' 'love' is sometimes lacking -- or inadequately recognized -- *force*.[25]   Here enters some touch of the quill-pen . . . the poet's pen . .
          . . . the philosophers are perhaps more terrifying than the poets.
          Whatever may be doubted, the actuality of consciousness cannot be doubted. 'Therefore consciousness in itself,   of itself carries the principle of actualness'   This is indeed the law and the prophets [cf. CP 253]
          It can happen in the poem.   Perhaps this should have been the meaning of 'objectivism.'

To Jerome Rothenberg
[Autumn? 1974]   TLs with AL postscript   UCSD 10, 60, 14

Jerry
          '- - - Its meaning (crucial meaning) is that it is now part of a mass movement' you most excellently told me once
          Group-poetry, vernacular ritual, chant, the naming   Possibly a part of the exodus from the cities, certainly an expansion in itself   Some possible liberations
          Possibly even a part of political defeat   Did, does the new left ever want a political victory?
          thanks for the greeting   Excellent as *Technicians*   on the whole Awaiting us the day we arrived[26]

                                        regards   congratulations
                                                  George

(Mary still talks of your reading at S F State

To Jerome Rothenberg
[Autumn? 1974]   TLs with AL postscript   UCSD 10, 60, 14

Jerry
          spent the day reading rev of the word - -
          mood nostalgic   but no reunion of the old school to me.   I thought: I was a stubborn old codger at an early age.
          I think the times failed.   (no fault of the present editor)
          ((no visible faults in the present editor)

(my memory - - probably faulty is that Bob Brown's Eyes appeared in Transition, circa 1930) [typing apology]

George

To Jerome Rothenberg
[Autumn? 1974]   TLs   UCSD 10, 60, 14

Dear Jerry:

Rev of the Word - - - fine job: I speak mildly I suppose because I had assumed it would be - -

I believe the only revision of my sense of these elders is in the case of Mina Loy whom I had drastically under-rated - - I had no memory of the 'wit' of her poetics - -

(autobiographical: The greats, the heroes of Paris and elsewhere . . . . . we were very conscious of being a generation younger than they - - - - - and were rather youthfully scornful of such recent history

- - - I mean, of them as people.   Thought them rather absurdly immodest.   We were immodest?   Not at all: we were simply the heroes of the story.   No, not the heroes, simply the protagonists

Don't know, simply don't know whether my attitude is 'conceited' or modest. Perhaps simply un-scholarly

- - - - nevertheless, spent the night reading

Too groggy to type, as you can see

George

My impression -- not of the editing but of the work -- is that it's inadequate.   My own too

To David McAleavey
[before October 9, 1974]   TLs   David McAleavey

Dear David:

I am entirely pleased by your essay --[27] no demurers - - - I am in fact quite moved --- well, very moved, by me and you

'by me and you':   I mean the phrase to sound not lame or small at all

Your discussion of avant-garde   pleased me indeed --- I cannot

remember that I had ever set myself to enter the avant garde on the page
- - - - I felt the avant-garde of time, of time itself - - - if we would rescue
love . . . etc

but as for avantgardism of technique - - - - I wrote as I could   I
found, if I could, and find if I can,   a way to say it - - -[28]

well, yes,   some sense of teleology is it?   or just that I don't
dislike the world.   I have sense enough to be afraid of it, of course, and
so I was quite moved by me and you   And several others, and so thanks
for your essay

George

garden   forest   an awning

fluttering   four-lane

highway the instant

in the open the moving
edge and one
is I

((quoting from myself: a poem in process)) [CP 247]

To David McAleavey
[early October 1974]   TLs   David McAleavey

Dear David:

converting image, that is, experience   ('what makes my image of
him an image of him?')   into parable - - - a necessity of the essay.   No
other way to do it.   I would offer no 'corrections' of any importance

-- and most moved by your scrupulousness.

(startled by your going back to the Aiken anthology.[29] Thought it just
a little story of my Western adolescence. And perhaps it is.   But I was
startled to discover that I remembered almost every poem you cited, tho
I had forgotten the names of many of the contributors to Objectivist anthology!

-- almost as in coming to understand a dream.

-- the essay has its own life, its quartering of the field, in Duncan's
phrase: leaps across the poems, journeys thru the poems to explicate - -
the essay itself an adventure, a work of art   In fact I found it very moving

(this merging of the poetic and the philosophic: their epistemo-
logies inseparable
     and thank you for it

                George

(their ontologies inseparable.   Their ethic indistinguishable)
     Inextinguishable
     tho the letters of the alphabet become gibberish   well, neverthe-
less, nevertheless, we make our meanings
              and they mean.

To David McAleavey
[October 1974]   TLs   David McAleavey

Dear David:
     having omitted   this minor protest, I find it still on my mind:
     Closed Car : Joy, all joy, tending to the joy of prominence   And
prominence becoming isolation, anaesthesia, ignorance.   Ignorance [CP
6]
     Little less than terrifying.
     The key word is *closed*   The car at the curb was closed, and later
the man closed in it.
     Yes, I am at fault in the Dembo interview

                George

To Anita Barrows
[October 1974]   TLs   Anita Barrows; carbon UCSD 16, 2, 28

Anita
     was thinking -- after our conversation:
     the phrase 'black is beautiful' was a life-saving slogan.   A blaze of
light, I think it lit many lives
     so: it was poetry
     The man, woman who said that knew it had the force of poetry
     To repeat it is 'political poetry.'   That is, to repeat it is to recite
poetry

Reciting poetry and writing poetry are not the same thing   (no objection to reciting poetry of course)

((Whitman celebrated America   Because he had seen it, it came to *him*

I hope that by the year two-thousand   *black is beautiful* will be something in the nature of Fourth of July oratory.   Recitation.

> (nice visit)
>
> George

(re-   cite)

To Anita Barrows
[October 1974]   TLs   Anita Barrows

Anita:

[. . .]30

(Lorine?   ;   touching, very touching and brave including the bravery of skill, an acerbic bravery - -- The neatnesses a little too marked? and the distances too great, that is, too small

> distance from the 'full foamy
> folk'31

not to dismiss people.   not that I want to dismiss people and poems, but

sauve qui peut

or in another phrase of fluent French, it is not forbidden to lean out the window32

((I'm just being 'clever --- it is, in its way, a saving poetry   And 'perfect' . . . . . Perfect: saves without hope.   But, in the end, saved her.

———

[. . .]33

> - - --George

[During 1974, Oppen also corresponded with Paul Auster, Philip and Margaret Booth, Michael Cuddihy, Rachel Blau DuPlessis, Michael Hamburger, Michael Heller, Stuart Lavin (published in *Four Zoas Journal*),34 Armand Schwerner, Diane Wakoski, and Douglas Worth.]

1975

[The issue of *Ironwood* devoted to Oppen appeared in March; also, on March 12, Oppen introduced Carl Rakosi, who was reading at San Francisco State University. In May, the Oppens gave two interviews, on May 1 to Reinhold Schiffer and on May 25 to Kevin Power.[1] In Maine, Mary Oppen was writing her memoirs, *Meaning a Life*. On September 1, the Oppens went to Israel, in residency at Mishkenot Sha'ananim in Jerusalem.[2] They returned, after a brief stop in Greece, in October. Oppen's *Collected Poems* was published on October 23.[3]]

To Carl Rakosi
[1975]   TLs   Houghton Library, Harvard University

Carl:
        I am honored by the dedication[4]

            look long distances
        but inside are small
        from sweetness of the knowledge of mortality[5]

        or: *Enter an heroic line, disguised.*

            'It has been Englished'[6]

        The poems are very, very fine, and I am honored, old friend[7]
                                George

To Carl Rakosi
[1975]   TLs   Houghton Library, Harvard University

Dear Carl
        Ex Cranium - - a marvel   Above all, perhaps, the 'Poet' section
- --- Or perhaps the Day Book --- tho it might also be the letters written

in the persona of a woman - - - or   or   --in fact, all are mar-
vels

     I don't know, I don't know: is it the words or the light behind the
words?   I don't know, but it's a marvel   Is it the tone, the brilliance, or is it the force of the words

     (it is what we mean when we say *poetry*)

     Poetry is a word with comparatively few referents

George

To John Taggart

[January 25, 1975] TLs Homer Babbidge Library, University of
Connecticut, Storrs

John:

     worked my way thru accumulated mail   Hurriedly. Can't re-
member what I may have written concerning 'technique'[8]   Can't imagine having said anything much in opposition to what you say of it --

     'an acquisition, like any skill, because of deep need --' and the mu-
sic indeed is the crystal of your book

     fellow me airs, fellow me airs, it is form makes the thing, the poem,
graspable the pure and the visible crystal[9]

     did I say otherwise   ?   I retract.

     there is the problematic generality   But if we speak of experience,
speak *to* experience, the cadence, the sound the form . . . . . did I say otherwise?   surely should not have

     thanks for your care and tact in Shippensburg

George

To Carl Rakosi

[February 19, 1975] TLs Houghton Library, Harvard University

Old Friend:

     -- and a tough old bird also, o marvelously elegant old bird, thanks
for your words.[10]

George

     ((I'll see you in March   Right? at the San Francisco Museum (among the exhibits of antiquities?)   ((observe the vest-buttons, the guide will say))[11]

((I say nothing of fly-buttons, hoping you will read that poem concerning your fly-less self in the bathtub))[12]

that byzantine eye - - do please read it.[13] I begin to ponder my Byzantine 'introduction'

To James Laughlin
[February 1975]   TLs   James Laughlin

Dear J:

Thanks for your note.   I'll be interested in Kenner's remarks.

(Kenner invited us to visit Santa Barbara a few years ago - - pondering an offer of poet-in-residence, I supposed, and because I did not intend to accept -- or perhaps out of pure perversity -- I persistently talked of Sherwood Anderson. Causing Kenner considerable pain, of course.

But not really pure perversity in me: I wanted to have a look at Anderson, sentimental and populist and touching: Anderson in the light of Kenner's aristocratic brilliance.   Or to have a look at Kenner in the light of Anderson?

Anderson and those like him launched on a kind of secular pilgrimage.   And on the mid-west landscape   We, at least, have a debt to them

(we, Mary and I, barely touched the last moments of all that -- were there to receive its last breath, as it were, and feel a kind of paternity back there   ) rather immature, as perhaps we'd prefer our fathers to be.

(being driven to the station by Mrs Kenner, we passed Kenner on his small motorcycle headed for the college and looking for all the world, in that green landscape, like an Irish Gentleman on his fine Irish Hunter))

I'd be interested to read Kenner on G O   No one I'd be more interested to read on that subject.[14]

Best wishes   and to Ann
George

———

Peter Glassgold sends some queries concerning details of the ms   Very clear and scrupulous: I think we'll have no difficulties

To James Laughlin
[between February 25 and March 26, 1975]   ALs   James Laughlin

J:

lost *all* our papers in 1950 - - - A bad blow to us. I have only two
short notes from Williams: One is a little note to say he enjoyed our visit,
and to say some kind words about *The Materials*.   The other is permission
to quote him on the back-cover of The Materials. These notes dated very
near the end of his life - -

To send the first is obviously self-serving on my part - - and the
second positively embarrassing;   it was a rather shabby act - - and pretty
shabby to display them now, so I'll refrain.[15]

--we much enjoyed your visit and Ann's, by the way

George

To Harvey Shapiro
[after March 1975][16]   TLs   Harvey Shapiro

Dear Harvey

'frivolous letter' you say   An entrancing letter   You seem to
me, tho probably not to yourself, the only city man I know   now as
Rezi recedes into history, tho to me the most vivid and living history,
perhaps the only history I *feel*

(as to one's impression of oneself vs other's impression: Rakosi
read at S F State and stayed two days with us.   Rakosi's first words on
the threshold: 'You're taller than I thought you were

Me: no I'm not

certainly, I felt, *I* should know how tall I am.

Hilton Kramer did indeed visit   Which we enjoyed very much,
and so thanks

his admiration for your work very profound   We too, as you see 'decided to be social' and also feel cheered   Cheered and - - what?   Vague
feeling that there's a meat grinder somewhere that we cannot quite visualize and which all these people are telling us about

we feel we're missing something unknown, we feel rather flatulent
like a whole side of beef

we feel somewhat unbutchered and neglected   But this is not Hilton or Rakosi really: it is apropos of the whole, I think, of Stony Brook

and certainly the whole of Sumac, plus Jerry Rothenberg and others who foregathered - - - - -

Flattering   I kept trying to look profound, fatherly in a bony Jewish manner   Didn't, I don't think   Didn't quite not -----

cannot bring ourselves to plan a stop in N Y   Mary just will not   Says, kindly, that I could   I can't face it, airport or any of it.

CAN YOU NOT MAKE A LITTLE TRIP AT LEAST TO MAINE????
we'll sail you to islands, we'll - - - - walk you in forests,   whatever you want

((Rakosi talks with unmitigated sub-sociological sentimentality about poetry, including his own, and writes, as you've noticed, with considerable glitter and pride - - -   )) Notice he hasn't read me   Or you   He's deep in the sense of Jewishness: I loaned him Battle Report[17] -- which he'll mail back

he's confident and at ease in a class room, by the way   Probably a good teacher   Why do I report all this?

George

To Michael Cuddihy
[March 1975]   TLs   Michael Cuddihy: copy in UCSD 16, 3, 53

Dear Michael:
the meaning of the book,   the value of the book   (and I think it is very high value)   is your own love of poetry --[18]

what shines even from the cover of the book is your love of poetry, I become almost dizzy to find myself playing a part in it

and another step into beauty beyond belief with the photo on the page where Mary's eyes look across the page to Mary's prose, eyes and prose in the same light, reflecting the same light, everything becomes clear at this moment   The light that *matters*.

Michael, no way to thank you for this labor of love   A love that picked, among other things, me.   But it's your love, Michael,   it's yours   A lot of praise for me in the book, but I blush sheepishly: what shines, is Michael's capacity for love, and care, and I thank you   Tho it is impossible to thank you.

George

(I seem to have been very lucky, Michael: it is astonishingly lucky to be lucky)

I am lucky in my friends   :   Charles Tomlinson, Carl Rakosi, Rezi, Diane Wakoski, Ted Enslin, Serge Fauchereau, Bruce Andrews, [Larry] Dembo and Charles McBride and John Taggart and David McAleavey and Rachel Blau DuPlessis, and others[19]

And Zukofsky, who would not reply, but from whom I learned some crucial matters, and others who are not poets   (and this fact too has been extremely lucky)

To Robert Duncan
[after March 16, 1975]   TLs   Poetry/Rare Books Collection, SUNY-Buffalo

R'bt:

interested in your remarks about the recent poems. Didn't perfectly follow. You were saying the recent poems are incomprehensible   ?   I don't really think so.   And was not thinking of that which cannot be said in language -- of that indeed silent however unwillingly.   I was confused by the entry of Wittgenstein --

- - do, however, think of that which cannot be said except thru the poem. Nothing very wild about this: the line-break is as much a part of the language as the comma   the period   the paragraph?

(this is not a debate.   Maybe a foot-note)

a fine day, a fine walk.   Love

George

((it is true there has been a remarkable silence about those poems.   And R Blau, whose opinion I also respect, wrote simply that they made her dizzy[20]   Bit troubling, yes. But I thought I was simply pointing to things -- and clearly enough or accurately enough   Perhaps not.   I'll see how they look later

((thought the eyes of the Tiger pretty damn *clear* [CP 244]!

((Mary, reading this, reminds me that you mentioned Heidegger. Yes, I see.   I point: it is true I don't think everything has already been named, yes it's true.

To Rachel Blau DuPlessis
[March 21, 1975]   TLs with AL postscript   R. B. DuPlessis

Rachel

>   questions in your letter:

>   don't know that I'm 'seeking' a basic element.   Maybe.   My spon-
taneous feeing is that I *look*   If there's a basic element, I assume we'll
arrive there

>   yes, I suppose I assume a basic element.   I would not want to look
away,   to disregard this.

>   Soli: used your words because they were perfect.[21]   I was
thinking of the young women, the young women in small towns and farm-
lands   (the countryside itself rose up at the end and perhaps dominated
the poem -- or no, that scene finally of the coast described their (our) isolation.

>   'I feel too vulnerable, with no poem, just looking, and thinking'

>   these are the wonderful things you say,   I mean this is one of them.
And of course I feel sometimes too armored with all those poems *written*
- - - - - written, I would like to be adrift again - - I am afraid, I mean, that
I might lose the sea

>   *Have talked too much!*

>   'why me,' you say 'plus Pound?'   not sure of the reference here[22]
But answered above: not you, but your words   I simply stole 'em

>   (You can see why I couldn't credit the lines to you)   (even tho you
may partly have meant yourself, or a fear for yourself)

>   This is a funny letter, like an interview

>   Better come visit.
>   George

Advice: stop writing poetry.   Write prose.   Without telling yourself   that
prose has to be different from poetry, or longer, or anything else.   Just
don't use line breaks, line divisions and then it's prose.[23]

To Rachel Blau DuPlessis
[April 17, 1975]   TLs   R. B. DuPlessis

Dear Rachel:

>   a form of doodling: - - - going backward and forward in a poem

that won't form - - - your essay comes into my mind again ---- "he simply turned his back" - - - Biographically true   -- or somewhere very close to it --- the sharp phrase startled me, as it should: it is beautiful and sharp essaying.[24]

--- but may not be true of the poems or not quite if you consider "And Their Winter and Night"[25]   the images of war again (politics by other means)   and the reference to Blake and the songs of Innocence and the Songs of Experience paralleling and contradicting each other poem by poem - - -

even that it's the Nurses Song has some reference to the Old Left - - - -[26]

not complaining: I could hardly approve the essay more, or any essay more   But here's a letter; thinking I would like to talk

George

(my birthday's the 24th   Take a plane and I'll have a birthday party

IT IS

if it is not
a small
truth to be held
in the hand a groping
down a reaching
down even a machine
does not reveal
only itself it is
connected to all
other things meaning
is the mind among
things indeed
what is
lived

(the poem that won't form.   Probably the poem knows best)
((times when a crippled poem will turn and look at me and
say   George........?

To John Crawford
[after May 1, 1975]   TLs with AL inserts   John Crawford; photocopy UCSD
16, 3, 48

Dear John:
  [cut; discussion of a Crawford poem] (And there we come to the real prohibition of love between equals, adequate love between equals in the Left)
  Mary and I knew we were not professional revolutionaries, not really, because we loved each other. But then the war. How does one say he is 'in favor' of a war, meaning he is in favor of someone else fighting it?
  -- and still I am not sure (and Mary is perhaps too kind to say) what-all was at work in that decision)
  [cut, more discussion of the poem by Crawford]
  ((I once read thru 10 years worth of Soviet Lit Today and of Chinese Lit today
  Every peasant woman (heroine of the story, and Stakhanovite) who exposed (of course) the saboteur, thereafter left her husband and married the Farm Manager, Communist organizer, or whoever was highest in rank in her purview
  Every male Stakhanovite of equal merit also joined himself in holy deadlock with a Stakhanovite lady (with a record, of course, slightly below HIS
  as for China: ditto But no need to go into it: there was the famous Sons and Daughters (have I the title right) which sold several trillion copies or whatever
  [written in margin] Mary says I have the name wrong (in fact the name of a medieval novel.) I mean a novel that appeared in the 50's

———

  Alright, alright Spender (was it?) wrote of Bourgeois love: 'to be good to one or two --' yes I know. But love is a bit strained, it don't quite fall like the dew
  I don't mean an attack: this isn't 'politics' And no one should starve for someone else's love. The poem must work it out
  -- yes: something of it is there in the father's death in your poem.

((and still I don't think it can be done.   Not, surely, with the approval of the Left.

Simply: the revolutionary proposal is that we must sacrifice at least a generation.   I don't reject the proposal.   But where such staggering proposals are made there is one thing, one classic virtue we MUST have, and that's honesty

which the Left almost thematically rejects: It appears as liberalism, at least in thought. Let the leftist speak honestly [citations from Crawford's poem]:

'I can't love one'

(it's the 'hard-eyed man' whom I trust not one inch.

To Eric Homberger
[May 30, 1975]   TLs   Eric Homberger

Dear [Eric]:[27]

I thank you for the research - - - I could not have brought myself to do it, fearing to find myself in the dim and dusty past among my elders - - -

Startled to see that none of these reviewers had the least idea of what I was saying, speaking of -- Williams, I think, simply defending the 'modern,'   and the others spluttering about it   Tho Bill did choose the Cat Boat poem to display -- choosing the poem that one might well think unmistakable, the most infectious - -[28]

(Pound, despite the Browningesque swagger he chose for himself, saw the poems clearly.   Saw also the tentativeness of their 'success.'   He said, 'sensibility,'   not 'Here we are, completed,   done and said - -'[29]

(the young writer says 'me too,'   but cannot know if the 'too' is justified.   'I know too,' he says.   But they read neither the world nor themselves as he read them.

Trials of one's youth - - - knowing, in those times, least of all about one's contemporaries.   (we in our early twenties: 'everyone'   was older than we)

Thanks again for finding these.   Hope to see you soon again- - we enjoyed the evening immensely

George

To Carl Rakosi
[June 16, 1975]   ALs   Houghton Library, Harvard University

Dear Carl:

"Lordy I've been lucky" - - Don't know, don't remember the context in which I said it; but I have

- - probably meant lucky in my friends. Including Carl R.[30]

(and your remarks about Denise at Yaddo - ('could have been me in the old days')   tells me the depth of your political commitment in those old days which I had suspected but you didn't say - - and which makes our friendship not so new as we said it was to each other talking to each other from the bottom and the top of those Brooklyn-like   stairs.[31]

love
George

To Paul Auster
July 8, 1975 (dated)   ALs   Middlebury College Library

Dear Paul:

The circumstances of the moment being a small shack on an island in Penobscot Bay - - and the small shack being very damp at the moment - - I can't write adequately of your incomparable essay on Charles Reznikoff[32]

. . . . To have seen the space (which is the world) between the words

'Each word the sign of an exile . . . One's place, from now on, is the world'

- - - I write for the joy of repeating these words   .   And would want to repeat all the words of your piece

with thanks
George

To John Wilson
[Summer 1975]   ALs   John Wilson

Dear John:

In fact I am very moved by Taggart's essay.[33]   I feel myself to be a stubborn old codger . . . and yet there is no joy greater than the joy of being heard.   Heard - - I don't believe there is a name for this rhetorical figure - - but I will say: heard so eloquently.

The temperature here is in the forties;   we sailed our way home from Camden - - or groped our way home - - in cold and blinding fog - - - I'm far from complaining, it was a marvelous trip, a pair of seals followed us for an hour, and other wonders and delights - - but I'm sitting with my feet in the stove and answering a package of mail, so I'll ask you please to quote me to John T. - - with messages of love

- - - and I thank you for Occurrence and all its contents[34]

George

To James Laughlin
[September or October 1975]   TLs with AL inserts   James Laughlin

Dear J

We are, as you see by the letter-head, in Israel: we having been invited on a sort of cultural exchange program[35]

We are dazed and heartsick.   Wonderful conversations -- [Yehudah] Amichai, Abba Kovner, and others, all treating us as if we had known each other forever.[36] And there are the armed guards -- perfectly useless, and there is no possibility of anything but war forever and of course everyone wants to ask us why we don't immigrate, and we are ashamed to answer, for the Israelis are bargaining for their lives, and any 'concessions' will cost lives, Israeli lives, and there is no where else they can go -- nowhere that ALL of them can go -- and they're too polite to force us to an-swer - - -, and we are heartsick

and dazed for here are the archeological sites, David['s] castle and Solomon's temple and the cave where Ben Kothbar and the last of his followers died, it is just where it was said to be--- letters and memo-randa: 'send us two carcasses of beef if you can for we have no more food'[37] - - - - - And here is the via dolorosa, it is here, and it is a street . . . . .   And here are the inscriptions, the words and the history of three great religions,   and sometimes we wish that we would come to an ancient inscription saying: Sometimes I feel like a motherless child.

it is not a 'vacation.' It is not a vacation in Maine

———

We received the books   thru N D's miraculous ingenuity
I think I wrote of this to Jim [Fred?] Martin: we asked the young

lady at the information desk at N Y airport for directions to the Catholic Chapel, and as we left she said -- somewhat less than half-lightly -- Say a prayer for me.   The Father was not in, so we left a note for the Father with his secretary, telling him this story and adding, "so I pray for her happiness."   The secretary must have read this note after we left, for she ran after us and said: Say a prayer for me too.   So I did that too - - at the Praying Wall, and it is not a vacation in Maine.

I find that Mary has the invoice. We will send a check from S. F.[38] We are stopping in Athens to see our son-in-law's mother, and stopping in Austin to visit our daughter and son-in-law - - - - both of which we had to promise to do - - - we will arrive in San Francisco, I'm afraid, taxy-ing in, quite literally taxying in on our last energy

Thanks again for the books
George

(I write this on a borrowed typewriter having a strange key-board --- Hebrew? Ancient Greek?   Phoenician? --- and must hope that it is decipherable)

To Harvey Shapiro
[Fall 1975?]   TLs   Harvey Shapiro

Harvey
        I cannot 'answer' your last letter   caught in similar dead-ends
Cannot write an adequate poetry either   The second time around for
me
        A story in the times: Tel Aviv: the Play, *The Queen of the Bathtub* has been withdrawn here . . . offensive to the armed forces . . . . deputy premier so-and-so denounces it . . . . particular exception to the portrayal of a father who wanted his son killed so that he might appear as a bereaved and heroic parent - - - - - - - - - - - -
        disturbances by members of the audience - - - - - -[39]
        here we go again.   Are they wrong?   a people girding itself, needing all of its courage, all-but superhuman courage, all of its self-love and

self-respect - - - - - - Is it a time to bother them with ----- with poetry or anything but this?

     as the hungry in the 30's   As the victims of Fascism   As the draftees and the Vietnamese now - - - - A world war   possibly final approaching   Second time around

     I did write -- I forget which poem --- this question   --Sing? to one's fellows ?---   that is, to one's 'equals'   a song, I said, full of treason [CP 91]

                       well, that's it
                           Other factors also.

     Perhaps Mary and I searched for 'trouble'   and for the problems of children, a child's world - - a parent's world (which is the same thing)   Not that Mary and I were unhappy, but that we were not   The Happy Ending -- which is an end.   And so we looked for the children   Or The Workers   or - - something beyond the Happy Ending which was, in a way, an end

     all this and - - - it would be a very long and contradictory letter   I cannot resolve it   Unless in the treason of - - - well, of the discrete series, perhaps.

     These words of your friend won't strengthen you, I'm afraid   Unless 'Me too' is strengthening[40]

                       our love to you, though,
                       or also
                       George

To Harvey Shapiro
[mid-October 1975][41]   TLs   Harvey Shapiro

Dear Harvey:

     someone phoned from N Y a few days ago (second day of our return or thereabouts to ask me to read with you in N Y

     I've been postponing this letter because it's going to involve me in some messy confessions more suitable to the ear of a therapist - - In fact, I've read nowhere since that festival in Michigan -- unable to bring myself to do so - - -- AND trouble with my work, unable to be sure of it -- I've sent nothing for publication, or almost nothing, short poems, and unsure of them - - - and I've done no readings at all - - - two or three years isn't it since the Michigan doings?[42]

you said something once about your sense of personal drama   My drama is the role of David with his home-made sling-shot;   I fall down dead in the role of Goliath, and even the minuscule 'recognition' of the last few years - - - - I make a miserable Goliath.   It's a minuscule and almost secret 'fame' I've attained, but it's too much for me - - -   it's not the drama I can sustain.   Just can't do it.   I really am in serious trouble with this damn neurosis, trouble with my work, I mean --- my voice shakes and I get sick thinking of myself even as the least of star performers - - poor Mary.   But this neurosis in fact was my escape from the poor little rich boy, and the basis of my adult life   I have to protect it, let the Shrinks fall where they may

but indeed I could wish I was otherwise -- I think of you reading the three old Jews who look down -- and I reading some of the most recent poems in the collected - -[43] Well - - - - the three old Jews including Freud look down and cluck their tongues, they always did, they've always been there, I've heard them clucking - - - they sure clucked over me as a G I, and they're clucking now like crickets in a summer evening

and so, I'm afraid, are you.   For which I'm sorry.   And poor Mary.   (who in fact doesn't mind

(that's her neurosis)

I am 'laying low'   Or perhaps lying-in.   And may give birth.

George

To Harvey Shapiro

[Fall 1975]   TLs with AL insert   Harvey Shapiro

Dear Harvey:

I don't think I meant a lecture - -.[44]   The situation at my typewriter was this: I could write, 'the poems are brilliant.'   The same little lecture (alright: a lecture) would have been there in the failure to say more.   So I said what I said: said why I couldn't find a way to say more - -.   Friendship and a real admiration for the force of the poems notwithstanding

to all of which you answer.   Cogently indeed.   'My sense of personal drama,' and the question of who the hell reads me or ever heard of me --- all cogent indeed

-- but,   then, that's my sense of personal drama.   David,   Not Goliath: I go to pieces (as Goliath did) in the role of Goliath

David: a sensitive Jewish boy.   With, however, a little home-made sling-shot

(it is true I learned a little   carpentry from the Butler: God knows I couldn't have learned it from any relatives - -

--- and yes, I thought the same of the photograph: an idle, sensitive Jewish boy.   Fortunately Mary had never seen one before.[45]

Difficult to manage 'tone' in this correspondence: I hope, for God's sake, that we're friends   I'll assume we are

as for the argument from [Erica?] Jong - - - I am not in a position to judge, since I've not read the Jong, but I suspect the argument is not valid - -- there was once someone named - - - - - I forget the names.   But that's the point.

George

((and my correspondence is a mess.   Also a number of other things   Senility: no other word for it.   I cannot remember what happened yesterday: I fail to recognize people I know well - - -.   67:   a little early for such things- - -   I cannot do simple arithmetic: I mis-read clocks - - Maybe I went too far in the home-made slingshot business - - - It is very extreme.   Been talking to a doctor: he begins with no coffee, no tea, no alcohol, and of course no tobacco, but I don't find that possible. - - I see myself walking about supported by Mary's elbow - - - pretty soon   (Or is Mary's elbow a stimulant, and therefore forbidden?)

[written in margin with a line drawn to the last paragraph] This is the news: you wanted news.   This is it.

To Michael Heller
[after mid-November 1975]   TLs with AL insert   Michael Heller

Dear Mike

-- I'd seen your note of me --- Wasn't sure of the etiquette of replying to praise ---- all the more in that I was delighted[46]

(the experience of Discrete Series,   the insistence that it COULD not be understood,   leaves me in danger of weeping in friendship,   in companionship,   over such an essay on the work   - - that work and the new work.

yes: the word *presentness*   :   central to me too

(((yes: read quite a bit of Merleau-Ponty (tho not the book you mention. I'll look for   it)[47] - - - More moved by Maritain - - -- Maritain of the *Creative Intuition in Art and Poetry* - - - only that book of his, in fact -

and Heidegger -- whom I quoted on a fly-leaf: "the third path, the arduous path of appearance"

(any chance of your appearing sometime in S F?   It would be pleasant to talk

George

To Sharon Olds
[November 18, 1975]   TLs   Sharon Olds

Dear Sharon Olds

flatly impossible to read all the magazines that are delivered to my helpless door   Troubles me, for I had once dreamed of becoming old and being as responsive and perceptive as Bill Williams and Ezra had been - - -Foolish dream;   I'm not fitted for it, aside from lacking their influence

But I possess a guardian angel - - I've been aware of this for some time   Glancing thru the deluge of mags in the most cursory and unconscionable way, I read what I should read.   I've noticed this before. And still I'm amazed that among the 19th century lithographs of Kayak I come upon a poem as fine and powerful as *Satan Says*   Your angel-devil watches over me among the pin-cushions

(and thanks to him-her)[48]

George Oppen

To Linda Oppen Mourelatos
[November 22, 1975]   TLs with AL additions   ucsd 33, 1, 19

Lindy dear:

(my typewriter, as you'll see) needs repair --- I'll try to manage - - -

of the list, as you said, of people ruined or injured - - It would be a very long list.   and some --- [Friend's Name] spoke of this --- some who had been ruined before they became what they meant to be and would

have become --- [Friend's Name] himself;   Trumbo had already become Trumbo, and, even black-listed, was the man who had written major
scripts - - the injustice was visible   Whereas [Friend's Name] was
blacklisted as one of the major studios was about to accept a major
script - - -

and others.   Several thousand schoolteachers in N Y blacklisted --
-- whole groups of lawyers and of doctors - - - it would be a very long list.

(I wrote a small note about one of the poets -- Tom McGrath --
which is reprinted in that Ironwood issue - - - I said: 'I do not know
how many'[49]   But they were very many, they were very many   The public and the juries refused to believe (because it was frightening to believe)
that the FBI, the CIA, the police, the judges - - -the whole of government --- lied.   Were lying.

--and for all the mistakes, and worse than mistakes of the Left, there
is this fact: During that time, all the major countries of the world became Fascist or near-fascist   (Italy, Germany, Spain) or moved leftward
--- Labor Party, Front Populare, New Deal - - - - - - - - - - -   despite all
that was wrong with the Left.   That's what it was, that's the history of
the time.

((I'll Xerox -- if I get 'round to it -- a poem or two of Naomi Replansky's - - that speak of these things in their own way))

I think it is true that we could not have done otherwise than as we
did   I think that   to have done nothing, nothing at all - - - I think
we'd have lost each other. - - I mean, me and Mary

((it is strange now reading these 'revelations' -- for they are not
revelations, everyone always knew.   They merely were not shocked.   And
suddenly they're shocked   ?   it is very strange, very strange
with our love, Lindy dear [typing apology]
Pop

To Harvey Shapiro
[end 1975]   TLs   Harvey Shapiro

Dear Harvey:

Muse,
Once   you made this chaos shine[50]   Still, in a way, shines.

the whole book perfect, powerful - - - and yes it's chaos, and in a way it shines

Harvey: I wouldn't say this except that you say in the poems that you're troubled by under-recognition - - -:   A lack of   'world-view'   Must be something wrong with what I'm saying that I need such a hyphenated expression, but in a way the poems can't be understood, the anger seems merely your own.   Which means, it can't be understood- - - -

this is the public resistance to the poems.

I don't mean to dismiss them   It would be hard to do, there is very great force in them

In The Room is the major marvel.   And it does, in a way, tell the story: it tells that you can't tell

I can't sleep.
Love has fixed my head.
Now this girl, now that.

certainly better than Skunk Hour.   But it doesn't tell, it's locked in itself, this is the problem

(Lowell saved it a little with the image of the skunks.)[51]

((some implication of the force of the given))[52]

I don't know   Can't help.   They are powerful poems
George

To Jonathan Griffin
[end 1975]   TLs   Jonathan Griffin

Dear Jonathan:

the syntax!   moves of its own force, moves in the force of the world, it restores light and space to poetry.   It is what the poetry of England has lacked for -- how long? - - -

'She!   the
fairest of her daughters Earth'[53]

it is an event   And the poem, the poems are events.   I mean they *matter*! It's become a rare thing

- - - - - - well, it always has been

(Shakespeare has been a good master to you)

George

To Robert Kelly

[before December 22, 1975]   TLs   Poetry/Rare Books, SUNY-Buffalo

Dear Robert Kelly:

thru stupidity?   or, more charitably stated, thru pressure on my time and the startling deluge of mail which is somehow generated by modern times, I have neglected to read you with any approach to adequacy   And am now grateful indeed to Black Sparrow who have sent me The Loom

-- above all, at first reading for the section numbered 22, and the marvel of its last lines[54]

((I continue to look for excuses: there IS such a deluge of magazines, of poetry, and   is bad?   No, it is a network of poets, and not to be deplored, but - - - - - -

and I rely on my destiny: I do finally come upon what there is

ALL BEST WISHES

George Oppen

(my impression that you have learned a good deal from Zuk   -- from whom indeed much can be learned   ?   would it be absurd to suggest Eliot also   ? --yes; absurd; the differences so great.   Less absurd if I had said Rilke   ?   ---- in the movement, the 'narrative'   ?

(my respect for Rilke so great that I tend to hear him whenever a sufficient depth is reached - - - this trick of my mind has nothing to do with hunting 'sources'

(((and my respect for the Quartets somewhat greater than is fashionable at the moment

[In 1975, Oppen also corresponded with Stephen Berg (for The American Poetry Review), Philip Booth, Theodore Enslin, Serge Fauchereau, David and Maria Gitin, Michael Hamburger, Shirley Kaufman, David McAleavey, Gerard Malanga, Sister Patricia Ryan, Armand Schwerner, Tony Stoneburner, John Taggart, Charles Tomlinson, Sarah Appleton Weber, J. D. Whitney, and Barbara Wright (of the Poetry Center, San Francisco State University).]

1976

[On January 22, Charles Reznikoff died; in late January or February, George and Mary Oppen discussed Reznikoff, interviewed by Charles Amirkhanian on Pacifica Radio (KPFA).[1] In March, Oppen's *Collected Poems* was nominated for the poetry prize of the National Book Award; the prize in fact went to John Ashbery. New Directions brought out a paperback edition of the *Collected Poems* on October 4. In the summer, the Oppens went to Maine, and in the fall, they considered buying or renting a "shack" in Tomales Bay or Marshall, California.]

To Diane Meyer
[1976]   TLs   UCSD 16, 7, 29

Andy:
        in Mexico we were the age you are now.   Not an easy time.   Very nearly lost each other   among other things.
        Not broke   but persecuted.   Every now and then in hiding   Fairly close equivalent, isn't it?
        also (1958)   Linda had started college.   Very nearly lost her   Did, somewhat, lose her
        Also (1958)   that I confessed to myself that I possessed a marked ability - - and that it wasn't carpentry
        Not an easy time of one's life.
        our experience seems to show that there's another side to come out on   Hang on, Andy
                                                George

To Rachel Blau DuPlessis
[April 13, 1976]   TL with AL inserts   R. B. DuPlessis[2]

Dear Rachel:
    to occupy the 'idea'; to live in it - - this is simply and precisely the undertaking of poetry
    there is no prescription for the doing
    Talk in the poems as if speaking to divinity . . . does this phrase help? Speaking to divinity - - i.e., the vertical dimension - - -
    'vertical dimension':   one of the things the line-break is *for*
    (when one is not in the vertical dimension, when one is talking only to the reader, the lines *lengthen*

    Paul Auster visited, full of unlimited praise for your essay on my work[3]
    Don't know if I've answered, I mean I am sure I have not
    But I do know this: you analyze too much: you set yourself too much of a program- - - The program prevents you from sinking *in* ((into the-thing-before-the-words))

                                          [unsigned]

To Rachel Blau DuPlessis
[April 29, 1976]   TL   R. B. DuPlessis

Dear Rachel
    I send you this for whatever you may feel about it --- whatever, not excluding indignation - -[4]
    send it - - I don't know -- just because I did it. The principle not, I think,   any scheme of prosody but - - that the words -- an attempt to connect each word, as nearly as I could in a hurry connect *each* word AT BOTH ENDS - - - connected at the beginning and the end of the word - - which *is*, perhaps, 'the vertical dimension'   (which phrase you accepted)
    --Open of course to all other possibilities, and you may simply dis-agree altogether, but - - -- - - but, to me --- narrative itself must at certain points STAND STILL - - - -
    which is approximately what I was trying to do in this ver-sion - - -[5]

If you feel it's wrong, O K, O K - - - I've only meant to feel my way, maybe to feel *our* way, I don't know

(I have an advantage: I write such godawful prose that I am not tempted to prose procedures)

I am moved by the poem --- and can't keep my hands off it

love

[unsigned]

((I made the experiment, as you see, only on the first page of your ms

To Naomi Replansky
[April 29, 1976]   ALs   Naomi Replansky

Dear Naomi,

can't type (strained my back somehow. And don't know if my handwriting is legible- - (and what a strange thing! Your ms arrives the day after I had been re-reading Ring Song!⁶

These things happen

Very moving poems in The Darkening Green - very very moving - - and still the wit of parable and the wit of language, wit of form (perhaps above all, for me, in *I met my solitude* - - or, how to choose - - many others

I see the tightness, the force you gain (a spider-kiss scuttling / thru a close-mouthed rhyme) ((who could fail to see it?)) from the form you demand of yourself, and yet I think that if you should experiment with free-er forms you would - - - well, what to say? or how to say it - - - - - you would find *another* poetry, new to you; another landscape . . . . to explore. I don't mean any reservation against the poems - - Just that I'm thinking of possibly still *another* landscape that could open up for you

and thanks for the poems

George

Do the poems lack a vertical dimension? They are so entirely *social* - - (I don't mean 'political')

To James Laughlin
[about May 6, 1976]   TLs with AL postscript   James Laughlin

Dear J:

we went, of course, to Bunting's reading here.   A triumph, a magnificent reading - -

Mary delighted by the number of women who had rushed to the
platform to kiss Bunting - - who, when Mary congratulated him, said he
had kept count, and gave the number as four hundred

four hundred and one, therefore, counting Mary.

In the rather gloomy S F Museum of Art, a red-letter day.

Four hundred and one, counting Mary, who counts indeed ---- so
since you have a nice review from the TLS [*Times Literary Supplement*],
would you send me a copy? - - I haven't seen it

George

(yes, Ashbery not a disgraceful choice for an award - - - I had feared it
would go to Dugan, which would have been annoying[7]

To Diane Meyer
[Summer 1976]   ALs   UCSD 16, 7, 28

Dear Andy:

Eve's 'collapse' -- 'collapse' being the wrong word: as you say, she
never lost her own ground.   Never will.[8]

(That's even part of the sorrow: it remains just *one's own*
ground?

(Mary + I: *our own ground?*

Experiences so shared that it becomes almost the same thing,   Where
are all the others? It is almost the same thing.   Anything can happen:
nothing guaranteed.   It is often double jeopardy, and we are often afraid.
We arrived in such poor physical shape that we were startled: have had
to change our way of sailing a bit.   But there are interesting people on the
island this summer: we've talked more, and sailed less--- less 'magic' of
the cruises, but - - maybe not a bad thing.   Or, at least,

all our love,
George

it rains and rains. We become cosier and cosier and, in these woods, indistinguishable from the old, old souls of the 19th century - - - disregarding the fact that we arrived and will leave by jet-plane, and that we have an elaborate little boat in the harbor   (nylon sails, jiffy reef, plastic hull, weather radio   and, and, and - - -[9]

George

To John Martin
[August 9, 1976]   TLs   John Martin and UCSD 9, 22, 4

Dear John Martin:
     It seems clear that I must have sent these poems to Rezi, but I have no memory of doing so. The Oppen of my name written on the fly leaf is in my hand-writing: I find it impossible to believe that the name George was ever at any time the way I wrote those letters.   Can't explain this. Maybe Rezi's notation for neatness -- or even for filing.[10]
     I did bring Rezi a copy of Discrete Series, when the book was printed. Rezi spoke only of the poem with the line 'O City Ladies'   (he liked the line) [CP 12]   I see that that poem is not in this ms, so this is not what I remember showing Rezi. Evidently an early ms of the poems, revised before the book was printed.
     I may have made more than one copy to show to friends, for Pound, of course, must have seen the ms before he wrote the introduction for Discrete Series.   This ms sent to Rezi can not be the ms Pound saw, or, at least, Pound saw also another and later ms for he included the poem beginning Brain All nuclei in his Active Anthology, and that poem is not in this ms.[11]
     ***-----   (I see I've become confused, typing this hurriedly. No doubt the poem beginning Brain all nuclei was written after the publication of Discrete Series) As you see, little can be expected from my memory since I become confused so easily even in the narrative present. Sorry that my memories fails me -- and you [sic].
     (I see that I felt 'the pigeons fly from the dark bough' to be a failure, or inadequate. I do remember working on that poem in our Brooklyn apartment - - - I see again that it is inadequate, but feel that I might well have included it nevertheless. Perhaps the poem should have been on the page following the poem beginning

burns
beside the wall
he has chosen a place
with the usual considerations
without naming them . . . . etc
[CP 6]

best wishes,
George

To the Mourelatos family
[approx. August 11, 1976]   TLs   UCSD 33, 1, 19

L/A:

thought no doubt you'd have heard of the Floridoran hurricane moving this way;   tried to make arrangements with the postmistress to phone you to say we were safe ashore.   Don't know if she did, the postmistress being a rather dreamy type   But if you heard of the hurricane, no doubt you heard also of its   turning out to sea, and its dispersion

Meanwhile on this island, the atmosphere of a nineteenth century novel: the men of the island plus Mary hauling the boats up the beach and tying them down,   a large yacht making its way in a hurry to one of the safe harbors cutting too close to the point of the island and running aground, balancing wildly high on a rock as the tide went down, pulled free by the gathering of the men, and all this under the grey skies and the peculiar feel of low barometric pressure - - - - scenes from, say, Victor Hugo

Strange event: all of us working with all our strength to save the toys because we knew of no way to save the houses. This shack would surely not have survived the hundred-mile winds predicted - - but what does one do?   Well, I've told you what one does: one hauls   up the toy boats

actually, there's one brick house on the island: I think we all meant --- all of us little pigs meant -- to go in there in the huffs and the puffs that would surely have blown our house down

Hope you got the news   of the hurricane warnings   retracted before this letter (the mail-boat, which of course had not ventured out should be here this morning)

Wish you'd seen us toilers of the sea, tho   magnificent in our sea-
boots

love to you
G/M

((going now to help put the toy boats back in the water: typing hurriedly
to get this letter in the mail boat. Decipherable I hope

To Helen Plotz
[September 1976]   TLs with AL postscript   UCSD 16, 8, 23

Dear Mrs Milton Plotz:

It seems to me that a footnote would be remarkably insulting to the
reader and the poem -- the supposition that a footnote is needed.   Surely
it is clear that the reference is biblical.[12]

I see that you've used the words of one line of the poem to identify
it in your letter. The title of the poem in which that line appears is *Of
Being Numerous*. -- a long poem of which the section you wish to use is a
part.   Please identify the section you wish to use as   'from the poem *Of
Being Numerous*' Or, better, 'From the long poem *Of Being Numerous*'
which would explain your using only a part of the poem.

with best wishes
George Oppen

((the Covenant, in my poem,   is not a covenant only with my people.
'The covenant is' that in this unlikely world,   'there shall be Peoples'
And people.

But footnotes?   That was not in the covenant.   We may omit
them[13]

To John Martin
[September 11, 1976]   TLs   John Martin

Dear John Martin:

Thanks for the notices of Rezi's work.   I seem to have spoken
gloomily to several people, for a number of friends send me   notices of
Rezi's work, obviously meaning to say, George, not everything gets lost,

stop worrying about the N Y Museum of Modern Art with its young men trying to shock their maiden aunts, and the New Yorker and the academics and such, so I stop.

(but do send me what you come across: it is a great pleasure to read[14]

all regards and thanks
George

To Paul Auster
[September 21, 1976]   TLs   Middlebury College Library

Dear Paul:
'journalistic' you say   Which underestimates the essays[15]   Charles I know would have been delighted by your response, by your sense of enough, by your trust in the poems
'Joy' you said of Charles's work   And the first, I think, to have seen this. Joy and, strangely, elegance   Elegance: a man who could experience joy in reading the words *Elevate them guns a little higher*
and thanks for the Xeroxes from Poetry   Those poems went thru more revisions even than I had remembered.   And needed to
best wishes to you and Lydia [Davis]

George

(strange to come on my twenty-odd year old odd self)
(((apropos   of speaking of Charles,   I found this among my closets full of notes which   I seldom if ever re-read -- and in which I neglect to surround with quote marks --so I don't know if this is mine or a quotation, but will write it here again: -- since we speak of Rezi:
'the created world,   as in childhood,   rises around us,   an unfamiliar and absolute truth

To John Martin
[before September 24, 1976]   TLs with AL insert   UCSD 16, 7, 17

Dear John Martin:
a proposal: I wrote this poem -- simply that I was thinking of Charles and of his work   It occurs to me now that it might do very well,

and better than the note I wrote at your request, on the back cover of   the
book   of Charles'

We would not, of course want to impose a sample of myself on
Charles' audience, but this could be solved very simply by simply putting
no signature on the poem - - no author's name. If the result is slightly
mysterious, it will do the book no harm.

You decide . Simply let me know your decision. ((and please
return the ms in any case))   envelope enclosed[16]

again with regards
George

To Sharon Olds
[September 28, 1976]   TLs   Sharon Olds

Dear Sharon Olds:

yes, I will say, yes, I am yes   (I am)[17]
Best wishes
George Oppen

To Michael Heller
[October 1976]   TLs   Michael Heller

Dear Mike

'meaning gains shine'
(cringe in its light)
- - - you're one of the few poets with sense enough to be afraid of
poetry - - - - - not lack of sense, really: just too much literary gossip, etc.

finding ourselves in good invited company, we're thinking of going
to England and to France - - Stop-off in N Y, of course, if we do ----[18]

don't count on it, tho - -- I mean, if you have a chance to come West,
do it! Would be pleasant indeed to see you   We could whirl you around
no end, no end - - it's a pretty place   And much fine talk.   tho
- - - well, it's tearing itself apart for some reason or other like the rest of
the country   Puritanism replaced by a strange viciousness without
pleasure - - a freedom of sexuality which is an attack on sexuality, etc etc
- - Maybe strangest here on this very pretty bay, and the mountains across
the bay - - --

how'd I get into this?   It's a pleasanter place than most cities, I meant to say. and still   and still: all these people desperately eager to board the sinking ship - - well, it's reasonable -- they want to be 'in the swim' - - how else but from a sinking ship

Me? I'm the ancient mariner   Tied round the albatross's neck. That half-witted bird

best wishes (we would indeed like to see you

George

To the Mourelatos family
[October 1, 1976]   TLs   UCSD 33, 1, 19

Dear L Dear A:

we bought a car   !!!! a Volkswagen bug It's a bug alright, no question about that, and I think it's a car   ?   It's very like a car - - - -

little bit old (8 years) Bought from the Budapest Garage -- as remarkable an institution as I have ever seen

but they did a remarkable job.   Guarantee offered -- and therefore they went over the bug, discovered it needed new brake-linings (which I could not have discovered for myself without tools - - - etc etc   All Hungarian mechanics - - A strange   (a rather wild)   atmosphere with some ten or twelve mechanics, the owner, manager, the Mamma of the owner-manager very much present - - - - And a Black girl running errands on a motorcycle. How (being insane) could we resist it?

((not quite so wild or eccentric as I am making it sound: Mary has acquired a business manner --- neither rough nor gruff nor suspicious, but - - - - I guess 'unhurried' would be one word for it.

-- I have acquired the manner of an idiot, an idiot who has been entrusted with various papers, licenses, etc, and who cannot find any of them. Perhaps an excellent tactic: a seller who does not try to take advantage of me is a saint   Or at least a member of the Rotary Club

- - - I now carry a license, a social security card, a car registration, a - - - - well, there are about six pieces of paper tucked away in my clothes, and our generation is not accustomed to this   (I remember our fury when we first went to France because the French police demanded that one carry an Identity card!! we used to fight about it.

Times change. We don't. Or we do, but we make quite a fuss about it.

------

this whole venture of The Shack In The Country is going to work
out, I think.

we found -- on our most recent expedition, a boat-yard plus - - I
don't know. Primarily boat yard -- a few trailers   (house-trailers for rent
scattered about the woods near the waterfront ---- Large boat-storage and
boat-building sheds, into some of which small apartments have been built
for rent - - this whole thing run by two very young people, man and wife
--- with infant child   And a goat! - - - - very flexible people: I think
we'll work something out

(one proposal we and they are considering is that since they have
room for another apartment in one of the boat-houses, but lack money to
undertake the work, we made a tentative proposal that we put up the
money for the undertaking, and subtract from our rent accordingly

etc

may work.   Anyway, we have a great time looking and concocting
ideas--- many of them wild.   Some of them perhaps possible

AND the bug: it alters our personality. A bug is efficient, but it
won't drive smoothly or with any great dignity - - - - - I'm teaching it a
few things, but without anger, for we will use it only in the country --
small roads and even non-roads -- and there is little occasion either for
dignity or slick characters in the driver's seat

We're pleased with ourselves.   So far.   Tho SO far . . so very far . .
Country characters   ?

------

all this (above) not in Inverness, which we were exploring, but the
other side of Tomales Bay. Marshall is the town name. Inverness too arty
-- too many young poets wishing to be too helpful   ('Poets,' above, means
would-be or non-poets, who have achieved Bohemianism but not poetry.
Their attention to us not entirely altruistic

I think Marshall will be free of these literary ambitions   Or comparatively free . . . . it is devoted rather to boats and boaters

- - - well, we'll see.

We've accepted an invitation to read at an international (as they say) poetry

Linda Oppen Mourelatos and George, Bolinas, California, 1977.

festival in France -- accepted (tentatively) because it seems to work out as to date with an invitation from England which we tentatively accepted a while back ---- We haven't decided, but -- we'd see various friends and such things - - - May do it   Maybe we've stalled too long.   We may do it.

All love to you both

Pop

To Serge Fauchereau
[October 15, 1976]   TLs with AL inserts   S. Fauchereau

Dear Serge:
'too short for trend - - -'[19] *Trend*, tendency, direction of forces   (that about the ship's cable might enter a nautical reader's mind   So much the better.   It derives from the same meaning --- the angle of the cable indi-cates the direction of forces -- tide and wind.   I think you can translate as *tendance* tho this loses the *earth* some feel of the earth, the land, in

trend --- No such earthiness in French so far as I know since Villon -- let it be *tendance*

the 'mouths' are human. The Rims (of eyes)--a vividness,   (of the human) a brightening, and then the geraniums, small, local, vivid, his life's eyes -- -- this has been said over and over again in Discrete Series

------

'Orienté' won't do for *trend*   Too static
Existant dedans seems O K   Existing in the place, existing in the *trend* (tho it was denied in the previous line -- 'too small for trend'-- and yet there is trend - - (perhaps *direction* does better than *tendance*?
((the poems of Discrete series cannot *really* be translated)
(can any poem?)

('his life's eyes'   - the image, the vivid the local, the shock of music, (the music of the poem)

I can't judge Série Discrète   vs   Discrete Series. Discrete series is a mathematician's term, meaning a series empirically (not mathematically) derived   If discrete Series -- if in that phrase the English shows thru the French I would not object - - if it seems strange in French, so much the better --- it's an American poem. (but find if you can the mathematician's phrase in French

[Autograph marginal note, boxed] USE THE ENGLISH TITLE; *Discrete Series*. We say Fleurs du Mal -- I never heard anyone call it anything else. Why should they?

[']He finds himself by two'   the existence of another -- finds himself by confrontation, the existence of another [CP 35]

page 55   where the roots are, this place where the roots are (human roots): it is a slum. I don't know of a French word   You may have to alter the poem   This would be   O K:

If the city has roots they are in filth,
it is impoverished, even the sidewalk
rasps under the feet[20]

(with this punctuation - - How it sounds in French I do not know: but this English is acceptable - - perhaps can better be put into French than the original can be

[Autograph insert] Yes: *slum* means a whole district as well as the room itself - - and the poem in English uses that meaning, both meanings. But if a choice must be made between indicating a poor house or a poor district,   it is the poverty of the whole district which is important

'taper down' - - beautiful feet, a woman's feet   The contrast of a woman, beauty of a woman (I was thinking in fact of Wyatt's   'They flee from me who sometime did me seek. . . -----'   For still, still, there might be a beautiful woman in this tenement - -

In some black brick apartment
of poverty a woman's body[21]

Glows the gleam the unimaginable - - - - -[22]

Of course you cannot use *coup de pied*.   'Taper down the ankles   ? ? ? or ankle ? ? ? ? ?   yes, ankle, the singular   maybe that would do

'to the wooden floor   .   .   Maybe not too bad.   'taper down' her *feet* taper (is it possible that coup de pied means the instep of the foot?)[23]

———

The People, The People
I don't understand the problem here. The people -- common in English usage to mean the common people, the mass - - don't know if gens or peuple is better here -- Don't understand at all why the same word cannot be repeated here --- it becomes an exclamation -- without which the poem is meaningless   The poem needs this outcry - - -

((the people, the people, we know who they are, they are that mountain to whom   we all go . . . . seems clear enough[24]

or are you speaking here of page 96?

'that they are
that force within the walls   '   ?   *force* here is a noun   They are that force which - - etc

Yes, *directeurs* and *mecaniciens* seems best
they resound *down* walled avenues, not *in*   (page 96.[25]

page 255 --anything BUT Romanesque   Romance, romantic
--- Two Poems Of Romance is possible[26]
     [page] 102 Eros: Maze -- commoner English for a labyrinth

---

     page 250 The Lighthouses --   I strongly urge you to substitute for
this poem *Of Hours* (page 210)-- a very much better poem of the same import

---

     Eros, 102 a maze   The image of the buildings appears in the
word heavy A heavy weight --- (do you have a difficulty: *poids lourde* meaning *truck?* - - -- Find some word   *ponderous* ?? -- must be *some* word[27]
     page 255–56[28]
     all that goes before --- the words, the rain's small pellets   small
fountains that live,   the face of the water,   dilations, the heart of
the republic -- are the subject of the verb *skips* the heart skips a beat
where these things touch it.
     power of the scene I said the small paved area' --- just leave it
unpunctuated for the rapidity of movement, all these things and I don't
know how to say it   I say all that I can' [CP 255]
     we'll be in France for that conference ------
     we can talk about this then if you wish
                                        regards
                                        G

I would urge upon you to use the Anniversary Poem, page 219

(I think the date of the Discrete Series poems had better be indicated
(1929–1933)

To James Laughlin
[October 18, 1976]   TLs with AL addition   J. Laughlin

Dear J:
     pleasant to hear from you --- and a very pleasant letter   Alas,
at this moment, at just this moment, embarrassing, for just now,   just be-

fore the morning's mail and your letter arrived, Mary and I -- Mary as well as I -- confronted the fact that we can't, can't or are not willing to undertake these travels, these 'Festivals.'[29]

We cannot bring ourselves to undertake it.   Physically hard-- an ordeal-- but it is not that that stops us, it is a violation of our sense of ourselves and of the meaning of poetry and of our lives - - - - we can't, we can't, and I feel guilty toward N D -- AND I am concerned that the book should sell enough to justify print, but I find I can't go junketing

(perhaps the current Presidential campaign increases one's queasiness   ?   One would like at least to retain more dignity and pride than a Presidential candidate - - - No time for 'festivals'   Maybe a time for hermitage.   And yet I am concerned that the book should justify print.   I think it will

(I notice that N D seems to subscribe to a clipping service only for newspaper clippings.   A number of very fine and sometimes superlative reviews and essays have appeared in periodicals.   Somewhere   (Encounter)? the assertion that the poems 'will be read as long as English is spoken' - - - Hudson Review has an excellent article *and* a great many others: I have a shelf-full of these enthusiasms: readers who *read*. - - - - - I think I'll continue to justify print

well: let's hope so. I cannot go performing.   Not the place for me   (my sense of the matter -- unlike the young, the television generation -- is that the poem is primarily on the *page*)

> Best wishes to you and to Ann
> George

To Henry Weinfield *et al.*
[late 1976 or early 1977][30]   TLs   Henry Weinfield

Dear Henry Weinfield, Paul Auster, The Mysterious Barricades and all others of Barricades #4: congratulations

'a knowledge of the real world' that hath us creatures in it

and for the first adequate notice of Bill Bronk

-- for all of which congratulations and thanks

(I once happened upon a book written by a Canadian reporter who to his amazement found that he had somehow received a visa to visit China without having asked for it - - evidently some error.   Dependent on a translator, of course, and what his eyes can do for him, he writes what he can as best he can, quietly and modestly and not un-moved.   At the end, they bring forward a young woman who launches bravely into her speech: 'we were the slaves of slaves, but our great Chairman - - etc.   All of which said reporter transcribes, and remarks, mildly, at the end (the last sentence in the book)   'But why do the Communists find such terrible liars to tell the truth'

it is a question that haunts me, why O why, and what will come of it and for how long

Therefore best wishes
George Oppen

(re-reading, my letter sounds to me flippant: I don't mean it so.   A race against time, perhaps

[In 1976, Oppen also corresponded with William Bronk, Ed Cox, Michael and Mary Cuddihy, Donald Davie, Frances Jaffer, S. R. Lavin (printed in *Four Zoas Journal* 3, 1976), Audrey Nicholson, Steven Schneider, and Harvey Shapiro.]

1977

[Although he had been invited to poetry festivals in both Cambridge (England) and Paris, Oppen canceled both appearances. The Oppens spent the summer in Maine; it was their final summer on Eagle Island, as the terminal illness of Oppen began to manifest itself more clearly. Mary Oppen worked on *Meaning a Life*, for which she had signed a contract on March 4. In the fall, Oppen completed *Primitive* with the secretarial help of Mary Oppen—marking a change in his writing practice.]

To Serge Fauchereau
[January 5, 1977]   TLs   Serge Fauchereau

Dear Serge:
        I cannot come to France   In a few months I will be 68   [69]   I cannot come to France, I --- we -- simply do not have the strength.   And I do not want to show off. The poems are mine -- they are for myself, myself and Mary, our lives and deaths   I mean to remain in the areas I speak of
        I enclose the new poem.[1]

                                    regards
                                    George

((the poem is perhaps more lucid than this apologetic (and hurried) letter)

To Stuart Lavin
[January 17, 1977]   ALs   Middlebury College Library

Stuart:
        I too dream, I've noticed, mostly of *rooms*   or sometimes buildings and of speech. Voices in my dreams.   usually abruptly

(the word eleven, it's true, would be very strange   Don't know if I could dream eleven --- another world or a hole in this one
     (XI, however, would be quite a forthright dream![2]

                                        George

To Sharon Olds
[January 25, 1977]   TLs   Sharon Olds

Dear Sharon Olds
     O no O no, I do not 'hate to be praised.' I am pitifully happy with praise. And so happy to have you with me

     'the exit is thru Satan's mouth

                    the dancers'

     ruby eye . . . .'

     'come out (up, down)' ---- I am so happy to have you with me, and in love with clarity   And in love with courage.[3]
     -- a pleasure (tho maybe not good for me) to read praise of myself   Perhaps not good for me because I must get on, get further. Finding it sometimes difficult. Afraid that it is becoming difficult for me -- Afraid that I am afraid.   I hope not.
     Above all happy (reading your letter) that you are with a truly beautiful man. Therefore also: thanks.[4]

                    ———

     Sitting down to answer your letter, I went to the bookcase to read again your work, and noticed a pamphlet with a paper tag on it because the pamphlet of course had no spine on the back to carry a name, but the paper tag glued to it had the name Sharon Olds .   Kayak #39.   The first thing my eye saw in the book case.
     Miracles -- Which are the commonest things in the world   (the only things)

                    ———

     Here is the story of that poem that moved you.[5]
     a young friend and his girl --- the girl's mother coming to New York to visit - - - They wanted us to meet the mother to display - - - I don't know.

George and Mary, Polk Street, 1977. *Photo Stephen Johnson.*

Adult approval, adult connections - - - Adult respect   ? -- I don't know. But of course we obliged.   Pete [Young] -- the young man -- said: let us go for a walk, and we walked thru Greenwich Village, and out the 14th Street pier - - nine or ten o'clock at night, the pier populated by drunken men   . We sat down on the string-piece - - both the mother and the young girl dressed very stylishly.   - - I was not sure it was a very wise thing to be doing - - - or very reassuring to the mother as a sample of the wise adults   ? - - - and indeed a very drunk man, a tremendous man and very drunk came over and wedged himself between me and the dainty mother - - - - talking loudly to us, a bullying manner unmistakably - - -

I interrupted. .   I don't know: maybe not altogether merely scheming, merely being clever - - - there was something in the man's face. There truly was. And yet it was mostly being clever on my part: I said to him: "What was your father's name"

. . . . . . O my god, it came pouring out, pouring out   'My father was a good man, my father was a good man, I'm glad he can't see me now . . .'   O my god.   And me being clever.

We talked   .   We talked awhile. It was getting late   We said good bye, and stood up and walked back down the pier, the man following us, and telling and telling, and we listened - - - What could we do?   We should say: come home with us - - - and of course we were not going to say that, and it would be useless . . . I did not know what to do, the man following behind us, what would we do - -

and then Mary stopped,   and turned back to the man, and put her arms around him, and kissed him, and said: now we must leave   -- for we knew it could only be this moment for him - - -

and we walked off. It was then he said, Good bye momma, good bye Poppa - - - -

––––––

you will see that I have not exaggerated Mary's beauty, total beauty, confidence, strength of beauty   I wrote the poem.   As well as I could.

and thank you for reading it so well

George

I am sorry that I cannot   Cannot   type decently

To Tom Sharp
[early 1977?]   TLs   Tom Sharp

thanks for your letter -- and poem

You say something about lack of compression - - I don't feel that you need a greater compression --- If there is anything lacking in the poem, I think perhaps it is a disregard of music, for music used, not as a stretching-out of the poem -- above all, not music used as a stretching-out, but as a part of meaning - --- of why you say what you say, why it is worth saying.

music   will tell us.

but I don't mean to carp against the poem

--- Or, better, as you say, not to take the *I* for granted

delighted that you speak of R. L. Stevenson. Do you know his little essay *Silverado Summer*?[6]   It is the only meaningful writing about early

California that I know of (the business men of the Bohemian Club and their desire to be sophisticated, plus the humorists such as Bret Harte, made a total mess of the thing, leaves nothing but Stevenson, Stevenson and perhaps some of Jack London as a record of this coast

so no, don't go to France.

As to becoming a professor, I cannot answer

also the matter has been much discussed by wiser heads perhaps than mine

again thanks for your generous letter

Since, as you see, I can't type, why not come sometime and visit

(apologies for the illegible typing-- ache[s]   and pains, Difficult for me to spend adequate time at the typewriter

George

To Donald Davie
[April 6, 1977]   TLs   Beinecke Library, Yale University

Dear Donald:

thanks, many thanks, for your generous letter --- and the discussion of   of Bunting (et al)

a *mind*!   an operative mind --- What other companionship is there on this stopping train?

-- and the danger to poetry today is not the bogeys we fought in the thirties, but the lazy minds, the lazy minds

again thanks - - - - Let us somehow arrange for another talk some-time

George

To Rachel Blau DuPlessis
[April 15, 1977]   TLs   R. B. DuPlessis

Rachel
[a few sentences cut]

(interested in your phrase *humanly transformative* as a feature of women's writing   (meaning, I think, ethically transformative - - - - unable to find the right word, I am letting ethically here mean relations between

people)   Yes, surely marked in women's work   easy to understand:
women as 'the other' who however speak or attack (protest) from *inside*
     --- immediacy of feeling, emotion, immediacy of emotion, aesthetic,
in your phrase meaning the contrary of anaesthetic - surely true of most
women's writing   (I know too little of H.D.'s work to have known this of
her work

> with love, Rachel
> George

To Frederick Martin
[April or Spring 1977]   TLs   UCSD 16, 8, 20[7]

Dear Fred: (and J L
     I know, I know.   And I am not immune to the delights of fame and
the security of large sales   But I must guard my life (as tho it were my
life)   (as tho it were my poetry)
     goose-poets laying golden eggs (and golden girls)   all over the
place   all must
     like chimney sweepers come to dust[8]
     And who knows? maybe someone will come to dust me and I shall
look bright and new among the raggle taggle Gypsies O
     - for I remind you again: I am sixty-nine years old. I will complete
what I have to say, such as it is, but I will need time.   I need my time

-----

     delighted to hear of the nautical adventures---- and thanks for the
copy of the review

> George

To Milton Hindus
[late spring 1977]   TLs   Milton Hindus[9]

Dear Milton Hindus:
     beginning with an apology: my typescript. I cannot, at the mo-
ment, do better - - - leaving, momentarily for a summer in Maine, and an
abominable typist at best, but I am delighted to hear from you and do very
much wish to reply even among the suitcases and other disorders for since

1928 or it may have been 1929 when I first encountered Reznikoff's work, I have thought of him as among the truly great, the truly permanent poets - - - not, of course, 'taking a position' in the manner of Eliot: I mean only to speak of what I have felt, and what has mattered to me.

(I was with   ((tho perhaps not very useful to)) the U S infantry in France during the Second World War, and in the final days of that war found myself trapped in a fox-hole, slightly injured, and with no apparent means of escape, certainly no possibility until night-fall. I waited, I think, some ten hours, and during those hours Wyatt's little poem -- 'they flee from me . . . ,' and poem after poem of Rezi's ran thru my mind over and over, these poems seemed to fill all the space around me and I wept and wept [CP 242]. This may not be literary criticism, or perhaps, on the other hand, it is

---

I have read the essays you mention other than the piece in The Old East Side, which I will obtain.[10]   As for the Charles in the boat and in my poem - - it was another Charles ["Philai Te Kou Philai," CP 75–76]. Charles Humboldt, but indeed it might have been Rezi - - it is his vision of things - - somewhat like the anthropologist finding our rubbish on the hillsides - - - in a way it was Rezi in the poem, tho not in the boat

Again: I am truly pleased to hear from you, to feel almost that we know each other - - and I thank you for the Xeroxes

will all regards,

George Oppen

Might it be possible for you take a small vacation in Maine this summer?   We could show you a very beautiful island - - and we could find sleeping room for you - - tho very, very primitive - - - ? Eagle Island, Maine - - - about forty miles from Bangor - - - It would be a pleasure to talk

To June Oppen Degnan
[early summer 1977]   ALs   UCSD 17, 5, 10

June Dear:

weather beautiful but cold. We seem amazingly debilitated & clumsy physically - - - hope to improve during the summer - - - Been a hard year somehow :   the new poems were a strain - - - and it seems that walking is not enough exercise - - - - -

well, it's strange. On a little path fifty yards long from here to the road (and which I've been over a hundred times) I somehow got lost! Mary said: I'm not far behind you. I said: There's something worse; maybe you're just seven months behind me (Mary's birthday is Sept. [November] 28th)

well: we will, I think, get our bearings - - (the nautical term is obviously appropriate)   It's true that we're dazed: things had somehow got away from us - - (My relation to the mail in S.F. was the relation of the running man to the structures [?]   he's got hold of: he can't let go or jump on - - - alright, alright, we'll heal in Maine.   If not, we won't *never* come home

love

George

To Diane Meyer
[June 16, 1977]   ALs   UCSD 16, 7, 28

Andy Dear

Yes, I think you are right: a change in the tone in the new poems

-- I no longer have time, time, time to force the meaning, the statement on the reader   Time to argue. I must trust him, her, to know where we are. To TRUST himself, herself: to TRUST me: to say yes. To say yes, we know, we are also here

'possibly more youthful,' you suggest. It may be. You could call it youthful or you could call it old. To complete the circle.

George

To Michael Heller
[early to mid-September 1977]   TLs   Michael Heller

Dear Michael:

--couldn't deal with New York --- Dazed by the wreckage[11]

--- afraid to look back at my Of Being Numerous. Couldn't have written it now - - we've become alien   (alien to streets in Brooklyn where we knew, I think, almost everyone in every apartment   Alien then, no doubt, in that we had lines of retreat open to us that we never admitted ----   and now, perhaps, their revenge.   And where are we?   As the walls fall   I think my destiny lies with the Romans, however reluctant they and we may be as allies.[12]

I know so little about these men and these women, and surely they take me for a fool.

Not that I agree - - but . . . .? Well, that is to say, I'm sorry we missed you.

George

To Eric Homberger
[September 22, 1977]   TLs   Eric Homberger

Dear Eric:
The Art of the real -- . or the reality of art ---   a fine, and reassuring book[13]

(yes, it does somewhat skimp me --- that is to say, I am   rather notably of the art of the real   (a line in one of my poems reads   "A poetry of the real," and in fact I have been rather embattled among the fashionable solipsists [CP 195? or 196?]

(and there is the fact that Discrete Series was published in 1934 --- the poems written some three or four years earlier, which makes me something of a pioneer (tho of course not alone in the realism of 'image'

(don't, for God's sake take this remark as an assault)

((sorry to hear of the 'savaging' of your book. English bards and Scotch reviewers - - - England no longer in need of the Scots: the English   (Why?)   do their own savaging   It seems to be a game   A game beginning on the playing fields of Eton?   Marvelously regrettable, whatever the origin.

regards to you - - and from
Mary
George

To Eliot Weinberger
[September 28, 1977]   TLs   Eliot Weinberger

[No salutation]

All possible congratulations on Montemora 3   Jonathan Griffin alone makes a red letter day[14]

Surprising lack, in the issue as a whole, of the quality of song, of music --- Chance: editorial preferences, straw in the wind - - -?? Unpleasant to chew straws as a steady diet in *any* wind

((even the selections from Bronk's work lacking music   !!   nothing could be more unexpected

Bunting becoming school-teachery?   The last resort of scoundrels, tho Bunting is of course no scoundrel   But does he think the poet helpless in the hands or tongues of the language?   (recognition in England more dangerous even than in the U S ? the wounds of the playing fields of some Eton??

———

none of this reproof   Nor pontifical   Just wanted to talk   A fine issue   An amazing issue

George

To Henry Weinfield
[later 1977?][15]   TLs   UCSD, Additions to Papers 1989, 3

Dear Henry

could of course argue here and there with your letter   More important to me is the degree and the force of our agreement

Yes: the question we discuss is 'almost a conflict between the heroic and the epic modes '

(((you malign Kenner: I am sure he did not mean merely that   I needed time - - - He was aware that I needed to know,   to see,   to test, and be there - - - - I am sure that he did

--or am I sure?   But it is what the phrase meant to me   I think he knew   And that he knew, the fact that he knew - - - - itself had meaning.

a sad meaning.   In view of all the blood-shed   Which means that poetry might sometime ---- you know I do not *want* to put forward this kind of self-aggrandizement of the poet - - - but it means that poetry might sometime be primary

       ---given decency about us - - - might be primary.

                           all regards   and to

                           Christine

                           George

(((an eloquent and brilliant letter   More enlightening to disagree with some matters   than agreement with most of what is written would be

To Armand Schwerner

[1977 or 1978]   TLsc with AL postscript   UCSD 16, 10, 23

Armand:

       A great poem[16]

       A joy to say so, for I remember (you may not) that you were angry years ago when I objected to your manner of reading The Tablets - - - reading as comedy, tho the poem was tragedy

       But of course this poem is the contrary ((and maybe the child) of the Tablets, for the poet-translator was a lost man, the words were disappearing, whereas here the work, the joy, the triumph of the will is a great poem. And I thank you

                          George

(if you can send me three or four copies I would like to mail them to the (few) intelligent editors I know of

[In 1977, Oppen also corresponded with Paul Auster, William Bronk, Jane Cooper, Cid Corman, Ed Cox, Michael Cuddihy, Eli Goldblatt, Frances Jaffer, David McAleavey, Tony Stoneburner and family, and John Taggart.]

1978

[*Primitive* was published by Black Sparrow Press; Oppen's author's copy was sent on April 24, which was, coincidentally, his seventieth birthday. On June 15, Mary Oppen's memoir *Meaning a Life* was published, also by Black Sparrow.[1] On May 12, Louis Zukofsky died. The Oppens spent the summer in Marshall, California, in large part because the sailing was simpler and more manageable than in Maine.]

To John Martin
[January 23, 1978]   TLs   John Martin

Dear John Martin:
    I find myself with a group of new poems written since the Collected poems--- the group would come to some fifteen or twenty pages in print.   I think very well of the poems, but it is clear that I will not have a book-length collection for some time - - several years, I would think. New Directions has, thru my contract with them, the 'right of first refusal.' I have corresponded with J. Laughlin, who has no objection to my printing this short collection as a chapbook, and has instructed me as to how copyright notice should read, etc., etc. This leaves me free to offer the group of poems to Black Sparrow. Would you let me know if you would be interested
                              with regards
                              George Oppen

To John Martin
[January 31, 1978]   TLs   John Martin

Dear John Martin:
    thanks for your letter. I'll take a little while to go over the manuscript again.

I'll need your assurance that the book will be published within a year from now in order to give the book a sufficient time to sell before I have a book-length ms for New Directions

Of course I have no objection to the letterpress

again thanks

New Directions gives rights for one time use, and retains book rights   Copyright then returns to George Oppen

George Oppen

To John Martin
[February 15, 1978]   TLs   John Martin

Dear John:

I send you (enclosed) a new poem. It should be the last poem in the book

Incidentally, I do not know if you intend to number the pages in the book   (I myself see no reason to do so)   But if you intend to number the poems [i.e., the pages], I will go over the ms carefully, and make final decisions as to the order of the poems. If, however, the pages will not be numbered, I can take a great deal of time for these decisions   and I would like to   give myself   a great deal of time--

-- not only a matter of time, but to see the poems in type before committing myself

(the weight of the thing falls slightly differently in type)   and the sequence of the poems might involve or suggest slight revisions

let me know at your leisure

George

To John Martin
[March? 1978]   TLs   John Martin

Dear John:

still one error left: 'The Dream,' page 21 -- a number of lines lost. No harm done: in looking the poem over once more, I see that 'The Dream' should be omitted[2] - - so that the poem Gold On Oak Leaves will follow the poem Populist

George, Charles Tomlinson, and Mary. Polk Street apartment, probably
January 1980.

     -- and of course the pages re-numbered
     ---- as you say, we're getting close: this will surely be the last
correction
George

To Robert Duncan
[after May 13, 1978]   ALs   Poetry/Rare Books Collection, SUNY-Buffalo

Dear Robert:
     I thank you for the praise, and for the beauty of your letter 'The
heart answers' which is why we live[3]
George

[In 1978, Oppen also corresponded with Cid Corman, Ed Cox (to his poetry workshop for senior citizens), Michael Cuddihy, Linda Gregg, Gary B.
Pacernick, Carl Rakosi, John Taggart, and Henry Weinfield.]

1979–1981

[In 1980, Oppen received two major honors. On May 21, 1980, the American Academy and Institute of Arts and Letters gave him an award "in recognition of his creative work in literature." In July, Oppen was one of eight recipients of a one-time award for an "extraordinary contribution to contemporary American literature over a lifetime of creative work." During 1979–80, George and Mary Oppen sometimes wrote letters to each other (although they were together), trying to sort out their feelings of love, confusion, and pain at Oppen's worsening condition; he stated in one of these letters, "my intelligence is intermittent."[1]

In 1981, a special Oppen issue of *Paideuma* was published, followed by the volume *George Oppen: Man and Poet* in 1982—both by the National Poetry Foundation. He received the PEN/West Rediscovery Award in December 1982. In 1982, Oppen was diagnosed as having Alzheimer's disease. In 1983, a special tribute for his seventy-fifth birthday occurred on April 24 in San Francisco.[2] On July 7, 1984, Oppen died.]

To Linda Oppen Mourelatos
[March 5, 1979]   TLs with AL additions   UCSD 33, 1, 20

Lindy Dear:
Yes, these questions arise.   I've often been faced by them   If someone said to us, 'sometimes I feel like a motherless child'   would we not weep?   And why then all this strangeness of art?   And why then all this strangeness of technique overwhelming the joy of dance - - or of horses or of song?   Technique overwhelming the dance and the joy of dance   --
Our own dance
But perhaps we need not decide   and cannot decide,   for what is ourself decides   If we are free - - - and sometimes even if we are very nearly chained down, the self answers - - the answer inherent in us.
- - there's no other happiness - - -

———

It is necessary that the world be bright enough   ('*world*   meaning
the central strangeness
Not necessary that we dance on our heads

———

Linda: we love you more and more as you and we grow older

———

———

((((I do now really have excuse for my typing - - - - heaps and heaps
of unanswered letters, and I cannot sit long enough to reply
But I am getting over this pain - - an end to it I think really in sight
- - by way of exercise (including swimming), chiropractor, doctor, M.D.,
and a few etceteras I really am getting thru it[3]
((you'll be the first I write to legibly)

Love
Poppy

(I've tried to give examples ('images') in my own work - - - e.g., the
bright pebbles under shallow water . . . [CP 167]
- - it's *meaning* - - it is meaning if it means to you and me
[on the back of the letter] (Pound, defending my first book from the
charge of being obscure reminds the reader that Browning was considered
incomprehensible, and added that no adult 'today' found him impossible
to understand
- - there is involved here a something like historical optimism - -
tho Pound would surely not deliberately have subscribed to such a belief

To James Laughlin
[before June 19, 1979]   AL   UCSD 16, 8, 10

Dear J.
I can well imagine the number of recommendations, urgings, etc.
as to what you should print, and I can easily imagine that such correspondence becomes annoying if not in fact infuriating, but I would like to
remind you that I have carefully refrained from advice (with the single

exception of having, thru June Degnan's participation, induced N.D. to print Reznikoff and William Bronk, whose recognition came slowly--in the case of Reznikoff almost at the end of his life, but whose work is spoken of everywhere, and it seems to me that my record is pretty good

I hope you'll agree, for I want now to call to your attention John Taggart's *Peace on Earth*. I think, quite simply that it is a very great poem--a tremendous poem. I can't believe that it will ever be forgotten, and I can't refrain from writing this note of more-than-recommendation. I think that nothing--nothing at all--could contribute more to the glory of ND than to print this book-length poem which is not merely 'like music,' but is actually music and as moving as music.[4]

(cf. also Robert Duncan's remarks on Taggart's work)

[unsigned]

To Eliot Weinberger
[Fall 1979]   [TLs?]   published in *Montemora*[5]

Dear Eliot,

Yes--a lot of very bad poetry floating around   Maybe it has its place / out of anger and fear some will rise into poetry.   I think we will.

George Oppen

To Ethel K. Schwabacher
[1979–1980?]   TLs   Christopher C. Schwabacher

Dear Ethel,

Your writing comes out of your life-- a life of contemplation and a search for peace, using art;   your painting,   drawing--   all that you are still doing.   In the writing of this journal the proof that this is indeed your life, a life of art, a life in art, which is the only life that lives.[6]

With all love, Ethel

George

To Jonathan Griffin
January 17, 1980 (dated)   TLs [signed by Mary Oppen]   Jonathan Griffin

Dear Jonathan,

Your book and Charles Tomlinson's arrived on the same day. Maybe our common language yet may *outsing*.[7]

George

To Paul Auster
March 8, 1980 (dated)   TLs   Middlebury College Library

Dear Paul,

Very tempting-- a pleasant prospect to see you again, and to talk.[8]   What worries me is the question of whether or not I can say anything that I have not already said-- *And*   my own condition at this moment which is something alas, very like senility--   I am not being very brilliant these days, and I have not writ anything since *Primitive*

It is not that I fear being less than brilliant: I find that my only recourse is to admit to myself and to others that on familiar streets   I cannot find my way home.   I am not attempting to deny this fact, but,   "Alas; how the mighty mites have fallen. /"

What will you manage to report of me that will be interesting enough to be a credit to your ability as an interviewer?

It would nevertheless be a great pleasure to me and to Mary to talk. I'll do my best if you go ahead.

Regards,
George

To Tom Sharp
May 18, 1980 (dated)   TLs   Tom Sharp

Dear Tom,

I thank you for your essay--[9]   Not   only for its praise of my work, but for its insights and a host of memories attaching themselves to Louis' letter, generous letter recommending me to Pound - - I had not known of this letter - - - or perhaps had forgotten it.

Reading your essay I remember   Rilke's words: 'amazement is my heaven'

I think also of Isaac Newton's 'The great ocean of truth.'

i.e. the ocean of events. And time.

Regards,
George

To Linda Oppen Mourelatos
[May 20, 1980]   AL   UCSD 33, 1, 20

Linda Dear, Linda Dear, there is no way to thank you sufficiently for your lovely, lovely letter

- - I am not afraid of age - - for I could say,   as Rilke said: 'amazement is my paradise[']

And our love for you, Lindy - - - and your love for us is also happiness

(Your counting my books has also served to give me peace with myself. I had not thought to count

[unsigned]

To Henry Weinfield
August 14, 1980 (dated)   TLs   UCSD Additions to Papers 1989, 3

Dear Henry,

Thanks for the sonnet: Very vivid: the communist in the midst of things somehow   feels himself above them[10]

(We remember)

[and yet we could say that the C. P. rescued the pride of many thousand   what if they had not?][11]

Sincerely
George

To Henry Weinfield
December 17, 1980 (dated)   TLs   UCSD Additions to Papers 1989, 3

Dear Henry,

I have been haunted, and infuriated, by the accusation of being

George, Mary, and Mark Linenthal of San Francisco State University, probably on the occasion of Oppen's 75th birthday celebration, April 24, 1983. *Photo © Charles Amirkhanian.*

difficult or perhaps incomprehensible. Your essay on *Of Being Numerous* should put an end to that, and I thank you for it.[12]

(I would swear that I write simply, and in a simple language if anyone has ever done so, and I thank you,

Sincerely

George

To Dan Gerber
[Christmas 1980]   TLs   Dan Gerber

Dear Dan,

A whole life coming to a moment, which is to say: a poem (and the flexing of memory--   a whole life and it speaks again on my desk

George Oppen[13]

To Charles Tomlinson
January 25, 1981 (dated)   TLs with AL postscript   Charles Tomlinson

Dear Charles,
        Reading your *Some Americans* with great pleasure and a little
guilt: we were very young, and perhaps did not fully recognize Louis'
brilliance. But need I thank you for the essay: I dream of walking with
you over the ground and hills of Gloucester?[14]
        any chance of your coming here?   we could bed you down.
        Love to Brenda and a loving hug for Justine   and Juliet. Send them
for a visit   ?   We'd show them the town
        With all best wishes, and in friendship
                                                                George

To Rachel Blau DuPlessis
February 5, 1981 (dated)   TLs   R. B. DuPlessis

Dear Rachel,
        When I was in high school or possibly earlier, I drew up a scale of
the sound of words.   i.e.: the word *down* happens to be lower in pitch
than the word *he*.   And I am still amazed -- and still bothering Mary by
asking in annoyance why on earth people write   *poetry*   if they disregard the sounds of the words they use?
        And then there is Zukofsky's dictum: Poetry moves toward mu-
sic as its upper limit.[15]
        If the 'O' sound is tremendous: it is almost a world[16]
                                                with love,
                                                        George

To Anthony Rudolf
[June 6, 1981]   TLs   Anthony Rudolf

Dear Tony,
        I think there is no light in the world but the world.   And I think
there is light. My happiness is the knowledge of all we do not know.[17]
                                                George Oppen

To June Oppen Degnan
September 25, 1981 (dated)   TLs   UCSD 17, 5, 11[18]

June:

I have the little figurine in exactly the right place [spot][19] and I remember my mother in the garden by the sun-dial and the Rothfeld grand-mother who asked me not to play [the piano] so loud and I said, 'It's supposed to be loud.' And the man across the street who said, 'Hello Bud,' and the manicurist who came at intervals, and the Saxon automobile with me sitting on my father's lap and steering, and the slope down-hill toward our house at Circuit Road and the bicycle I got for Christmas and I insisted it must belong to the delivery-boy-   I couldn't believe it was mine,   and a great many other things--   all in the little figurine,

And me climbing on my mother's bed, and the people said to come down and someone said, let him be - - - -[20]

[unsigned]

To Claude Royet-Journoud
September 26, 1981 (dated)   TLs   C. Royet-Journoud

Dear Claude,

I am truly sorry to refuse anything that you ask of me, but I cannot bring myself to write poetic "exercises."[21]   We come back to that old say-ing: a poem is a poem is a poem.   (and never an exercise)

it is tied to the world, and the stones of the villages.

Again sorry to refuse to do anything you ask of me,

Best wishes,

George

[In 1979, Oppen corresponded with William Bronk, Eli Goldblatt, Jona-than Griffin, Tony Stoneburner, and John Taggart. In 1980, Oppen also corresponded with William Bronk and Harvey Shapiro. In 1981, Oppen sent a thank-you note to contributors to the Oppen issue of *Paideuma*.]

Correspondents

Charles Amirkhanian (1945–), composer and Music Director of KPFA-FM, Pacifica Foundation listener-sponsored station in Berkeley, California. Produced programs with and about Oppen.

David Antin (1932–), poet, cultural critic, and Professor of Visual Arts, University of California at San Diego. Edited *Some/Thing*, 1965–70 with Rothenberg; author of *definitions* (1967), reviewed by Oppen in 1968; *code of flag behavior* (1968); *Meditations* (1971); *Talking* (1972); *Talking at the Boundaries* (1976); *Tuning* (1984).

Paul Auster (1947–), poet, novelist, translator from French. *Disappearances: Selected Poems* appeared in 1988. His prose works include *The Art of Hunger* (1982), *The Invention of Solitude* (1982), *The New York Trilogy—City of Glass* (1985), *Ghosts* (1986), *The Locked Room* (1986); *In the Country of Last Things* (1987), and *Moon Palace* (1989). Wrote on Reznikoff in the mid-1970s and edited the *Random House Book of Twentieth Century French Poetry* (1982).

Anita Barrows (1947–), poet, child psychotherapist, and translator from French (Kristeva, Duras) and Italian. Author of *Emigration* (1972); *The Limits* (1983). Represented in feminist and Jewish anthologies.

Philip Booth (1925–), poet, Professor Emeritus, Syracuse University; elected a Fellow of the Academy of American Poets, 1983. Author of *Letter from a Distant Land* (1957), *The Islanders* (1961), *Weathers and Edges* (1966), *Margins* (1970), *Available Light* (1976), *Before Sleep* (1980), *Relations: Selected Poems, 1950–1985* (1986).

William Bronk (1918–), poet and essayist, worked in family business. Author of numerous collections of poems including *Light and Dark* (1956); *The World, the Worldless* (1964); and *Life Supports* (1981); and *Vectors and Smoothable Curves: Collected Essays of William Bronk* (1983).

Ron Caplan (dates unavailable), poet and publisher; republished *Discrete Series* in 1966. Author of *A Sampler* (1967).

Jane Cooper (1924–), poet and Professor Emerita of English at Sarah Lawrence College; numerous honors and awards. Author of *The Weather of Six Mornings* (1969); *Maps & Windows* (1974); the chapbook "Threads: Rosa Luxemburg from Prison" (1979); *Scaffolding: New and Selected Poems* (1984).

Cid Corman (1924–), poet, translator from Japanese and French, essayist, editor and publisher of *ORIGIN* and Origin Press. Over a hundred titles, including *In Good Time* (1964); *Sun Rock Man* (1962, 1970); *Nonce* (1965); *livingdying* (1970); *O/I* (1974); *Word for Word* (1977) and *At Their Word* (1978): two volumes of essays; *Aegis* (1983), *And the Word* (1987); *Of* (2 volumes, selected poems; 1989–90).

John Crawford (1940–), poet, editor of *West End* Magazine (1971–76) and Press (1976–current); Lecturer in English, University of New Mexico, Valencia Campus. Wrote on Oppen in 1972; committed to multi-ethnic and left culture in his editing; has published, among others, Meridel LeSueur and Tom McGrath.

Robert Creeley (1926–), poet, novelist, Gray Professor of English at SUNY-Buffalo; author of many books including *For Love, Poems 1950–60 (1962); Words* (1967); *Pieces* (1969); *Was That a Real Poem & Other Essays* (1979); *Collected Poems 1945–75* (1983); *The Complete Prose* (1984); *The Collected Essays* (1988); editor of Charles Olson's *Selected Writings* (1967), and co-correspondent with Olson in their multivolume *Complete Correspondence*.

Michael Cuddihy (1932–), poet, translator from French, publisher and editor of *Ironwood* (1972–89); author of *Celebrations* (1980) and *A Walled Garden* (1989); translator of Maritain (1968). Cuddihy published two issues of *Ironwood* completely devoted to Oppen, 5 ([March] 1975) and 26 (Fall 1985), and Oppen poems in numbers 1, 9, 12, and the final issue, 31–32.

Donald Davie (1922–), British poet, critic, editor, translator from Russian, former Professor of English at Stanford University (1968–78), and Andrew W. Mellon Professor of the Humanities, Vanderbilt University (1978–88). Thirty years of poems assembled in *Collected Poems: 1950–70* (1972) and *Collected Poems: 1971–83* (1983); author of *Articulate Energy* (1955), *Ezra Pound: Poet as Sculptor* (1964), *Thomas Hardy and British Poetry* (1972), *These The Companions: Recollections* (1982).

June Oppen Degnan (1918–), Oppen's half sister. Publisher of *San Francisco Review*, and publisher, with New Directions, of Oppen's second and third books. Member of the Democratic National Committee (1972–80); National Director of Americans for Democratic Action (1962–68). Served as National Finance Chairman for Eugene McCarthy's presidential campaign (1967–69); Vice-Chairman of George McGovern's presidential campaign (1970–72); one of the founders of Daytop Village (a therapeutic community for substance abuse). Trustee of the Kennedy Center for Performing Arts (1981–).

Aubrey Degnan-Sutter (1940–), psychologist. Regional Psychologist, U.S. Department of State, West Africa (1984–86); daughter of June Oppen Degnan and niece of George Oppen.

L. S. Dembo (1929–), critic, editor of *Contemporary Literature*, and Professor of English, University of Wisconsin-Madison. Author of *The Confucian Odes of Ezra Pound: A Critical Appraisal* (1963), *Conceptions of Reality in Modern American Poetry* (1965), *Detotalized Totalities: Synthesis and Disintegration in Modern Fiction* (1989). He interviewed the Objectivists in 1968 and wrote on Oppen, Reznikoff, and Bunting, as well as on modern Jewish fiction.

Robert Duncan (1919–88), poet, critic. Author of *The Opening of the Field* (1960), *Roots and Branches* (1964), *Bending the Bow* (1967), *Fictive Certainties* (essays, 1985), *Ground*

Work: *Before the War* (1984), *Ground Work II: In the Dark* (1987); *The H.D. Book*, correspondence, and collected poems forthcoming from the University of California Press.

Rachel Blau DuPlessis (1941–), poet, critic, Professor of English, Temple University. Author of *Wells* (1980), *Tabula Rosa* (1987), *Writing Beyond the Ending: Narrative Strategies of Twentieth-Century Women Writers* (1985), *H.D.: The Career of that Struggle* (1986), *The Pink Guitar: Writing as Feminist Practice* (1990). Has written on Oppen.

Serge Fauchereau (1939–), French poet, essayist, art critic; editor of *Digraphe* (Paris), affiliated with *Critique*, *Les Lettres Nouvelles*, and *La Quinzaine littéraire*. Author of *Lecture de la Poésie Américaine* (1968); *Expressionisme, dada, surréalisme et autre ismes* (1976), *La révolution cubiste* (1982), and numerous other books on poetry and art.

Theresa Zezzos Fulton (1921–85), artist and Professor of Art at University of Southern California, Claremont Graduate School, and member of Art Department at Queens College. Coauthor of *Looking at Modern Painting* (1957, rev. 1961 and 1970) and contributing author of *The Humanities and the Library*.

Dan Gerber (1940–), poet, novelist, and journalist, coeditor of *Sumac* (1968–71) with Jim Harrison, and editor of Sumac Press (1969–78). Author of *The Revenant* (1971), *Departure* (1973), *The Chinese Poems* (1978), *Snow on the Backs of Animals* (1986), in fiction *American Atlas* (1973), *Out of Control* (1974), *Grass Fires* (1987).

Jonathan Griffin (1906–), British diplomat until 1951; poet. Made Knight of the Order of Saint James of the Sword, in Portugal, and awarded the French Order of Arts and Letters for his translations. Author of *The Hidden King* (a verse-play, 1955), *The Oath* (1962), *In Time of Crowding* (1975), *In This Transparent Forest* (1977), *Outsing the Howling* (1979), *The Fact of Music* (1979), *Commonsense of the Senses* (1982), *Collected Poems* (1989).

Eve Haight (1954–), English Instructor at City College of San Francisco; grandniece of George Oppen, in her teens at the time of their correspondence.

Michael Hamburger (1924–), British poet, translator from German (Hofmannsthal, Hölderlin, Trakl, Büchner, and modern German poetry). Author of *Reason and Energy* (1957), *Weather and Season* (1963), *The Truth of Poetry* (1969), *A Proliferation of Prophets* (1983), *Collected Poems: 1941–83* (1984), *After the Second Flood* (1986), *Selected Poems* (1988).

Charles Hanzlicek (1942–), poet, Professor of English and Director of Creative Writing, California State University at Fresno. Author of *Living in It* (1971), *Stars* (1977), *Calling the Dead* (1982), *When There are No Secrets* (1986); translated *Mirroring: Selected Poems of Vladimir Holan* (1985).

Michael Heller (1937–), poet, critic, and faculty member at New York University's American Language Institute. Author of *Conviction's Net of Branches: Essays on the Objectivist Poets and Poetry* (1985), which includes an essay on Oppen, and several volumes of poetry: *Accidental Center* (1972), *Knowledge* (1980), and *In the Builded Place* (1989).

Milton Hindus (1916–), critic, Edytha Macy Gross Professor Emeritus at Brandeis University. Editor of *Leaves of Grass: One Hundred Years After* (1955); of the American Writing section of the *Encyclopaedia Judaica*; of *Charles Reznikoff: Man and Poet* (1984);

author of *The Proustian Vision* (1954, 1967), *Essays: Personal and Impersonal* (1986), and *The Broken Music Box* (poems, 1980).

Eric Homberger (1942–), critic and Reader in American Literature, University of East Anglia (Norwich, England). Edited *Ezra Pound: The Critical Heritage* (1972); author of *The Art of The Real: Poetry in England and America since 1939* (1977) and *American Writers and Radical Politics, 1900–1939* (1986); in both of which Oppen figures.

Lita Hornick (1927–), author, publisher, and editor of *Kulchur* magazine (with Jones, Sorrentino, O'Hara, Berkson, LeSueur); ran the alternative press Kulchur Foundation in New York from 1966. Author of *Kulchur Queen* (1977) and *Nine Martinis* (1987).

Charles Humboldt (1910–64), critic and editor. Wrote a regular column for *Masses and Mainstream* (1958–60); was an associate editor of *The New Masses* and an editor of *Mainstream* until 1959 when he became cultural editor of *The National Guardian: a progressive newsweekly*. Was in Mexico at the same time as the Oppens.

David Ignatow (1914–), poet, teacher, Professor Emeritus of CUNY, lecturer in the Writing Division, Columbia University; President Emeritus, Poetry Society of America; recipient of many awards. Author of *Figures of the Human* (1964), *Poems 1930–69* (1970), *Notebooks: 1934–1971* (1973), *Open Between Us* (prose, 1980), *New and Collected Poems: 1970–1985* (1986), *The One in the Many: Literary Memoirs* (1988).

Frances Jaffer (1921–), poet, associate editor of *HOW(ever)* (1983–89). Author of *Any Time Now* (1977), *She Talks To Herself In The Language Of An Educated Woman* (1980), *ALTERNATE Endings* (1985).

George Johnston (1913–), Professor Emeritus of English Language and Literature, Carleton University, Ottawa, translator from Old and Modern Scandinavian, and poet. Author of *The Cruising Auk* (1959), *Happy Enough: Poems 1935–72* (1972), *Auk Redivivus selected* (1981); internationally known scholar of Icelandic sagas and translator of *The Saga of Gisli* (1963), *The Faroe Islanders' Saga* (1975), *The Greenlander's Saga* (1976).

Shirley Kaufman (1923–), American poet and translator from Hebrew, lives in Jerusalem. Author of *The Floor Keeps Turning* (1970), *Gold Country* (1973), *From One Life to Another* (1979), *Claims* (1984); translator of Amir Gilboa and Abba Kovner.

Robert Kelly (1935–), poet and Professor of English at Bard College. Author of many works, including *Kali Yuga* (1970), *Flesh Dream Book* (1971), *The Loom* (1975), *The Book of Persephone* and *The Convections* (both 1978), *Kill the Messenger* (1979), *Spiritual Exercises* (1981), *In Time* (essays, 1971).

Hugh Kenner (1923–), Andrew W. Mellon Professor of Humanities, The Johns Hopkins University. Author of *The Poetry of Ezra Pound* (1951), *The Pound Era* (1971), *A Homemade World* (1975), which discusses Oppen; many other books on Joyce, Eliot, Beckett, Buckminster Fuller, and Irish and Anglo-American modernism.

Elizabeth Kray (1916–87). The Executive Director of The Academy of American Poets (1963–81); originated the Poets-in-the-Schools Program in 1966. Author of *Four Literary-Historical Walking Tours* (1982); *Chelsea 1904–1913: John Sloan's Neighborhood and Neighbors* (1985).

James Laughlin (1914–), poet, founder (1937) and editor of New Directions Publishing Corporation and the New Directions Annual (1936–). Author of *In Another Country* (1978), *Selected Poems* (1985), *The Owl of Minerva* (1987), *Pound as Wuz* (1987), a memoir of Pound. Publisher of Williams, Pound, Levertov, Snyder, Oppen, Rothenberg, and many others.

S. R. Lavin (1945–), poet, teacher at Castleton State College, Vermont, editor of *Four Zoas Journal of Poetry and Letters* (1972–present). Author of *Let Myself Shine* (1979); *The Stonecutters at War with the Cliffdwellers* and *Cambodian Spring* (1973).

Denise Levertov (1923–), poet, translator, and Professor, Stanford University. Author of *With Eyes at the Back of Our Heads* (1950), *The Jacob's Ladder* (1961), *O Taste and See* (1964), *The Sorrow Dance* (1967), *Relearning the Alphabet* (1970), *The Freeing of the Dust* (1978), *Breathing the Water* (1987), and two volumes of essays: *The Poet in the World* (1973) and *Light Up the Cave* (1981).

Philip Levine (1928–), poet, translator, Professor of English at California State University at Fresno and Tufts University. Author of *Not This Pig* (1968), *They Feed They Lion* (1972), *The Names of the Lost* (1976), *Don't Ask* (essays and interviews, 1981), *Selected Poems* (1984), *Sweet Will* (1985), *A Walk with Tom Jefferson* (1988); recipient of many awards.

Robert M. MacGregor (1911–74), editor, vice president, and trustee of The New Directions Corporation, 1950–74.

David McAleavey (1946–), critic, poet, Associate Dean, and Professor of English, George Washington University. Did Cornell University Ph.D. dissertation on Oppen, compiled the Oppen bibliography for *George Oppen: Man & Poet*. Author of *Sterling 403* (1971), *The Forty Days* (1975), *Shrine, Shelter, Cave* (1980), *Holding Obsidian* (1985).

Frederick Martin (1937–88), editor and vice president at New Directions, 1967–83.

John Martin (1930–), editor and publisher of Black Sparrow Press from 1966 to the present; publisher of Oppen's final book, *Primitive*; Mary Oppen's memoir; the collected work of Charles Reznikoff.

Diane [Andy] Meyer (1928–), Oppen's niece, daughter of his sister Elizabeth (Libby). B.A. from University of California at Berkeley (1950). Mother of Mari (b. 1951), Hannah (b. 1958), Eve (b. 1954), and Paul (b. 1961); painter, founder of the San Francisco Children's Art Center in 1973, and its director until 1985.

Alexander Phoebus Dionysious Mourelatos (1936–), Professor, Department of Philosophy, The University of Texas at Austin. Married Linda Oppen in June 1962. Author of *The Route of Parmenides: A Study of Word, Image, and Argument in the Fragments* (1970); editor of *The Pre-Socratics* (1974).

Linda Oppen Mourelatos (1940–). Dressage horse trainer and instructor. Only child of George and Mary Oppen. Literary Executor of the Estate of George Oppen.

Aleksandar Nejgebauer (1930–89), writer, translator from Serbo-Croatian, professor of English in Novi Sad, Yugoslavia. Has written on Oppen in Serbo-Croatian. Author of *Traditional and Individual Elements in Shakespeare's Sonnets* (1971), *English Literature in the Age of Romanticism* (1981), four books of poems, among them *Haiku* (1975).

Sharon Olds (1942–), poet. Author of *Satan Says* (1980), *The Dead and the Living* (1984), *The Gold Cell* (1987).

Anita Pepper (1927–). Taught in the Department of Epidemiology and Public Health, Yale University School of Medicine (1962); now Professor of Epidemiology for Nursing, School of Nursing, St. Louis University.

Max Pepper, M.D. (1930–). Director of Mental Health Planning in Connecticut (1962); now Professor and Chairman of Department of Community Medicine, St. Louis School of Medicine. The poem "Sara in Her Father's Arms" is addressed to him.

Panthea L. Perry (1929–88), niece of Oppen; daughter of his sister Elizabeth (Libby). Psychologist (Ph.D. in psychology), founding member Allied Health Associates, was faculty member Columbia Pacific University, and served on panels for the State Department of Health and Department of Vocational Rehabilitation in California.

Allan Planz (1937–), poet. Author of *Wild Craft* (1975); *Chunderhara* (1977).

Helen Plotz (dates unavailable), anthologist. Editor of *The Gift Outright: America to Her Poets* (1977); *Eye's Delight: Poems of Art and Architecture* (1983).

Ezra Pound (1885–1972), poet, critic, translator. Vital to the formation and dissemination of twentieth-century poetry. Author of *Hugh Selwyn Mauberley* (1920), *The Cantos* (1919–72), and such books of practical and cultural criticism as *ABC of Reading* (1934), *Guide to Kulchur* (1938), *Literary Essays* (1954).

J. H. Prynne (1936–), poet and teacher, Fellow of Gonville and Caius College, Cambridge. Author of *Kitchen Poems* (1968), *Aristeas* (1968), *The White Stones* (1969), *Brass* (1971), *Into the Day* (1972), *Wound Response* (1974), *High Pink on Chrome* (1975), *News of Warring Clans* (1977), *Poems* (1982), *The Oval Window* (1983), *Bands around the Throat* (1987).

Carl Rakosi (1903–), poet, social worker, and psychotherapist (retired in 1968). Author of *Selected Poems* (1941), *Amulet* (1967), *Ere-Voice* (1971), *Ex Cranium, Night* (1975), *My Experiences in Parnassus* (1977), *Droles de Journal* (1981), *History* (1981), *Spiritus, I* (1983), *Collected Prose* (1983), *Collected Poems* (1986).

Naomi Replansky (1918–), poet. Author of *Ring Song* (1952, rpt. 1962), *Twenty-One Poems: Old and New* (1988), *The Dangerous World* (unpublished).

Charles Reznikoff (1894–1976), poet, publisher/printer, editor of law textbooks. Published his first works in 1918; author of *By the Waters of Manhattan: Selected Verse* (1962), *Testimony: United States* (vol. 1, 1978, vol. 2, 1979), *By The Well of Living & Seeing: New and Selected Poems* (1974), *Holocaust* (1975), *Poems 1918–1936* (1976), *Poems 1937–1975* (1977), *The Manner Music* (fiction, 1977).

Martin Rosenblum (1946–), poet, editor, musician, administrator at The University of Wisconsin-Milwaukee. Author of *Home* (1971), *The Werewolf Sequence* (1974), *Music Lingo* (1987), *Conjunction* (1987); has written on Carl Rakosi and is editing *The Objectivist Casebook*.

Jerome Rothenberg (1931–), poet, teacher, and editor. Founded Hawk's Well Press (1958–

65); influential anthologies such as *The Technicians of the Sacred* (1968), *Shaking the Pumpkin* (1972), *America, a Prophecy* (with G. Quasha, 1973), *The Revolution of the Word* (1974). Author of *A Seneca Journal* (1978), *Poland/1931* (1974), *Pre-Faces* (essays, 1981), *Khurbn and Other Poems* (1989).

Claude Royet-Journoud (1941–), French poet, editor of *Siècle à Mains* (1963–70); his translations of George Oppen appeared in *Vingt Poètes Americains* (1980). Author of *Le Renversement* (1972; trans. Keith Waldrop, 1973), *The Maternal drape, or the restitution* (trans. Charles Bernstein, 1985), *La notion d'obstacle* (1978; trans. Waldrop, 1985).

Anthony Rudolf (1942–), British poet, editor, publisher of The Menard Press (1969–). Editor of *European Judaism* (1970–75) and the anthology *Voices Within the Ark* (1980); author of *The Same River Twice* (1976), *After the Dream* (1980), *Byron's Darkness: Lost Summer and Nuclear Winter* (essay, 1984); translator of essay on Balzac's *The Unknown Masterpiece* (1988).

Steven J. Schneider (1934–), writer and translator of poetry and fiction, including under the name "Samuel Klonimos." Director of several companies (Europe). Author of professional articles and books on wine and wine economics. Administrator of arts patronage fund (The Andarrios Fund). Old friend of the Oppens from Mexican period; strong contact in the early to mid-1960s. Nephew of Julian Zimet.

Ethel Schwabacher (1903–84), painter, writer of *Arshile Gorky* (1957), and diarist of a meditative journal, *The Tortoise and The Angel*. Cousin of George Oppen. Did a series of paintings called "Women" in 1951, paintings of the civil rights struggle, and visions of mythic figures such as Orpheus and Eurydice, Prometheus, Antigone, and Abraham in the late 1960s.

Armand Schwerner (1927–), poet, translator from Greek, German, French; performance work; Professor, College of Staten Island, CUNY. Author of *The Lightfall* (1963), *Seaweed* (1969), various collections of *The Tablets* (1968, 1971, 1974, 1975, 1976, 1988), *Bacchae Sonnets* (1977), *Sounds of the River Naranjana and The Tablets I–XXIV* (1983).

Hugh Seidman (1940–), poet, technical writer, technical editor, faculty member at The New School for Social Research. Author of *Collecting Evidence* (1970), *Blood Lord* (1974), *Throne / Falcon / Eye* (1982). Studied with Louis Zukofsky at the Polytechnic Institute of Brooklyn.

Harvey Shapiro (1924–), poet, editorial positions with *The New York Times Magazine* (1957–75; 1983–current), editor of the *New York Times Book Review* (1975–83). Author of *The Eye* (1953), *The Book and other poems* (1955), *Mountain, Fire, Thornbush* (1961), *Battle Report* (1966), *This World* (1971), *Lauds* (1975), *Nightsounds* (1978), *The Light Holds* (1984), *National Cold Storage Company* (1988).

Tom Sharp (1952–), poet and technical writer. Author of *The Problems* (1972), *The Balancing of Grinding Wheels* (1979), *Synopsis of Signal Systems* (1979), *Ezra's Book* (1980), *Important Beater Instructions* (1985). Has written on Oppen and the Objectivists.

Mary Ellen Solt (1920–), poet, Professor of Comparative Literature, Indiana University. Author of *Flowers in Concrete* (1966), *The People-mover: A Demonstration Poem* (1978);

editor of *Concrete Poetry: A World View* (1968); *Dear Ez: Letters from William Carlos Williams to Ezra Pound* (1985).

Gilbert Sorrentino (1929–), poet, novelist, Professor of English, Stanford University; numerous fellowships and awards. Author of *Black and White* (1964), *The Sky Changes* (1966), *Imaginative Qualities of Actual Things* (1970), *The Orangery* (1978), *Mulligan Stew* (1979), *Selected Poems: 1958–80* (1981), *Something Said: Essays* (1984), *Odd Number* (1985).

Sherman Stein (1926–), Professor of Mathematics, University of California, Davis. Author of *Mathematics: The Man-Made Universe: an Introduction to the Spirit of Mathematics* (1965; 1969; 1976).

Tony Stoneburner (1926–), Professor of English, Denison University, associate editor of *East-West Review* (1964–73) and *Anglican Theological Review* (1974–84); has written on David Jones, Denise Levertov, Gary Snyder.

John Taggart (1942–), poet, Professor of English, Shippensburg University, editor of *Maps* (1966–74). Author of *To Construct a Clock* (1971), *The Pyramid Is A Pure Crystal* (1974), *Dodeka* (1979), *Peace on Earth* (1981), *Dehiscence* (1983), *Loop* (1989); wrote a Ph.D. dissertation on objectivist poetics in 1974.

Charles Tomlinson (1927–), poet and painter, Professor of English, Bristol University. Author of *The Way of a World* (1969), *Written on Water* (1972), *The Shaft* (1978), *Notes from New York* (1984), *Collected Poems* (1987); in prose, *Some Americans* (1981), which discusses Oppen; *Poetry and Metamorphosis* (1983); editor of *Marianne Moore* (1969), *William Carlos Williams* (1972), *Oxford Book of Verse in English* (1980).

Diane Wakoski (1937–), poet, Writer in Residence, Michigan State University. Author of *Coins and Coffins* (1962), *The George Washington Poems* (1967), *Inside the Blood Factory* (1968), *The Magellanic Clouds* (1969), *The Motorcycle Betrayal Poems* (1971), *Trilogy* (1974), *Cap of Darkness* (1980), *The Collected Greed: Parts I–XIII* (1984).

Sarah Appleton Weber (1930–), poet, translator from French. Author of *Theology and Poetry in the Middle English Lyric: A Study of Sacred History and Aesthetic Form* (1969), *The Plenitude We Cry For* (1972), *Ladder of the World's Joy* (1977).

Brenda Webster (1936–), writer, translator from Italian, and critic. Author of *Yeats: A Psychoanalytic Study* (1973), *Blake's Prophetic Psychology* (1983), *The Sins of the Mothers* (a novel); coeditor, with Judith Emlyn Johnson, of the journals of her mother, the painter Ethel Schwabacher, *The Tortoise and the Angel*.

James L. Weil (1929–), editor and publisher, poet. Publisher of The Elizabeth Press (1961–82); of James L. Weil, Publisher (1982–current). Editor of *Elizabeth* (March 1961–December 1971). Author of *Quarrel with the Rose* (1958), *The Correspondences* (1968), *Your Father* (1973), *Portrait of the Artist Painting Her Son* (1976), *Uses* (1981), *Houses Roses* (1985).

Eliot Weinberger (1949–), writer, editor of *Montemora* (1975–82), translator from Spanish. Author of *Works on Paper: Essays* (1986), *19 Ways of Looking at Wang Wei* (with Octavio Paz, 1987). Translations include *Altazor* by Vicente Huidobro (1987), *Seven*

Nights by Jorge Luis Borges (1984), and *The Collected Poems of Octavio Paz 1957–1987* (1987).

Henry Weinfield (1949–), poet, founding editor of *The Mysterious Barricades* (1972–76), faculty member, Humanities Department, New Jersey Institute of Technology. Author of *The Carnival Cantata* (1971), *In the Sweetness of the New Time* (1980), *Sonnets Elegiac and Satirical* (1982); has written on Oppen and Bronk.

Frederic Will (1928–), poet, critic, translator, and editor-founder of *Micromegas*. Author of *A Wedge of Words* (1963), *Literature Inside Out: Ten Speculative Essays* (1966), *Archilochos* (1969), *Our Thousand Year Old Bodies: Selected Poems 1956–76* (1980), *Shamans in Turtlenecks* (1984), and the trilogy *The Fall and the Gods* (1988–).

William Carlos Williams (1883–1963), poet, essayist, novelist, and physician. Pivotal American modernist; author of *Spring & All* (1923), *In the American Grain* (1925), *Paterson* (1946–58), *Selected Essays* (1954).

John Wilson (1948–), editor of *Occurrence* (1973–78).

Julian Zimet (1919–), screenwriter and novelist (under the name of Julian Halevy); author of *The Lovers, a novel* (1955). Uncle of Steven Schneider.

Louis Zukofsky (1904–78), poet and critic. Editor of *An "Objectivists" Anthology* (1932) and *A Test of Poetry* (1948/1964); author of *Bottom: on Shakespeare* (1963), *After I's* (1964); *All: The Collected Short Poems 1923–1958* (1965), *Prepositions: The Collected Critical Essays* (1967), *Little: for Careenagers* (1970), and *"A" 1–24* (1978).

Notes

Introduction

1 Oppen's poems, as he wrote in a letter of January 1966 to Steven Schneider, contain "many of the issues. . . that are issues between us" and that were established in their correspondence; letters were an integral part of Oppen's poetic practice. There are moments when citations from his letters directly enter as lines of his poems, moments when letters come from, or turn into, notes and jottings which inform the poetry's process of thought, and a few moments when what correspondents write back to him become lines of his poetry.

2 "In its very form of ongoing response and reply, the correspondence [here of George Sand and Flaubert] presents the dynamic movement of self-consciousness as it comes to know, express, and even shape itself by confronting otherness." Wendy Deutelbaum, "Desolation and Consolation: The Correspondence of Gustave Flaubert and George Sand," *Genre* 15 (Fall 1982): 299–300.

3 This is my answer to the interesting question posed by Charles A. Porter in his consideration of the functions of letters (a message-bearing object between two people) and the genre of correspondence (the extension of that transmission beyond the addressee to further readers). Porter asks: "Just exactly *what is the 'plot'* of a writer's correspondence?" "Foreword," to *Men/Women of Letters, Yale French Studies* 71 (1986): 14. Sometimes, of course, that dual function became strained and contradictory.

4 The "Objectivist" agreement to form a publishing cooperative was made, upon the failure of an earlier enterprise, To Publishers (1931–32), for which Oppen was publisher (and financial supporter), Louis Zukofsky was the editor, and Pound was the guardian angel *cum* mentor. A number of other poets became more strongly affiliated with the "Objectivist" enterprise later: Niedecker, Rakosi, and Bunting, although they were active poets in the early thirties. I have retained Zukofsky's quotation marks around the name of this "group."

5 Although Pound and Williams are more familiar mentors on whom Oppen and Zukofsky continued to meditate, Williams's essay on Marianne Moore (1925), published by To Publishers in 1932, in which Williams tries to characterize the formal innovations and express the excitement which Moore's work generated in him, seems to have a special possibility as an initiatory "Objectivist" statement, one with a great impact on Oppen, and possibly Zukofsky. Williams emphasizes a new kind of spatial, constellated, rhetoric, the heterogeneity of codes and even the critique of any unifying subject (his "multiplication of impulses"), and a protoprojectivism in the "anthology of transit." He proposes a combination of specificity and metonymy to characterize an objectivist poetics.

6   Niedecker, the only woman in that generation of Objectivists, is an exception to other of these generalizations; a nonJew, she is also nonurban, living most of her life (with the exception of a few years in Milwaukee) in the country; she is, however, firmly political from the beginning of her poetic career, and throughout, with a democratic populism expressed in both theme and formal/generic issues.

7   Ron Silliman, "Third Phase Objectivism," *Paideuma* 10, 1 (Spring 1981): 85–89, a very important contribution to a new literary history. The first phase is of course 1929 to 1934/35; the second phase is polemically construed as the absence of Objectivists, which created an extremism in the New American Poets of the 1950s as they tried to formulate an "open-form, speech-based" poetics that would connect them to Williams and Pound, an extremism Silliman argues was tempered by the reemergence of Objectivist work in the mid-1960s.

8   Charles Altieri in a number of statements such as "From Symbolist Thought to Immanence: The Ground of Postmodern American Poetics," *boundary 2* 1, 3 (Spring 1973): 605–41; "The Objectivist Tradition," *The Chicago Review* 30, 3 (1979): 5–22; and in *Enlarging the Temple: New Directions in American Poetry During the 1960's*, Bucknell University Press, 1979. Marjorie Perloff in *The Poetics of Indeterminacy: Rimbaud to Cage* (Princeton University Press, 1981); *The Dance of the Intellect: Studies in the Poetry of the Pound Tradition* (Cambridge University Press, 1985), especially "Pound/Williams; whose era?" Both are preceded by a very important essay registering this opposition: David Antin, "Modernism and Postmodernism: Approaching the Present in American Poetry," *boundary 2* 1 (Fall 1971): 98–133.

9   There is correspondence from 1971 (UCSD 16, 8, 22) about the possible inclusion of work by Oppen in the first *Norton Anthology of Modern Poetry*; six poems altogether were chosen. It is not known why they were finally excluded. The second edition of this "canonizing" anthology not only excludes Oppen, but Zukofsky as well, who had been present in the first edition. There are, at the same time, significant critical readings of Oppen, in *George Oppen: Man and Poet*, ed. Burton Hatlen (Orono, Me.: The National Poetry Foundation, 1981), with both critical studies and bibliographic apparatus, in *Paideuma* 10, 1 (Spring 1981), in *Ironwood* 5 (1975) and 26 (Fall 1985), ed. Michael Cuddihy, and in *Not Comforts/But Vision: Essays on the Poetry of George Oppen*, ed. John Freeman (Devon: Interim Press, 1985). Also Michael Heller, *Conviction's Net of Branches: Essays on the Objectivist Poets and Poetry* (Carbondale: Southern Illinois University Press, 1985). In *Ironwood* 26, John Taggart has pointed to the situation of Oppen vis-à-vis anthologies, suggesting, provocatively, that Oppen is unanthologizable. The Hatlen volume henceforward cited as GOM&P.

10   For Oppen's published essays, see David McAleavey, "A Bibliography of the Works of George Oppen," *Paideuma* 10, 1 (Spring 1981): 155–69. My interim "Bibliography of Interviews of George and Mary Oppen, Chronologically Arranged" has been published in *Sagetrieb* 6, 1 (Spring 1987): 137–39. Excluding a few letters published as statements (e.g., by *The Four Zoas Journal*), there are more interviews than essays and reviews in the Oppen canon. See also an "Interview with Mary Oppen" conducted in July 1987 by Dennis Young, *The Iowa Review* 18, 3.

11   "An Adequate Vision: A George Oppen Daybook," ed. Michael Davidson, *Ironwood* 26 (1985): 5–31; " 'Meaning Is to Be Here': A Selection from the Daybook," ed.

Cynthia Anderson, *Conjunctions* 10 (1987): 186–208; "Selections from George Oppen's 'Daybook'," ed. Dennis Young, *The Iowa Review* 18, 3 (Fall 1988): 1–17; "The Anthropologist of Myself," ed. Rachel Blau DuPlessis, *Sulfur* 26 (1990). In his work cataloging The Archive for New Poetry George Oppen Register, Bradley Westbrook distinguishes between two groups of working papers: "Notes, Jottings," (UCSD 16, 13–18), and materials bound into packets by Oppen (whether by staples, with pipe cleaners, or nailed; UCSD 16, 19A and B). Sometimes drafts or carbons of letters occur in these notes, for there is some fluidity in the generic border between the two; both are kinds of working papers. It is important to note that virtually none of these working papers is dated, and no sequence has been suggested by Oppen for the great majority of these papers.

12 Indeed, the existence of a chronologically arranged letters might assist the dating and correlation of the working papers.

13 The family name was changed by Oppen's father in 1927; the change was registered in San Francisco Superior Court.

14 UCSD 16, 1, 2. The letter was written to JOD after Libby's death in January 1960; see also David McAleavey, "The Oppens: Remarks Towards Biography," *Ironwood* 26 (Fall 1985): 317–18. Linda Oppen Mourelatos suggests that the note was in the possession of Elizabeth Oppen Hughes (Libby), for she saw it after Libby's death.

15 Oppen, ed. Anderson, *Conjunctions* 10 (1987): 193–94. This abusive relationship had complex resonances throughout his life.

16 Mary Oppen, *Meaning a Life: An Autobiography* (Santa Barbara: Black Sparrow Press, 1978)—henceforward abbreviated *MAL*—and interview/discussion with RBD, October 17, 1986. An Oppen note (UCSD 16, 14, 13, early 1960s?): "My father was in fact charming witty kind and princely and a great trouble to me—a long and desperate struggle to save myself."

17 Mary Ruth Colby was born November 28, 1908, in Kalispell, Montana, to Alice Conklin (1878–1947), a schoolteacher, and Ora Colby (1874–1923), a postmaster. She had three older brothers—Wendell, Noel, and Paul. In 1918 the family moved to Seattle, and in 1919 or 1920 to Grants Pass, Oregon. In 1925, she entered the University of Oregon at Eugene, skipping her last year of high school, but by 1926 she had transferred to the branch at Corvallis.

18 June Oppen Degnan remembers the monthly income from this bequest as $400; Mary Oppen remembers $500.

19 MAL, 68–70; done because he was underage and feared family interference. This subterfuge they were later pleased with, claiming, in semiteasing fashion, not to be really married, which seemed to give them a sense of continual and renewed choice in their deep commitment.

20 Information from June Oppen Degnan (notes to interview, September 1986); Pelham, a town neighboring New Rochelle, had slate sidewalks.

21 They also heard "a speaker who explained fascism in Italy" who "had observed Mussolini's march on Rome." Young interview, 47.

22 In the Reznikoff Papers at The Archive for New Poetry (UCSD 9, 22, 4).

23 The outtakes from the Dembo interview of 1968, "Oppen on His Poems: A Discussion," in GOM&P, 202.

24 This press should be placed in the context of a continuing struggle and set of plans

to publish a "Poundian" group (1927–36), which began with *The Exile* and culminated in the founding of New Directions by James Laughlin in 1936. Tom Sharp, "The 'Objectivists' Publications," *Sagetrieb* 3, 3 (Winter 1984): 41–47. Pound's active interest in the establishment of an effective press is documented in Barry Ahearn, ed., *Pound-Zukofsky: Selected Letters of Ezra Pound and Louis Zukofsky* (New York: New Directions, 1987).

25   For instance, in a letter of 1958 to LOM (UCSD 33, 1, 13) from Mexico, Oppen praised "historical materialism": "It really makes sense of history, and so far as I know no one else does." By the same token, given the fact of organizing for basic social services, Mary Oppen has characterized the thrust of the day-to-day organizing as "liberal." Young interview, 39.

26   This argument about instrumentality is replayed in 1962 in exchanges about "The Mind's Own Place," especially in a letter to Charles Humboldt, included here.

27   Some of my argument here was prefigured in my "The familiar/ becomes extreme: George Oppen and Silence," *North Dakota Quarterly* 55, 4 (Fall 1987): 18–36.

28   The Hatlen-Mandel interview, June 1980, "Poetry and Politics: A Conversation with George and Mary Oppen" GOM&P, 25.

29   Young interview with Mary Oppen, 38.

30   FBI file; the FBI also knew, in its first report of 1941, exactly how Oppen had voted in 1936. This file is unpaginated.

31   Personal communication to RBD, May 1988. This pact was, of course, one of the numerous crises of and for twentieth-century Communism as a movement; it corresponded to an attack on Roosevelt and the New Deal, and marked the end of the efflorescence of Communist influence in the United States.

32   American Campaign Medal, Purple Heart, Good Conduct Medal, European-African Medal, Eastern Campaign Medal with two bronze stars, World War II Victory Medal; he later called these the "normal 'decorations' and condolences." *Contemporary Authors: A Bio-bibliographic Guide to Current Authors and Their Works*, ed. Clare D. Kinsman, vols. 13–16 (Detroit: Gale, 1975), 329. For the severity of the injuries, see McAleavey, *Ironwood* 26: 309–10.

33   This is known from both *Meaning a Life* and the FBI files.

34   Letter of Mary Oppen to RBD, June 18, 1988.

35   Dembo, 175.

36   Letter of Mary Oppen to RBD, June 18, 1988. By "McCarthy" is probably meant not only Senator McCarthy's Permanent Subcommittee on Investigations in the Senate, but also HUAC, and the management of a "Red Scare" in general.

37   The FBI called his remarks on June 24 a "tirade." The verbatim account from the file: "[Oppen] said that if the FBI has authority to ask questions concerning political beliefs of Communists, then tomorrow they will have authority to investigate a person because he is a Republican or Democrat. Oppen then went into a tirade concerning reports that telephone lines of private citizens are being tapped and civil rights are being infringed upon."

38   Peggy Dennis's memoirs suggest the analysis then current: "With these convictions, the State sought to outlaw a legal, minority political party by so-called 'legal' processes. All minority opinion and action would then be intimidated and strait-jack-

eted." *The Autobiography of an American Communist: A Personal View of a Political Life, 1925–1975* (Westport: Lawrence Hill, 1977), 176.

39   Peter L. Steinberg, *The Great "Red Menace": United States Prosecution of American Communists, 1947–1952* (Westport, Conn: Greenwood Press, 1984), 182–83. There were Smith Act prosecutions in various cities from 1950 to 1952. The mandate to go underground of the central Party leadership was, in Steinberg's view, a decision contributing to its isolation and sectarianism.

40   Dembo, 175. In the 1987 interview with Young, Mary Oppen said, "we were about the next echelon which was due to be picked up," 29.

41   See *Meaning a Life*; the MO letter of June 18, 1988, said: "We went forth with petitions against the Korean War on the crowded beach at Redondo—couldn't supply forms enough for people to sign. These were our own petitions, just our names and address on them. The next day, and thereafter a person here, another there came to ask that their names be blanked out—Scared—shit-less—in the after thought of what wd happen to their kids—to jobs. We took the names off."

42   This post hoc reconstruction of their reasoning has been done in cooperation with Linda Oppen Mourelatos. Because HUAC had the right to subpoena witnesses (from 1940), any witness thus was in potential danger of being cited for contempt of Congress. As Eric Bentley ironically presents the case: "At best they would then go to jail, at worst spend some uncomfortable, expensive years keeping out of jail. . . ." *Thirty Years of Treason: Excerpts from Hearings before the House Committee on Un-American Activities, 1938–1968*, ed. Eric Bentley (New York: Viking Press, 1971), 947.

43   To France when Oppen attempted unsuccessfully to apply for a passport to go there. A December 14, 1953, memorandum from SAC (Subversive Activities Control) in Los Angeles to the director of the FBI tabbed the Oppen file COMSAB and DETCOM. These were catch-all categories—the first meant Communists with potential for sabotage, whether by training or by their position in vital industries; the second indicating "top functionaries, key figures, and individuals labeled under COMSAB and other individuals"—the "DET" suggesting plans for detaining or incarcerating such people. There seems to have been internal debate about "DET" status, for Oppen was explicitly removed from "DET" tabbing in June 1955 with the notation that such tabbing was not warranted. Steinberg, 182–83.

44   In June 1957 the U.S. Supreme Court (6 to 1) had reversed the conviction of the California Smith Act defendants. This *Yates* decision marked the end of U.S. government prosecution of American Communists.

45   Oppen designed furniture which was spare and modern in style—Shaker or Bauhaus in influence.

46   The Humboldt papers at Beinecke Library, Yale University, do not, unfortunately, reveal this among its holdings.

47   See MAL, 199–201. Apparently Oppen never even learned Spanish, although Mary could manage in that language and Linda became fluent. A further consequence of the exile is that Oppen lost all his "literary papers and correspondence," as he reports in a letter of [March 1975] to James Laughlin.

48   One bit of evidence suggests that the dream may have dated from 1956, the analysis of it from 1958; it is more likely that both occurred in 1958.

49   MAL, 201–2; see also the Hatlen-Mandel interview, GOM&P, 27–28 in which Oppen offers an alternative punchline: "You dreamt that you're not going to rot." A third telling of the story, with transcription problems, in the David McAleavey interview (January 1978), *Ironwood* 26:311. In the working papers (UCSD 16, 15, 11) Oppen notes the importance of his sister June leading him to these miscellaneous papers, and finding this "work ON PAPER" which instructed him how to prevent rust.

50   He says proudly ([1960?] letter to JOD, UCSD 16, 1, 2) that the poem "discloses the guilty fact that I was not Yeatsing on the green, nor Pounding, nor Eliotizing in the middle thirties."

51   There is intrafamilial debate on this; the coroner's report of Los Angeles County ruled a "probable suicide," and June Oppen Degnan insists from personal evidence the assumption or finding is wrong. Under her (then) name of Libby Danysh, Elizabeth had published a book of poems in 1940 called *Deny the Day*; Oppen always liked, and felt paradigmatic, her poem called "Step into My Parlor": "Caught in the awful maze / The sticky spider-web of being me / Spinning outward to affix / Untidy threads to every passer-by. / But surfaces are smooth and glassy / I remain the spinner and the victim."

52   Sailing was a primary experience of meaning for them throughout their lives; see MAL 102, 106.

53   These three books, as well as Oppen's third book, *This in Which*, were brought out under the dual imprint of New Directions–San Francisco Review with James Laughlin and June Oppen Degnan as joint publishers. One is struck by the fact that disseminating "third phase Objectivism" was to a large degree the work of Oppen as editorial advisor with his sister as publisher, as well as the work of Corman, publishing Zukofsky.

54   June Oppen Degnan solicited comments (UCSD, 17, 5, 12); a letter from Marianne Moore, dated September 25, 1965, said: "In THIS IN WHICH by George Oppen, the straight order of words is a relief from easy writing and the content has the flavor of courage." Moore added this postscript: "I am trying not to read books with a view to comment, but this book has the right ring."

55   The interviews appeared in an issue of *Contemporary Literature* under Dembo's editorship: 10, 2 (Spring 1969): 159–77.

56   On February 22; entitled "Four Major American Poets," this event used videotapes of Frank O'Hara and Charles Olson (who were both then dead).

57   Ted Berrigan substituted for Jonathan Williams; it is at this time that an Oppen and Berrigan interview occurred, later published in *Chicago* (London) 1 (October 1973).

58   This is essentially the last set of public appearances; Oppen canceled invitations to read in Cambridge (England) and at the Centre Georges Pompidou (Paris) to have taken place in 1977. There are meditative comments upon this, or this kind of, choice in his working papers, *Ironwood* 26 (1985): 9.

59   Her help involved typing clean copies and typing fresh drafts, but in subtle ways helping the book into its final form. Mary was also completing the memoir for which she had signed a contract in March 1977.

60   These, in the distinctive loose writing of his last years, are distributed among the boxes of notes; there is also "George Oppen's Last Words," those aphorisms found on his study wall at his death (UCSD 16, 19, 18).

61   Along with Meridel LeSueur and Janet Lewis.

Editorial Comments

1   In order to indicate year-by-year recipients I have appended, to each year, a list of those to whom Oppen wrote letters which were not selected for this edition. This should be taken as a general indication; obviously when letters could absolutely not be dated, I could not list the recipient in the proper year.

2   The little note (UCSD 16, 16, 2) glosses "bad character": "I am in the habit of asking correspondents to inject the phrase 'I think' whenever it is appropriate. I tend to omit it."

3   Sharon Hileman, "Autobiographical Narrative in the Letters of Jane Carlyle," *A/B: Autobiography,* forthcoming. I am grateful to Professor Hileman for a prepublication typescript of this article, with its pertinent comments about letters as a genre.

4   Conventional abbreviations are used: TL = typed letter; c = carbon or photocopy; AL = autograph letter or autograph section of a letter; PC = postcard; s = signed; d = draft; prov. = provenance. TLs with AL insert means "typed letter, signed, with autograph insert"; TLTs means "typed letter, typed signature." In addition, abbreviations may be used for family names: MO = Mary Oppen; LOM = Linda Oppen Mourelatos; JOD = June Oppen Degnan; APDM = Alex Mourelatos; DM = Diane [Andy] Meyer.

5   He had letterhead for both Henry Street and Polk Street addresses. My biographical headnotes to each year will give a sense of the places from which he was writing.

6   With all difficulties of transcription I have consulted Linda Oppen Mourelatos and/ or Mary Oppen. Diane Meyer provided typescript transcriptions of letters to her, which I consulted along with the originals.

7   In this case "reasonable assurance" generally means all postmarked dates, which are uniformly given in square brackets.

8   That is, he elides them back into words. Or even, into "things." When he is writing to authors themselves, this tactic has the effect of confronting them with their titles unsanctified by the authority of normal notation. This tactic is worth pondering at least for its commentary on the boundaries of an artwork and for its claims of the necessary power of unadorned words.

9   "On Armand Schwerner [a review of *Seaweed*]," *Stony Brook* 3–4 (1969): 72.

10 The exception is in the treatment of Oppen's wayward quotation marks, often given in such pairs as " for open quotation, but ' for close quotation, and often hanging at some distance from the citation. See below. Incidentally, Oppen seems to have confused the semicolon with the colon; while annoying, this has not been corrected.

11 For example, as a justification, it is clear that Oppen's irregular indentation almost always followed an impeccable logic. Oppen would change paragraphs or units of thought by double-spacing after a thought had (apparently) ended; this double space left the margin "set" exactly where the last word ended, but two lines farther down the page. This is a visual code for a "discrete series"—a phrase with tremendous importance to him: that mathematical term which he used as the title for his first book, that mark of what "really was out there," and how it was situationally and functionally organized. The task visually to notate not only *how* but *that* he got from one thought to the next is given to this particular scoring of the page which offers both connection and gap, continuation and surprise.

12 It is also true that Oppen sometimes did not indent but spaced between square-block paragraphs. These paragraphs have been normalized for visual clarity and consistency. It is also true that several statements, centered on the page by Oppen, are replicated here on this page.

13 This will give such forms as "alright," which serves an expostulatory function for Oppen, and "thot"—the twentieth-century poet's respelling of "thought."

1931–34

1 He also set about being informed about the literary scene, reporting in an [October 1931] letter to Pound that he read *Hound and Horn, Pagany, Blues, The Morada, The New Review,* and *Contempo.* The *Morada,* edited by Donal McKenzie and Norman Macleod, from Albuquerque, New Mexico, published four issues between 1929 and 1931; it seems to have aimed to present both politically and formally radical literature. *Morada* was originally mentioned by Pound to Zukofsky when LZ had just gotten asked (October 1930) to edit an issue of *Poetry,* and Zukofsky was receiving much interesting advice in numerous letters from Pound. Indeed, Pound's original description of what turned into the "Objectivists" issue of *Poetry* was, "The people D. McKenzie believes in & that you LZ are willing to write about" (Barry Ahearn, ed., *Pound/Zukofsky: Selected Letters* (New York: New Directions, 1987), 44). In a letter to the editor of *Contempo* of May 24, 1932, held at The Harry Ransom Humanities Research Center, the University of Texas, Oppen wrote, "I've been intending for some time to thank you for Contempo-- it's been a pleasure to see that a serious magazine can be so unembarrassed." He also sent a contribution which reads:

> The search-light
> Diagonal: (the
>
> Short but wide night).

2 In letters from Pound to Zukofsky, Pound was concerned (January 29 and 30, 1931) that the firm that had contracted to do his collected prose had gone "bust" (Ahearn, 88). On October 15, 1931, Zukofsky wrote to Pound: "Geo. Oppen is planning a publishing firm--TO, Publishers, and I'm the edtr" (Ahearn, 104). Oppen glossed this choice of name in a letter to Pound of October 11, 1931 (Beinecke Library), "The name is To Publishers (when questioned we say something about the dative)." Zukofsky stated, "The names of our presses were my ideas: To--as we might say, a health to--To." (" 'The Best Human Value,' " *The Nation* 186, 22 [May 31, 1958]: 501). On October 28, 1931, Pound wrote Zukofsky that Oppen wanted to do the " 'collects of EP' " (Ahearn, 101). As a further inducement, Pound proffered the possibility that the firm which could successfully bring out the collected prose would have the right to publish *The Cantos.* Pound also queried Zukofsky about Oppen's sources of "inkum" and inquired how he came by $100, and "if so what is he???" (Ahearn, 102). When Pound wanted formal assurance from Oppen, GO replied, November 24, 1931 (dated letter, Beinecke Library), "We will have sufficient funds to publish one book every two months irrespective of sales. It is not necessary

that the business should support itself for some years: at any rate we will complete any series on which we have started."

3   A gloss on "distribution" in a letter of Oppen to Pound of December 4, 1931 (Beinecke Library); the pun on the name of the press seems unintentional: "We need to sell about 1600 copies to break even. What you probably know (and I do not) is, To whom do we need to sell to get rid of 1600 copies?"

4   RBD has found no Oppen letters from 1933. In January 1933, Zukofsky proposed to Pound a "Writers Extant" cooperative, so writers would finance their own publication. In February, Pound was asked by Faber & Faber to edit *Active Anthology*; in April 1933, Pound approved, in a letter to Zukofsky, of Oppen's poems and selected several for the anthology. The anthology was published in October. Also in October 1933, Objectivist Press—the writers' cooperative—was formed. In a one-page note (Reznikoff Papers, UCSD MSS 9, Box 19, Folder 3), Reznikoff noted that the members of the group were "acquaintances of Zukofsky" who did not, poignantly, have the money to publish a book of his own.

5   Responding to Williams's thanks for *A Novelette and Other Prose*; Wallace gives official publication date as January 1, 1932; it appears to have been published a month or so later. In a letter of January 24, [1932,] held at the Beinecke Library, Oppen wrote to Williams: "To have the Note on Pound and the Note on Modern Poetry included in your volume would delay publication as the first galleys have already been corrected." The works by Williams most likely to fit these descriptions are two works from 1929: "A Note on the Art of Poetry," *Blues* 1, 4 (May 1929): 77–79 (Wallace C132), and "A Tentative Statement" (about Pound's *Cantos*, *The Little Review* 12, 2 (May 1929): 95–98 (Wallace C134). And/or works from 1930 and 1931, both eventually printed in Williams, *Selected Essays*: "Caviar and Bread Again: A Warning to the New Writer," *Blues* 9 (Fall 1930): 46–47 [Wallace C153], and "Excerpts from a Critical Sketch: The XXX Cantos of Ezra Pound," *The Symposium* 2, 2 (April 1931): 257–63 (Wallace C161).

6   Oppen had begun writing *Discrete Series* in 1929. On March 6, 1930, Zukofsky told Pound that he could send thirty-two pages of poetry by Oppen (unpublished letter in Beinecke Library; paraphrased by Tom Sharp in "George Oppen, *Discrete Series*, 1929–34," in GOM&P.) And on June 18, 1930, Zukofsky reminded Pound that he had not yet given a response to the Oppen materials, which apparently also included an essay (see Ahearn, ed.). Because the number of pages is exactly equivalent to the pages in *Discrete Series*, it is plausible that a complete manuscript of *Discrete Series* was in circulation. Indeed, in reference to an Oppen letter of [1972?], John Martin of Black Sparrow Press informed me that among the Reznikoff papers at UCSD, there was a "home-made copy" of *Discrete Series* among the papers. "I asked George about it, to find out if this was a unique copy made for Charles or whether he had actually prepared a small handmade 'edition' of this text for private distribution. Apparently he had done the latter and distributed copies to Charles and I would think also to Zukofsky and other poet friends. In effect, this makes these copies the first (private) edition of his first book" (personal communication, September 8, 1987). Oppen's response to Martin's query is included here, see 1972.

7   *Contact* was edited by William Carlos Williams from February 1932 to October 1932; there were three issues. A letter of Williams to Nathanael West indicates that

Contact was planning to publish Oppen; *The Selected Letters of William Carlos Williams*, ed. John C. Thirlwall (New York: McDowell, Obolensky, 1957), 128.

8 In a letter of July 19, [1932], Oppen had told Pound that "my income will be reduced by the new income tax." But on July 23, [1932], Oppen wrote to Pound, "Losses so vaguely reported have nothing to do with income-tax, it turns out, but with the general flop, mess, etc. [¶] Our income becomes almost non-extant [¶] So if the system won't even support the capitalists--"

9 In a letter of August 8, 1932, Zukofsky wrote Pound that *To Publishers* could not be continued, and that Zukofsky's salary was to stop at the end of "the year." LZ was not certain about the exact cutoff date, since he and GO had made no formal agreement (Ahearn, 132). Until then, LZ received $50 a week. As well, Oppen gave Zukofsky the $3 per contributor as a fee for those in *The "Objectivists" Anthology*, prompting Pound to say, in a letter of August 16, 1932, "Op / is sposed to be broke" (Ahearn, 134).

10 Oppen's address on this letter is c/o Thomas Cook & Son, Paris.

11 The last issue of *Contact* came out in October 1932.

12 Oppen had received Pound's "Preface" to *Discrete Series* and had responded the day before, on February 8, 1934 (dated).

13 The nature of those intentions can be gauged by a statement from the February 8, 1934, letter (Beinecke Library): "I need a poem to end the book which will not get an emotional extra-ness by being the last in the book" (see CP 14); the book ends "Successive / Happenings / (the telephone)."

14 For this oblique passage, perhaps a pun: discrete/discreet.

15 The allusion to Stein seems untraceable; the allusion to the economic crisis is clear.

16 Williams, *Collected Poems 1921–1931*, with a preface by Wallace Stevens (New York: The Objectivist Press, 1934).

1958

1 Poems by Zukofsky mentioned here are "Mantis," and possibly " 'Mantis,' An Interpretation," *All: The Collected Short Poems, 1923–1958* (New York: W. W. Norton, 1965), 73–80; the "sonnet" is harder, but is probably the sonnet(s) which open "A 7", 39, since the urban sawhorses making letters is a passage Oppen liked; the "mother's shoes" passage occurs at the end of "A 6", 38; "A" (Berkeley: University of California Press, 1978). In later statements on the war years, Oppen drops the mention of LZ's poems.

2 The citation which opens this letter is from a Replansky poem called "The Hunters," *Ring Song: Poems* (New York: Charles Scribner's Sons, 1952), 4.

3 I date this letter as before LOM visited Louis Zukofsky on or just before October 25, 1958, and before the Oppens visited Linda in November for Thanksgiving; the enclosed poem is later called "Man's Time" or "Man's Life." Certain of the stanza units in this poem appear in poems on CP 37 and 170. In a later letter from fall 1958, Oppen made a packet for her with eight of his poems from *Discrete Series*.

4 A labor leader and friend.

5 Oppen made carved bas-reliefs out of wood during his time in Mexico, and studied

at Esmeralda School of Painting and Sculpture. They were planning to visit over Christmas 1958.

6   This may allude to her call on the Zukofskys; it also recalls a funny and warm letter from 1958, but not included here, about the cure for vapor lock in cars.

7   On United Nations Day, October 24, Pablo Casals, the cellist, performed at the UN, breaking a thirty-year self-imposed ban on appearances in the United States because of its recognition of Franco's regime in Spain. The gesture was made in support of the influence of the UN on world peace.

8   LOM's English teacher assigned a paper on "the role of the river in Huck Finn"; GO shared LOM's delight at the topic.

9   In another letter (UCSD 33, 1, 13) of [November 1958], Oppen wrote to LOM about Mark Twain: "The weakness is though a sort of journalese. Huck and Jim for instance are not really talking to each other, they are talking for the benefit of the audience. It's a contrivance, though a very very entertaining one. The river is really there, and they're really on it, without any nodding and winking at the audience to make the point. It makes the book a novel[.]"

10 A comparison of their friend, Pete Young, to a character in a William Dean Howells novel sent GO to the English Language Library in Mexico City.

11 David Alfaro Siqueiros (1896–1974), Mexican muralist and communist.

12 Russel Wright (1904–76), American designer.

13 The Reznikoff poems alluded to are two sections from Jerusalem the Golden (1934), numbers 23 and 40; in section 40, Oppen substituted his word "rubble" for Reznikoff's word "rubbish." The old man "pulls off a bit of the baked apple, shiny with sugar, / eating with reverence food, the great comforter": section 18 of Five Groups of Verse (1927).

14 Jules Feiffer, Sick, Sick, Sick: A Guide to Non-Confident Living (New York: McGraw-Hill, 1958). At the end both of this book and of one of Feiffer's notable modern dancer cartoons—one called "A Dance to Autumn"—a single leaf drops, and the dancer says, "He heard."

15 J. D. Salinger, Franny and Zooey (Boston: Little, Brown, 1961). The story "Zooey" came out in The New Yorker in 1957.

16 Walt Kelly (1913–73), creator of Pogo and other inhabitants of the Okefenokee Swamp, a comic strip which also made political comment.

1959

1   Poems dated January 1959 in the UCSD collection are "To Town" (which will go into "Of Being Numerous"), "Generation of Drivers," and "Man's Time." Between 1958 and 1959, Oppen completed "Time of the Missile," "To Date [Blood from a Stone]," "O Western Wind," "Carpenter's Boat," "Man's Time," "The Town," "Generation of Drivers," "Near the Beginning," "A Debt."

2   June Oppen Degnan was trying to start a general interest magazine, called PACIFICA, about the nations on the Pacific rim.

3   This letter, dated by GO December 30, 1958, is in The Harry Ransom Humanities Research Center, University of Texas-Austin.

4   This credo is an amalgam of Wordsworth's "My Heart Leaps Up When I Behold"
    and transposed lines from William Blake's "Auguries of Innocence": "To see a
    World in a Grain of Sand / And a Heaven in a Wild Flower / Hold Infinity in the
    palm of your hand / And Eternity in an hour. . . ."

5   Eliot, "Burnt Norton, II," *The Four Quartets*, in *Collected Poems 1909–1962* (London:
    Faber and Faber, 1963), 191. In his citation, completely accurate, Oppen has, as he
    will say, left off the final line of the statement and the section: "But reconciled
    among the stars."

6   "Buddy" was Oppen's childhood family nickname. Linda Oppen Mourelatos re-
    membered that he tolerated, but felt burdened, when the "Buddy" (sign of his being
    "Junior" to a man also named George A. Oppen[heimer]) was used beyond the
    family circle, and also well past his childhood (Phone conversation, Winter 1988).
    His niece Diane Meyer pointed out that, with her, he used the name "Buddy" until
    such time as he again felt secure in his literary career, noting that before *This in
    Which* (1962–65), Oppen generally signed his letters to her "Buddy"; after 1965, he
    used "George" (Conversation, Winter 1986). Oppen once remarked to her, "We can't
    talk about *Buddy's* prosody." It is interesting to note that Oppen's letter of 1934 to
    Reznikoff which squared away The Objectivist Press's finances was signed "Buddy"
    (UCSD; not reprinted here).

7   "Choruses from 'The Rock'—1934," in Eliot's CP 159–85. Anglican poetry, a pag-
    eant commissioned from Eliot to raise money for the building of new churches,
    whose accomplishment led directly into Eliot's first play, *Murder in the Cathedral*
    (1935); see Peter Ackroyd, *T. S. Eliot, A Life* (New York: Simon and Schuster, 1984),
    209–10; 213–15.

8   Alfred, Lord Tennyson, "Break, Break, Break," citing the first two lines; the second
    line Oppen cites does not, however, come from that poem, but from William Words-
    worth, "She Dwelt Among the Untrodden Ways," whose final stanza reads "She
    lived unknown, and few could know / When Lucy ceased to be; / But she is in her
    grave, and, oh, / The difference to me!"

9   Robert Burns's "A Red, Red Rose" begins: "O My Luve's like a red, red rose / That's
    newly sprung in June."

10 Tennyson, "Crossing the Bar."

11 Often cited by Oppen, from Reznikoff's *Jerusalem the Golden* (1934), in *By the Waters
    of Manhattan*, 30.

12 It is not clear that this next material, in UCSD 16, 1, 1, on a separate page, is attached
    to this long letter, but it might well be, and so is included precisely here by RBD.

13 Oppen did not, in fact, have poems in *New Directions* #1. A second letter to Laugh-
    lin, not reproduced here, dates from April 7, 1959; at that point Oppen sent poems
    (not named in the letter) and information about some bookstores in Mexico which
    have an interest in "advanced or unguarded poetry."

14 In April 1959, Zimet sent Oppen several pages of close scrutiny and comment about
    the packet of poems Oppen had sent in February. From the Zimet letter, graciously
    made available, one has the titles of the poems. (1) "Generation of Drivers,"
    (2) "Man's Time," (3) "The Town," (4) "The Biblical Tree," published in *Poetry* 95,
    4 (January 1960), but uncollected in book form; (5) "Infantry," (6) "Time of the
    Missile," first in *The Materials* (CP 49); (7) "Near the Beginning," (8) "Wood, Water,

Carpenter, Wind," (8) "O Western Wind," first in *The Materials* (CP 53); (9) "To Date": comparable with "Blood from a Stone" (CP 31–33).

15   The text of the poem, from UCSD 16, 1, 1, dated January 1959.

Generation of Drivers

America, America,
Brand new America,
Old codgers' home.

'Fix anything'   a village sign.
       He tells them 'Treat er easy now'
       Designers, engineers,
       Not one of whom can drive.

'Fixed a bed up here.
This's the stove
I got a boot in these,
Needs tires--'

Past it, thru it,
Down the highways, past the trailer camps
(They see them? See the trailer camps?)
Half private down the eight lane roads,
The young
To find it-- find their own.
But who the fathers? How the sons?

And who loves who?

An entity
Of two, and which they love?

16   Zimet said: "I suspect that the real tale is on another level, and that the missile time is just another way of saying we are all going to burn in hell, and another way of saying this is the way the world ends, or we are here as on a darkling plain. . . ." Letter of April 1959, provided by JZ.

17   Another citation from the JZ letter, with its anthology of allusions to hegemonic examples of the lyric.

18   "It makes me ashamed": LOM said, "One of the few bits of Spanish GO had, and a favorite."

19   In comparison with "Blood from the Stone," the first section of "To Date" has an additional stanza which reads:

We loved each other. Loved ourselves.
Bird from a bush
Or a bird lights--- down
In eyes of love.
And a child's tight love.
The ground on which we stood. Our ground.

20   Continuing the presentation of the differences of "To Date" from its revised version in "Blood from the Stone," section II reads: "The 'Thirties. And / A spectre, sure. / A world, world of people. / Discovery; the least law / Everybody knows and always knew: / Nobody by law, shall starve. // In every street, / In all inexplicable crowds -- / For them, what they did then / Is still their lives. // Thirty in a group / To home relief-- the unemployed-- / Within the city's / Intricacies, lives. / The subway turnstile is a piece of oak, / hip high. / Simple to step over it, stoop / Under. Bolted wood confronted by a / Different circumstance-- /   Belief. / Humanity is God, or will be? / Answer! what do we believe / And live for? Answer! / Not to find, invent; / Just answer-- all / That poetry attempts. / And can we somehow add to each other? // - Still our lives."

21   In the version of "To Date" used as a base here, that word does not occur, and there is virtually no change between "To Date" and "Blood from the Stone" in section III except the expansion of line three in the earlier version: "There is a simple ego system in a lyric."

22   In section IV, the first stanza is verbatim, but the second two stanzas of the earlier version read: "Fifty years of / Planetary time. / Orphans of a stone dead dam. Mother: / Nature! Because we find the others / Deserted like ourselves-- and therefore brothers. Yet, // This is how we lived / And chose to live / And what we did / Felt the world! // These were our times."

23   Published in *Poetry* 95, 4 (January 1960), but not included in any book-length collections.

24   Reznikoff, *Inscriptions: 1944–1956* (New York: privately printed, 1959), 14. The lines are "Penniless, penniless, I have come with less and still less / to this place of my need and the lack of this hour." A letter dated December 15, 1959, in which Reznikoff responds to Oppen contains this paragraph (UCSD 16, 9, 42): "It is very pleasant to be praised, especially by you, but I still wince. I suppose the reason is that I compare my own work to other work I admire and I can not help thinking of all I want to do but am too busy with a lot of trivia to do. It should be easy to shake off the trivia without dying. I realized this clearly enough in the hospital [CR had just had pneumonia] but now that I am out I find myself in the same routine. I am even entitled to Social Security payments now and should be able to re-arrange my life sensibly."

1960

1   Oppen believed that his sister committed suicide; the death was ruled a "probable suicide" by the coroner of Los Angeles County. There is intrafamily debate on this issue; June Oppen Degnan has said (conversation with RBD, September 1986) that she has circumstantial evidence to the contrary. Elsie Rothfelt Oppenheimer was the mother of George Oppen and Libby Oppen Hughes; she took her own life in 1912.

2   A report in the May 1, 1960, *New York Times* states that the protest by dockworkers and seamen against Arab blacklisting of American ships that deal with Israel occurred because such a blacklist cost the seamen jobs.

3   Origin Press published *"A" 1–12* in 1959.

4   The conviction of Colonel Rudolf Ivanovitch Abel had been upheld by a 5–4 decision of the U.S. Supreme Court on March 28, 1960; the issue was not whether he was a Soviet spy, but whether he had been convicted on evidence seized from him in violation of the Fourth Amendment prohibiting unreasonable searches and seizures.

5   Inferentially dated by the existence of a May 23 [1960?] letter to Williams (Poetry/ Rare Books Collection, SUNY-Buffalo) which invites him to dinner. It is most likely, given the strokes which Williams had suffered, that the Oppens went to New Jersey. A letter from WCW dated November 31, 1960 (UCSD 16, 11, 46), comments on Oppen's work: "They fulfill what you have promised to do with the poetic line, to keep it clean and succinct, not overburdened with metaphors blown up past what they have been asked to carry. [. . .] You have never varied in your direct approach to the word as the supreme burden of the final poetic image." The last sentence, with pronouns changed, is cited on the dust jacket of Oppen's CP.

6   From a letter of [July 10, 1960] to LOM, (UCSD 33, 1, 14): "It occurs to me that the hardest to recognize is a major poet. Anyone can recognize a minor poet -- it's more of the same. People looking at Charles' work the first time must ask themselves, where's the whatsit, where's the whosis, where's the assonance the dissonance the ambiguity the Eliot the etc. If they could once approach it as major poetry they would find themselves at once considering whether it is better or less good than Eliot or than Yeats. But it would require a new effort of sensibility, in fact a revolution of sensibility [a]s for any major poet. I realize no introduction that doesn't make this point will really do him any good."

7   This letter was preceded by one [July 27, 1960] in which Oppen said "Louis Zukofsky tells me he has written to you of my work. I am glad to send these poems. You'll let me know if you can use them" (Special Collections, Middlebury College Library). Large portions of this and the subsequent letters to Corman were published in *Origin*, fourth series, 20 (July 1982): 34–37. It is not clear what poems Oppen sent beyond "Retirement" and "Travelogue."

8   Charles Olson's essay "Projective Verse" appeared in *Poetry New York* (1950), and was excerpted in *The Autobiography of William Carlos Williams* in 1951.

9   CP 23; Oppen had sent Corman a version slightly different in punctuation ("Abruptly mine!") and in line break. The changes occur in the final two stanzas. From the version Corman received: "Self-involved, strange, alien; / Leaving. The familiar / Flesh walking. I saw his neck, his cheek, // And called, called, / Deserted; unimaginably robbed."

1961

1   "The English in Virginia," section 44 of *Jerusalem the Golden* (1934), 31; the old man, section 18, from *Five Groups of Verse* (1927), 8; the shoelace, section 33 of *Inscriptions; 1944–1956* (1959), 105–6; all in Reznikoff, *By the Waters of Manhattan* (New Directions–San Francisco Review, 1962).

2   Paul Zukofsky, violin recital at Carnegie Hall, February 3, 1961; the *New York Times* review the next day commended his technical abilities but criticized his interpretive powers. He was then seventeen years old.

3   A later letter (UCSD 16, 1, 3) reveals that Oppen suggested reusing the title *By the Waters of Manhattan*, alluding to Psalm 137. The King James version translates, "By the rivers of Babylon, there we sat down, yea, we wept, when we remembered Zion. . . . How shall we sing the Lord's song in a strange land?" The version from *The Writings, Kethubim*, as translated by the Jewish Publication Society of America: "By the rivers of Babylon / there we sat, / sat and wept, / as we thought of Zion. . . . How can we sing a song of the Lord / on alien soil?" Reznikoff had used the title *By the Waters of Manhattan* twice before: once, in 1927 for a privately printed "Annual" of prose, memoirs, and verse; a second time for a novel published by C. Boni in 1930.

4   Oppen noted, in a letter of [late 1961–early 1962?] to Naomi Replansky (prov. NR), "I stumbled on Williams, Reznikoff, Pound when I was nineteen or twenty. And forced myself to confront them. God knows what they thought. Pound and Williams probably regarded me as posterity. So they may have been interested: they could scarcely have been reassured. Nor was I. But I am very glad to have found at that moment some sense of a contemporary literary world. I don't really know what I'd have done without that sense. The sense that somebody actually extant had an idea of literature, and of a future for literature."

5   A 1959 letter to LOM (UCSD 33, 1, 14) elaborates on this moment, or a parallel one. "Challenges me: what's a Jew? I tell him solemnly: 'A Jew is what you and I are.' Then I prove to him that I could cease to be a Jew, but only by lying. So, I say, if I had to lie in order not to be a Jew then I must really -- etc. Almost as a really tight philosophic proof."

6   In a letter of [before March 14, 1961] to JOD (UCSD 16, 1, 3), Oppen had said about Bose and Bengali poetry: "I finally understand the situation: they cannot get printed in American or English publications. They feel that it must be because their English versions aren't good enuf; they want an English-speaking poet to correct them. But of course they want only verbal corrections, including better rime, which is not enuf to get them printed. I did a literal translation of the To Memory for him -- from his literal translation, of course [cf. CP 65]. Followed the rime scheme without any rime-word that wasn't in his version, and translated line by line; that is, the whole sense of one line of his version in one line of mine, even reproducing run-overs from his version. Can't do more. But of course I didn't poeticize the language in English-- and he surely is not happy with it. That is; he likes his own. As how not? But he agrees to my 'arrangement.' "

7   Dated February 26, 1961 (APCs, UCSD 9, 4, 4), it includes these remarks: "I am more and more enthusiastic about the Objectivists. You did remarkable things for the time--much that looks 'new' in Creeley, same kind of compression, etc. Reznikoff is very, very fine--wonderful, amazing control of the long line--an attempt I assume to incorporate structural elements of Hebrew poetry into our speech."

8   Al Lewin is the friend whose searching critiques of his precision helped define Reznikoff as a writer; section 130 of Reznikoff's *Early History of a Writer* (1969) describes his impact: "Now doing just what Al did, / I saw that I could use the expensive machinery / that had cost me four years of hard work at law / and which I had thought useless for my writing: / prying sentences open to look at the exact meaning: / weighing words to choose only those that had meat for my purpose /

and throwing the rest away as empty shells.[. . .] leaving only the pithy, the necessary, the clear and plain." *By the Well of Living & Seeing: New and Selected Poems, 1918–1973* (Los Angeles: Black Sparrow Press, 1974), 134–35.

9   A large horse with colic who once tried to sit on Linda's lap when she was six.

10 June Oppen Degnan noted (conversation, April 1988) that this trip—Oppen's first to Europe since World War II, evoked many complex memories of the war.

11 Replansky, *Ring Song: Poems* (New York: Charles Scribner's Sons, 1952).

12 "The Hunters" and "The Invisible Man," in *Ring Song*, 4 and 3, respectively. "The Hunters": "They went hunting lions / But a flea attacked them / And their hunters' passion / Narrowed to a flea. // Can they tell their story / When the other hunters / Stand around like fountains / Headless in the dawn? // In the bloody morning / They will tell their story. / They have still their tongues, who / Never lost their heads," 4.

1962

1   In an ALs letter to June Oppen Degnan (UCSD), which should be dated [late 1961–early 1962] about the same time as this, Oppen discussed the prospective collection, *The Materials*, in these terms: "The important thing for me is to get this group out, away, finished, off my mind. I'm having trouble getting further -- and these *should* have been written in 1940."

2   An allusion to Rimbaud's 1871 letter to George Izambard.

3   In contemporaneous letters to Steven Schneider and Naomi Replansky, Oppen's anti-symbolist aesthetic is glossed more. To SS, [January 9, 1962]: "What life is, what things mean, it must be said in very small art. ... But surely small art: the ontogony, the onta, the things that exist[.]" And to NR [early 1962?]: "If we had the word *onta*, meaning the things that exist, I would use it. We seem to have only the word 'reality' which has been pretty badly messed up. Maybe 'the authentic' would be better." The latter word is an allusion to Denise Levertov's poem "Matins," which opens with the exclamation "The authentic!" *The Jacob's Ladder* (New Directions, 1961), 57.

4   A letter to Naomi Replansky (prov. N. Replansky) from [late 1961–early 1962] stated, with regard to *Ring Song*, and to Oppen's preparations of a manuscript: "Copiousness --. Would be nice. I envy it too. On the other hand there's no junk in your book, which is also a nice thing. I had a book out when I was twenty-two or so. Sort of rushed into it. A very small book, but not more than three or four of the poems should have been printed. I'll try not to do that again. If only out of a sense of wasted paper." In a letter of [December 20, 1962] to his niece Panthea Perry (prov. Panthea Perry), Oppen wrote about the reception of *Discrete Series*: "[. . .] I always tell the story that way, making myself a sort of hero of modernism. The fact is, that that little book was amazingly well treated: of course such verse was not reviewable at the time in the NY Times and such, but I remember quite a sheaf of reviews from the little magazines. [. . .] So it was really success, or 'success,' and even in that very small world, which I was unable to face. Interesting to realize. And scarcely heroic."

5   Apparently Oppen also sent a copy to Charles Reznikoff. In a letter of February 7,

1962 (UCSD 9, 4, 4), Reznikoff responded: "Dear George: [¶] I can't tell you what is good or bad in this book of verse. The only one who can decide that is you yourself in answer to the question what do you really want to say, what do you feel you must say. I can only tell you what I like and why I like it. But you must not let yourself be misled by that--and you won't be. [¶] As for the technique of saying what you want to say, you know as much about it as I do. You have sufficient interest in the meaning and sound of words and sentences and you know that the sound and rhythm is part of the meaning: that is why we write in verse-- [¶] C."

6   Ethel Schwabacher, *Arshile Gorky* (New York: Macmillan, 1957).

7   Ginsberg, *Kaddish and Other Poems* (San Francisco: City Lights), first published in 1961. From the "Hymmnn" section of *Kaddish*, the line Oppen cites is cited in the Ginsberg from the "last letter" of Naomi Ginsberg, whose death AG mourns: " 'The key is in the sunlight at the window in the bars   the key is in the sunlight'," *Collected Poems of Allen Ginsberg, 1947–1980* (New York: Harper & Row, 1984), 225. Correspondence with Henry Rago (Lilly Library, Indiana University), not published here, reveals that between January 25 and February 11, 1962, Oppen wrote "Three Poets" for *Poetry* (published August 1962), which reviews *Kaddish and Other Poems*, as well as work by Michael McClure and Charles Olson.

8   "The Mind's Own Place," originally published in *Kulchur* 10 (Summer 1963): 2–8; reprinted in *Montemora* 1 (Fall 1975): 132–37. Oppen wrote to Degnan [March–April 1962, UCSD 16, 1, 3] that the title comes from Milton: "Milton put it in the mouth of Beelzebub, so to the Puritan Milton it is the devil's doctrine[.]" *Paradise Lost* I, 254. In context: "Hail horrors, hail / Infernal world, and thou profoundest hell / Receive thy new possessor: One who brings / A mind not to be changed by place or time. / The mind is its own place, and in itself / Can make a heaven of hell, / a hell of heaven."

9   Dating and sequencing the materials dealing with "The Mind's Own Place" is a challenge; in this letter "a little discussion of the essay" might mean the discussions with Steven Schneider and Max and Anita Pepper alluded to in letters that are sent after the June 12, 1962, wedding of LOM and APDM. In that case, this letter also occurs after June 12; I have placed it here, with the Humboldt letter following, because the allusion to Levertov's poem "Song for Ishtar" suggests it came soon after the May 10 (postmarked) letter to Mary Ellen Solt.

10   In a letter of [May 10, 1962] to Mary Ellen Solt: "Disappointed by Denise's poem, tho it was well done. But it's impossible to decide what one feels about making love by considering in turn the word shining and the word grunt. Remains the same act. It isn't really words that think and feel and see -- Bill's [WCW] wrong about it." Levertov's poem, "Song for Ishtar" appeared in *The Massachusetts Review* 3, 2 (Winter 1962) and later in *O Taste and See* (New Directions, 1964), 3.

11   T. S. Eliot, "Morning at the Window," *Collected Poems, 1909–1962* (London: Faber and Faber, 1963), 29. "They are rattling breakfast plates in basement kitchens, / And along the trampled edges of the street / I am aware of the damp souls of housemaids / Sprouting despondently at area gates."

12   Much to Oppen's chagrin, the essay was rejected by *The Nation*, for which it had been written.

13   In a letter to Steven Schneider (mid-1962) (UCSD 16, 10, 8), another parallel state-

ment. "The article was written for the Nation on their request, and refused. I was thinking that the bad old times of the hole and corner poet were over, etc. etc. I cannot set myself to write 'printably' I must get a mimeograph or something of the sort, preferably something less inky, and use it as a means of communication. Absurd to undertake to speak for the editors rather than for myself. A bad profession, an absurd vocation. Fortunately, not mine."

14 The echo of a famous statement by Hillel: "If I am not for myself, who is for me? And if I am only for myself, what am I?" from the *Mishna*.

15 Humboldt, "A Film about Nazis—for Americans [review of Stanley Kramer's *Judgment at Nuremberg*]," *National Guardian: The Progressive Newsweekly* 14, 10 (December 18, 1961): 7.

16 Williams, *Pictures from Brueghel and Other Poems* (New York: New Directions, 1962), containing "Asphodel, That Greeny Flower."

17 In the poem "An die Nachgeborenen" [To Posterity], *Selected Poems*, trans. H. R. Hays (New York: Grove Press, 1947), 172.

18 From "The Mind's Own Place," *Montemora*, 136.

19 The film by Truffaut (1961), playing in New York in 1962.

20 The official publication date of *The Materials* was September 28, 1962.

21 Under the general title "Five Statements for Poetry," *Kulchur* 7 (Autumn 1962): 63–84 reprinted Zukofsky's "Program: 'Objectivists' 1931," "Sincerity and Objectification, with special reference to the work of Charles Reznikoff," and " 'Recencies' in Poetry." *Kulchur* 8 (Winter 1962): 75–86 reprinted "Poetry For My Son When He Can Read (1946)"; *Kulchur* 10 (Summer 1963): 49–53, which reprinted "A Statement for Poetry" (1950), was also the issue in which Oppen's "A Mind's Own Place" appeared.

22 A letter of Oppen to Cid Corman, from the Middlebury College Library Special Collections (and unfortunately not datable except inferentially to 1962), includes this paragraph. "What did you have in mind in the matter of printing Louis? A Collected poems, a Selected poems? Seems no chance at the moment of a Collected, of which of course I have spoken. If a Selected, what would you have in mind? I mean to ask only your own opinion, tho obviously no one can speak for Louis. But I don't think he should be bothered with this at the moment since I have no way of predicting SFR-ND's decision. But if you present a proposal that might be more appealing than anything I've outlined so far, I'll discuss it with them."

23 George and Mary Oppen, along with Linda and Alex Mourelatos, and Oppen's cousin Ethel Schwabacher, attended the film of Euripides' *Electra*, starring Irene Papas, opening in New York in December 1962. This play is, incidentally, the source of the phrase "Philai te kou philai" ("Here, one loved and not loved, we cover with these veils," ll. 1230–31) which GO used as the title of a poem written before March 1963 (CP 75). Translation from a January 1963 PC from APDM to GO (UCSD 16, 1, 21).

24 Oppen first wrote to Bronk on June 24, 1962, praising Bronk's poems in *Origin* V (April 1962); on [December 14, 1962], GO wrote to Bronk that he had sent June Oppen Degnan a group of his poems with the comment: "I can't tell you how much I think of these poems. They are absolutely coherent in thought and in form, they are staggeringly profound, and they are at moments overwhelmingly beautiful. I

know of no other writer who could put down with quiet, classic confidence the title 'Virgin and Child, with Music and Numbers.' Indeed it is set to music, music which appears in the quietest voice in which it is possible to read. And I know of nothing like the description of love inherent in the flesh and clumsy in Skunk Cabbage. And the first thing to say about such poems as The Feeling and Not My Loneliness but Ours ('The human loneliness / is the endless oneness of man') is that once it's been said, you know forever that it's true. That is to say, poetry is a test of truth, not of someone's rhetorical equipment. And these poems are perfect, they are really perfect, without, as you say, silly-seasoning" (UCSD 16, 3, 9).

1963

1 There is a considerable correspondence about details and particulars of Bronk's manuscript, which is not proportionately reflected here.

2 RBD has put the four pages of this letter in this order; however, it is possible that the order is incorrect. Hence, I have noted page numbers in square brackets, so readers can also assess the sequence. There is also a strong question of the sequence relationship between this letter and the letter to Bronk of [January 29, 1963].

3 Levertov, "Poetry: Pure and Complex [review of The Materials and Reznikoff's By the Waters of Manhattan]," The New Leader 46, 4 (February 18, 1963): 25–27.

4 A number of phrases in this letter ("test of truth," "test of sincerity," "test of conviction," "rare poetic quality of truthfulness") also occur in "The Mind's Own Place."

5 Sorrentino, "Poetry Chronicle" (an omnibus review of Oppenheimer, Hollo, Oppen, Reznikoff, Williams, Eshleman, Meltzer, Rothenberg, Spicer, and a mini-anthology called Four Young Lady Poets, including Bergé, Moroff, Owens, and Wakoski), Kulchur 9 (Spring 1963): 69–82. Sorrentino's dislike of "a kind of flirting with the 'surreal'" (71) would have appealed to Oppen, as well as these remarks: "What Deep Image seems to be is a contempt for that thing which is given, a contempt for things as they are as merely crust, or surface, or shell. This must inevitably lead the poet away from his task of interpreting the world qua world, into a position from which he imposes his will upon the things of the world.... [Deep Image] is the creation of seemingly intelligible forms, but the avoidance of extracting intelligible forms from seemingly unintelligible things (which I see as the artist's main function). It is Plato vs. Aristotle, Aquinas vs. Kant: it is the Romantic ego under a new name," 80.

6 The last sentence is a simple exhortation to read Spicer. The last two pages of the review concern Jack Spicer, about whom Sorrentino says, "It is Williams' 'no ideas but in things' extended, further, into: things are ideas, and ideas must be, ultimately, things—for the poet." The other candidate for a "last sentence," also 82, might be "... the poet must make reality useful through the employment of the imagination, and conversely, imagination, to be legitimate, must be inseparably linked to reality." It is also possible that Oppen meant the Aquinas vs. Kant material, on the bottom of 80.

7 Oppen translated the Latin in a letter of [December? 1962] to June Oppen Degnan: "Truth follows the existence of things."

8 "O Taste and See," title poem from *O Taste and See* (New York: New Directions, 1964), 53.

9 Levertov, "One of the Lucky" (Review of Paul Goodman, *The Lordly Hudson: Collected Poems*), *The Nation* 196, 15 (April 13, 1963): 310–11.

10 Oppen's first letter to Tomlinson [April 29, 1963] contained a statement, which Tomlinson retranscribed, with line breaks, and sent back to Oppen. The original statement: "One imagines himself addressing his peers, I suppose -- surely that might be the definition of 'seriousness'? I would like, as you see, to convince myself that my pleasure in your response is not plain vanity but the pleasure of being heard, the pleasure of companionship, which seems more honorable." This became the poem "To C. T" (CP 142) which Tomlinson sent Oppen before [May 31, 1963] (UCSD 16, 11, 12).

11 With the first letter to Tomlinson [April 29, 1963], a response to his praise of *The Materials*, Oppen had sent one of his three copies of *Discrete Series* and the remark that there were "three or four [poems] I would preserve."

12 *The Autobiography of William Carlos Williams* (New York: New Directions, 1951), 264.

13 This ambiguously worded sentence could be a unique instance of Oppen's stating that he did write during the "silence." However, it is far more likely that it should be interpreted as LOM did: that Oppen kept none of *Discrete Series*, or early writing, and no magazines from the early poetic career in his house during the twenty-five years of silence. And therefore he had not seen the essays of LZ's for "some twenty years."

14 In fact, their plans changed, and the Oppens and Tomlinsons met in New York City during the first half of August 1963.

15 This is an early version of "Guest Room" (CP 87–90). Published in *Sulfur 25*.

16 Allusions, respectively, to one of the more notorious of Williams's short lyrics, originally from *Spring and All* (1923), and to Oliver Wendell Holmes, "The Chambered Nautilus."

17 "Rape..." was eventually in *Poetry* in May 1964; "Bahamas" in *The New Yorker* in November 1963; "Narrative" in *The Paris Review*, Winter/Spring 1965.

18 The poem 'To --" was eventually called "A Narrative" (CP 132–40); this section of GO's letter is a gloss on an early version of "A Narrative." It is quite likely that Denise Levertov is the name Oppen effaced in his title.

19 Another letter to JOD from [summer 1963, UCSD 16, 1, 4]: "So here we are, rocking about in small boats, visiting people in their kitchens, getting a grip on something? or losing our grip on everything? I don't know. We'll know a year from now. But a strange experience. Rather dazing."

20 Mourelatos had written a doctoral dissertation on Parmenides, which Oppen had read.

21 An earlier letter to Tomlinson [July 27, 1963] (prov. CT) alluded to the possibility that Zukofsky might appear with ND-SFR: "The first years' poetry schedule [of ND-SFR] consists of Oppen, Reznikoff, and William Bronk, in which my advice is obvious enough. My recommendation of course included Zuk, but the suggestion -- as you see -- has not been acted on. It is by now too awkward for me to discuss the matter with Zuk at all, but it is my impression that they would be more likely

to do a Selected than a Collected poems, if only for budgetary reasons. I can't really urge Louis to submit a ms. since I have no assurance at all that they would accept it. But you might urge him to try it if you think it worth the risk -- to him -- of a rejection. If they had a ms. under consideration I could re-open the discussion.''

22 The work may be Carl Jung, *Memories, Dreams, Reflections* (New York: Pantheon Books, 1963). It also could be *Psychological Reflections: An Anthology of the Writings of C. G. Jung*, selected and edited by Jolanda Jacobi (New York: Harper & Brothers, 1961). Oppen owned the latter book; his slightly annotated copy is in the UCSD Archive. This letter is representative of a three-letter "Jung series" clustering in September 1963. Others are published in *Ironwood* 26.

23 A letter of September 3, 1963, sent by fifteen-year-old William Kaplan to his friend GO, rather critical of *The Materials* for being a "sombre" or even "fatalistic" work. Both the original letter and Oppen's reply, which among other statements is rather pleased with the youth for his challenge, are at UCSD 16, 6, 3.

24 Niedecker attended Beloit College for two years beginning in 1922; she returned home to Black Hawk Island, Wisconsin, in part to care for her deaf mother. In 1930, her brief first marriage had ended. See Lisa Pater Faranda's essay in *Dictionary of Literary Biography: Vol. 48: Modern American Poets*, ed. Peter Quartermain (Detroit: Gale Research, 1986): 304–19.

25 Niedecker died in 1970; her work history, as Faranda's biographical essay tells, is more complicated. She was a proofreader until her eyesight became severely impaired (1950); she was quite reclusive and did not have a paying job after the deaths of her parents in 1951 and 1954; she began working in maintenance in the hospital in 1957. Also, her small house was not a farm.

26 The book was *My Friend Tree* (Edinburgh: Wild Hawthorn Press, 1961). Oppen's citations from Niedecker are virtually accurate with the possible exception of certain line breaks; Oppen cites from *New Goose* for the punctuation of "Remember..." cf. *From This Condensery: The Complete Writing of Lorine Niedecker*, ed. Robert J. Bertholf (Highlands, N.C.: Jargon Society, 1985), 22, N 313 and also 130, N 329 which says "In one year..." was originally enclosed in a letter of June 5, 1962, to Zukofsky and does not give subsequent publishing history.

27 Reznikoff, *Inscriptions* #38: "Of course, we must die. / How else will the world be rid of / the old telephone numbers / we cannot forget? // The numbers / it would be foolish-- / utterly useless-- / to call." *By the Waters of Manhattan*, 107.

28 Although Oppen, in a 1964 letter, talks of events in 1924, the allusion to leaving the family values might have been strengthened by memories of 1946 or 1947, when Oppen, Mary, and Linda, in the postwar period, returned for a family visit, only, according to a striking undated one-and-a-half page memoir by GO, to be disgusted by the manifestations of wealth, privilege, and corruption he saw in his San Francisco family and their friends. The memoir ends: "As for us: we were on our own. There was no danger ahead of us anywhere equal to the danger behind us" (UCSD 33, 1, 21).

29 President John F. Kennedy was assassinated in Dallas, Texas, on November 22, 1963. His alleged assassin, Lee Harvey Oswald, was thereupon killed by Jack Ruby while in police custody.

30 Oppen wrote a two-page meditation on the Kennedy assassination (dated November

Notes: 1963–64 **385**

24, 1963) based on this and the preceding paragraphs of the letter of JOD; it was
sent to Ethel Schwabacher as well as to JOD. The rest of the statement reads: "If
Oswald was not the assassin, he must have been elaborately framed. And by the
Dallas police. Since the Dallas police permitted a 'friend' of theirs, a man known
to carry a gun, to approach Oswald in the police station, it is possible to believe
that they deliberately connived at his murder. If indeed they did, what is to be made
of the District Attorney's statement that the case of Oswald was closed by his murder, and would not be further investigated, nor further evidence given to the public.
Birmingham is not necessarily the only city in the south whose police chief is
involved with racist groups. Those groups have not made a secret of their fury
against Kennedy. This would be a picture of crisis, of violence which has got out
of hand. It may well be an accurate picture of the state of affairs."

1964

1 This was a major family gathering, including JOD's daughter Aubrey, Rich Beauvais,
Andy Meyer, and her children, Linda and Alex.

2 In November 1964 a report passed from the New York City Subversive Activities
Control to the FBI recommending that Oppen be included on "Section A of the
Reserve Index in view of the following subversive activity [blanked out] coupled
with his employment as a writer."

3 DM has discussed with GO the dance/performance work of Renée Shedroff.

4 "Memory at 'The Modern'" was published in *Elizabeth VI* (October 1963): 1 and
Sulfur 25 (1989). "We had seen bare land / And the people bare on it / And men
camp / In the city. The lights, / The pavement, this important device / Of a race, I
wrote then, / Twenty three years old, / Remains till morning. Nobody knows who
died / On the roads of that time, of the fact of roads. / I am a man of the Thirties /
/ 'No other taste shall change this' [.]" The final line alludes to Pound's Canto IV.

5 The poem also involved Schneider's family. Oppen had written to SS in March 1964
that "The poem 'To—' opens with a plagiarism from a letter of mine to you. And
includes a quote from Toby [Armour]." The quotation was "They're just BOY'S
rooms!" about seeing Keats's room. Oppen commented, in a letter to SS (prov. SS)
of [June? 1964] "I'm sure they were; a poet's room is a boy's room.... This in
which I live is a boy's world, and I don't in the least mean that I particularly urge
it on anyone, or recommend it. I just say that I know, like any grubby small boy,
how to fail. A miserable talent. Except that nobody knows how to succeed. Leaving
me with a talent so small as to be almost useful."

6 This letter followed a July 4, 1964, letter praising *The Lightfall* (New York: Hawk's
Well Press, 1963), and responded, for the second time, to Schwerner's long poem
about Akiba called "Prologue in Six Parts," *Seaweed* (Los Angeles: Black Sparrow,
1969). Oppen later reviewed *Seaweed* for *Stony Brook* 3–4 (1969): 72.

7 A similar kind of sentiment in an [August 8, 1964] letter to LOM (UCSD 33, 1, 16);
when appealed to about civil rights, Oppen essentially responded how long a task
to bring blacks and the poor into the mainstream of American society, and said, "I
just try to hang on to the principle that I have only one life and I've done a number

of things and right now I want very much to do this, to write poetry. God knows if one has a 'right,' but I think it is what I'm going to do. I really will not be able to face the idea of not having done it."

8   Some time before [August 31, 1964], Oppen had sent Tomlinson a copy of a book by Heidegger (unspecified) and the Hawk's Well books by Wakoski and Schwerner. In that letter too, this paragraph: "I don't suppose I really think of the 'state of poetry' in terms approaching the statistical. It's a matter of one or two poets in any country, and England has C T and the peopled landscape. A difficult thing for an American poet to feel that of his own country.   I think of the people -- I think there is such a thing as humanity, and moreover that no one could exist without it. And I think also of the land, Of the people and the land. And they seem to be standing on a pane of glass. And I would so very much rather say otherwise. I keep dreaming of a poem of final affirmation. Can't, probably, be done. The ear itself knows better, and rebels. We can say something of -- well, what I think I've got hold of a little at the end of the Narrative [CP 132–40], and we can speak of a peopled landscape -- even the Americans in their own way -- and I think that's all we will have. We will live by that if by anything."

9   Oppen had written to Diane Wakoski, July 4, 1964 (dated) (prov. University of Arizona) in praise of *Coins and Coffins* (New York: Hawk's Well Press [1962]): "The 'arrows do not always reach / their targets' and the following lines -- and in fact that whole series is most in my mind at this moment -- on first reading. 'Innocent' lines, but a fathomless expression of the feminine, of feminine tragedy --." A letter to Wakoski of [June 1965] (prov. University of Arizona) again expressed his appreciation of her work; of *The George Washington Poems*, seen in manuscript, he said, "The terror of the human consciousness packed somehow into a material body has never before been expressed in specifically feminine terms. Your whole self, whole weight, is flung at the reader, absolutely without sentimentality, in a voice which will not be forgotten--[.]"

10 Bronk, "Displacement: The Locks on the Feeder Called *The Five Combines*," in *Life Supports: New and Collected Poems* (San Francisco: North Point Press, 1982): 98–99.

11 Bronk, "Virgin and Child with Music and Numbers," *The World, The Worldless* (New Directions–San Francisco Review, 1964), 19.

12 Oppen wrote both to Leonard Wolf, the teacher of the class at Columbia University, and to Bronk after the class, telling which poems he read, and some of his interpretations. To Wolf (UCSD 16, 12, 4): "If, I said, one may think of one current of American poetry as deriving primarily from Williams and Pound, and a second stream as deriving from Eliot thru Auden and including -- a bit remotely -- Stevens, then Bronk is in the current of Eliot and Stevens."

13 On the letter, "Not sent" is written by GO.

14 The response is, apparently, to an invitation to try marijuana; a letter to LOM (UCSD 33, 1, 16 and 16, 12, 7) contains a one paragraph "report on the commerce between me and marijuana" which noted "I do not in the least like it; I continue to believe that I know my actual size, and my actual size seems to me to be an essential part of the matter, as it seems to me that the whole point of anything is that it is as it is. We fall again and again into the idea of higher realms, other spheres, higher and

dimmer heavens in which wonderful things will happen and all doubts be answered. But I think in this way we answer the doubt before it is felt, and solve the mystery before we have encountered it. The mystery is that there is something for us to stand on" [cf. CP 143].

15 A copy of this letter was also sent to JOD.

16 In an unusual move, as he rarely repeated letters to different correspondents, Oppen sent a verbatim copy of this letter to Steven Schneider, who was critical of the longer version of "Armies of the Plain."

17 The two poems are "Technologies" (then called "Wisdom, a Technology") and a longer version of "Armies of the Plain," more clearly based on Oppen's response to the Warren Report. In a letter to Charles Tomlinson [October 9, 1964], Oppen noted "Armies of the Plain -- To make a clean breast of this matter, one means to refer to Arnold - - - 'Where ignorant armies clash by night.'"

1965

1 An inference: this letter occurs before fall 1965, because the prose statement foreshadowing a section of "Another Language of New York" ["Of Being Numerous"] that emerges in this letter circulated in the copy of the poem sent to John Crawford, answered by him in [September 1965].

2 *Hardware Poets Occasional Software* was a newsletter of poetry and other writing edited by Diane Wakoski; the first issue appeared in February 1964. The fifth issue, appearing in late 1964 or early 1965, was a "Dream Sheet," with a strongly worded poem by Carol Bergé which began "i piss on you / in your bed / in your navel / where you lie / not dreaming / because I say / you must not dream. . . ." Special thanks to The Department of Rare Books and Special Collections, Memorial Library, University of Wisconsin-Madison for access to this rare periodical.

3 At the end of this letter comes a poem, numbered 4, which eventually splits and becomes the whole of 6 and part of 8 of the long poem "Of Being Numerous" (CP 150–51). "We are pressed, pressed on each other, / We will be told at once / Of anything that happens // And the discovery of fact bursts / In a paroxysm of emotion / Now as always. Crusoe // We say was / 'Rescued' / So we have chosen // *Amor fati* / As the dead tongues said, / The love of fate."

4 Although the war was undeclared, the early part of 1965 saw a marked escalation of the war in Vietnam, including a secret air war in Laos and air strikes over North Vietnam. Sustained bombing of North Vietnam—Operation Rolling Thunder—continued from February 13, 1965, to October 31, 1968. In this context came the April 19–20, 1965, meeting in Honolulu in which notable military and civilian leaders agreed to double U.S. Military Forces from 40,200 to 82,000. A letter of GO to Steven Schneider of [April? 1965] (UCSD 16, 10, 15) repeated and elaborated: "I remember now why we once believed in revolutionary action at any cost. Nothing less than an immediate march on Washington and the arrest of the president could restore the possibility of talking of ethics, morality --. Such words become nonsense, and we must find some other basis on which to define ourselves. I am not in favor of revolution -- therefore I am going to try not to talk of ethics again."

5   In late March 1965, Schneider had lent Oppen Yves Bonnefoy, *Du mouvement et de l'immobilité de Douve* (Paris: Mercure de France, 1959), in a version translated by Schneider.

6   In a letter of [April? 1965] to Schneider, Oppen had stated: "Unless to say this minimum: that a morality is possible within a family. It is, as you say, 'in the chromosomes.' It can make an area of human life possible. If it disappears, we will produce no sane people again" (cf. CP 184) (UCSD 16, 10, 15).

7   Andy's daughter Eve Haight was at that time between eleven and twelve.

8   John Crawford had made notes to and comments about the Berkeley Poetry Conference (1965) which he had sent to Oppen; these included a one-page description of the "Personal Predispositions of Creeley and Olson," four pages of notes on lectures by Robert Creeley, three pages of notes on lectures by Charles Olson, and a paragraph on Gary Snyder. Oppen had responded to these notes in a [June 1965] letter just preceding this: "Too much, too much noise, too big a show, too close to the proposition that a poet need neither mean nor write, but *be* --- a proposition at the roots of most bad poetry. Inflation, a tremendous straining. Most certainly an excess of 'message,' a wilderness of message, almost a morass" (photocopy UCSD 16, 3, 46).

9   Crawford reported, paraphrasing a Creeley lecture at the Berkeley Poetry event, that to exemplify the poet's creation of an activity in the poem, Creeley "wrote, spaced, on the board 'There is going to be [a war]' Erase the words one by one from the end and you will see the internal possibilities of the poem as object making itself. There are crucial areas in the writing of a line where the poem must make choices or confront difficult junctures of the language. e.g. between 'going' and 'to be.'"

10 The occasion of this letter was Oppen's response to Felix Pollack's "Soirées," a snide and scurrilous parody of Levertov's "Matins," a poem Oppen much respected. Pollack's text was published in *Kulchur* vol. 5, #18 (Summer 1965): 52–55. Pollack closed the parody with a long note, itself ending, "A breathlessly waiting world will be able to judge by whether a poem of mine will ever appear in THE NATION, if Miss Levertov could take the above in the spirit in which it was dished out: the spirit of good dirty fun." Levertov was then poetry editor of *The Nation*, Hornick, the managing editor of *Kulchur.* In May 1982, during a discussion of his letters with MO, GO, and RBD, this letter to Hornick was read to Oppen, who quipped: "Let's send it again."

11 Oppen had written to Schneider that he had completed the "other Language of New York during the summer. 31 sections." When the poem was totally finished, as "Of Being Numerous" it was 40 sections long. Antin read an interim "final" version, as did Crawford and DuPlessis, cf. subsequent letters.

12 The occasion of this letter was GO's reading of a RBD graduate school paper on William Carlos Williams's *Paterson;* the second part of the letter, cut here, concerns her poem "Parading." Oppen said there, "I've said too often by now that I think a poem is itself a process of thought, a means of thought -- but it is what I think. A poem which begins with an idea -- a 'conceit' in the old use of the term -- doesn't learn from its own vividness and go on from there unless both terms of the conceit or one at least is actually *there*." Some of these letters to RBD were published in *Ironwood* 24 (Fall 1984): 121–38.

13   Randall Jarrell's essay offers a brief discussion of the imbedding of letters from 'Cress' [Marcia Nardi] in the text of *Paterson*.

14   The issues of "what happens" and "accident" continued in a letter of [September 11, 1965] to DuPlessis, in which Oppen remarked: " 'Accident' is easily as mysterious a word as any; it means anything can happen! [¶] Poetry seems to me a thing to do when it is absolutely beyond, out of sight beyond the me-too of art. And whether the poems are perfect or imperfect, the leap is made at the first sight of 'the girder, still itself among the rubble'   (which is quoted from Charles Reznikoff)[.]"

15   Crawford's almost five-page letter discussed "Another Language of New York." This letter by Oppen in response includes several pages of comment on Crawford's poems, which have been cut here.

16   Crawford had said: "I boggle almost uniquely at 'Tho they said God once and behaved worse than we' [a line among three later cut from section 17] -- referent? The Church that Dante speaks of? But they hardly said 'God' at all, in any viable way. The Inquisition? the Calvinists? Perhaps you mean an age, when men were generally ruthless in the prosecution of the claims of their Ideal. The context around the line disturbs me *about* the line: 'One will finally say god / Or one will be unable to say anything.' The logic is Anselm's; the vision is either (1) despair or (2) mysticism. That is, if you put the weight on the *first* line you have (as I think you mean) ontology; on the *second*, you have the despair of the rationalist and the vision of the mystic. One can imagine Voltaire and Blake sitting in the audience; apart. I ramble. I mean to say, that coming after 'nobody here but us chickens' the next two lines cover a great deal of 'Folly'--of the history of a sentient being before what is incomprehensible to him and trying yet to retain sense, form *and* vision--these are very important lines. History is exhausted in them, they are larger than it. Then-- 'Tho they said God once. . .' a specific reference (though I don't see from context *when*)--a weakening particularity."

17   Crawford had said, "I'm moved by the difference, an honest difference, of your voice, which seems to come here [in the lines "And one may honorably keep // His distance / If he can"] as in other places in the poem. It is the distance of a 'one'-- of one--distanced in form, in the short stanzas and discrete lines--I have the feeling you *measure* your lines, not with a ruler but you know what I'm trying, badly, to say: to scale."

18   These lines, modified with pungent silliness, originate in T. S. Eliot's "The Love Song of J. Alfred Prufrock"; they are a motif for Oppen. In a letter of [July–August 1965] also to John Crawford, he had done it as: "Shall I wear my trousers? Shall my trousers wear me rolled? Has a peach eaten me? Did someone think to sing to me?" (UCSD 16, 3, 42).

19   Robert Louis Stevenson, "Rain," *A Child's Garden of Verses* (New York: Charles Scribner's Sons, 1905), 7. Oppen has altered Stevenson's second line, which actually reads, "It falls on field and tree."

20   David Antin, "Who are my friends," *Code of Flag Behavior* (Los Angeles: Black Sparrow Press, 1968).

21   In a letter of [October 20, 1965], to Rachel Blau DuPlessis, Oppen talked disapprovingly of the work of Frank Kuenstler, remarking, "And I once noticed that

Phyllis Wheatley wrote 'th' optic orb' for 'eye.' Time can be exceedingly cruel." That letter also elaborated a Poundean precept, stating "But poetry must be at least as well written as prose, etc. It must also be at least as good as dead silence. The caterpillar *said*: Begin at the beginning."

22 In a letter of [April 16, 1965] to LOM (UCSD 33, 1, 16), Oppen had said "What could be stranger than to insist IN the name of originality, on writing as everyone else is writing? . . . A less domestic test of originality would demand not so much that one write differently from his grandfather as that he should be distinguishable from his contemporaries."

23 The occasion of this letter was RBD's response of October 1, 1965, to "Another Language of New York," in which she posed the query that now stands at the head of section 9 [CP 152]: "Whether, as the intensity of seeing increases, one's distance from Them, the people, does not also increase."

24 Slightly misquoted from Lewis Carroll, *Alice in Wonderland*.

25 This letter is dated by a cross-reference in a letter to JOD of [November 11, 1965]: Laughlin "sent me a ms of Rakosi's (returned from the dead) asking me for my report on it -- return postage and all. I liked it very much, as he probably knew I would." Rakosi's note in *Amulet* says, "I did not write again until April 1965." This is a twenty-four-year silence (V. UCSD 17, 5, 10; Rakosi to Laughlin).

26 Carl Rakosi's *Amulet* was published by New Directions in 1967. The page numbers Oppen cites in parentheses are manuscript pages; I shall give the book pages for the poems in square brackets.

27 The final lines from Rakosi's "Time to Kill" read, "The poor small / wood louse / crawls along / the bark ridge / for his life" (*Amulet* 11).

28 June Oppen Degnan of *The San Francisco Review* had copublished, with New Directions, Oppen's *The Materials* and Reznikoff's *By the Waters of Manhattan* in 1962.

1966

1 This is Oppen's "rust in copper" dream; see Mary Oppen, *Meaning a Life*, 201–2: Oppen dreamed he had found, in the papers of his recently dead father, a note titled "How to Prevent Rust in Copper." He was puzzled and amused, because copper does not rust. The psychiatrist whom he was seeing said, " 'You were dreaming that you don't want to rust.' " He took this as a charge to begin writing poetry again after twenty-five years. The version of this generative event in the Crawford letter is significant because, unlike the account by Mary Oppen and by George in an interview with Hatlen-Mandel (*GOM&P* 27–28), Oppen here stated that two years went by before he began again to write. This would date the dream to 1956, two years after his father died. He began writing again in 1958, when his daughter was accepted at Sarah Lawrence College.

2 It is probably appropriate not to be able to know if "word" is, as I suspect, a typographical error for "world." This paragraph alludes to "Psalm" (CP 78), as well as to Wordsworth.

3 Enclosed with this letter was the long poem "Another Language of New York" in thirty-three sections. Seven sections were eventually added, and the title changed

to "Of Being Numerous" by mid-1966, probably June. The circulation of the poem to various friends and some of the provocative comments that resulted, created some of the conditions which allowed Oppen to complete the poem, in part by incorporating "phrases, comments, cadences of speech . . . which are derived from friends" (copyright page, CP), among whom was Steven Schneider.

4 In 1965, Schneider had sent the Oppens his translation of Yves Bonnefoy, *Du mouvement et de l'immobilité de Douve.*

5 Bunting, "Briggflats," *Poetry* 107, no. 4 (January 1966): 213–37.

6 Around the time of a thirty-seven-day pause in the bombing of North Vietnam; on January 31 the bombing resumed. Twenty-five of one hundred senators were opposed to the resumption of bombing.

7 In a letter of [February 1966] to John Crawford, not included here (UCSD 16, 3, 47), Oppen said: "See, in this regard, Basil Bunting's long poem in Poetry - - - and the line 'Shining slowworm part of the marvel' - - - - slowworm is the poet   in any case and by all means see Bunting's poem. Rather the completion of something than the beginning, but magnificent - - (I met Bunting in 1930 - - He is in the Objectivist Anthology;   returned like me to *Poetry* as from the dead, apparently but do read the poem. A completion no doubt; but bed rock, magnificent."

8 Bombing was resumed with statements that the U.S. government had shown sincerity in peace overtures.

9 To date, this allusion is untraceable, but it may be Brecht's "To Posterity."

10 Merton, *Conjectures of a Guilty Bystander* (New York: Doubleday, 1966), pp. 318–20.

11 A copy of the following statement is also included in a letter [late spring 1966] to John Crawford. A very slightly different version, perhaps a draft for the letter, is published as an autonomous daybook document in Michael Davidson's selection in *Ironwood* 26 (Fall 1985), 14–15.

12 Parmenides of Elea, Fragment #3 (Diels-Kranz). There are a number of alternate translations, due to the intense syntactic ambiguity of the line; for some, see *Fragments, A Text and Translation*, with an introduction by David Gallop (Toronto: University of Toronto Press, 1984), 57. "The same is to think and to be," Freeman's rendering, used by Oppen, deliberately leaves the syntactic ambiguity in place. Oppen may have known of Fragment #3 from as many as three sources: Alex Mourelatos's (his son-in-law's) doctoral dissertation in which there was a long discussion of the ambiguities of that fragment; Kathleen Freeman, *Ancilla to the Pre-Socratic Philosophers* (Oxford University Press and Basil Blackwell, 1956), which he owned in a copy given by APDM; Heidegger's *An Introduction to Metaphysics*, which devotes considerable energy to the discussion of Parmenides, translating the fragment, "The same is apprehension and that for the sake of which apprehension occurs," or, "There is a reciprocal bond between apprehension and being." Translated by Ralph Manheim (New Haven: Yale University Press, 1959), 139, 145. It is of some interest that Mourelatos's confrontation with this fragment was APDM's "conversion" to his interest in Parmenides and the pre-Socratics, while the Reznikoff fragment may be said to have served a similar function for Oppen and poetry. Mourelatos and Oppen had several discussions of the fragment, and Oppen knew about the ambiguity of the construction, which APDM summed up as depending on whether one takes "the same" as subject or as predicate. As subject—the same thing which is

there to be is the thing which is to think—there is no tension between the mind's conception of things and the way things are. This would be a realist position. Taking "the same" as predicate—the same is to think and to be—identifies thinking and being in an idealist fashion. Because in this letter Oppen capitalizes "the Same," Mourelatos suggested that it is used as a subject, and thus Oppen would interpret the line as a realist would. I am indebted to Alex Mourelatos for this information.

The Reznikoff is Oppen's oft-repeated modification of an epigram from *Jerusalem the Golden* (1934). "Among the heaps of brick and plaster lies / a girder, still itself among the rubbish," *By the Waters of Manhattan* (New York: New Directions and San Francisco Review, 1962), 30. Because Oppen modified this epigram into a fragment, I have argued (in *North Dakota Quarterly* 55, 4) that among its other functions for Oppen, the Reznikoff is a "place-holder" for his own work, and that his continual citation of this recasting is a deflected way of stating his own poetic ambitions.

13 Oppen often referred to the coincidence of his 1929 poem and Martin Heidegger's July 1929 Inaugural Lecture at Freiburg University, "What Is Metaphysics?" "Knowledge and rational opinions are certainly one kind of disclosure [states David Krell], but Heidegger located a more generalized and primary sort: Dasein [contextual, temporal human existence] is disclosed as such in the *moods* in which man finds himself, such as joy, boredom, excitement, or anxiety." "What Is Metaphysics?" concentrates especially on what can be learned about human existence—especially its necessary inflection with nothingness—from the mood of anxiety. Heidegger, *Basic Writings*, ed. David Farrell Krell (New York: Harper & Row, 1977), 92.

14 While technically this is not a letter, it seems appropriate to include this three-page note here. One minor but interesting point: the note is dated with extreme precision, in contrast to Oppen's usual practice in his working papers, and further, another departure, provides an exact bibliographic reference to a work important to him.

15 To date, no Fred Siegle can be identified; Barry Ahearn has suggested the Fred Siegel thanked by Hugh Kenner in the acknowledgments to *The Pound Era*. Oppen spoke of Heidegger and this incident to Frederick Will in a subsequent year.

16 Section 13 of the poem "Route" ends, "Substance itself which is the subject of all our planning' // And by this we are carried into the incalculable" (CP 195).

17 The six-paragraph units that come after the dividing line above were typed on this note, possibly at a later date; the note itself, in the text I am using, is a carbon copy.

18 This letter (with a half-page cut) and a subsequent letter (not published here) concern the work of Jo Pacheno, Crawford's friend, as a paradigmatic case of issues for women writing. Oppen opened section 34 of "Of Being Numerous" [CP 174] with two lines from a poem by Jo Pacheno.

19 The first citation is Sappho, J. M. Edmonds, trans. and ed., *Lyra Graeca*, 111; the second is Emily Dickinson, Thomas Johnson, ed., #465, "I heard a Fly buzz—when I died—."

20 Oppen was fascinated by "the feminine" in poetry, and by the task of women poets, about which he was both forthright and ambivalent. Some discussion of the "man-woman business" occurs in a letter to DuPlessis of [September 10, 1965], which instructed: "((read sometime Denise Levertov's *Matins*, in The Jacob's Ladder. The

speckled egg that we must break --- if we would be nourished. A most wonderful of speckled eggs that I stole from her -- with acknowledgement -- in Mayan Ground [CP 119]. Not that Denise, so far as I know, thought again about that egg. Poem after poem of technology, the technological prescriptions of wisdom literature, specifically How to be good. The trap which has engulfed most women poets -- if you can bear more of this man-woman business from me. Whereas you were saying that the fascination of the real involves -- now -- the question; what is chance? And indeed it does. The theory of games; 'What am I, What can I know, What must I do and --- What are my chances? But that for the sake of the joke. Actually, the question is What is chance? But it is a question about the nature of reality. . . .'"

21   This letter, along with the letters of [July 25, 1966] and [October 14, 1966], appeared in "Three Oppen Letters and a Note," *Ironwood* 5 (1975), 78–85.

22   In a letter to Fauchereau of [July 4, 1966], not published here, Oppen offered these suggestions for Fauchereau's reading: Bunting's *Loquitur*; Rakosi's *Amulet*; The "Objectivist" issue of *Poetry*; the five of Zukofsky's essays reprinted by *Kulchur*, "including the introduction of the Anthology and the introduction to the Objectivist Issue of Poetry"; Zukofsky's *A 1–13*; Oppen's *The Materials* and *This in Which*; Reznikoff's *By the Waters of Manhattan* and *Testimony: The United States (1885–1890)*.

23   In fact, Rexroth, Zukofsky, and Williams were the poets most extensively represented in that anthology.

24   A statement by Robert Creeley.

25   This sentence appears in "Route," section 4 (CP 186). From other citations of "Route" in an autumn 1966 letter to Michael O'Brien, it appears that Oppen is citing an already written poem; but it is also possible he was just finishing the poem.

26   The half page RBD has cut from this letter make an amalgam of lines from Crawford's long poem "Letters" with comments.

27   William Carlos Williams, "Introduction to *The Wedge*" (1944): "A poem is a small (or large) machine made of words." *Selected Essays of William Carlos Williams* (New York: Random House, 1954), 256.

28   Tomlinson had asked for biographical information "re *Seven Significant Poets*, an anthology [edited by Tomlinson] never published because Zukofsky refused to appear with Oppen and Reznikoff." See Tomlinson, *Some Americans: A Personal Record* (Berkeley: University of California Press, 1981), 71. Later in the letter Oppen continued a motif he often assumed with Tomlinson—punning on "son."

29   The allusion to T. E. Hulme's "Autumn," cited, as are all other of Hulme's "poetical works," in Ezra Pound, *Personae* (New York: New Directions, 1949). The poem reads: "A touch of cold in the Autumn night— / I walked abroad, / And saw the ruddy moon lean over a hedge / Like a red-faced farmer. / I did not stop to speak, but nodded, / And round about were the wistful stars / With white faces like town children," 252. In a letter of Fall 1977 to Michael Heller, Oppen alludes to Heller's catching his miscitation: "I am a slightly red-faced farmer -- tho I don't feel myself bound to quote a foolish line correctly--"

30   Zukofsky, "An Objective," *Prepositions: The Collected Critical Essays of Louis Zukofsky*, expanded edition (Berkeley: University of California Press, 1981); the open-

ing paragraph, 12, had also appeared in *Poetry* (February 1931) *"An Objective: (Optics)—The lens bringing the rays from an object to a focus. That which is aimed at. (Use extended to poetry)—Desire for what is objectively perfect, inextricably the direction of historic and contemporary particulars."*

1967

1 This important letter is very difficult to date; unfortunately, Elizabeth Kray's illness and death in 1987 made any consultation impossible. I locate it in these years (and would venture between late fall 1966 and the summer of 1967) because during that time Zukofsky's *All: The Collected Short Poems 1923–58* appeared, and was reviewed twice by Robert Creeley, in an essay called "Paradise / Our / Speech" appearing in *Poetry,* October 1965, and in an essay called "Louis Zukofsky: All: The Collected Short Poems. . . ," *Agenda* 4 ([August] 1966), an issue in which Oppen also appeared, and thus would have been likely to have read thoroughly. Also Creeley wrote "A Note" about Zukofsky's *"A" 1–12* which served as the introduction to the edition published by Doubleday in 1967. In none of these comments does the word "juncture" appear (which Oppen uses in this letter as if cited from Creeley). The typewriter Oppen used is also not the sans serif Correspondence Gothic font of mid-1964 through Fall 1966. The Creeley essays in *A Quick Graph: Collected Notes & Essays,* ed. Donald Allen (San Francisco: Four Seasons Foundation, 1970).

2 *An "Objectivists" Anthology* (Paris: To Publishers, 1932) reissued by Folcroft Ltd. and Norwood Editions, 1977. Niedecker was in neither the *Anthology,* nor the "Objectivists" issue of *Poetry*; in fact, she had originally contacted Zukofsky in response to that February 1931 issue of *Poetry.* Her first important publication occurred in the first *New Directions* annual (1936).

3 Published in Ashland, Massachusetts, by Origin Press in 1961; published as the prefatory piece to *Ferdinand* in London, by Jonathan Cape in 1968.

4 The first pleasure of the San Francisco move is noted in a number of letters; to Harvey Shapiro [February–March 1967] (prov. HS), Oppen said: "San Francisco full of corners, little wooden-housed corners that we remember very vividly. A strangely blithe town." A letter of [March? 1967] to June Oppen Degnan [UCSD 16, 1, 6] talked, with excitement of the "feel of bareness, of the Northwest"; "And we still have the Alaskan feel, and the Robinson Jeffers, early Robinson Jeffers feel about this coast." A letter of [1967?] to Diane Wakoski stated: "We take bus trips to anywhere and just get off   somewhere. A beach twenty yards long and one headland occupy us all day. . . ." A letter of [December 24, 1968] to Charles Tomlinson (prov. CT) says: "I've thought always of the East as a home-coming. Maybe a delusory home coming wrapped in the myths of childhood, a homecoming to childhood. But S F is a homecoming to my adolescence. And, sure enough, it gets under my skin a little, my thin, unfamiliar, adolescent skin[.]"

5 This letter is sent from 2154 Mason Street, after the abrupt move at the end of February.

6 The motif of the north is important to Oppen. From a letter to Diane Wakoski of [June 1965] (University of Arizona), speaking of Maine: "That it [Maine] is north, the fact of northerness, and Eastern extension into the sea --- I cannot tell you what

it means to us. The other antiquity, the northern antiquity, the alternative to the classic -- [CP 105] [¶] I can't say why. Same thing that happened when I first encountered the Middle English."

7   Will had sent Oppen a copy of *Literature Inside Out: Ten Speculative Essays* (Cleveland: The Press of Western Reserve University, 1966); the essay called "Heidegger and the Gods of Poetry" was one that Oppen noted particularly.

8   In a draft of this letter, UCSD, Oppen continued, after the "massiveness" citation: "Some such word also in my mind. Heidegger I think does not assume the permanence of man, and indeed, how can we? This is the difficult thing to confront: we begin to confront it in that word." Oppen wrote of the Heidegger incident in a note to himself in 1966.

9   This letter's return address is 2154 Mason, San Francisco.

10   Stein's liberal arts math text, *Mathematics: The Man-Made Universe*, was first published in 1965; this letter is dated to 1967 by Stein's reply to Oppen's letter, August 4, 1967. Therein Stein says: "I will confess. I think that there is a universe out there (or in here) or ... on which we stub our toe. To assign it a place is as absurd as to assign it a color. BUT WE CAN BEHAVE AS IF IT DOES NOT EXIST. This is meant to cheer the reader of my book; he is not reading about Talleyrand or Julian the Apostate through the clouds of time or about riots instantly blurred by his own proximity. So your question-answer is being answered-questioned in the most avant-garde mathematical circles" (UCSD 16, 10, 46).

11   A letter from Spring 1967, to Frederic Will (UCSD 16, 11, 44): "I send the opening lines of a poem I am now working on (cf page 33 of the Speculative Essays [Will, *Literature Inside Out*, see note 7, above]. [The poem follows titled] A Morality Play:

> Preface
> The play begins with the world
>
> Piety
>
> We who once said
> Objectivist
>
> A play exposed and jagged
> On the San Francisco hills

12   This is a one-page note beginning "The Categorical Imperative" and it is printed here after this letter.

13   The Oppens used an inflatable rubber kayak to get ashore.

14   As should be clear, Oppen wrote Camden, then corrected himself; I have changed to the correct place throughout.

15   Philip Booth's memory offers some more drama in the entrance, including a line squall in Castine harbor, and a full narrative of the meeting; "Seascape: George and Mary in Maine," *Ironwood* 26 (1985): 32–37. Booth said of them: "Nobody sailed so often, or so far, in so small a boat."

16   In a letter to Philip Booth (prov. PB) of [August 1967], after this meeting, Oppen underlines the allegorical nature of the contrast: "to find ourselves so alien in Belfast and among friends in Castine is . . . I was going to end this sentence otherwise, but

is, probably, something we always knew and knew so well that we played dangerous games. Games? Well, whatever." Booth cites from a part of this short letter, *Ironwood* 26, 33.

17 The suggestive "goo" for "goût" is an intended judgmental pun repeated here and in other letters.

18 APDM had asked for GO's help in translating Parmenides fragment 14, "nyktiphaes peri gaian alômenon allotrion phôs." This line playfully appropriates a Homeric formula as an expressive vehicle for Parmenides' pioneering astronomical discovery that the moon's light comes from the sun. In a letter of August 9, 1967, APDM presented the Greek, transliterated into Roman alphabet, discussed the meter and pitch, offered a literal translation with syntactic comments, and discussed the subtler aspects of the citation, setting the terms in relation to aspects of Parmenides' thought. Oppen's translation of the line appeared in Mourelatos, *The Route of Parmenides: A Study of Word, Image, and Argument in the Fragments* (New Haven: Yale University Press, 1970): 225, n. 12. It reads: "Astray over earth / Bright in darkness / Its light also a wandering foreigner."

19 APDM had noted that the phrase *allotrion phôs, a foreign light* is a pun on two unrelated Greek words: the masculine noun *phôs* (with a circumflex), which means *chap* or *guy*, and the neuter homonym, which means *light*. Changing the Homeric formula *allotrios phôs*, "a foreign guy, a stranger," into the homonymous neuter, Parmenides is saying at once that "the light is not the moon's own" and that "the man in the moon is a stranger."

20 In "Neighbors," a poem in *Primitive*, Oppen recasts the Parmenides fragment: "...and the voice of the poem a wandering / foreigner more strange / and brilliant / than the moon's   light the true / native opening / the nooks and the corners and the great / spaces clear. . . ." *Primitive* (Santa Barbara: Black Sparrow Press, 1978), 28.

21 Bronk, "Copan: Historicity Gone," *Vectors and Smoothable Curves: Collected Essays* (San Francisco: North Point Press, 1983): 35; the citation comes from the final paragraph of the essay, which reads: "The world or what we term the world, that medium in which we find ourselves, and indeed whatever of it we set apart and term selves, is not related to what we make of it and not dependent on what we make of the world or make of ourselves. It is not in the least altered, nor is our basic nature altered, by any cosmology or culture or individual character we may devise, or by the failure or destruction of any of these, as all of them fail. If they seem for a time to succeed, they blind us as though they were real; and it is by our most drastic failures that we may perhaps catch glimpses of something real, of something which is. It merits our whole mind. The good society and the good life are more than we could imagine. To devise them or to assert and defend their devising is not the point."

22 "Displacement: The Locks on the Feeder called *The Five Combines*," *Life Supports: New and Collected Poems* (San Francisco: North Point Press, 1982), 98–99.

23 "A Message from Rabbi Nachman," later to be published in *This World* (Middletown, Conn.: Wesleyan University Press, 1971); the final stanza reads: "*There are stones— / How else will the house / Be built— / Like souls / That are flung down / In the streets.*" The "friend" alluded to in Shapiro's poem is, in fact, Oppen himself.

1968

1   There were also apparently readings which I have not been able to verify, at Long Island University (in May) and at Carleton University, Ottawa (before November 26).

2   In a letter to David Ignatow on the occasion of DI's review of Oppen, appearing in the *New Leader* (July 1968), 20–21. In a letter to Eliot Weinberger of [November 27, 1968], Oppen remarked, "Took me a long time to get clear of Numerous. I was, as a matter of fact, afraid. I seem to be alright."

3   A draft of this letter also exists at (UCSD 16, 7, 29); because it alludes to *Of Being Numerous* as a book, I have chosen 1968, perhaps arbitrarily, as the date for this letter.

4   The biography of George Eliot by Gordon Haight confirms that "Dickens was one of the few to discern a feminine hand in the author of *Scenes of Clerical Life*" (1858) (New York: Oxford University Press), 251.

5   Crawford has ascribed this letter "probably 1968."

6   Oppen later found he had a slipped disc.

7   Bronk, *Life Supports: New and Collected Poems* (San Francisco: North Point Press, 1982), 98.

8   Also to Bronk [May 25, 1968] (UCSD 16, 3, 11): "I too am elated by the rioting students, the rioting world. They perhaps carry the thing further, carry further the experiment of life or of consciousness. 'Further' meaning, as always, toward its end. Strangely, they are zealots of catastrophe   Resembling, in this way, the poets."

9   Rachel Blau DuPlessis. In a letter of [July 1968] to June Oppen Degnan (UCSD 16, 1, 6), GO cited the "Whether, as the intensity..." statement again, and noted: "occurs to me: Perhaps one's distance from any gang of people increases: perhaps one's distance from humanity does not[.]"

10   Oppen is responding to Mourelatos's comments about "Of Being Numerous."

11   An account of this meeting, quite similar, is preserved in a letter of [July 1968] to June Oppen Degnan; there GO notes the presence of Elizabeth Hardwick and that Lowell spoke of JOD.

12   It had been republished in 1966 by Ron Caplan of Mother/Asphodel Press in Cleveland.

13   In Rothenberg's anthology *Technicians of the Sacred: A Range of Poetries from Africa, America, Asia & Oceania* (Garden City, N.Y.: Doubleday, 1968). Gassire's Lute, 184.

14   This remark gains resonance with reference to CP 215, "Some San Francisco Poems," and the fact that the Adam and Eve material was more prominent in drafts and comments from 1967–68 than it may appear to be in the poem as finished.

1969

1   After Charles Amirkhanian and Carol Law married, in December 1968, they received some lines commemorating a hike they had taken with the Oppens to the top of Mt. Tamalpais. CA reports that "the perspective at that vantage point is skewed surrealistically" a gloss on Oppen's "bent ocean." In a letter to Amirkhanian of [January 1969] (prov. CA) Oppen said: "An abnormal Epithalamium, but here are the first lines of a poem I had written starting from that climb: [¶] The Impossible

Selected Letters of George Oppen

Poem // Climbing the peak of Tamalpais one looks to the front / Not down and sees the loose gravel // And outward streaks of fog in the sky / And the city shining with the tremendous wrinkles / In the hills and the winding of the bay / Behind it, it faces the bent ocean // Niwcomen man   the newcome man. . ." cf. CP 226.

2   The chapbook contains "Alpine," "But So As By Fire," "A Barbarity" (not in CP), and "The Song" (a shorter version of "Song, The Winds of Downhill").

3   Oppen's memoir of this meeting, "Pound in the U.S.A.," *Sagetrieb* I, 1 (Spring 1982): 119.

4   At least one was, and perhaps the other two of the first three readings (those in San Francisco) may have been given; an audiotape of the October 29 event at San Francisco State University exists in the American Poetry Archive. Other readings may have been scheduled.

5   The Heidegger books in Oppen's personal library (UCSD) were *Being and Time* and *Existence and Being*; the latter is a selection of a number of works including "An Account of 'Being and Time' "; "An Account of 'The Four Essays' "; "Hölderlin and the Essence of Poetry"; and "What Is Metaphysics?"

6   Duncan, *Bending the Bow* (New York: New Directions, 1968); this letter is dated by this allusion and by Oppen's allusions to his *Of Being Numerous*, published in 1968. Duncan's use of the word "IT" occurs in a whole section of his "Introduction," so titled, vi–viii, which speaks of "a poetry of all poetries, *grand collage*," and says, "It has only the actual universe in which to realize itself. We ourselves in our actuality, as the poem in its actuality, its thingness, are facts, factors, in which it makes itself real. Having only these actual words, these actual imaginations that come to us as we work." Oppen's is "Of it, the word it, never more powerful than in this / moment. Well, hardly an epiphany, but there the thing / is all the same // All this is reportage," CP 193.

7   The two Duncan poems mentioned are "Tribal Memories, *Passages* 1" and "Orders, *Passages* 24." They appear in *Bending the Bow*, 9–10 and 77–80.

8   Stein's revision of his liberal arts math textbook, *Mathematics: The Man-Made Universe*, had appeared in 1969; Stein had given Oppen a copy.

9   The autograph additions to this letter are difficult to read, and not clearly relevant, but they say, "(((True that I don't object: Simply, I think the future hazardous))) (for N.Y.)."

10   In her suicide note. The statement haunted Oppen. For some discussion of her note, see the interview conducted by David McAleavey, "The Oppens: Remarks Towards Biography," *Ironwood* 26 (Fall 1985): 317–18.

11   Enclosed with this letter is "But So As By Fire," now section 10 of "Some San Francisco Poems," CP 227–28. There is only one verbal change between the enclosed version to DM and the published poem: in line 6 "coastal woods" has become "Eastern woods." In a letter of [January 8, 1969] to Linda Oppen Mourelatos, Oppen had enclosed at least "A Morality Play: Preface," " 'And their Winter and Night in Disguise'," and "But So As By Fire," which knowledge offers some possibility that this letter to DM can be dated [early 1969], or even [late 1968]. Also included was a poem, at this point either fourth or fifth in the sequence, but not part of the final version, called "The Footing"; it begins, "Potrero, its grassy top. . . ."

12   The corresponding letter (undated) from DM includes the statement, "A man sees

the ocean takes a boat, an oar or a sail and grapples with it. I have spent my life hanging over the edge not wanting to use the tools" (UCSD 16, 7, 26).

13 By Eve Haight.

14 An allusion perhaps untraceable. It may allude to the eighteenth-century adventure of one Jørgen Jürgensen (1780–1845), the "convict king" who attempted to become monarch of Iceland.

15 A draft of this letter, at UCSD 16, 5, 33, says about the importance of 'that non-classic antiquity': "You'll have noticed in the poems - - - I am tempted here to adduce even the small boy's normal interest in Arthur and the Welsh . . . . . [¶] Arthur. The small boy. Courage. And from there to my word 'timidity' Despite Browning-Pound-Hemingway and all that, what poet isn't 'timid' I didn't mean any lack of courage. I understood that."

16 With this letter was enclosed a packet of poems whose typed title is "A San Francisco Sequence" and whose autograph title added is "Epistle to Harvey." These seven poems are a version of "Some San Francisco Poems," differing in many interesting ways, including the existence of poems not, in toto, in the final version, like "New Year," and "The Footing," but with lines which get salvaged and used.

17 This comment suggests that later 1968 is a possible date for this letter; other contextual evidence as well as HS's memory place it in 1969.

18 A letter to Duncan that might fit this description, undated, but clearly the first letter in a relationship (prov. SUNY-Buffalo): "My wife and I have recently moved to this city -- it is actually a return. A return, it happens, neither to my childhood nor to Mary's, but to both my adolescence and to within a reasonable distance of Mary's Difficult return. We're equipped at last with a apartment capable of producing a dinner for four, and I would very much like to meet and to talk [¶] This undertaking is a little awkward in that I am not entirely sure that you know my name, but it is possible that you do. If you would care to make an appointment, I would be very pleased if you will phone."

19 In a letter of [March 1969] to Betty Kray [prov. the Estate of Elizabeth Kray], Oppen wrote of seeing Duncan: "Enjoyed Duncan (on a previous meeting) very much. Literature as fortress, a compound, at least, from which one must fire a new shot, a new weapon: I have no sense of myself as being within that fortress - - - - But nevertheless there is something very lovely about Duncan. Including the rapidest mind I can remember encountering, and a pure joy for that. I feel ponderous, but pleased."

20 Shapiro had written (on [March 23]) GO an account of a symposium held on March 21, 1969 (including Nat Hentoff, Robert Brustein, Paul Goodman, Judith Malina, Julian Beck), on "Theatre or Therapy" which was broken up by members of the Living Theater and The Theater of the Absurd, shouting down the panelists (except for Malina and Beck), spitting at, insulting, and yelling obscenities at the audience. "Their point as far as I can understand it [wrote HS], was to demonstrate that theatre is happening all the time, that it does not take place in a theatre under authoritarian direction, that it is created by people freed of their blocks, and therefore an evening of discussion (lousy words) such as this is absurd & shd not take place."

21 Ezra Pound, "Sestina: Altaforte," an early poem in the voice of Bertran de Born,

whose third line is "I have no life save when the swords clash." There is an exclamation mark after Pound's "Damn it all!"

22 In a contemporaneous letter to George Johnston (prov. The Public Archives of Canada), which recapitulates this discussion, GO underscores this reversal: "and ended by my reversing myself when, finally, I narrowed it down to a little lyric   Which said pretty much the contrary of what I had been furiously and bitterly saying to myself- - - -"

23 In response to the original Shapiro letter, Oppen made about one page of citations about the incident at the March 21 symposium and used them as what he called a "preamble" to the first poem of his current version (called "A San Francisco Sequence") of "Some San Francisco Poems." GO says in another in this set of letters "(((your letter seemed to be what I needed in a struggle to get loose from Numerous and reminiscence[.]" The citations have been cut from the final version and never appeared except in drafts.

24 The letter is printed, unexcerpted, in *Ironwood* 24 (Fall 1984), 132–35; the last half page, the material cut here, cites approvingly from RBD's letter.

25 The interviews with Oppen and the other "Objectivists" were published in *Contemporary Literature* 10, 2 (Spring 1969); Dembo was the editor and had conducted the interviews. Oppen's copies of the journal had been delivered the day before, just after he had been awarded the Pulitzer Prize for Poetry.

26 Zukofsky, *Bottom: on Shakespeare*, begun 1947, completed in 1960, published in 1963, Austin, Texas: Ark Press for the Humanities Research Center, The University of Texas.

27 As part of an exchange in the Dembo interview of Reznikoff, *Contemporary Literature* 10, 2 (Spring 1969), 195. By dropping the word "on," Oppen changed the meaning of the statement.

28 From Ezra Pound, Canto LXXXI, "What thou lovest well is thy true heritage."

29 Oppen expressed similar sentiments about the prize to William Bronk, Rachel Blau DuPlessis, Michael Heller, and George Johnston; this letter best summarizes his various remarks.

30 In this letter "RE" was a nonliterary childhood friend of Oppen, "with whom he went to dancing school"; "he was surprised she understood poetry." The Strand review was a review *of* Mark Strand's work; Oppen did not think Strand's success was merited. Athenaeum's refusal occurred when June Oppen Degnan offered *This in Which* to them for joint publication, something she told to GO only considerably after the fact—indeed, after he had won the Pulitzer Prize. These identifications, courtesy of JOD.

31 The "Icelandic" trope because Johnston was a professor of English and translator from Old and Modern Scandinavian, including the *Saga of Gisli*.

32 The Apollo 11 moon shot departed on July 16, 1969, and arrived on the moon July 20, 1969. In a letter of [after July 20, 1969] to June Oppen Degnan (UCSD 16, 1, 7), Oppen said: "didn't mean to object *that* they went to the moon, but how   The how was not a technical necessity -- and was, in all common sense technically inadvisable, it was a display of para-military apoplexy, and it frightened a great many people I am sure. Including me[.]"

33 Oppen was to mention his poor typing increasingly; I have, from this moment on, cut these apologies with the notation "typing apology."

34 Title poem from Cooper, *The Weather of Six Mornings* (New York: Macmillan, 1969), 48–51.

35 In Cooper's book "The Builder of Houses" is dedicated to Sally Appleton [Weber], 23; "For My Mother in Her First Illness, from a Window Overlooking Notre Dame," 18, has as its last line "how can I tell which one of us is absent."

36 Oppen enclosed his version of "The Weather of Six Mornings" which omitted section 4, let 6 stand as "too beautiful to touch," removed certain explanatory statements, and excised the final line, the summarizing and placing line, from each of the other sections.

37 Cooper had "told George about studying with Robert Lowell at the University of Iowa in fall 1953. But also, no doubt, I'd mentioned to him how important *Lord Weary's Castle* had been to me in the 40's, when I first started to write seriously"; Cooper mentioned "Lowell's rhetoric, and his baroque, powerful, wrenched music."

38 Cooper's poem "The Builder of Houses" begins: "What was the blond child building / Down by the pond at near-dark. . .?" Elizabeth Barrett Browning's poem "A Musical Instrument" (1860) begins with the lines Oppen cited.

39 In a letter of October 12, 1969 (UCSD 16, 4, 7), Dembo had posed eleven biographical questions for Oppen to answer. When the question is not implicit in the answer, I shall interpolate it, or a summary, in square brackets in the text. Oppen's rough dates should be checked against the biographical summary in the Introduction here.

40 The Williams letter, August 2, [1932], to Nathanael West, about a new issue of *Contact*, planned to include "Oppen's fragmentary poems." *The Selected Letters of William Carlos Williams*, ed. John C. Thirlwall (New York: McDowell, Obolensky, 1951), 128. The Pound letter from January 7, 1934, notes the possibility of his editing an annual anthology of younger poets' work; Oppen, as well as Rakosi, are mentioned as potential contributors: "Oppen (if energy don't fail)." Pound, *The Letters of Ezra Pound: 1907–1941*, ed. D. D. Paige (New York: Harcourt, Brace & World, 1950), 250.

41 "The Circumstances" served as a provisional or transitional title for *Primitive*.

42 Dembo, "Individuality and Numerosity," *The Nation* (24 Nov. 1969): 574–76.

43 As late as September 12, 1969, in a (dated) letter to Kray and the Academy of American Poets, Oppen had confirmed that he was to read on November 25 at the Guggenheim Museum. Just a little before, in [September? 1969], he wrote to Kathleen Norris, Kray's assistant, to confirm a reading at the Rhode Island School of Design; Norris and Kray were helping him set up readings.

44 Oppen mentioned in a postscript to Kray's copy of this letter that it was being sent to "some 15 people." An elaboration of his position occurs in a letter to Charles Tomlinson of [late October 1969] (prov. CT): "I had (most brashly) arranged myself a reading tour here --some twelve readings   And woke up one night in the absolute certainty that I could not do it   Sent wires cancelling   Mess, mess, you can imagine the mess   But everyone startlingly kind ¶ but cannot, cannot, perhaps particularly with the expansion of voice in Numerous   I cannot make a Chatauqua of it, cannot put myself so thoroughly INTO it, so irreversibly into it   like a Ginsberg. Can't   Or it wouldn't be good for me."

45 Because of his Pulitzer Prize, Oppen had received a certificate of honor from the Board of Supervisors of the City of San Francisco. This was his response. He also sent a copy of this letter of acknowledgment, with a covering letter, to the political editors of the *San Francisco Examiner* and the *San Francisco Chronicle*, with the final paragraph: "I believe the Board of Supervisors would indeed speak for the serious interests of the city if they should address a resolution to the President, Senate and Congress to this effect."

46 Indeed, University of Texas at Austin both published *Bottom* (see note, above) and is the major repository of Zukofsky manuscripts. No Oppen letters are listed in Marcella Booth, *A Catalogue of the Louis Zukofsky Manuscript Collection* (Humanities Research Center: The University of Texas, Austin, 1975), although some were found there for this edition through the good offices of LOM and the special collections library staff.

1970

1 The poem, "Rises in the Dark," about Oppen, which is a section of "Thistles," a poem sequence dedicated to Oppen, in *They Feed They Lion* (New York: Atheneum, 1972): 51–62; Levine sent GO a copy of the poem before its appearance in book form. The relevant lines about the "60 yr old wanderer" are, "Always a new dark / the cup rests in the stained hands."

2 Both Oppen's mother and his aunt committed suicide; about the death of Libby (his sister) in January 1960, there is intrafamilial debate. She had made suicide attempts; these, along with the coroner's report of probable suicide, seem to have inflected the interpretation of certain family members, notably Oppen and Libby's daughter Andy, on the cause of her death; however, her half sister June, with certain empirical evidence, disputes whether her death was self-inflicted.

3 "The Drum Thing," periodical publication in *Maps* 3 (1969) and *Some / thing*, nos. 4–5 (1968), book publication in *To Construct a Clock* (New Rochelle, N.Y.: Elizabeth Press, 1971).

4 *Origin* series 3, no. 14 (August 1969) featured Taggart's work.

5 In a letter of April 7, 1970, Taggart had inquired how "Of Being Numerous" was put together: "as serial argument worked out day by day or what; did you work from a larger design" (UCSD 16, 11, 2).

6 An unattached second page (UCSD 16, 3, 42) of a letter to John Crawford may be used to further gloss the question of "thought." "There are thoughts easily available to me because they have already been thought. There is an almost audible click in the brain to mark the transition between thought which is available because it has already been thought, and the thinking of the single man, the thinking of a man as if he were a single man . . . 'Of Being Numerous' is constructed around that click, of course - - and the poem ends with the word 'curious.' I had set myself once before to say forthrightly "We want to be here," [CP 143] and the long poem ends almost jokingly with 'curious' [CP 101 and 179]. But it is not a joke entirely. If I were asked, Why do we want to be here --- I would say: it is curious - - - the thing is curious - - - [¶] Which may be referred to, briefly, as O's Affirmation." In a letter to an

unidentified correspondent (UCSD 16, 12, 5) Oppen says, "I ended with the word 'curious,' of which the root is *curia*: care, concern[.]"

7   Alludes to "Leah"; the letter is filled with allusions to this poem and to "Poem," "In Thy Sleep," and "No One Talks About This," all in *Sumac* (Winter / Spring 1970). Rakosi has noted that this "must have been his first letter to me"; the two did not meet until May 1971.

8   The interview by L. S. Dembo, in *Contemporary Literature* 10, 2 (Spring 1969).

9   In a letter of [early 1970] to Harvey Shapiro, Oppen said: "My own work thins, is what's happening, thins in the influence of the California skies and the sea- scape   Something happening to the solidity of objects and the sense of city   Those islands, those things which seem at the same time uncompromisingly to exist and to be lost still in my mind but the emphasis shifts for me to the thing they are lost in -   Well, there we are: This In Which, which I seem to have spoken of before, but the center of the picture changes for me   ---"

10 They were published in Mary Oppen, *Poems & Transpositions* (New York: The Mon- temora Foundation, 1980).

11 Eugene J. McCarthy, announced presidential candidate of antiwar Democrats in 1968. The Democratic ticket in fact was Humphrey and Muskie. June Oppen Degnan served as the national finance chairman for the McCarthy campaign.

12 An allusion to the title of Booth's first book, *Letter from a Distant Land* (New York: Viking, 1957).

13 Eugene McCarthy, *Other Things and the Aardvark* (Garden City, N.Y.: Doubleday, 1970); in his preface, McCarthy noted: "The book is a tribute to American poets like Robert Lowell, William Stafford, Reed Wittemore, James Dickey, Philip Booth and the many others who have written of this country and of its people. . . ."

14 A Shapiro letter of June 22, [1970] (UCSD 16, 10, 31) said that Wesleyan University Press had accepted *This World*; HS asked whether he might use an Oppen intro- duction to a Shapiro poetry reading as the jacket comment on his work.

15 Shapiro had, in a letter (UCSD 16, 10, 32) of November 1, 1970, asked Oppen what he thought of Hugh Seidman's *Collecting Evidence* (New Haven: Yale University Press, 1971), which had won the Yale Younger Poets Prize. About this time, a correspondence between Oppen and Seidman began. The "long story" to which GO alludes is "The Modes of Vallejo Street," 12–30. In this poem occur the lines: "This poisoned needle / lodged in the upholstery," 21.

16 A letter dated October 8, 1970, to Stuart Montgomery, publisher of Fulcrum Press (TLc, UCSD 16, 4, 43) contains this statement: "If I should speak of myself as pos- sessing such a thing as a career it would be necessary to speak in a small voice, but insofar as I do possess such a thing I have lost a year of it in England at least"; Oppen goes on precisely to delineate the degree of delay that "would constitute an inexplicably malicious injury to me," but later tempered legal threats.

17 Cited from Seidman's letter of November 10, 1970 (UCSD 16, 10, 25).

18 The substitle of Zukofsky's "Sincerity and Objectification" is "with special refer- ence to the Work of Charles Reznikoff." It was not reprinted in its original form in *Prepositions* and must be sought in *Poetry* (February 1931) or in *Charles Reznikoff: Man and Poet*, ed. Milton Hindus (Orono, Me.: National Poetry Foundation, 1984): 377–88. It is in *Prepositions*, revised edition.

19 Levertov, *Relearning the Alphabet* (New York: New Directions, 1970). "Matins," mentioned subsequently, from *The Jacob's Ladder*, is a poem for which Oppen had a great regard, and from which he cited in "The Mayan Ground" (CP 119).

20 Etheridge Knight, *Poems from Prison* (Detroit: Broadside Press, 1968). In a letter of [December 22, 1970] to Robert Vas Dias (TLS, University of Virginia; TLc, UCSD), Oppen further discusses Knight: "((thru Dan Gerber of Sumac I've seen work by Etheridge Knight --- who will have or has about now a book. Lost my record of the publisher - - I mean name and address. Black poet -- the point not being one's political duties but that, writing in answer to Gerber I found myself talking about Sherwood Anderson - - - -a starting from the beginning, new ground - - - -"

21 Sherwood Anderson, "Song of the Soul of Chicago," *Mid-American Chants* (New York: John Lane, 1918: 62–63). The poem has eight verse paragraphs. The last three read: "We'll stay down in the muddy depths of our stream—we will. There can't any poet come out here and sit on the shaky rail of our ugly bridges and sing us into paradise. [¶] We're finding out—that's what I want to say. We'll get at our own thing out here or die for it. We're going down, numberless thousands of us, into ugly oblivion. We know that. [¶] But say, bards, you keep off our bridges. Keep out of our dreams, dreamers. We want to give this democracy thing they talk so big about a whirl. We want to see if we are any good out here, we Americans from all over hell. That's what we want." Oppen incorporated his version of the Anderson line in "Disasters": "to whom and // to what are we ancestral *we wanted to know* / / *if we were any good* // *out there. . .*" *Primitive*, 11.

22 The extra "n" has been crossed out by hand in both "cannons."

23 From Seidman's letter (UCSD 16, 10, 25) of December 18, 1970: "I was for instance talking to Selden Rodman yesterday who is putting together a new version of his anthology and for him it is men like Olson, Duncan, Creeley, Zukofsky, etc. who have betrayed the desire for a 'common order of language' (Zukofsky's phrasing if you will) by making poetry into an esoteric game for the initiated that excludes the rest of us (whoever we are). Not exactly my view, but in many ways I cannot but agree with him (again mathematics vs. A12) and that is the odd part because in the flesh Louis was always saying how the common order was what he was after and would amaze me by his preferences for things on the level of the most simple folksong—turning about to write with the obvious immense complexity of syntax, etc. Almost playing some strange game with the world, which of course I guess he always has, turning away with one foot and reaching forward with the other. . . ."

24 In Feld's letter of December 15, 1970 (UCSD 16, 4, 28). "The artificial" is the moment of winning a prize or honor; "our humiliation" is the extreme difficulty of working, unacknowledged, at the practice of poetry.

25 Zukofsky, toward the end of "A–12," "A" (Berkeley: University of California Press, 1978), 260 and 261.

26 There is no closing, and no second page; in editorial discussion, Meyer confirmed the possible lack of a second page.

1971

1 He wrote to L. S. Dembo [April 26, 1971]: "a new book, after long long false starts and confusion now beginning to take on shape (San Francisco coloring everything,

an obsession I can't break if I wanted to. And S F is not my idyllic early childhood of boats and etc nor my adulthood but a lost lost adolescence   And a coast essentially untouched by literature." To LOM, November 9, 1971 (UCSD 33, 1, 18), he characterizes "Some San Francisco Poems" as a work "with its meaning for me, autobiographical, and, I think, a more historical meaning -- This distance, this edge of the country,   and the thing beyond or outside the sense of metropolis[.]"

2   "Peanut butter can" was Meyer's summary image for the reality of women's daily life with children. As with all Meyer's letters, this is very difficult to date. In its *Ironwood* appearance (26 [Fall 1985]: 176–78), this letter was attached to another Meyer letter beginning, "I want to say some things that we did not say yesterday. . .": this conjoining of the two letters is inaccurate.

3   Rakosi, *Ere-Voice* (New York: New Directions, 1971); in Rakosi's *Collected Poems*, 68–69.

4   Rakosi responds to this statement in one of the meditative passages in *Ex Cranium, Night* (Los Angeles: Black Sparrow Press, 1975), 102: "When George Oppen first read my poem, 'In Thy Sleep / Little Sorrows Sit And Weep,' it seemed to him that if it had ended on the line, 'the crow slept,' it would have been 'absolutely immovable.' By that he meant so solid that it couldn't be reduced any further. [¶] The strange thing is that ending the poem there ends it before anything has happened. *That* poem looks into eternity in a very different way. It is as if nature, and the poem, were more self-contained and clairvoyant when they were still, and had more gravitational pull and magic while they were still brooding and imminent."

5   Tomlinson, "Elegy for Henry Street," in *Written on Water* (Oxford: Oxford University Press, 1972). The Oppens' Brooklyn address was 364 Henry Street.

6   The eagle seems to come from T. S. Eliot's *Four Quartets*; the umbrella from familiar photos of Eliot.

7   Sarah Appleton Weber, *Theology and Poetry in the Middle English Lyric* (Columbus: Ohio State University Press, 1969). This version may not have been sent; carbon of another version (UCSD 16, 11, 26).

8   RBD has cut nineteen lines by Sarah Appleton Weber as revised by GO; seeing them is not necessary for the argument.

9   An allusion to Appleton [Weber's] book *The Plenitude We Cry For* (Garden City: Doubleday, 1972) which opens, "This is the record of one season's growth of a horse chestnut tree in 1964 at Northampton, Massachusetts," 7.

10   In a letter to Sarah Appleton Weber of [after March 8, 1971], Oppen wrote of some of the cost of child-rearing to poetry. "I've known people turned irremediably heavy by these years, and people forever superficial by the lack of them -- all, I'm sometimes afraid, of the recent poets   Duncan, Olson -- I count em as recent -- - - not very far from pure foolishness   calling on everything, anything, to hide this fact   Trying to drown it   in copiousness and digressions - - and in the proliferation of theories   in . . . [¶] ((Ginsberg's Kaddish the marvel among these things)" (UCSD 16, 11, 26).

11   Gerber and Oppen were exchanging letters just prior to this about Gerber's long poem "Departure." Among other issues was the title, and in a letter of [June 12?, 1971] Oppen had said, "I like the title 'from Tamalpais' because it seems to acknowledge this shift of focus, shift to distance, shift between interiority and notation

- - and I think quite possible this alteration of focus, of the meaning of distance is something to be retained, not revised 'out' - - but handled more consciously??" In a letter of [June 17, 1971], Oppen remarked, "I think, have always thought focus, depth, what the painters once called aerial perspective - - change, control   understanding of depth, of focus is crucial[.]"

12 Cuddihy had, in September 1971, solicited work from Oppen for *Ironwood* (which MC was starting); Oppen responded with what he called, in a letter of [after September 11, 1971], "a small poem   small   atypical   I think the poem works   If you'd want to give it a page to itself, I think it would hold, a-typicalness and all - - -" The poem, published in *Ironwood* 1 (Spring 1972): 12, but uncollected is "A Poem About the Garden":

> carpel
> filament the brilliant
> center pollen-gold
>
> crimson stirs in a girl's
> eyes as tho one had entered
> a flower, and been a stranger

13 "Ditch" is a word that recurs in Oppen's poetry.

14 "Book of Hours," *Sumac* 3, number 2 (Winter 1971), 9–11; this is "Of Hours" (CP 210–12), which concerns Ezra Pound, Oppen's Jewishness, and World War II, among other subjects.

15 The citation is from Emily Dickinson's poem #288 (T. Johnson, ed.) which begins, 'I'm Nobody! Who are you? / Are you—Nobody—Too? / Then there's a pair of us?" Another letter to Harvey Shapiro from approximately the same time formulated other of Oppen's responses to the poems in *Seascape: Needle's Eye*: "I think the new poems are good   Sparse, but they move   And yet I wanted them to move elsewhere   Toward greater self-satisfaction?   I guess that's it. Greater complacency   Drift and drift and drift: the image everywhere in the poems is the sea and its horizon   Everywhere in my mind too."

16 Heller's letter of November 20, 1971 (UCSD 16, 5, 5), to which this and a previous Oppen letter of [after November 20] respond, contains the following: "I feel, as I put it in a poem, the times are entropic, and many minds accept a kind of Spenglerian winding down of life and world, and make a poetry from the self-pity of such a condition. I feel you--almost alone--have faced this situation without retreat into these false elegies, you are almost the first poet to write directly into the teeth of what has happened to all of us: the sense that the age has virtually lost the capacity to apprehend the kind of energy the poem is. . . . I think you are very aware of just the difficulty here, of listening and hearing what is possible without stepping back from either truth or decency."

17 In the first letter to Heller, in an oblique discussion of political action and writing, Oppen produced a definition of the "directly political": "Something one wants to do and without which he will not possess his own life   and the 'retreat from decency' which is the failure to act --   anguish and shame   Not the anguish but the shame probably erodes his honesty. I can't answer

'. . . and the women and children were sold' Herodotus, Josephus, Thucydides and anyone else   the heart freezes. Every time. No end to it, it can freeze you in ice, destroy the poetry, the will to poetry, no one can hear it - - Sick, paralyzing, rational despair - - Fear   --but the 'act' is opposed to the poetry because . . ? We both know. We both want to face this bluntly and without indecent defenses, but we both know[.]"

18 Webster's essay is "Yeats' 'The Shadowy Waters': Oral Motifs and Identity in the Drafts," *American Imago* 28 (Spring 1971): 3–16.

1972

1 In an interview between Charles Tomlinson and Oppen, recorded May 22, 1973, for the BBC, Oppen offered a context for the title when asked by CT about the "greater fluidity" of his San Francisco poetry: "Well, it is the scene, it is the edge of a continent, and it's a bare edge of a continent. You come . . . you stand on a little beach, you can stand on one little rock and look out--if you saw far enough you'd see Honolulu. There's nothing between. It's a bare, bare edge; it's a metaphysical edge. What happens there--the symbol of the needle's eye is the horizon, the horizon at sea, in which these dimensions close, coincide. The . . . the detail, the objectivism in the sense it was usually understood, and the sky, the unlimited space, the un-limited. At that point almost touch leaving a needle's eye." Interview and reading copyright © by The British Broadcasting Corporation as recorded May 22, 1973, on BBC Radio 3, produced by George MacBeth.

2 Introduced by Mark Linenthal; an audiotape exists. He was also apparently in residence at San Francisco State for a week in 1972.

3 A letter to Dan Gerber of [October 7, 1972] (prov. Dan Gerber) characterized the weather: "the summer was a marvel, a great wonder   Strong winds, great speeds   hundreds or thousands was it of small harbors entered in wild seas[.]"

4 "Horizon" is *Seascape: Needle's Eye*; the letter is to Dan Gerber (prov. DG), from [October 7, 1972], and expresses eagerness to see the book in print.

5 This is a carbon draft (unsent?) of another somewhat less frank letter, dated 1972 by Kaufman. It begins, "again, thanks for the evening   Worth it to hear the liturgy very well worth the evening   ((of the rest, Eckhart said it of the equivalent Christian 'services' 'that god is not god enough for a flea'   -each holds the religion he is capable of. It makes very little difference whose Bingo party he goes to[.]" *Sunday, Bloody Sunday*: the 1971 film, directed by John Schlesinger, based on the screenplay by Penelope Gilliatt. Bergman's *The Touch* is also a film from 1971.

6 Kaufman translated "My Little Sister" from the Hebrew of Abba Kovner, in *Abba Kovner and Nelly Sachs: Selected Poems* (Baltimore: Penguin Books, 1971); it was reprinted in *A Canopy in the Desert: Selected Poems* (Pittsburgh: University of Pitts-burgh Press, 1973). A revised version in Kovner, *My Little Sister and Selected Poems, 1965–85*, translated by Shirley Kaufman (Field Translation Series, vol. 11: Oberlin College, 1986).

7 The sent letter says, "the Introduction very fine   above all those last paragraphs [. . .] Those faces in the pool are not so clear for me - - - or, rather, they are not all

Hebrew faces -- but there is nothing, nothing at all I value so much as that some of them *are*   Beautiful dark faces among the 'classic'[.]"

8 Gerber, who was then in the Soviet Union, had apparently sent a picture of the Kremlin.

9 As published in "Myth of the Blaze" (CP 242), these lines have become, ". . . Wyatt's / lyric and Rezi's / running thru my mind / in the destroyed (and guilty) Theatre / of the War   I'd cried / and remembered / boyhood   degradation   other / degradations. . . ."

10 That page of Duncan's *The Truth & Life of Myth: An Essay in Essential Autobiography* speaks of Duncan's weeping: " 'Garcia Lorcia stole / poetry from this drinking-fountain' [an initial poem in *Ceasar's Gate*, "The Waste, The Room, The Discarded Timbers," 2] I wrote in one of the poems of *Caesar's Gate*—I almost came to weeping as I wrote and had to retreat from the idea as best I could.[. . .] The numen is not only awe-full; it moves us to tears."

11 A statement by Oppen presented by Cynthia Anderson in *Conjunctions* 10 (1987) may illuminate some aspects of the extremes. "Duncan: he can put the actual honey in the poem. I can't do that   I cannot come near it Perhaps he has more control of sound than I, the syllables are deeper, the syllables are whole   My 'little' words rattle sometimes   his syllables are whole, are deeper, are whole," 202. There are also some notes on Duncan in the Davidson "Daybook" selection, *Ironwood* 26 (Fall 1985).

12 On March 13, 1972, *Playboy* sent Oppen "Seven Poems by Mao Tse-Tung: The Classical Verse of a Revolutionary," trans. by Nieh Hua-Ling and Paul Engle, forthcoming in the April 1972 *Playboy*. This letter occurs in TLc (draft), and TL, both UCSD. The apparently more final version is used here. The other instance occurred in 1971, asking Oppen to comment on a "profile" of James Dickey. He did, succinctly: "Maybe 'My Land'?   or 'Laws-a-Massy'?" (UCSD 16, 9, 19).

13 This deeply modified allusion to the end of T. S. Eliot's "The Love Song of J. Alfred Prufrock" occurs as well in the final poem of *Primitive*.

14 With this letter, Oppen enclosed a copy of "Song: The Winds of Downhill" on which he noted that this was his sixty-fourth birthday, with the wondering tag he often used about aging: "an odd thing to happen to a child."

15 Dembo had identified Maud Blessingbourne who " 'approached the window as if to see / what was really going on'," a talismanic gesture for Oppen, as coming from James' "The Story in It," *The Complete Tales of Henry James, Volume 11 (1900–03)*, ed. Leon Edel (Philadelphia: J. B. Lippincott Co., 1964).

16 From *The Poems of Saint John of the Cross*, "Del Verbo Divino" (Of the Divine Word), translated by Willis Barnstone as, "Pregnant with the holy / word will come the Virgin / walking down the road / if you will take her in" (Indiana University Press, 1968). Oppen modified this, in "Route," to "Virgin / what was there to be thought/ / comes by the road" (CP 192). See also CP 207. In her *Poems & Transpositions*, Mary Oppen rendered this as, "what is *there*   to be thought // comes by the road / if you will give it shelter" [n.p.]. In a letter of [May 6, 1969] to George Johnston (prov. The Public Archives of Canada), Oppen cited this passage after saying: "Words of desire which bring one to tears: word of reality which brings one to 'religion'   religion in quotes because if it retains its root meaning and if the

"bond" means a bond tying a people together, it is nowhere in my experience - - - a descendent of a number of generations of German Jewish merchants, two generations behind me at least powerfully assimilationist and argumentatively atheist, Christianity and Judaism are about as exotic to me as Zoroastrianism -- and yet I stumble over these stories, the Christian and Jewish stories, the Christian writings --- increasingly for many years." The St. John of the Cross lines follow.

17   From a [June 1972] letter to Brenda Webster somewhat later in this exchange: "you must start now to work without knowing or wanting to know if anyone 'likes' it and without thinking about whether or not anyone will 'like' it, and there is, in my opinion, no other way you can begin to reach the ground of poetry."

18   Jacket copy intended for Davie's *Collected Poems*.

19   In a letter of October 20, 1972 (UCSD 16, 4, 5), Davie had addressed the gulf between them. "You are not English; I am not American (nor Jew either, but that's something else again, and much less to the point I think). [. . .] I believe I do accept more responsibility for English society as a whole, for the English historical record, for what have been the distinctively English life-styles, than Charles [Tomlinson] does or Basil Bunting. [¶] You must not suppose (perhaps you don't—I can't tell) that what you call 'wit of form' is something I opt for on settled principle. If I did, how could I respond to poetry so different as for instance yours or Pound's? I write the best I can, as we all do, and 'wit of form' is just the way it worked out for me." Oppen drafted a second, short statement not for publication (UCSD 16, 4, 5) which began: "A work so strongly within a national, a racial tradition, a work of unfailing wit within that tradition -- it is a poetry the most distant from me; in its distance, its brilliance fascinating almost shattering to me."

20   Oppen, "Three Poets," *Poetry* 100, 5 (August 1962): 329–32; Oppen argues that Olson is Pound's epigone. The Olson rejoinder in *Maximus Poems IV, V, VI* (London: Cape Goliard Press, 1968), n.p.; it reads, "I want to open / Mr Oppen / the full inherited file / of history."

21   "Trevenen" is an epistle in tetrameter couplets based on the life of eighteenth-century Captain James Trevenen; Edmund Burke and James King are among its dramatis personae. Davie, *Collected Poems, 1950–1970* (London: Routledge & Kegan Paul, 1972), 283–92.

22   A postcard from Davie dated October 21, 1972, noted that he despaired, given what he saw as Oppen's making so little of his work (UCSD 16, 4, 5).

23   Two drafts of this letter exist at UCSD Archive; the longer of the two is chosen here.

24   Rakosi, "Nine Poems from The Everyday Book," *New Directions in Prose and Poetry 25*, ed. James Laughlin, with Peter Glassgold and Frederick R. Martin (New York: New Directions, 1972), 138–43. A poem called "The Poet" is dedicated "to George Oppen"; it is retitled "When He Sat Down to His Desk" without the dedication to Oppen in Rakosi's *Collected Poems*, 225.

25   A relevant paragraph—the main one—from the shorter letter by GO to CR (UCSD 16, 9, 35): "'If you were starving, you wouldn't concern yourself with' -- the fanciness of, they mean --- 'poetry'? You mean that sort of thing? But the fact is, it is in extreme situations of hunger, fear, oppression, catastrophe, an enemy world that a given man is affected by everything he, that given man, has known of art; is touched again by everything that has ever touched him of art - - I've reported

something of the sort   This, I think -- and the circumstance that I know this -- marks the space separating our thinking in this regard."

26   Simic, *White* (New Rivers Press, 1972), 11 is the source of these lines, from the first poem in the poem sequence. Simic has written: "Out of poverty / to begin again: // With the color of the bride / And that of blindness, // Touch what I can / of the quick, // Speak and then wait, / As if this light // Will continue to linger / On the threshold." Oppen cited the Simic lines in "Song, The Winds of Downhill" (CP 213).

27   A letter to Shapiro (UCSD 16, 10, 30) could gloss this: "((on my use of Simic's lines, which annoyed you -- THAT can be answered. As you say, it's been said 'by everyone.' Therefore quoted Simic   for the sake of the quote marks   O K on that?)"

28   At UCSD 16, 5, 8, there is both a draft of this letter, with other formulations, and a copy, with AL additions.

29   From the draft (UCSD 16, 5, 8): "I begin to understand that the earlier books have been taken to be a simple realism - - I was in these books speaking of Being: I had thought I could arrive at the concept of Being from an account of experience as it presents itself in its own terms - - Needle's eye is perhaps more familiar, more personal, or seems so - - - a man more immediately and more individually facing the fact of his own temporality - - - - - It will be taken as less than I meant it to be if it is not taken in the light of the previous books.[. . .] ...I was sure I had said, managed to say - - - - - - *Being* - 'the most obvious thing in the word' [sic] 'ob via   the obvious,' [CP 205] a simple realism."

30   The citation is from a traditional African-American spiritual.

31   The allusion is to D. H. Lawrence, "The Ship of Death."

32   *The Waste Land: A Facsimile and Transcript of the Original Drafts including the Annotations of Ezra Pound,* ed. Valerie Eliot, had been published by Harcourt, Brace, Jovanovich in 1971. At Christmas 1972, Laughlin published a privately circulated pamphlet, which reprinted Harry Levin's "*The Waste Land* from UR to ECHT," from the Mexican journal *Plural,* ed. Octavio Paz.

1973

1   A letter to JOD (UCSD 16, 1, 7): "Rezi, Rakosi and Duncan at Michigan were a joy, of course, a joy to talk to people whose work one does actually take seriously. . . ."

2   Duncan, *The Truth and Life of Myth: An Essay in Essential Autobiography* (Fremont, Mich.: The Sumac Press, 1968, reprint 1972). According to the Bertholf bibliography of Duncan, the reprint edition was not published until January 1973; that fact provides at least a year date for this and the subsequent letter to Duncan.

3   Heller had published *Accidental Center* (Fremont, Mich.: The Sumac Press, 1972).

4   In a letter of Heller to Oppen, December 26, 1972 (UCSD 16, 5, 6).

5   Titled "Out of the Whirl Wind (demiurgos)" and dated "as of Jan 6, '73," with a heading "(from a series parallel to the Book of Job)," the work reads: "argot / of the purchasers slang / of the buyers and 'the commonplace // lost' the mills of the godless / grind slowly but grind / very fine we   the greasers // in the path of tornado the words // piled on each other lean / on each other deadweight / on garage floors

serving the dancing / valve-stems the last words // survivors, will be tame / will stand near our feet / what shall we say   they have lived their lives / they have gone feathery / and askew / in the wind from the beginning carpenter / mechanic o we / impoverished we hired / hands that turned the wheel young / theologians of the scantlings wracked / monotheists of the [w]eather-side sometimes I imagine / they speak." Compare CP 238, where this draft becomes a section of "The Book of Job. . . ." On January 20 Oppen sent to Heller a version of that poem much closer to the published version, bearing the epigraph: " 'the loss of the commonplace' Mike Heller."

6   In his letter of December 26, 1972, Michael Heller had cited a passage of Erich Heller from "The Artist's Journey into the Interior": "What really is appears at such times like the vision of a visionary, and the realism of great poetry becomes 'meta-physical': not, however, by wilfully deserting the physical world, but by being left outside through a peculiar contraction of the circumference of the real" (UCSD 16, 5, 6).

7   While writing an essay on Oppen, Crawford had posed a number of significant questions about Oppen's work, based in part on JC's response to the recent Dembo article. Crawford, "An Essay on George Oppen," *New*, 25 & 26 (1975): 131–40.

8   Crawford's question, from his letter of January 23, 1973: "Did you have any back-ground in the American empiricists, James, Dewey, etc. -- or was the 'nominalism' Dembo speaks of Hegel plus observation, e.g., just *living*? Also, any early interest in phenomenology, and if so, could you lead me to a book?" In a letter to Oppen of August 1, 1981 (UCSD 16, 3, 44), Crawford wrote: "I found [a letter] where I asked you whether something I thought was Marxist in your work came from reading or, I believe the phrase was, 'only experience.' I wonder where I was then, whether anyone ever knocked on my door, and if they did, what on earth they tried to say to me."

9   William Langland, *The Vision of Piers Plowman*, from the section called "The Vision of Holy Church": "Truth telleth thee that Love is the treacle of sin, / A sovran salve for body and soul. / Love is the plant of Peace, most precious of virtues. / Heaven could not hold it so heavy was love, / Till it has of this earth eaten its fill" (London: J. M. Dent, 1912), 20.

10   Crawford's question: "With Chartres, do you feel any Marxist orientation to the materials treated in the poem? Men make not only the things they produce, but themselves through the things they produce, and the ethical nature derives from the material; then the spirit of the cathedral is the production of the hand carving the single stone?"

11   Crawford: "Referring later to 'situations . . . in which people would not be willing to live . . . without some concept of sharing in history or humanity,' are you simply referring to the experience common to you, Camus, and the millions of others who shared the 30's, the war? [. . .] a greater awareness of humanity through the suffering of war?"

12   Davie, *Thomas Hardy and British Poetry* (New York: Oxford University Press, 1972; London: Routledge & Kegan Paul, 1973).

13   Hardy, "The Voice"; its central section reads: ". . . Let me view you, then, / Standing as when I drew near to the town / Where you would wait for me: yes, as I knew

you then, / Even to the original air-blue gown! // Or is it only the breeze, in its listlessness / Travelling across the wet mead to me here, / You being ever dissolved to existlessness, / Heard no more again far or near?''

14   In a letter of February 7, 1973, Davie proposed this gloss: "I and the better British [writers] are not afraid *enough*, as you and the better Americans are, being so much further on and nearer to the edge. . . ?''

15   This term is discussed by Oppen in the subsequent letter of [before February 20, 1973] (Beinecke Library): "Surely I am not 'radical.' Consciousness in itself, and of itself, (I think Descartes might have said) establishes the fact of *actualness*, for it, itself, is undoubtedly actual. And so we have the fact of actualness   Which is the miracle. If I saw things differently ('visions') I would report my existence differently. The difference would not be of great importance to me. This is the 'antinomian-ism'[.]''

16   Davie, "Notes on George Oppen's *Seascape: Needle's Eye*," originally published in *The Grosseteste Review* 6, 1–4 (1973): 233–39; reprinted in *George Oppen: Man and Poet*, 407–12.

17   The final sentences of Davie's review are "I would call that ["Exodus," CP 229] (although the word may give offence) elegant as well as touching. And I would say indeed that the elegance and the touchingness depend upon each other."

18   Nejgebauer noted: "The word 'Adventure' is a reference to a long article I was writing on George, called 'The Adventure of George Oppen,' and which was pub-lished in Serbo-Croatian—'Avantura Dzordza Opena,' *Mostovi*, Belgrade, 17 (Janu-ary–March 1974), 3–14."

19   Pound's *Drafts & Fragments of Cantos CX–CXVII* had been published by New Direc-tions in 1968. In a note (UCSD 16, 16, 8), Oppen says about "the meeting with Pound": "So we wept on each other. I don't know why. Maybe for all the people we each had tried to kill." See Oppen's brief narrative, "Pound in the U.S.A., 1969," *Sagetrieb* 1, 1 (Spring 1982): 119.

20   Sherwood Anderson, "Song of the Soul of Chicago," *Mid-American Chants* (New York: John Lane, 1918), 62–63; "We want to see if we are any good out here, we Americans from all over hell." Cited more fully in note to a Gerber letter, 1972. This line of Anderson is used in Oppen's "Disasters," *Primitive*, 11.

21   An indicator arrow is drawn from this phrase back to "Let the poems sit a while   I mean to also." Taggart had edited a Louis Zukofsky issue of *Maps* (#5, 1973).

22   A letter to J. H. Prynne of [before March 16, 1973] responded to the invitation tendered to Oppen to read at Gonville and Caius College, Cambridge.

23   The allusion to the "Ode to the West Wind" by Percy Bysshe Shelley, whose last line, "If Winter comes, can Spring be far behind?" is widely interpreted to express a revolutionary hope.

24   Prynne, *Aristeas* (London: Ferry Press, 1968); *Kitchen Poems* (London: Cape Goliard Press, 1968); *Into the Day* (Cambridge: Saffron Press, 1972).

25   Assistance with transcription was provided by both Mary Oppen and Linda Oppen Mourelatos. The letter was occasioned by Nejgebauer's invitation to Oppen to gloss two lines from "Of Being Numerous." From section 7 (CP 151): "Obsessed, bewil-dered // By the shipwreck / Of the singular // We have chosen the meaning / Of being numerous"; the lines are "By the shipwreck / Of the singular."

26 "The Book of Job and a Draft of a Poem to Praise the Paths of the Living," dedicated "in memory of Mickey Schwerner" (CP 236–41), one of three civil rights workers for CORE murdered in Mississippi in 1964, and a cousin of Armand Schwerner.

27 Rothenberg, ed., *The Revolution of the Word: A New Gathering of American Avant Garde Poetry, 1914–1945* (New York: Seabury-Continuum, 1974); Oppen's work on 181–89.

28 The series of letters to Andy Meyer about Simone Weil was also published in *Ironwood* 26 (Fall 1985): 170–76, including DM's side of the correspondence. DM writes as introduction: "I had read Simone Weil's letters. I had been awed, stunned and in some sense repulsed.

"The next day a four year old girl, the daughter of a Catholic politician, had said to me 'God does not want us to eat fish,' and then added abruptly, 'But it's alright if we do.'

"The child's statement came to me as a kind of relief from the uncompromising rigor of Simone Weil.

"George's response is letter 1."

29 Simone Weil, "The Love of God and Affliction," *Waiting for God* (New York: Harper & Row, 1973), 134–35. The second paragraph actually begins, "Extreme affliction, which means physical pain . . . ." With thanks to DM for this reference. This Weil citation appears in CP 210.

30 During the late fall 1973, Cuddihy proposed that a special issue, or a part of an issue, of *Ironwood* be devoted to Oppen. Oppen approved of these plans, saying he was "very moved by such a labor of love" [letter after November 23, 1973, UCSD 16, 3, 51], and cautioning MC that he held to a strictly noninterfering policy, although he did not want the "Book of Job" (re)printed if not in the context of a full issue; it had appeared in whole or in part in three British journals: *European Judaism* 8, 1 (Winter 1973–74); *Grosseteste Review* 6, 1–4 (1973); *Poetry Review* 66, 1 (1975).

31 The relation of this letter and the next is not clear, nor is the date any but conjectural.

32 Duncan, *Caesar's Gate*, poems from 1949–50, originally published in 1955 by Divers Press, was revised and reissued by Duncan in 1972. But the Bertholf bibliography of Duncan notes that the edition of *Caesar's Gate Poems 1949–50* (Berkeley: Sand Dollar, 1972) was actually published in Winter 1973, which gives a putative date for these letters. The poem alluded to in this letter is the four-part "What Is It You have Come to Tell Me, Garcia Lorca?" 44–46. The bee is central: "In the honeycombs the golden bees waiting / cross to the land of the dead and back"; later, "each least bee enormous with spirit." See also *Caesar's Gate*, xxxv.

33 It appears, from the context, that Oppen meant that works by Planz "have seen this landscape," for an autograph line at the bottom of this letter says, "You've written the poem, or part of the poem, I've been trying to write."

1974

1 In a letter of [summer 1974] to Diane Meyer, UCSD 16, 7, 27, Oppen described it: "island in the middle of the bay - - the ocean seas come rolling past - - a hundred islands around us - - this a steep island, heavily wooded, rock base, farmland on

the summit, old barns more or less falling apart - - little shacks (*camps,* they call them) in the woods, paths cut to them - - -"

2   In a letter to Michael Heller of [September? 1974], such poems as "The Little Pin: Fragment."

3   Duncan, "A Preface Prepared for Maps #6," *Maps #6* (1974), 1–16. *Maps* was edited by John Taggart.

4   Very likely alludes to Reznikoff, *New and Selected Poems* (Los Angeles: Black Sparrow, 1974).

5   "She comes up the stairway of lost breath," from "Grandmother in Heaven," *1933* (New York: Atheneum, 1974), "Zaydee" [GO: Zayda] also from this book; "They feed they lion," from *They Feed They Lion* (New York: Atheneum, 1972).

6   Stoneburner had written, December 31, 1973: "My etymological discovery for the mythology of Christmas this season was *exuberance*: its root is a word for udder: the Child at Mary's breast is example of exuberance; so is the Milky Way, & all the galaxies." Carol Elizabeth, Stoneburner's child, had learned to float by imitating bladderwrack lifted by the tide.

7   McAleavey had posed such questions as the "history of your involvement in politics," and whether "your money funded the Objectivist Press" in inviting Oppen to write autobiographical information.

8   See Mary Oppen, *Meaning a Life,* 158–63.

9   Oppen had enclosed two pages of bibliographic lists of work by and about him.

10   Jane Cooper reported in an explanatory letter to RBD, February 14, 1984: "Some time in late '71 or early '72, as nearly as I can remember, I found a box containing 80-odd poems I'd written between 1947 and 1952, which I thought I had destroyed." This whole experience is described in detail in Part II of *Maps & Windows,* in the essay "Nothing Has Been Used in the Manufacture of This Poetry That Could Have Been Used in the Manufacture of Bread."

11   This letter, probably [1974?], was apparently provoked by a discussion of an article on right brain and left brain thinking which appeared in *Psychology Today* (May 1973); placed here it illuminates the issue of women's poetry as not or non-metaphysical, which Oppen had discussed with Jane Cooper, above.

12   RBD cut now-obscure editorial comments about the note "Non-Resistance, etc. Or: Of the Guiltless," which Oppen wrote for *West End* 3, 1 (1974): 5.

13   Brecht, "An die Nachgeborenen [To Posterity], a poem from 1938 (in the Michael Hamburger translation): "Even hatred of vileness / Distorts a man's features. / Even anger at injustice / Makes hoarse his voice. Ah, we / Who desired to prepare the soil for kindness / Could not ourselves be kind." *Modern German Poetry, 1910–1960,* ed. Michael Hamburger and Christopher Middleton (New York: Grove Press, 1962), 231.

14   "The love-cars" is an allusion to Robert Lowell's "Skunk Hour"; the end of the letter seems to claim that Oppen is another kind of confessional poet.

15   It should be noted that, in using the sum of "45," Oppen includes as his work the time he was not writing or publishing.

16   In a letter of September 6, 1974, Laughlin urged Oppen to use the term "collected"—because of "the mentality of librarians and prize committee judges"; Oppen agreed in a letter of September 19, 1974.

17   "Rosenblum on George Oppen," *Margins*, No. 3 (1972).
18   Describing a wedding, DM had used the phrase "the professional men and their cushy wives."
19   Respectively Democrat, Alabama, served in the House 1969–79, and Democrat, New York, in House 1971–. Oppen had spelled Rangel as "Wrangle," thus making more evident the humors characters of Jonsonian comedy.
20   This letter is dated in the context of the Watergate affair. From July 27–30, the House Judiciary Committee adopted three articles of impeachment against President Nixon. This letter occurs before President Nixon's resignation of office on August 8, and probably just after his statement (on August 5) about witholding information about his knowledge of the Watergate break-in six days after it had happened.
21   "Intending a Solid Object: A Study in Objectivist Poetics," Ph.D. dissertation for Syracuse University; revised portions later appeared in *Louis Zukofsky: Man and Poet*, ed. Carroll Terrell (Orono, Me.: National Poetry Foundation, 1979) and in *Credences* 2–3 (Fall/Winter 1982).
22   Oppen, rephrased from "The Mind's Own Place" (1963).
23   An allusion to Taggart, *The Pyramid is a Pure Crystal* (New Rochelle, N.Y.: Elizabeth Press, 1974).
24   The lines occur at the end of "A-12."
25   The apostrophe of possession, apparently wrong, I have left uncorrected, as it adds grammatical possibilities to this already convoluted sentence.
26   *Revolution of the Word: A New Gathering of American Avant Garde Poetry 1914–1945* (New York: Seabury-Continuum, 1974); Oppen's *Discrete Series* was republished in full in *Revolution of the Word*. The allusion to "the day we arrived" could place this letter in the autumn, after their late September return from Austin (where they often stopped after summers in Maine to visit Linda and Alex).
27   McAleavey had shown Oppen the almost final version of his Ph.D. thesis (Cornell, 1975), *If to Know is Noble: The Poetry of George Oppen* (Ann Arbor Microfilms, 1975).
28   The force of this remark can be glossed by a statement in a letter of [September 22, 1973] to Eric Homberger: "in fact I know nothing about techniques. I can, when I am lucky, unbelievably lucky, it seems to me, find a way to make the poem: don't remember that I've ever found a choice between two possible ways -----" A similar expostulation in a letter (unsent?) to John Crawford (UCSD 16, 3, 42): "John, for Christ's sake!   I have never in my life found two ways to write the same poem. Don't know that anyone ever has. [. . .] ANY problem of the poem can be solved. Any vowel you need you can get, any structure, any order of phrase that you need. Occasionally lines write themselves, but a line may take weeks or months to write, and sometimes very much longer   But there is no reason why every syllable should not be perfect. Of course you must test each syllable for yourself -- one must certainly not be thinking about what other people may or may not have got away with. You just have to make EVERY syllable perfect. But that's ALL there is to it. EVERYBODY knows that except the poets --"
29   Conrad Aiken, ed., *Modern American Poets* (New York: The Modern Library, 1927); the poets included were Emily Dickinson, E. A. Robinson, Anna Hempstead Branch, Amy Lowell, Robert Frost, Vachel Lindsay, Alfred Kreymborg, Wallace Stevens, Wil-

liam Carlos Williams (one poem), John Gould Fletcher, H.D., T. S. Eliot, Conrad Aiken, Edna St. Vincent Millay, Maxwell Bodenheim.

30   Another letter from Oppen [October 1974], commenting on poems from Barrows's unpublished manuscript *The Small*, preceded this. The manuscript contains a sequence in honor of Lorine Niedecker. I cut some talk about the manuscript.

31   Probably an allusion to Niedecker's "In the great snowfall before the bomb . . ." wherein the lines "I worked the print shop / right down among em / the folk from whom all poetry flows / and dreadfully much else." *From this Condensery: The Complete Writing of Lorine Niedecker*, ed. Robert J. Bertholf (Highlands, N.C.: The Jargon Society, 1985), 108.

32   French train windows carry the formal warning that "il est interdit de se pencher dehors."

33   Lines by Barrows are cut.

34   The letter published in *Four Zoas Journal* 1974 (issue: Amnesty) is an amalgamation of material in a letter or letters which Lavin received from Oppen; the cuts are not editorially indicated and Oppen's syntax is somewhat distorted in the process.

1975

1   These were published in, respectively, *Sagetrieb* 3, 3 (1984): 9–23 and *Montemora* 4: 186–203 (1978).

2   When invited, he wrote to Shirley Kaufman in [June] 1975 (prov. SK): "Marvelous. Almost literally. For, no, I don't think I could become an Israeli : my sense of Jewishness is a vague sense of being foreign and therefore, in an American way, or rather one of the American ways, faintly aristocratic --- the word may not be the exact word, and the feeling may be hard to define, but it's mine, and I'm stuck with it."

3   There had been some correspondence with Laughlin about cover quotations (cf. UCSD 16, 8, 8). On October 19, Hugh Kenner reviewed the *Collected Poems* for the *New York Times Book Review*.

4   Rakosi, *Ex Cranium, Night* (Los Angeles: Black Sparrow Press, 1975) names Oppen among several to whom the book is dedicated.

5   Rakosi's sequence, "The Poet," in *Ex Cranium, Night*, section viii, 153. Also in *The Collected Poems of Carl Rakosi* (Orono, Me.: The National Poetry Foundation, 1986), 194. Oppen has altered the lines by underlining a word, and by dropping a comma after "small," which makes the third line a modifier of the second, not the case in Rakosi's poem.

6   Section v, titled "The Execution," from "The Poet," *Ex Cranium, Night*, 149, reorganized in *Rakosi Poems* into "The Poet, III," 226.

7   The "old friend" trope, often repeated in Oppen's letters to Rakosi, may have its origin in Rakosi's brief memoir of Oppen, in the "Observations" section of this book, which describes how the two men "became old, old friends in one night," *Ex Cranium, Night* [ECN], 138. Reappears in the section "Scenes from My Life" in *The Collected Prose of Carl Rakosi* (Orono, Me.: The National Poetry Foundation, 1983), 115.

8   Taggart may have been alluding to a letter Oppen sent him on ([January 16, 1975] UCSD 11, 17, 11), whose first paragraphs read "'to be able to say anything' -- yes, it is for me the prosody, skill, technique, the voice, the whole art   Glad you said that [¶] that the motion, and the emotion that creates language bring forth again and again ------ and that I must find again in each poem the subject - - as you say - - Must 'find' it for the reader ------ O well, yes it troubles me, delays me - -"

9   The Taggart book is *The Pyramid Is A Pure Crystal* (New Rochelle, N.Y.: Elizabeth Press, 1974); the phrase "fellow me airs" recalls the phrase in "Gold On Oak Leaves," in Oppen's *Primitive*: "fellow / me feminine / winds as you pass," 24.

10 In "Observations," *ECN*, 138 or "Scenes from My Life," *Rakosi Prose*, 115.

11 Rakosi was scheduled to read there under the auspices of San Francisco State University. Oppen introduced him.

12 "In a Warm Bath," originally published in *Ere-Voice* (1971), 4, now in *Rakosi Poems*, 99.

13 A prose piece appearing in "Day Book," from *ECN*, 93; in *Rakosi Prose*, 13.

14 Kenner, *A Homemade World: The American Modernist Writers* (New York: Knopf, 1975), 163–71, and 183–88.

15 Laughlin had inquired whether Oppen had letters from Williams for the edition of Williams's letters edited by Emily Mitchell Wallace.

16 After some thought, I have dated this letter from its allusion to the Rakosi reading in March 1975, not from the allusion to Reznikoff which might (but might not) concern his death in January 1976.

17 Shapiro's 1966 volume of poems, published by Wesleyan University Press.

18 Cuddihy edited *Ironwood*; the letter concerns the special Oppen issue.

19 Comparison of this list with the work published in *Ironwood* 5 shows it is broader and more inclusive. It may have been intended to note a few people not in fact published there; in at least the case of McAleavey, the exclusion occasioned some disgruntlement, of which Oppen was aware.

20 In a letter of March 16, 1975, from which this letter is dated. RBD had not intended "dizzy" as a term of reproach; quite the opposite.

21 In "The Speech at Soli" (*Ironwood* 5: 36–37), various lines from "a letter"—"young girls fell into [open] wells," "in the green [spring] storm" and "bringing to birth" are all from DuPlessis' poem "Elegies" (*Wells*, New York: The Montemora Foundation, 1980) n.p. The last phrase appears in an unpublished draft of the poem.

22 The reference is to Oppen's other citation in the poem, ". . . it will not // cohere it will NOT that other," which DuPlessis took to allude to Ezra Pound, Canto CXVI, "And I am not a demigod, / I cannot make it cohere." *Drafts & Fragments of Cantos CX–CXVII* (New York: New Directions, 1968), 26.

23 Written in the margin, this thought has a big exclamation mark next to it. This letter was published in *Ironwood* 24 (1984), 135–36.

24 "The most memorable fictive landscapes and actions of Oppen's recent poetry are born from the desire to move beyond the struggle with alternatives. Having argued, posited, and negated, he will simply turn his back and move away from the necessity for this struggle into a beautiful, stark landscape of awe, almost devoid of man-made objects and certainly empty of a mass of people" (*Ironwood* 5, 76).

25   "'And Their Winter and Night in Disguise'" is the title of the third poem of "Some San Francisco Poems," CP 217–18.

26   William Blake's "Nurses Song" ends: "Your spring & your day, are wasted in play / And your winter and night in disguise."

27   Perhaps in confusion with Michael Hamburger, the salutation is made to "Michael." However, this letter is to Eric Homberger.

28   Williams, "The New Poetical Economy," (a review of *Discrete Series*) *Poetry* 44 (July 1934): 220–25. The "cat boat poem" cited by Williams is "The mast / Inaudibly soars; bole-like, tapering. . . ."

29   The eighth and final paragraph of Pound's "Preface to *Discrete Series* (1934)" reads "I salute a serious craftsman, a sensibility which is not every man's sensibility and which has not been got out of any other man's books." *Paideuma* 10, 1 (Spring 1981), 13.

30   In a brief letter to Rakosi in May 1975, Oppen had said, "Old friend, lordy, lordy I've been lucky. For a stubborn man, incredibly lucky. Don't know that I deserve it, but I've been lucky. . . ."

31   Denise Levertov and Rakosi had political discussions at Yaddo, the artist's colony. Rakosi adds: "'those Brooklyn-like stairs' refers to the long, steep flight of stairs (dark too) to his apartment on Polk St. in San Francisco."

32   In *European Judaism* (Winter 1974–75). In a letter to Harvey Shapiro about the same issue of *European Judaism*, Oppen praised HS's "lovely description of Rezi!" and stated: "it occurs to me that Rezi (and, in fact, Louis) remain immensely important facts -- poles of meaning, facts about the world   A part of my love for the world (love for myself and my past?)"

33   John Wilson, the editor of *Occurrence*, had, in #3 (1975), published John Taggart's "Deep Jewels: George Oppen's *Seascape: Needle's Eye*," 26–36.

34   The issue had poetry by Hugh Seidman, Michael Heller, John Taggart, and Ronald Johnson, as well as reviews by Taggart, Theodore Enslin, and Ron Silliman.

35   The letterhead is Mishkenot Sha'ananim, a Jerusalem retreat for the creative. The Israel trip had many reverberations. In a letter to Diane Meyer toward the end of the summer in Maine (UCSD 16, 7, 28), Oppen had said: "and we'll soon be in Israel, thoroughly embraced, enwrapped, argued with - - 'It's home' (as our friend Julian [Zimet] wrote, 'and I'd leave it again' - -"

36   Both Israeli poets: Amichai, author of *Songs of Jerusalem and Myself, Travels of a Latter-day Benjamin of Tudela*, and the novel *Not of This Time, Not of This Place*; Kovner, author of *My Little Sister*. Kovner was a leader of partisans in the Vilna ghetto.

37   Bar Kokhba, leader of a Jewish revolt (132–35) against Hadrian, died in A.D. 135 C.E.

38   Invoice for the books. Oppen had cut a few sentences, not restored here, about his search for the invoice.

39   The play, by Hanoch Levin, is a controversial political satire written in 1972.

40   An allusion to a poem by Harvey Shapiro in which he alludes to Oppen. *This World* (Middletown, Conn.: Wesleyan University Press, 1971).

41   The dating and sequencing of this and the subsequent letters to Shapiro were done

in consultation with Harvey Shapiro; we have both done the best we could with inference, surmise, and memory.

42　In June 1973, the Oppens had attended the National Poetry Festival at Thomas Jefferson College, Allendale, Michigan.

43　The poem of Shapiro's is possibly "Adoration of the Moon," with the lines "Lean out of the abyss of origin four ragged Jews / Masters of wrath and judgment, gentled by the moon." From *Battle Report: Selected Poems*, 1966, 60.

44　This first paragraph seems to allude to an Oppen letter that was not found among Shapiro's papers.

45　About one of the photographs of the young Oppen in *Ironwood* 5 Shapiro had quipped, "George, you look like any other sensitive Jewish boy."

46　Probably Heller's review of *Seascape: Needle's Eye* in *The American Poetry Review* 4, 2 (March/April 1975): 1–4.

47　In his letter of November 15, 1975, to which this responds, Heller had mentioned Merleau-Ponty's *The Visible and the Invisible* (Evanston, Ill.: Northwestern University Press, 1969). The Maritain was published by Meridian Books in 1955.

48　Olds reported that this letter about her work in *Kayak* "came to me out of the blue. [. . .] It was largely because of his letter that that particular poem began to seem central to me, finally giving its name to my first book."

49　"A Note on Tom McGrath, &c," originally published in *West End* 1, 2 (Summer 1972): 10–11; reprinted in *Ironwood* 5 (1975), 42.

50　Cited from "In the Room," in Shapiro's *Lauds* (New York: Sun, 1975).

51　The allusion, of course, is to Robert Lowell, "Skunk Hour," *Life Studies* (New York: Vintage Books, 1959).

52　In a letter to Shapiro just after this, Oppen says, "Occurrences -- events   the heavy events - - - - and down or somewhere to the toys of everyday, small self-interest, the wings of the wasp - - -" This prefigures Oppen's poem "The Occurrences" (CP 206) which ends, "hopes / Which are the hopes / Of small self interest called // Superstition chitinous / Toys of the children wings / Of the wasp[.]"

53　Griffin had given Oppen a copy of *In Time of Crowding: Selected Poems (1963–74)* (London: Brookside Press, 1975); the lines cited are from "The Goddess," 12.

54　Kelly, *The Loom* (Los Angeles: Black Sparrow Press, 1975); the final lines of section 22 "[The Hallway of Isis]," 271, read: ". . . She / says nothing to him. / He's left his heart / to enter the room. / When he remembers that, / he knows he has only / one thing to say. / He says it to her, / quietly. I / am what you mean."

1976

1　"Memorial Broadcast for Charles Reznikoff, KPFA, Berkeley, California," was published in *Sagetrieb* 3, 3 (Winter 1984): 29–35. Sometime in 1976, the Oppens were interviewed by Michel Englebert and Mike West; this interview in *The American Poetry Review* 14, 4 (July–August 1985): 11–14.

2　This letter and the next were published in *Ironwood* 24 (Fall 1984): 136–38.

3　DuPlessis, "George Oppen: 'What Do We Believe to Live With?'" *Ironwood* 5 (1975): 62–77.

4 "This" is a revision-by-excision of the DuPlessis poem "Voyaging," dedicated to Oppen, which had also been discussed in an Oppen letter of [April 10, 1976], not published here. The poem is in *Wells* (New York: The Montemora Foundation, 1980).

5 This could be glossed with a citation from the letter of April 10, 1976: "still I do think that your very strong tendency to narrative conflicts with the image, the images, you want to trust."

6 Replansky, *Ring Song: Poems* (New York: Charles Scribner's Sons, 1952), reprinted in facsimile by the author in 1962. "I Met My Solitude," in Replansky, *Twenty-One Poems, Old and New* (New York: Gingko Press, 1988), 21.

7 In 1976, Ashbery won both the Pulitzer Prize and the National Book Award for *Self-Portrait in a Convex Mirror.*

8 Eve Haight, Oppen's grandniece; her mother, DM, glossed this as "experiences of doubt."

9 A parallel formulation from a letter to LOM of [August 11, 1976] (UCSD 33, 1, 19): "And Eagle Island itself is endlessly lovely and peaceful   Don't know why   we have need of escape from San Francisco, since S F is far from the worst of cities, but we do.   Forest, and the miniature landscape and sea scape   *and* the silence -- almost unbroken - - - -   luxurious to have both places. And we pay visits to old friends on Little Deer, arriving by sail, and feel like people out of the nineteenth century. . . . . a joke, an historical joke even to the natives: the nineteenth century with an inflatable canoe and other twentieth-century accoutrements added."

10 In the Charles Reznikoff Papers (UCSD 9, 22, 4), there is a unique copy of Oppen's *Discrete Series*, carbon typescript on 3-hole 6 × 9 paper, bound in a shiny brown cover to make a small book. Some of the poems are in a slightly different order and some are slightly different from the 1934 version; there is a strong sense of poems placed one against the other on facing pages. Opposite the poem "She lies, hip high" is the pigeon poem alluded to later in this letter (clearly related to Pound's "imagist" haiku "In a Station of the Metro": "The apparition of these faces in the crowd; / Petals on a wet, black bough."): "The pigeons fly from the dark bough / unleaved to the window ledge; /   There is no face."

11 One of five Oppen poems in the *Active Anthology*: "Brain / All / Nuclei / Blinking / Kinetic / Electric sign / A / Pig / Dances / Painfully / Cannon / Rockets / A curve // Behind / This / Eye / No / Further brain; // The tendon / The slots / Pianola / Into / Slots / Sound / A room's / Back- / Ground [.]"

12 An Oppen poem, section 24 from "Of Being Numerous," as well as "The Building of the Skyscraper," was reprinted in Helen Plotz, ed., *The Gift Outright: America to Her Poets* (New York: William Morrow, 1977). The section reads, "In this nation / Which is in some sense / Our home. Covenant! // The covenant is: / There shall be peoples" (CP 164).

13 Oppen's AL postscript which may be a draft from which he selected the postscript typed in the letter includes several more phrases of interest. The variant is: "The covenant is: there shall be people. And peoples. And my people. Please let the miracle shine forth even on my small page.   Without footnotes."

14 Black Sparrow had published *The Complete Poems of Charles Reznikoff, Volume I: Poems 1918–1936* in 1976, *Holocaust* in 1975, and *By the Well of Living and Seeing: New and Selected Poems, 1918–1973* in 1974.

15 About Reznikoff, Auster had written a "journalistic" piece for *Harper's Bookletter* (3, 1) in 1976 and an essay for *European Judaism* in 1974–75.

16 Charles Reznikoff, *Poems 1935–1975*, volume 2 of his *Complete Poems*, ed. Seamus Cooney (Los Angeles: Black Sparrow Press, 1977); on the back cover is the following: "who wrote / in the great world // small for this is a way // to enter / the light on the kitchen / tables wide-- // spread as the mountains' / light this is // heroic this is / the poem // to write // in the great / world small[.]"

17 Olds glossed this: "Sept. 76 - I was getting ready to teach a course on American poetry at the Theodor Herzl Institute here in Manhattan, and was starting with all poets with Jewish background. So I was writing letters to various poets saying Religious background?, etc., but to George I wrote my question outright -- are you?! & thus his charming reply." Alluding, of course, to the end of James Joyce's *Ulysses*. When asked in September 1978 by Gary B. Pacernick (UCSD) for poems "which speak of the Jewish experience," Oppen mentioned "From Disasters," "Sara in Her Father's Arms," and "Blood from a Stone." "From Disasters," was begun during Oppen's visit to Israel in 1975.

18 Serge Fauchereau had invited them to the Centre Pompidou; in his response of [September 27, 1976], Oppen said "among other things, will be good to see you again and I'd like very much to meet Octavio Paz whom we've just missed meeting several times."

19 Fauchereau is translating the penultimate poem in *Discrete Series*, which reads "Deaths everywhere----- / The world too short for trend is land- - - - - / In the mouths, / Rims // In this place, two geraniums / In your window-box / Are his life's eyes" (CP 14).

20 Oppen's poem, "The Source" (CP 55), begins almost exactly thus, but Oppen has provided an alternate phrase for the beginning of line 2 for Fauchereau to translate. The poem's text reads, "It is a slum" for "it is impoverished." As Oppen then says, he has altered the punctuation as well: the CP version uses three periods as terminal punctuation.

21 Again, this is Oppen's own paraphrase of the next lines of "The Source."

22 This is the wording of Oppen's poem, but the punctuation has been removed.

23 The section under discussion reads, "The gleam; the unimaginable / Thin feet taper down / The instep naked to the wooden floor!"

24 The poem is "The People, The People" (CP 112). Oppen's notes for a reading of this poem at the Guggenheim Museum (UCSD 16, 30, 4) indicate that it concerns the possible disappearance of the radical intellectual, and that it derives from his reading of Norman Mailer's novel *Barbary Shore*. The "she" of the poem is related to the character Guinevere; in both novel and poem she is "the people." Oppen has a long commentary on the novel in a letter to JOD [before April 1964] (UCSD 16, 1, 4).

25 Section 3 of "A Language of New York" (CP 96).

26 "Two Romance Poems" (CP 255).

27 "Eros" (CP 102–3) has the lines "Maze // And wealth / Of heavy ancestry and the foreign rooms // Of structures // Closed by their roofs / and complete [. . .]."

28 In glossing "Two Romance Poems," Oppen is glossing the final text in the *Collected Poems*.

29   From a letter to Laughlin of [September 25, 1976]: "---feel a little guilty toward N D
     -- and, in a way -- toward myself in that I've been refusing invitations to read in
     public -- Some reluctance - - hard for me to say why   Partly   that I want to
     move forward;   that I want *not*   to wander back into what I have already written,
     and I have little new work, tho what I do have I think is good[.]"
30   The date is based upon Weinfield's memory of the publication date of *Mysterious
     Barricades* #4.

1977

1   The title of this enclosed poem was not indicated by the recipient.
2   Stuart Lavin had written Oppen a letter about his dream of the number eleven,
    enclosing a poem beginning, "Two weeks where space raged *eleven,* / a new number,
    possessed and known."
3   The citations are from "Satan Says," the title poem of Olds's collection (Pittsburgh:
    University of Pittsburgh Press, 1980).
4   In her letter to him, Olds had commented on Oppen's poem "Of This All Things"
    in *This in Which,* which contains the lines: ". . . What distinction / I have is that I
    have lived / My adult life / With a beautiful woman, I have turned on the light /
    Sometimes, to see her // Sleeping" (CP 111).
5   The poem is "Night Scene" (CP 118).
6   R. L. Stevenson, "The Silverado Squatters" (1905), published in the Biographical
    Edition with "The Amateur Emigrant" (New York: Charles Scribner's Sons, 1908).
7   Two versions of this letter exist; both at UCSD 16, 8, 20. The salutation of one
    includes Laughlin; that longer version is used here. The opening of the unused
    version is more spare: "I know, I know. But I must be in my own room and in my
    own life   (I must guard my life as tho it were my life)   (as tho it were my poetry)."
    I have dated this letter in a literal-minded way; Oppen turned sixty-nine in April
    1977, and he usually called attention to his exact age around his birthdays.
8   William Shakespeare, "Fear no more the heat o' the sun" from *Cymbeline*; lines 5–
    6 read: "Golden lads and girls all must, / As chimney-sweepers, come to dust."
    Hugh Kenner glosses these lines: "in the mid-twentieth century a visitor to Shake-
    speare's Warwickshire met a countryman blowing the grey head off a dandelion:
    'We call these golden boys chimney-sweepers when they go to seed.'" *The Pound
    Era* (Berkeley: University of California Press, 1971), 122. "The raggle-taggle gypsies"
    is an anonymous folk song.
9   This letter is published, in facsimile, in Milton Hindus, ed., *Charles Reznikoff: Man
    and Poet* (Orono, Me.: The National Poetry Foundation, 1984), 279–80.
10 Milton Hindus, ed., *The Old East Side: An Anthology* (Philadelphia: Jewish Publi-
    cation Society of America, 1971).
11 The Oppens had planned a leisurely visit to New York City; they had borrowed
    Eliot Weinberger's apartment. Instead they found they could not stay.
12 For Roman, barbarian, Jew imagery see also the appendix to 1973 letters and the
    poems "Semite" and "The Lighthouses" in CP.
13 Homberger, *The Art of the Real: Poetry in England and America Since 1939* (Totowa,

N.J.: Rowman & Littlefield, 1977). The main section treating Oppen compares him favorably to Berryman and Lowell: "*Discrete Series* comes from another world of theoretical severity and artistic seriousness than *Dream Songs* and *Notebook*" 204.

14 *Montemora* 3 (Spring 1977), ed. Weinberger, featured twenty-five poems by Griffin, an interview with Basil Bunting, and assorted work of contemporary poets.

15 Weinfield had criticized Kenner for his remark about the gap in the writing career, that it had simply taken Oppen twenty-five years to write the next poem. HW to RBD: "It seemed to me at the time (and still seems to me) that Kenner was disregarding the real process at work."

16 Schwerner, *the work, the joy and the triumph of the will* (New York: New Rivers, 1978). Oppen probably saw the poem in manuscript. Schwerner's "The Tablets" in *Sounds of the River Naranjana and The Tablets I–XXIV* (Barrytown, N.Y.: Station Hill Press, 1983).

1978

1 Michael Heller reviewed both books on December 31 in the *New York Times Book Review.*

2 "The Dream" is a prose poem with distinctly articulated line breaks (UCSD 16, 27, 55). "I dreamed one night that I was in Northern France in one / of the red-brick industrial towns the doors / and the windows locked. I knocked on a door and entered / and I said to the family *I was here during the war, I was / in a house near here tho I cannot find it, it is near, you / can take me there they will know me.* I stood / in that room and they would not guide me. I was lost and / they could not guide me[.]"

3 Praising *Primitive*, Duncan had written, "Heart felt, feeling its way, the words moving in the eyes' reading the heart hears in a kind of answering" (UCSD George Oppen Papers, General Correspondence).

1979–81

1 RBD has seen these, through the kindness of MO; the letters were in a notebook of Mary Oppen. There is a two-page AL from GO, a five-page AL by GO with responses by MO, a one-page AL from GO, and responses by GO on a page by MO. The letters are not published here.

2 The participants were Rachel Blau DuPlessis, Robert Hass, Burton Hatlen, Hugh Kenner, Mark Linenthal, Carl Rakosi, Jerome Rothenberg; it was held at Intersection, and co-sponsored by Intersection and the Poetry Center at San Francisco State University.

3 Oppen suffered from sciatic nerve pain for more than two years.

4 Taggart, *Peace on Earth* (Berkeley: Turtle Island Foundation, 1981). In a letter to Taggart of [June 19, 1979], Oppen reiterated his praise for the poem: "Not 'like music,' but music itself. In this perhaps unique."

5 This letter was Oppen's contribution to a symposium on "The Poetry Business,"

provoked by a letter by Nathaniel Tarn; *Montemora* 5 (1979), 72–116. The Oppen letter, 90.

6   Schwabacher, *The Tortoise and The Angel: The Journals of Ethel Schwabacher*, ed., Judith Emlyn Johnson and Brenda S. Webster, ms. Schwabacher had turned to the journal in 1971, and increasingly in 1977, as the arthritis in her hands prevented her from painting.

7   Griffin, *Outsing the Howling* (London and New York: Permanent Press, 1979).

8   Auster had proposed to interview Oppen as part of the Writers at Work series for *The Paris Review*. There is a draft of this letter at UCSD.

9   Sharp, "George Oppen, Discrete Series, 1929–1934," in Hatlen, ed., *George Oppen: Man and Poet*: 271–92. Oppen had seen a typescript version of this paper; the Zukofsky estate did not give Sharp permission for this material to be cited in the printed version.

10   Weinfield, "Sonnet (For years I called myself a communist)," *Paideuma* 10, 1 (Spring 1981), 36.

11   On Weinfield's letter to Oppen (UCSD 16, 11, 40) is an autograph draft of this response which includes the statement in square brackets here; the letter Weinfield received ended "(We remember)."

12   Weinfield, " 'Of Being Numerous' by George Oppen" in Hatlen, ed., *GOM&P*: 375–79.

13   Oppen's signature is actually placed on the top of the page and thus opens the letter, which refers to a poem that Gerber had sent to them.

14   Tomlinson, *Some Americans: A Personal Record* (Berkeley: University of California Press, 1981); the essay is Chapter 2 "Objectivists: Zukofsky and Oppen."

15   In "A 12," 138 and 173; the former is the statement defining Zukofsky's "poetics": "An integral / Lower limit speech / Upper limit music[.]"

16   RBD had written to GO in response to a class discussion she had conducted about "The Little Hole," #2 from "Five Poems about Poetry" (CP 81). She wrote: "someone noticed all the "o" sounds—those open o's like hole, exposed, close, compose, home, alone, and so. That's a lot for such a small poem. And we were wondering about the presence of sound in poetry, and the level of consciousness or self-consciousness that a poet has about the presence of those sound patterns." A series of specific questions from the class followed; this letter was GO's response.

17   The occasion for the letter was the request for a message to the Cambridge Poetry Festival.

18   There is another version of this, autograph of Mary Oppen (UCSD 33, 1, 12), labeled, "George dictated to Mary-83" I have included in square brackets additions from this later telling of the story, which was otherwise the same as the letter here.

19   A copy of a clay sculpture of a dancing woman made by a woman friend of Oppen's father, dated 1913, now in the possession of Mary Oppen. JOD thought that Elsie (Oppen's mother) made it; MO ascribes it to the friend, who was a dancer.

20   When Oppen was four, his mother, after suffering from depression, was hospitalized for a suicide attempt; she subsequently died of those self-inflicted injuries.

21   Royet-Journoud had asked Oppen to send a one-line poem for an anthology he was editing with Emmanuel Hocquard. Oppen sent the following poem:

The Poem

A poetry of the meaning of words
And a bond with the universe

I think there is no light in the world
but the world

And I think there is light

When Royet-Journoud persisted in his quest for a one-line poem, Oppen wrote the letter of September 26, the last letter which RBD has found.

Index

NOTE: All of Oppen's allusions to writers are indexed using that writer's name as the main entry (e.g. Pound, Ezra; Heidegger, Martin). When Oppen mentions his own books and essays either by name or by inference, these are indexed by their individual titles under "Oppen, George." When Oppen alludes to, cites from, or talks about his published poems, these are indexed alphabetically by individual title under "Oppen, George: poems of." In alphabetizing, these poem titles are treated as they are in the New Directions *Collected Poems* index; the words "The," "O," and "A" in initial position are counted into and as the first word. Citations from uncollected poems are indexed under the subheading "poems, uncollected." Materials in the notes are indexed when they offer substantial information or interpretation, or when Oppen's letters are cited.

Rachel Blau DuPlessis is a Professor of English at
Temple University in Philadelphia. She is the author of
*Writing Beyond the Ending: Narrative Strategies of
Twentieth-Century Women Writers*, *H.D.: The Career of
that Struggle* and *The Pink Guitar: Writing as Feminist
Practice*. Her books of poetry are *Wells*, *Gypsy/Moth*,
and the recent collection, *Tabula Rosa*.

Library of Congress Cataloging-in-Publication Data
Oppen, George.
[Correspondence. Selections]
The selected letters of George Oppen / edited by Rachel
Blau DuPlessis.
Includes bibliographical references.
ISBN 0-8223-1017-1. — ISBN 0-8223-1024-4 (pbk.)
1. Oppen, George—Correspondence.   2. Poets,
American—20th century—Correspondence.
I. DuPlessis, Rachel Blau.   II. Title.
PS3529.P54Z48   1990
811'.52—dc20
[B]   89-23772 CIP